BEING ABOUT MUSIC

TEXTWORKS 1960-2003

J. K. RANDALL   **BENJAMIN BORETZ**

VOLUME 1: 1960-1978

OPEN SPACE

This publication is made possible in part by a grant from the Princeton University Music Department, which is gratefully acknowledged.

ISBN 0-9629865-0-X (2-volume set)

Published 2003 by Open Space Publications, 29 Sycamore Drive, Red Hook, New York 12571. Email: postmaster@the-open-space.org. Website: www.the-open-space.org.

Recognitions

Charles Stein was multitasking principal editor and omniprescient surehanded advisor in the assembly and execution of these volumes.

Keith Eisenbrey was intrepid music e-calligrapher.

Tildy Bayar was fail-safe textual problem detector, researcher, and copy editor.

Mary Lee Roberts was strenuously critical reader, technical supervisor, and administrative manager.

Reuben de Lautour was patient and expert scanner and magical restorer of graphics and texts, including all the pages of "How Music Goes" and "ADVT." (Randall), and *Language ,as a music* and *"Talk": If I am a musical thinker...."* (Boretz).

Origins:

text sources are as follows:

The Musical Quarterly, July 1961: "Current Chronicle: Evanston, Ill".

The Music Review, Vol. XXI #2, May 1960: "Haydn: String Quartet in D Major, Op. 76, No. 2".

Journal of Music Theory: Vol. 8, No. 2 (Winter 1964): *"Convertible Counterpoint in the Strict Style* (1906), by Sergei Ivanovich Taneiev"; *"Twentieth Century Harmony: Creative Aspects and Practice,* by Vincent Persichetti"; Vol. 33, No. 1 (Spring 1989): "The Logic of What?".

Cimaise, Fall 1964: "American Music".

Harper's, February 1967: "New Music, Old Words".

Music Educators Journal, November 1968, Volume 55, Number 3: "Electronic Music and Musical Tradition".

Journal of Philsosophy, Vol. LXVII, No. 16 (August 29, 1970): "Nelson Goodman's *Languages of Art,* from a Musical Point of View".

Proceedings of the American Society of University Composers, 1970: "Composing With Electronics: Sensitive Mirrors for Subtle Echoes".

Encyclopedia of Twentieth-Century Music, John Vinton, Ed. E. P. Dutton, 1971: "Milton Babbitt".

Perspectives of New Music, as follows:

Vol 1, No. 2 (Spring-Summer 1963): "*Serial Composition and Atonality,* by George Perle"; Vol. 2, No. 1 (Fall-Winter 1963):"Godfrey Winham's *Composition for Orchestra";* Vol. 3, No. 2 (Spring-Summer 1965): "A Report from Princeton"; Vol. 4, No. 2 (Spring-Summer 1966): "A Note on Discourse and Contemporary Musical Thought"; Vol. 5, No. 2 (Spring-Summer 1967): "Three Lectures to Scientists"; Vol 8, No. 2: *"The Acoustical Foundations of Music,* by John Backus; Vol. 9, No. 2/10, No. 1 (1971): "Stravinsky in Person"; "in Quest of the Rhythmic Genius"; Vol. 12, No. 2/13, No.1 (1973-74): "A World of Times"; Vol. 13, No. 2 (Fall-Winter 1974): "a soundscroll"; Vol. 14, No. 2/15, No. 1 (1976): "how music goes"; Vol. 15, No. 2 (Spring-Summer 1977): "Musical Cosmology"; "Reply to John Rahn"; Vol. 16, No. 1 (Fall-Winter 1977): "What Lingers On (, When the Song is Ended)"; "trobadores"; Vol. 18 (1979-80): "(a loss too soon)"; "ADVT. Repeat After Me."; Vol. 20 (1981-82): "forM(a music)"; "Talk: If I am a musical thinker..."; Vol. 22 (1983-84): "Afterward: a foreword"; Vol. 23, No. 2 (Spring-Summer 1985): "Are You Serious?"; "Interface, Part I: Commentary: The Barrytown Orchestra on Hunger Day": Vol. 25 (1987): "Interface, Part II: Thoughts in Reply to Boulez and Foucault: 'Contemporary Music and the Public' "; "A Conversation About *Perspectives";* Vol. 27, No. 1 (Winter 1989): "Relevance. Liberation."; Vol. 27, No. 2 (Spring 1990): "On Thinking About Various Issues..."; Vol. 29, No. 1 (Winter 1991): "The Inner Studio..."; Vol. 30, No. 1 (Winter 1992): "Some things I've been noticing..."; "Diaogue for JKR"; "Experiences With No Names"; Vol. 31, No. 2 (Winter 1993): "Regretting John Cage and Kenneth Gaburo: A Gathering of Texts"; Vol. 34, No. 2 (Summer 1996): "e: a reading"; Vol. 39, No. 1 (Winter 2001): "Music as Anti-Theater"*.

The Open Space Magazine: Issue 1 (Spring 1999): "Music, as a Music"; "Wiska Radkiewicz's 60-minute exercise"; Issue 2 (Spring 2000): "Notes for Open Space CD 10"; "Reflections on Cardew and Wolpe: Vignettes of Old Masters I"; Issue 3 (Spring 2001): "It's all yours"; "Introduction, for *Music Inside Out,* by John Rahn"*; Issue 4 (Fall 2002): "Prologue to ("Whose Time, What Space"); "("Whose Time, What Space")"; "Prologue and little reviews (Life in the Slow Lane)".

Audible Traces (Carciofoli Verlag, 1998): "music/consciousness/gender"(Open Space Video 1).

---

*First published in John Rahn, *Music Inside Out. Going too far in musical essays.* Gordon and Breach, 2001

Being About Music

Volume 1

Contents

PREFATORY NOTE

QUODLIBET 1, *Question 7:* Can an angel who has a habitual cognition of an object cause an actual cognition of that object in another angel without causing an actual cognition of that same object within himself?

— (Wm. of Ockham)

[Ockham's answer: "It depends …………………………………………….]

Ch. CXLV. The property of all the divine order frequents, and gives itself to, all inferior kinds throughout the secondary.

Ch. CXLVI. The ends of all divine progressions resemble their beginnings because they revert thereto; they, having neither beginning nor end, engirdle a circle.

Ch. CXLVIII. Every divine order is, by itself, made one, in a threefold manner, first by the supremity within itself, secondly by the mediocrity, and thirdly by the end thereof.

— (Proclus)

Perhaps you will allow "engirdles"; ——but will yet debate with Proclus whether order hierarchically descends, or adventitiously rises.

And if you suppose that your experiences of music are, precisely, your perceptions of its acoustic carriers, then you're most likely dead to the question posed by Ockham. (Worse, you're dead to his goading disinclination to ask the obvious: Can A1 cause *A2* to *actually* cognize what A1 actually and habitually cognizes? ((He's asking *not* whether *you*'ll get my message, but whether in sending it *I*'ll get it.)))

In fairness, Ben and I might be said to have run, from early to late, a strenuous gamut from somewhat in excess of Proclus to somewhat in excess of Ockham:

from the interpenetration of intricacy and grandeur in the divine order, or its simulacra (most classically, in Ben's Tristan analysis in METAVARIATIONS (publ. Open Space); or more talmudically, in my own Depth of Surface in the present collection)

to the shifty concretions of identity in the clutch of attention, or venue, or transmission, or report (as historical romance, in my own intimacy—a polemic; or as a psycho-ontologically engirdling questionmark, in Ben's scripts of the '90's and '00's, esp. m/c/q & I/O).

Even our more ephemeral pieces seem to me to point, usually (if modestly), along this trajectory.

Should you find it so, the terms "Being", "About", and "Music" will glimmer; and perhaps goad.

Current Chronicle

United States

Evanston, Ill.

In his remarkable discussion of Roger Sessions's Violin Concerto[1], Elliott Carter pointed out a major preoccupation that Sessions shares with most of the serious composers of our time: the development of articulated, continuous, and meaningful musical structures capable of fully absorbing and expressing the entire wide range of present-day musical materials. Carter's point is confirmed with special force in the case of Sessions's music, where the further insistence that such articulation must not be gratuitous, but that it must arise from the logic and necessity of the total musical procedure has led him to militant avoidance of any appearance of surface novelty, even of the "advanced" kind that guarantees a quick imputation of efficiency, economy, and, indeed, "originality" to otherwise undistinguished work. Thus, despite his own indigenous originality, Sessions has remained a "traditionalist" in his retention, particularly, of the ideal of the long, flowing line, as well as in his refusal to deck out the often neutral-sounding tissue that characteristically binds and frames his foreground development of ideas with ear-catching (or -splitting) scrimshaw.

The difficulty of finding a genuine connection to tradition, free of literalness but retentive of its still relevant and fruitful aspects, has led many "advanced" composers to a hard-line rejection of associative qualities *in toto.* But where the need forfresh procedures arises from fresh creative necessities rather than from the imperative of public attention, a frame of reference is still required, securely rooted in and evolved from a traditional basis, by reference to which new procedures can be assessed, and, even, perceived as authentically new. As Carter pointed out, the development of "a new and meaningful type of musical continuity . . . must be undertaken by slow, rather intuitive steps, since the condition of 'meaningfulness' presupposes a cooperative development in the

---

[1] *Current Chronicle,* July 1959. This is a brilliant, classic statement whose formulations (several of which are quoted in clarification of points raised in this report) have laid a firm foundation for future study of Sessions's work.

composer and in some qualified listeners of a grasp of musical relationships not previously clearly recognized, coupled with an ability to test them against some standard of interest and meaningfulness".

Clearly, in the sparseness of his early output and in his obscurity in the public awareness, Sessions has paid a heavy price for his artistic conscience. But of late he has reaped its rewards as well, in a burst of fecundity productive of a number of significant works that are unmistakably the work of a composer who has, at least, found himself.

A unique opportunity to test by experience this broad view of a composer's development was provided by the presentation in Evanston, under the joint auspices of Northwestern University and the Fromm Music Foundation(*), of a three-day festival of Sessions's music, during which more than half of his output since 1947 could be heard, along with a few earlier works. Even a brief examination of the more recent scores reveals how the techniques for meaningful coherence described by Carter in relation to the Violin Concerto have come to full and variegated flower in the latest period. The addition of certain new aspects, such as the use of twelve-tone derivations, seems to have helped clarify and direct the formal impulse, sometimes providing a firm basis for cohesion within a wide-ranging or rhapsodic structure, and at other times supplying, within an associative neo-Classic framework, workable substitutes to compensate for the loss of the articulative power of tonal functions. With this in mind, it may be fruitful to examine briefly some of the recent works to uncover the different points of view they take to musical continuity.

"More and more the notion of extended, continuously flowing sections during which ideas come to the surface, gain clarity and definition, and then sink back into the general flow has characterized Sessions's unique style."[2] The way in which Sessions has adopted twelve-tone procedures is entirely consistent with this characterization. The series is used in a directly melodic-motivic way, and does not also function as a more or less totally pitch-organizing principle. But the charge of irrelevance, leveled at music which, for no very compelling reason, "uses" such a serial base,

(*Disclosure, 2003: at the time of this writing (Fall 1960) I was employed as music consultant for the Fromm Music Foundation.)

[2] *Ibid.*

does not adhere to Sessions's work, since he has typically found a meaningful way to turn the row into the service of an important, if non-serial purpose. Series-derived materials, when present, are almost always in the principal voice, the foreground. Thus a voice unobtrusive in the "general flow" is suddenly brought to individualized life by participating in the exposition of the series without breaking its own chronological stride. In this way, Sessions is able to achieve individualized "entrances" without overtly changing the unity of the sonorous texture.

The opening movement of the Piano Concerto (1956) articulates by this, as well as other means, a coherent, forceful and original structure clearly paralleling a classic "sonata" design. The row reveals strongly defined intervallic properties which function, in the form, horizontally as well as vertically (Ex. 1).[3] An alternate form of the first hexachord provides maximum derangement, hence variety, possible without also losing the important intervallic characteristics (Ex. 1a).

I have indicated a division of the series into three-note groups since, except where the full series is stated, the formal procedure entails internal permutations of these trichords, while retaining their over-all integrity. The intervallic redundancies among the trichords are obvious, and the principal intervals dominate the texture of the movement. At the very opening of the slow introduction (Ex. 2), the minor and major seconds are vertically exposed in the gentle piano *ostinato,* while the fourth, tritone and major third are horizontally prominent.

These opening measures offer, in capsule form, a concise demonstration of all the many kinds of association that enrich and widen the expressive scope of this structure. First of all, the introduction of the bass-tone B♭ (which forces the ear to re-evaluate acceptance of C as the principal bass, and reconceives the initial

---

[3] All the Sessions examples are reprinted by permission of the copyright owner, Edward B. Marks Music Corporation, New York.

sonorities as, instead of "tonic" [C or E], a kind of "augmented sixth" whose normal "deceptive" resolution would be to B♭) presents new harmonic associations which lead directly to the statement of the "derived" hexachord. The first harmonic sound is a composite verticalization of the two kinds of seconds (B♭-B♮; B♭-C), while the second combines F♯ and E with B♭, yielding the pitch-content of the first trichord of the derived hexachord. The next bass-note, F (a perfect fourth below B♭, paralleling the upper voice of the *ostinato),* forms with C and B a perfect fourth and a tritone, the two remaining intervals important in the trichords, and also provides the pitch-content for trichord 2a. Note, too, that the first two tones of the derived hexachord are F♯-E, as in the piano *ostinato,* and are both harmonized in turn against the C-B in the piano.[4] One more point: as soon as the new exposition of the row

---

[4] By the same token, the clarinet's B♭ is harmonized with F♯ and E, thus vertically summarizing the *pitch*-content of the trichord 1a, while the clarinet C is harmonized with F♯ and D, yielding the same trichord's *interval*-content. Moreover, the bassoon and cello move to F♯-C♯ under C in m.5, yielding the interval content of trichord 2a, and again, permuted, as E-B♭-F. The E and B♭ are also associated with this bassoon's preceding F♯, relating them further to trichord 1a, and so on.

begins in the clarinet (whose riff runs through the entire concerto as an associative signal), the piano part loses its serial definition, and becomes background, formally as well as in acoustical fact; when it re-enters the acoustic foreground, its material is again serial. In these five measures, too, can be seen the beginning of the stepwise prolongation of the bass movement B♭-F-B♭ ("I-V-I"?) which characterized this introduction and clearly relates it to classical models (see Ex. 3).

Ex. 3

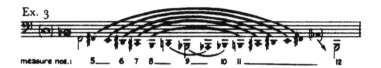

The formal articulation of the rest of the movement is, on a large scale, similarly determined by this associative-individualizing activity. The first thematic group, hinted at in the introduction, grows up through the texture into a fullblown statement of the basic series and several of its forms. The "second theme" is closely linked in pitch-content and sonority to the opening, centering on E♯ (F), the "dominant", as the first thematic group centered on B♭. At the same time, it is clearly separated from the first theme by its slower tempo, its largely non-row-derived material (since this is a piano solo, there is no question of being swallowed into the background), and its stepwise motion, compared with the intervallically and rhythmically jagged first theme. A fermata clearly articulates the structural division between the "exposition" and "development"; the beginning of the new section with the combination of the initial *ostinato* (slow) with a fast, even figuration from the accompaniment to the first theme auditorially characterizes this as "development". Other parallels to classic procedure are the "delay" of the tonic bass note at the beginning of the "recapitulation" (a detail that is made meaningful by the important neighbor-note bass progressions at other structural points), the enrichment as well as the compression of ideas and exchanges of function between solo and orchestra in this recapitulation, and so forth, all bonded firmly within the context of a personal style that never literally suggests the sounds or the attack patterns of Classical music.

"The second movement ranges itself alongside those other highly unified slow movements from Sessions's pen, which have as a point of departure a single dramatically expressive phrase centering around one wide melodic skip."[5] Although this was written about Sessions's Quintet, it fits the Piano Concerto equally well. The associations with the first movement will be clear from Example 4 (the clarinet riff is prominently recalled later on), but the intervallic emphasis has been changed to center on major-minor thirds. Another means by which this movement is distinguished is the alternation, rather than the simultaneous opposition, of piano with orchestra, which rarely play together. The piano sections involve ever more elaborated, never literal, repetitions of and departures from the opening idea. The orchestral sections are relatively unornamented (the clear separation in chronology and character of soloist and orchestra inevitably brings to mind Beethoven's Fourth Piano Concerto), and pick up, successively, two of the prominent intervallic suggestions of the solo passages. The Finale, a vigorously propulsive rondo-like movement, maintains a steady tempo throughout, has piano and orchestra playing almost all the time (with the piano notably here in an accompanying role) until the final cadenza, a strong and brilliant passage that leads to a powerfully conclusive ending clearly rooted on C. The effect of teleological finality clearly justifies Sessions's faith in the carefully constructed bass-line with which he defines polar movement, often without any apparent support from the superstructure, a circumstance that has led to criticism of it as being out of place and ineffective against the prevailing "dissonant" harmonic texture.

In the Fourth Symphony (completed 1958) one becomes aware of integrative and delineative strategies of an even wider range; the entire symphony, in fact, could be called an essay in the problem of large-scale musical characterization, if that description did not minimize the overtly "expressive" quality of the work. Sessions has himself given some outward indication of this preoccupation by naming his movements for aspects of the three types of Greek drama: *Burlesque* (for Comedy), *Elegy* (for Tragedy), and *Pastorale.* But anyone seeking, on the strength of this programmatic announcement, anything like the atmospheric idealizations of Impressionism or the monumental serenities of Stravinsky, will be disappointed. As with every Sessions work since

[5] Andrew Imbrie on Sessions's String Quintet, in *Current Chronicle,* July 1958.

Ex. 4 II. Adagio (♩=80)

the 1940s, there is nothing "appropriate" in the musical unfolding; as always, it is simply (or not so simply) Sessions's invariant private universe revealing a new aspect, but always unmistakably itself.

This presentation of the total musical personality in each work, whatever its ostensible object, must be regarded as an inseparable part of Sessions's creative identity. He does not, like some other recent composers, thrive on the kind of limitation that maps out a specific musical area as the framework for the channeling of the creative appetite; for Sessions, the frame of reference is always the full range of musical material at his disposal. Hence "effectiveness" is as alien to his creative impulse as it has often been a primary stimulant to Stravinsky's.

On the formal level, the three "character" contrasts of the Fourth Symphony are manifested in a tight, concise, and super-economical first movement, contrasted with an almost extravagantly rhapsodic second movement, full of furious but controlled contrast, and a deliberately, continuously evolving last movement, which seems, like the finale of the Second String Quartet, to be all of a piece — a single profile fully revealed only at its ultimate moment. The opening movement presents, in fact, an even more clearly partitioned and unified "sonata"-type design than does the corresponding section in the Piano Concerto. Here Sessions takes his jocularity rather obviously from the familiar *buffa* spirit of brisk Classic allegros, of which this is a jumbo-sized descendant. But he still finds the kernel of humor that Schoenberg totally missed in works like *The New Classicism* because he (Schoenberg) was parodying something he regarded with savage loathing rather than with bemused affection. So Sessions becomes more literally Classical than the classics: his surfaces are whimsically conformable to the prescriptions of the rule-book, while at the same time they construct a meaningful, ultimately original form. The first idea (Ex. 5) is dominated by a stereotypically "masculine" rhythm (downbeat beginning and ending), and includes other important motifs (as noted):

The second theme, whose rhythm has crept in, Sessions-fashion, during the exposition of the first, is clearly related to the opening, but is perfectly type-cast as "feminine" (upbeat beginning, demure ending; Ex. 6):

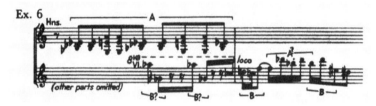

The development begins with the opening shout (up a fifth, of course), and includes a square fugue complete with inversions and stretti (and tuba bluster — Hindemth style), whose subject is row-derived like all the thematic material in the symphony. The recapitulation is straight-facedly regular; although the second theme is inverted strategically to retain its original focal point. The short coda (which includes a dry-bones xylophone solo) composts the rhythms of both themes.

The extraordinary achievement of the second movement is the juxtaposition of maximally contrasted passages that seem nonetheless to grow out of one another. Atmospheric fragments in the woodwinds alternate with extended dirges in the strings and furious fast episodes for full orchestra. Each successive "atmospheric" passage is further enriched: first harp is added, then vibraphone, then a kind of turbulence is brewed within the transparency, and finally, after the last allegro effusion, there is a long oration on trombone, accompanied by lower strings (an arresting piece of scoring with clarity in the darkest of orchestral colors), and the opening simple fragments again. Each return, then, carries one forward in a through-composed onward continuity, and simultaneously reveals the measure of precisely how far one has already gone.

The obvious "pastorale" aspects of the last movement are simple to indicate, but not especially compelling: six-eight meter (or, later, compressions and expansions thereof) dominates, there are "siciliano" rhythms, the English horn and oboe are featured, etc. But what there is more deeply of "nature" in this is rather a sense of a background of immutable continuity against which foreground "dramatic" events evanesce, and which envelops and survives all of them — rather in the spirit of Ives's *Unanswered Question,* but without Ives's literalness.. Perhaps there is some relevance in that the actual motivic identity of the series, present but unnoticed in the propulsion of the other movements, is here very strikingly audible, and contributes to the riverlike unending by appearing at the conclusion in augmentation.

For its own virtues, as well as for the context it supplied for more recent works, the stage presentation of *The Trial of Lucullus,* written in 1947 and Sessions's only opera to date (he is presently composing another on the subject of Montezuma), was especially welcome. It is distinctly "middle-period" Sessions; compared with the free continuity of later works, its continuous unfolding from the tiniest motif in an ever-widening expansion controlled rigorously by stepwise part-writing seems, for all its impressive integrity, to press its method somewhat relentlessly, as though in fear lest the careful system of tight connections break down, or risk the disrespect of its audience. The technique employed can be described, in conjunction with Example 7, as like the house that Jack built — a truly additive procedure in which, starting with the smallest germ, a unlimited range of disparate ideas can be made to seem to logically cohere. The output of this constricting method suffers by comparison with the freer range and bolder flair of recent works, though it is hardly wanting in gravity, substance, or commitment.

Ex. 7 *(Intro.)*

It has been said that, whatever its musical value, *Lucullus* does not succeed as an "opera". But (and should we not long ago have been spared the necessity of repeating this?) there is obviously no such thing as "opera", any more than there are the entities "symphony", "sonata", "suite", etc., divorced from their individual exemplifications. *Lucullus* is a Sessions kind of opera, a work, as one would expect, of exclusively "musical" music, from which dramatic features are as absent as they are from Sessions's other music. (*The Black Maskers,* as a matter of fact, is by exception quite uninhibitedly "operatic" — something noticed by Paul Rosenfeld back in 1923).

The text of *Lucullus* is an anti-war tract by Bertolt Brecht, poorly translated, and clearly revealing (by the continual presence of narration and equally consistent absence of stage action) its origin as a radio play. The words are, in truth, dreadful, but blissfully (once one has got the hang of the thing) without importance to the musical experience. They pour out as continuously, with the same feeling of inexhaustible flow, as does the music. In this context "set numbers" with word repetitions would seem disturbing or incongruous. By the same token, most of the polyphonic development is in the instruments; the voices usually sing alone — another deliberate evasion of "dramatic" possibilities. In all of Sessions's vocal music his predilection is for solo lines set against a polyphonic instrumental texture. This is obvious in the case of single-voice works like *The Idyll of Theocritus* (and who but Wagner or Sessions would have conceived — and executed — a forty-minute cantilena for soprano with orchestra?) and *On the Beach at Fontana,* but it is also true of the Mass for unison voices and organ, and of the chorally homophonic *Turn, O Libertad,* which has a fully developed two-piano accompaniment.

Of the other works performed during the prodigious festival the Second String Quartet and the String Quintet have previously been reported on in these pages, and made their usual profound impression. Only the earliest works seemed, by comparison, perhaps, somewhat less substantial. The *Black Maskers* is clearly the brilliantly polished climax of a youthful phase; the Three Chorale Preludes for organ of 1928 conversely represent an imperfect achievement of ideas of contextual harmony based on the extension of tonal principles, ideas that were later to crystallize into a point of compositional focus. The last of these, with its rhythmic energy and reminiscence of Bach's *Durch Adams Fall,* seemed the most fully realized.

It was startling, to a listener at this festival, to realize that all the large works performed during this weekend but hardly ever elsewhere, stand among the most significant monuments of American music. This is certainly a testament to Sessions's qualities of mind, determination, and native gift, which seem now to have brought him out of obscurity to the status of a serene old master, unburdened by the compulsion to struggle to the head of the mainstream, but content simply to insert one lofty work after another into its midst.

Indeed, the entire presentation strikes one as rather miraculous, as if the accumulated backlog of Sessions's neglect by our institutional musical culture required no less drastic compensation than the devotion of all the resources of one of our staunch Midwestern citadels of musical conservatism to such a festival, as a beginning toward the restitution of old injustices. The Northwestern University School of Music, which, in all fairness, has not heretofore been known for its zeal in the cause of advanced music, suddenly found itself responsible for the mass conversion of a large segment of its student body — most of whom had barely heard of Sessions, and who at first found his music incomprehensible and unplayable – into a disciplined and enthusiastic cadre of Sessions-performers and, evidently, admirers.

Thor Johnson, who conducted devotedly and well everything that needed conducting, was principally responsible, but the pianist Guy Mombaerts, by his thoroughly secure, sympathetic, and sensitive performance of the Piano Concerto, also inspired conviction in the students. Even in a report concerned primarily with matters internal to music, this phenomenon deserves notice for its indication that perhaps the prevalent dullness of our regular musical life is more self-imposed and needless than we may have supposed.

BENJAMIN BORETZ

12/60

Haydn: String Quartet in D major, op. 76, no. 5.

J. K. RANDALL

THE tonal organization of Haydn's string Quartet, op. 76, no. 5, derives from a progression of tonicizations stated in its opening section. Not only does each subsequent section derive tonally from the first by means of three basic operations; but, in addition, within each movement these operations appear in the same order. Furthermore, the special tonal characteristics of the individual movements form a progressive sequence, in which the final movement serves as a summation of the preceding three.

Although "tonicization" is the basic term of this analysis, I am not able adequately to define the general conditions under which it will be applied. So complex and interdependent are the relevant chordal, linear, durational and motivic influences, that ad hoc persuasion seems the safest course. It is hoped that ambiguous instances in a work by Haydn will be few enough to permit this indulgence in conventional camouflage.

For matters discussed as well as those not, a score at hand, with the measures numbered in each movement, will be indispensable.

MOVEMENT I

The opening section (meas. 1-28) of the first movement states the progression of tonicizations fundamental to the entire quartet:

Meas. 1-12   13(15) 16   17   18   19   20-28   29

(D⟷A),   D⟶b⟶G⟶e⟶D,   (A⟷D) ‖d

FIG. I.

- 14 -

(Essential for Fig. 1 is the interpretation of meas. 15, by analogy with meas. 3, as belonging exclusively to D, and not at all to the mildly tonicized G of meas. 14.) The tonicizations of Fig. 1 are all associated either with the head-motif of the theme[1] or with a cadence, and all state their "tonic" in the bass; the mild tonicizations of G in meas. 2, 6, 10, 14, 22 and 26 have been omitted from Fig. I because they lack all of these qualifications. The parentheses around meas. 1-12 and meas. 20-28 indicate the simple enclosure of A within D; by way of contrast, the tonicizations of meas. 15-19 are not thus individually enclosed: it is with this progression of "independent" tonicizations that most of this analysis will be concerned. Nevertheless, the parenthesized tonicizations signify a hierarchy decisive for the "independent" progression: all "independent" progressions in the quartet move from tonic to tonic (as in movement I), from dominant to dominant, or from one to the other. The local juxtaposition of tonic major and tonic minor (meas. 28-29), which occurs in this movement simply as a by-product of a sectional juxtaposition (cf. discussion of Fig. 2), will develop a significance of its own in movements II and IV.

The D minor section (meas. 29-57) of the first movement states a progression of tonicizations which shows some obvious partial resemblances to the "independent" progression of the opening section:

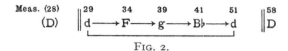

FIG. 2.

---

[1] In meas. 19 the head-motif rhythm is maintained, but the contour and harmonic rhythm are sharply modified so as to reproduce the melodic 7th-span A ⟋ G which followed the head-motif in meas. 1-2, meas. 5-6, meas. 9-10 and meas. 13-14. Meas. 20 moves directly to a cadence on the tonicized dominant, omitting any reference to the melodic peak of B in meas. 3 and its analogues. This omission is significant in view of the entirely different role for which the melodic fragment B-G-E-D-C sharp is being saved. This point will be discussed in connection with the finale.

Within the B flat section are several subordinate tonicizations whose exclusion from Fig. 2 needs explanation. The tonicization of E flat in meas. 45-46 is similar to that of G in meas. 2 and its analogues (cf. especially meas. 118-119). Notice particularly the approach to the 6/3 position, with the bass "tonic" appearing only on an eighth-note off-beat. The c of meas. 47, which also elaborates the 6/3 position, seems still milder by virtue of its function as a 5-6 exchange over the "tonic" of the preceding measure. Whether or not meas. 52 should be labelled a tonicization of F at all is difficult to decide. At any rate, since this measure is clearly enclosed within d, it should not be granted the rank of an "independent" tonicization.

Closer inspection reveals that the progression of Fig. 2 may be derived in its entirety from the "independent" progression of Fig. 1. For the sake of economy, let us incorporate the original D major enclosure of the Fig. 1 progression into a cyclic representation (Fig. 3a):

FIG. 3a.　　　　　　FIG. 3b.

By *transposing* this cycle up a minor third we obtain Fig. 3b, in which the direction of the arrows has been reversed to indicate the actual connections in Fig. 2. These connections are therefore *retrograde* with respect to Fig. 3a. But a glance now shows that the entire progression of Fig. 2 simply represents Fig. 3b read from its right-hand member. Thus, in relation to the "independent" progression of Fig. 1 (= Fig. 3a), Fig. 2 (= Fig. 3b) introduces not only transposition and retrogression, but also a *rotation* of the whole cycle.

It should be stressed that this particular rotation and this particular transposition capitalize upon predominating characteristics of the basic progression itself: the former upon the unique emphasis accruing to the relative minor relationship through immediate recurrence within the progression (D → b, G → e), and to b in particular through its cadential position in meas. 16; and the latter upon the primacy of the tonic enclosure—a primacy established not only by the "independent" tonicizations, but by the simple enclosures of the opening twelve measures. Retrogression of this rotation restores the original ordering of the relative major and minor pairs. But most important of all, the operations of transposition, rotation, and retrogression are necessary and nearly sufficient for the derivation, from the basic progression of Fig. I, of every subsequent progression of "independent" tonicizations in the Quartet. It is precisely these three operations whose order of application is the same within each of the four movements.

Measures 58-75 bring an abbreviated and melodically ornamented re-statement of the first section of the movement. The abbreviation affects only the dominant-tonic exchanges of the flanking phrases, reducing them to one on either side. The important modifications in meas. 73-75 will be discussed later in connection with the finale.

The concluding section of the 1st movement[2] presents a literal retrograde not only of the basic "independent" progression but of the total abbreviated progression of meas. 58-75:

Meas. 76   85   88   91   93   95   97   101   102
(D ⟶ A ⟶) D ⟶ e ⟶ G ⟶ b ⟶ D(⟶ A ⟶ D)   ‖

FIG. 4.

---

[2] Thematically a summation section, involving all of the characteristic melodic fragments of the preceding sections.

The subsequent tonicizations of G, especially the mild version of meas. 118-119 with the 3rd in the bass, provide a final retrograde flourish with reference to meas. 2 (or meas. 59).

We may now schematize the order of operations within the 1st movement—an order decisive for each of the remaining movements. Let us designate the initial statement of the "independent" progression as the "major" phase of the movement; the progression of the second section, derived by rotation, retrogression, and transposition, as the "minor" phase; and the concluding progression, derived by retrogression alone, as the "retrograde" phase. For the remaining movements, let us agree to call *"major"* any section most economically derivable (from the basic progression or one of its fragments) *by identity* or *by transposition alone; "minor"* any section derivable only through the three basic operations combined; and *"retrograde"* any section most economically derivable *by retrogression* with or without transposition, but *without rotation.* Let us also agree that our "retrograde" section must play an unambiguous retrograde role *within* the movement in question. (The reasons for this double restriction upon the "retrograde" phase will become apparent in our discussion of the 2nd movement.) Although these conventions are by no means adequate for the unique description of every possible fragment, those few ambiguous cases which do arise in the Quartet may be readily resolved in context.

We should also clarify at this point a distinction between "fragment" and "rotation": the earmark of the latter will always be the overstepping of the original enclosure, regardless of starting-point; in the absence of this overstepping, we will speak simply of a "fragment". For example, the fragment G → e → D (cf. Fig. 1) *does not* involve rotation, whereas the fragment e → D → b (cf. Fig. 1 and Fig. 3a) *does.*

MOVEMENT II

In contrast to the first movement, which operated in each of its sections upon the entire basic progression, the second movement operates exclusively upon fragments. The finale will play off the total progression and its fragments against one another.

The "exposition" of the second movement utilizes the fragment G → e → D of Fig. 1 transposed down a half-step, and therefore constitutes its "major" phase:

Meas. 1-13   14   18 |35
F♯ ——→ d♯ ——→ C♯ | c♯

FIG. 5.

Just as in the first movement the major 2nd approach to the tonic (meas. 18-19 of movement I) preceded the appearance of its parallel minor at the outset of the "minor" phase (meas. 29 of movement I), so in the second movement does the major 2nd approach to the *dominant* (meas. 14-18) herald the appearance of *its* parallel minor (meas. 35), and therewith the opening of the next "minor" phase. Were this analogy to be completed within the limits imposed by the three-membered fragment of the "major" phase, the "minor" phase would now follow the course c sharp → E → f sharp; an exact parallel, again by half-step transposition, to the d → F → g of movement I (cf. Fig. 2). In this way, the combined "major" and "minor" phases (F sharp → d sharp → C sharp → c sharp → E → f sharp) could be derived as a single unit from the series of *"independent"* tonicizations between meas. 17 and meas. 40 of movement I (G → e → D → d → F → g). Such a simple fulfilment does not come to pass, however. Other, subtler processes, conditioned by the impending retrograde phase and by the very presence of an F sharp major movement in a D major quartet, delay the required final f sharp through a transposition of (C sharp) → c sharp → E to (E) → e → G (brackets 2 and 2a) and a subsequent return to e:

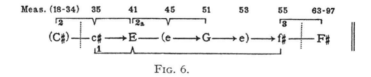

FIG. 6.

In order to justify relegating the segment e → G → e to the status of an "insert" into the "minor" phase (bracket 1)—as well as elevating so brief a segment as the f sharp—F sharp juxtaposition of "development" and "recapitulation" (bracket 3) to the status of the "retrograde" phase—we must show that, in spite of its sequential origins (bracket 2a), the segment e → G → e taken as a unit possesses characteristics unique within this movement. That such is actually the case is evident: this segment represents the only excursion of a movement in the "distant" key of F sharp major into previously defined tonal regions (cf. movement I: Fig. 1 and Fig. 4). Furthermore, the beginning of this excursion (meas. 45-47) is marked by a radical alteration of "accompaniment" texture-descending triple-octaves found nowhere else in the movement.

Now while this point of view makes fully plausible the sequential pro-liferation of the "minor" phase as far as G (meas. 51-52), it also creates new problems: not only does the return to e (meas. 53) seem redundant and schematically isolated, but in addition it subjects the G to enclosure, thereby depriving G of "independence" as a tonicization. Yet it is precisely this return to e which both consummates the orientation to the overall tonic of D and confirms the relations which will serve as the basis for the "retrograde" phase. The harmonies through which the "redundant" e is approached (meas. 51 plus the first half of meas. 52) stand so patently in the relation of IV and V7 to D *major* that their re-interpretation, effected by the rise of C sharp to D sharp in the viola (meas. 52), comes as an aural surprise. (The subsequent activity of the cello in meas. 58 and meas. 60 absorbs this suggestion of D major directly into the current tonic of F sharp.) Finally, the resultant enclosure of G suggests a "larger" progression of C sharp (meas. 18-34)—c sharp (meas. 35-40)→ E (meas. 41-44)—e (meas. 45-53), whose double statement of parallel major and minor is immediately followed by the retrograde of precisely that relation (f sharp—F sharp). Thus, although the basic derivation of the "retrograde" phase from D—d of Fig. 1 by retrogression and transposition is trivial in itself, the anticipation provided by the course of this movement (cf. our original twofold condition for the "retrograde" phase) invests this juxtaposition with a new significance.

Two difficulties remain: first, since G is enclosed within e, why not drop the G from the diagram (Fig. 6) and dissolve several of our problems at the outset; and second, should this prove untenable, why not call e → G the "retrograde" phase (cf. Fig. 4) and G → e a "re-statement" (cf. Fig. 1)? As to the first, the temporal distribution of G across a cadence (meas. 49-51) plus the lack of any established tonal priority of e (all previous "enclosures" have occurred within the *tonic*) would seem to oblige us to treat G at face value. As to the second, e → G, although identical with a segment of Fig. 4, does not fulfil the *second* condition for the "retrograde" phase: that it play an unambiguous retrograde role *within* the movement in question. The sequential relation of e → G (brackets 2 and 2a) to an unambiguously initiated "minor" phase simply makes such an identification incorrect by definition. On the other hand, the identification of G → e as "re-statement" cannot be called incorrect, and may even be found suggestive because of the resultant analogy in position between the "re-statement" phases of movements I and II. Yet the temporal disparity between this newly christened "re-statement" and its surrounding phases makes foolery of such an identification. Thus, it becomes apparent that the purely schematic ambiguities which beset such brief fragments are fully dispelled in the musical context.

MOVEMENT III

The minuet and trio misbehave under our analysis—not because of any lack of correspondences to the other movements, but rather because of the lack of a clear internal pattern. The direct progression from tonic to dominant (meas. 1-8), already familiar from the opening phrase of the Quartet, re-establishes the primary functions of D major. (This "re-establishment" is thematically quite literal, in that the first ascending F sharp major *arpeggio* of movement II is now transposed back to D major.) The return to D by way of a tonicization of E minor (meas. 9-11) is familiar as the final stage of the basic "independent" progression, and again heralds the appearance of the parallel minor. (Cf. the Trio.) The mild tonicization of G in meas. 26-27 (still with the 3rd in the bass) recalls the analogous event in the 1st movement, where this particular enclosed tonicization also appeared as a final appendage to the "independent" progression of a section (meas. 26 of movement I) and of the movement itself (meas. 111-112 and 118-119 of movement I). These patchwork parallels to the "major" phase of movement I do not, however, explain the absence in the Minuet of a larger controlling progression.

The Trio offers similar obstacles. The promise of a "minor" phase implicit in its D minor opening is not fulfilled. Instead, the appearance of the dominant minor as an independent sectional analogue to the dominant major (compare D → A :||: → D :|| of the Minuet with ||: d → a :||: → d :|| of the Trio) paves the way for the elaborate transformations of the dominant minor which will occur in the finale. (Notice that in movement I *tonic* major and minor appeared as sectional analogues; in movement II, tonic *and* dominant majors and minors appeared in local juxtaposition; and now, in movement III, *both* appear as sectional analogues.)

By means of a slight re-definition of our "major", "minor", and "retrograde" phases (in terms of most economical derivation from Fig. 1, Fig. 2, or Fig. 4, rather than in terms of the operations themselves), a re-definition equally serviceable in the other three movements, we might even construe the progression g → F → d (meas. 49-52) as a "retrograde" phase in relation to Fig. 2. Yet these gymnastics only emphasize the irrelevance of our descriptions *within* the movement. The final enclosed tonicization of G *minor* (meas. 5) yields, at most, a parallel to the tonicizations of G major already discussed.

In analysing the finale, we will return briefly to some additional characteristics of movement III which receive a more specific interpretation subsequently. This further dissolution of the Minuet into a pastiche of crossreferences to other movements will, of course, contribute nothing toward explaining the internal coherence of the minuet itself. In our concluding paragraph we will attempt to remedy this deficiency from another point of view.

MOVEMENT IV

The "exposition" presents the following progression of tonicizations:

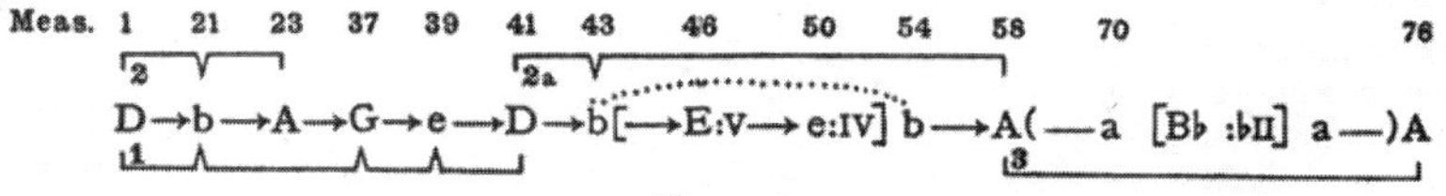

$$\text{D} \rightarrow \text{b} \rightarrow \text{A} \rightarrow \text{G} \rightarrow \text{e} \rightarrow \text{D} \rightarrow \text{b}[\rightarrow \text{E:v} \rightarrow \text{e:IV}]\ \text{b} \rightarrow \text{A}(\text{—a}\ [\text{B}\flat : \flat \text{II}]\ \text{a —})\text{A}$$

FIG. 7.

The most striking feature of this progression is its restoration of Fig. 1 (cf. bracket 1 of Fig. 7). Although we might avoid some labour by describing the A of meas. 23-36 as a "fill-in" or an "ornamentation" of this basic progression, these catch-all terms are absurd in the face of the durational and thematic priority of these measures. That these priorities in themselves create the unit shown under bracket 2 is obvious, as is its derivation (by transposition) from the remainder of the basic progression (meas. 37-42). But let us recall in addition that the F sharp → d sharp → C sharp "major" phase of movement II was derived in the same manner and stated in a similar temporal distribution. (Compare meas. 1-34 of movement II and meas. 1-36 of movement IV.) For these reasons it seems appropriate to speak here of a "superimposition" of the "major" phase fragment of movement II upon the total basic progression. This interpretation receives some confirmation in meas. 41-58, where the fragment D → b → A recurs, now detached from its larger context (bracket 2a). The "retrograde" phase will invest this unit with a new importance. We should also notice that D, b, and A in themselves had a special significance in movement I as the *only* cadential goals within the "major" phase, and that b and A were absorbed directly into D *in the order* D → b (VI) → A(V7) during the cadential modification of the "re-statement" (cf. meas. 73-75 of movement I). We might also hesitantly suggest that the a sharp in meas. 5 of the minuet indicates, in its faint—very faint—allusion to b, an intermediate stage in the gradual unveiling of D → b → A as an overt progression of tonicizations.

The description of meas. 46-49 as the dominant of A rather than as a simple tonicization of E requires explanation. If we confine our observation to these measures plus the last eighth-note of meas. 45, then we must certainly acknowledge a tonicization of E. In view of the durational disparity between the B dominant seventh and its flanking chords, however, it seems more relevant to evaluate E in terms of its connection with the preceding b of meas. 43-45, and then to relate B7 to the result. On this basis, E stands to b as V to II in A major, with B7 tonicizing E *within* an implied A major context. In this interpretation, meas. 54-57 make explicit these implications of meas. 43-49. The whole passage serves to underline the function of b as a transition from D to A; additional modifications, equally inescapable aurally, are introduced in the "retrograde" phase when the function of b is reversed.

Now it may be objected that all tonicizations may be reduced to a subordinate position in relation to other tonicizations, and eventually, if not immediately, in relation to the tonic itself. Yet this truism must not be allowed to obscure the innumerable types and degrees of subordination. Our previous use of the term "tonicization" has in every instance been influenced by the durational weight, with respect to the surroundings, of the harmonic components involved; and has usually received additional support from thematic associations. Our present case certainly involves no thematic priority within the progression B7 → E: on the contrary, thematic considerations segregate the tonicization of b (meas. 43-45) and the repeated E-B 5th (meas. 46-49) as distinct phases, neither of which involves the B7; likewise, the purely durational emphasis links b with E across the B7. Therefore, this "tonicization" of E is different from the events that we have hitherto described as "tonicizations", so that to place it as an equal partner among them would be inappropriate.

As previously, the major 2nd approach to the dominant (meas. 54-58: b → A) anticipates the entrance of the dominant minor (meas. 70). This event (meas. 70-75) is sharply differentiated from its surroundings rhythmically and includes as its most crucial feature the B flat major triad of meas. 72-73. In addition to the dominant major-minor relationship already exploited in the 2nd and 3rd movements, these measures create the possibility of reference to the dominant minor through quotation of its atypical and emphatic B-flat triad—a possibility which is unmistakably realized at the outset of the "development", where a similar rhythmic isolation and melodic descent over the sustained triad (meas. 126-129) initiate the complexities of the "minor" phase. Similarly, the enclosure of a within A will assume heightened importance in the connection of the "minor" with the "retrograde" phase.

The total progression of the "development" is as follows:

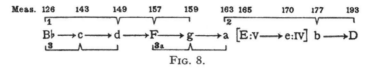

Fig. 8.

That bracket 1 yields the "minor" phase complete except for its failure to return to its new starting-point of B flat (derivation by a new rotation; compare with Fig. 2 and Fig. 3b), and that bracket 2 yields the "retrograde" phase at least in its segment b → D (cf. identity with Fig. 4) and perhaps in its entirety in relation to the already discussed D → b → A (Fig. 7) seems clear enough. But why the "minor" phase should be complicated by c, and why the opportunity for the exact "retrograde" A → b → D should be scuttled by the use of the dominant *minor*, calls for explanation.

First of all, let us observe that the particular rotation employed in the "minor" phase has been carefully prepared; not only by the already discussed B flat triad of meas. 72-73, but by the original statement of the "minor" phase in movement I (where the B flat tonicization represented both the most extended duration and the extreme degree of thematic modification), and also by the use of the fragment d → F → g as a self-sufficient unit in movement II (transposed to c sharp → E → f sharp) and in movement III (presented in retrograde at the original pitch in meas. 48-52); the detached B flat now being re-introduced at the "wrong end". Next let us recall that within the context of the finale the B flat of meas. 126-129 refers explicitly to its origins in the A minor of meas. 70-75; consequently, the progression of the "minor" phase to A minor[3] (meas. 163), rather than back to its new starting point of B flat, may be interpreted as the return of B flat to its own origins within the finale. Analogously, when this resolution is followed (meas. 166) by quotation of meas. 46*ff.*—with their already discussed implication of A major—we may say that A minor has, in its turn, been referred back to *its* own origins within the finale (cf. Fig. 7, bracket 3). Thus the progression of the "minor" phase, as

---

[3] This progression is somewhat foreshadowed in the Trio of movement III by the proximity of the A minor cadence of meas. 44 to the g → F → d of meas. 48-52. The intervention of D minor in meas. 45-48 spoils the analogy.

well as its connection to the "retrograde" phase, is controlled by the implications of the last stage of the "exposition" (meas. 58-120).

The above interpretation of the "minor" phase simplifies the problem of the "retrograde" phase. While the progression a → b → D is not derivable from the basic progression of Fig. 1 except in its segment b → D (a segment qualified in itself to constitute the "retrograde" phase); nevertheless, the quotation of meas. 46*ff.* in meas. 166*ff.* (discussed above) indirectly symbolizes the derivation of a → b → D by retrogression of the D → b → A of meas. 41-58. The reversal of the function of b between D and A is brought into "first-hearing" audibility by the unique harmonic modification of meas. 189-190, where, by analogy with every previous and subsequent statement of this motif, the note of the 2nd violin would be G sharp rather than G natural.

The C minor impurity in the picture developed thus far may now be explained. Immediately obvious is the sequential relation between B flat → c → d and F → g → a (Fig. 8: brackets 3 and 3a), the latter segment being independently entailed by the considerations adduced above. Yet we may ask why F → g → a, precisely because independently entailed, need appear in this *sequential* garb. First, notice that the superimposition of D → b → A upon the total basic progression in the "exposition" (cf. Fig. 7) creates as a by-product the unprecedented segment b → A → G, and that this segment receives gratuitous emphasis through the quotation of meas. 23 in meas. 35. Now the attempt to derive the segments B flat → c → d and F → g → a directly from b → A → G, by retrogression and transposition, leads nowhere because of the reversal of "quality" in each component. Yet this derivation cannot be entirely ignored, especially since the reversal of "quality" in corresponding components is in itself a by-product of the initial derivation of Fig. 2 from Fig. 1. In this light, the presence in the "minor" phase (of the finale) of sequential segments involving a reversal of "quality" in regard to a newly created byproduct of the "major" phase, may be viewed as a development suggested by a characteristic feature of the "minor" phase in general. Furthermore, throughout the quartet such newly created by-products or emphases have received development. For example, in the finale itself the new emphasis upon D → b → A became the source of the "retrograde" phase, just as did the new emphasis of the local juxtaposition of parallel major and minor in movement II. We have already dwelt at length upon the history of the suggestion contained in the last stage of the finale "exposition", which was in its turn suggested by the gradual liberation of the dominant minor in the course of the Quartet—a liberation which is only completed in the indirect A minor enclosure of the "minor" phase of the finale.

The sequential articulation of the "minor" phase is not merely schematic: on the contrary, it is made explicit in the musical context through the durational and thematic parallelism within B flat → c → d (meas. 134-153) followed by the entirely distinct durational and thematic parallelism within F → g → a (meas. 155-165). Yet despite the clarity of this articulation, a foreshadowing of d as the second component of the "minor" phase is not altogether lacking: cf. meas. 120-126, in which B flat is approached through an A dominant seventh, and stands therefore in its immediate context as VI to V7 in D minor. Thus, although the relation of meas. 126-129 to meas. 72-73 points back to A minor origins, and the relation of meas. 132-140 to their sequel necessitates the label of "tonicization", the initial small-scale harmonic context of B flat (meas. 120-129) still manages to allude to the impending direction of the "minor" phase.

The schematic possibility of deriving a → b → D from c → d → F of the "minor" phase by transposition alone may now be quickly disposed of. It follows from the above paragraph that the musical context provides no articulation whatever for c → d → F as a unit; so that such a derivation of a → b → D would rival in foolishness the hypothetical "solutions" offered at the end of our discussion of movement II.

The "recapitulation" of the finale, initiated by an ingeniously compressed version of the 1st violin part of meas. 8-12 in meas. 193-197 (2nd violin)[4] combined contrapuntally with the motif of meas. 1-6, brings back the basic progression of Fig. 1 in its original form:

---

[4] Notice particularly the transformation of meas. 12 (1st violin) into meas. 196-197 (2nd violin).

Meas. 193   198   200   202   205   207   208-220   221   225   229   233
D → b → G → e[→ A:V] D,   (A ↔ D),   [A:V → a:IV] e → D   ‖

FIG. 9.

The previously superimposed and appended fragment D → b → A (cf. meas. 1-23 and meas. 41-58) has, in effect, been "cancelled" by its retrogression in meas. 166-193.

The description of meas. 205 as the dominant of D rather than as an independent tonicization of A follows from the same considerations as those applied in meas. 44-46[5]. Yet the presence of this pseudo-tonicization within such a crucial phase of the Quartet in itself requires explanation. A glance ahead to meas. 221-236 reveals that the musical material of the now "cancelled" segment b → A (cf. meas. 46-61) is to be transposed to the still available segment e → D. Thus, the "ambiguity" of meas. 205 may be interpreted as an anticipation, by means of incorporation into the basic "independent" progression itself, of the impending transposition to A:V of the all-important E:V (→ e:IV) function of meas. 46-49 and meas. 166-169. This anticipatory relation of meas. 205 to meas. 221 is made unmistakable through the literal quotation of the 1st violin fragment B-G-E-D-C sharp (meas. 204-205) in meas. 220-221. Curiously, this melodic figure has not previously appeared in the finale—unless we are willing to call the 1st violin part of meas. 72-75 a "previous appearance". For the nearest literal statement of this series of tones we must return to meas. 74-75 of movement I, where the same melodic fragment, derived in turn from the peak of the opening phrase of the Quartet (meas. 3-4), was employed with exactly the same significance: to mark the end of a "re-statement" phase—the *only other* "re-statement" phase in the entire Quartet. This

---

[5] In this connection, we should observe the difference between meas. 204-205 of the finale and meas. 3-4 of movement I, where we have without much hesitation discovered a "tonicization" of A. While the G sharp of meas. 3 (last eighth-note in the cello) is hardly sufficient durationally to counter-balance the larger IV (or II) → V implications of meas. 3 plus the first quarter-note of meas. 4, the additional weight provided by the subsequent course of the cello in meas. 4 (together with the G sharp of the 2nd violin) seems to confirm the presence of a local V → I progression in A. No such subsequent confirmation occurs in meas. 205 of the finale: on the contrary, meas. 206 introduces a G natural in the viola. Not until meas. 208-209, after the confirmation of D, can we make any case for the label "tonicization of A".

virtuoso display of incorporation and cross-reference secures an additional advantage *within* the context of the finale: just as the segment b → A occurred twice in the "exposition", so does its transposition e → D occur twice in the "recapitulation".

The tonicizations of A in meas. 208-209 and meas. 212-213 (the latter dubious) offer no new problem, inasmuch as the basic progression of Fig. 1 was itself surrounded by tonic-enclosed tonicizations of A. Indeed, the "re-statement" (meas. 193-207) imitates its model (meas. 15-19 of movement I) rather closely throughout: notice once again the sequential head-motifs followed by the 7th-span A→G (cf. footnote 1) at the approach to the tonic (meas. 205-206, 1st violin). Although the chromatic activity of meas. 214-216 provides a modicum of grist for our mill in its suggestions of F sharp:V and E:V, we will forego discussion of this very brief passage which certainly yields no overt tonicizations.

That the divisions of each movement implied by this analysis correspond closely to conventional thematic and tonal divisions is evident. More interesting is the fact that each tonicization phase of the Quartet may be derived, after Schenkerian reduction, from middle-ground neighbour-note prolongations of the melodic level "5". These prolongations always involve the upper-neighbour 6 (or ♭6), and, more often than not, the lower-neighbour ♯4 as well. From this point of view, movement III is much less of a problem. The minuet itself elaborates a 5-1 *Urlinie* by means of double neighbour-note (♯4, then 6) prolongation of 5, while the trio elaborates the same *Urlinie* by means of analogous prolongations in minor. Also, from this point of view, our cross-references between movements I and IV in regard to the tonicization fragment D → b → A, the melodic sequence B-G-E-D-C sharp, and the triad of B flat major, deal not merely with minute identities of the foreground but with local reflections of the most fundamental middleground prolongation technique of the Quartet. Thus, a reduction analysis substantially clarifies certain details of this analysis; and, in addition, succeeds easily (in movement III) where this analysis failed. On the other hand, this analysis does bring out purely foreground determinants which might become obscured in the process of reconstruction from more basic structural levels.

Textual note.—The version of this Quartet given by the complete Pleyel edition (c. 1802) is sloppy and inconsistent throughout, particularly in its use of accidentals. While the vagaries of movement II (e.g. E sharp unmodified in the 1st violin and cello parts against E natural in the 2nd violin and viola parts in meas. 45) and movement III (the viola part *Allegretto*, the other parts *Allegro*) can hardly be called problematic; still, the maze of omissions and superfluities in meas. 154-162 of movement IV does require comment. This passage omits all naturals before C in the 2nd violin part, and all those of meas. 156-157 in the 1st violin part. Presumably, the superfluous final natural of meas. 155 is supposed to last through meas. 157 in the 1st violin. The missing naturals in meas. 157-158 of the 2nd violin must be editorially supplied on the grounds that their absence is vertically and linearly absurd. If the foregoing is correct, an additional natural before C in meas. 161 of the 2nd violin might now be introduced on the somewhat weaker grounds of motivic probability. As for the omitted flat before B in meas. 161 of the viola, B natural cannot be called musically absurd. On the other hand, if the note is not B flat, then why the superfluous cautionary natural before the following E? And above all, why is there no cautionary natural before the B itself? Unfortunately, this mode of reasoning requires the assumption that the cautionary accidentals of this edition are rationally employed—an assumption I would not wish to make.

The slightly earlier Artaria edition (1799) is of similar quality. The assignment of the same tempo to all instruments in movement III is compensated for by the disparity in the number of measures between the 1st violin and the other instruments in movement IV. Measure 45 of movement II shows the same distribution of simultaneous E sharps and E naturals. The accidentals of meas. 154-162 of movement IV are likewise exactly the same as in the Pleyel edition. For the purposes of this analysis, I have simply followed the line of strongest prejudice and accepted Wilhelm Altmann's version (Eulenburg edition) of the pitch content of this passage.

Author's Note (2003):

Hoping to elevate my negligible standing with my mother-in-law, I confided to her that my Haydn article (—my maiden voyage—) had just been accepted for publication by a highly respected music journal. Said she: In what way will such an article benefit anyone?

At the time, I was at a loss for an answer.

SERIAL COMPOSITION AND ATONALITY*

Reviewed by BENJAMIN BORETZ

UP TO NOW, the few available books attempting to deal generally with atonal and twelve-tone music have consistently failed to reveal much awareness of the significant approaches recently developed to the fundamental theoretic, analytic, and compositional implications of systematic pitch organization. For the most part, these works offer little beyond routine restatement of the traditional "rules" of procedure originally propounded as guidelines during the early stages of twelve-tone composition, which in practice almost immediately underwent extensive modification, and "analyses" consisting primarily of simple set identifications and note counting. The triviality of the actual material presented is often masked behind pretentious metaphysical and pseudohistorical, pseudoscientific "justifications" whose origin is in those similar statements by Schoenberg that constitute the least fruitful aspect of his thought.

This preponderance is particularly lamentable in view of the defenselessness of many readers against the fallacies and misconceptions that abound in such facile productions. Most of the genuinely rigorous thought in this field has been presented in articles of a highly specialized nature which are either inaccessible or require for their comprehension a degree of prior experience and training that is, to say the least, far from prevalent even among professional musicians. As a result, an important, perhaps the most important, development in contemporary musical thought has taken place and is rapidly expanding out of reach, in the absence of a comprehensive general statement of its principles and attitudes, of the majority of those for whom it has the greatest interest and consequence.

The present book takes an important step toward supplying this deficiency by examining "classical" atonal and twelve-tone works in terms of their relation to some of the central concerns

---

* *Serial Composition and Atonality,* by George Perle. University of California Press, 1962.

by which current theoretical work is motivated. *Serial Composition and Atonality* is, within this general realm, a personal approach that focuses on issues and instances that seem of particular importance to the author. Perle's deep and productive involvement, as composer and analyst, with this tendency and its elucidation, would alone suffice to justify the approach and to guarantee the book's value, were not its special merits of keen observation and concentration so powerful in themselves.

The subtitle, "an introduction to the music of Schoenberg, Berg, and Webern", is an important qualification of the book's objectives, making it clear, for one thing, that it is not intended to be a systematic synthesis of relevant theoretical constructs, and justifying, for another, its limited treatment of post-"classical" aspects of twelve-tone procedure except as they arise from specific features of the passages under discussion. Nor does Perle attempt a methodical or complete exposition of atonal and twelve-tone practice; as his title indicates, the emphasis is on composition rather than system, and systematic concepts are introduced in connection with compositional solutions rather than as a consequentially interrelated body of principles.

The advantages of such an informal method are ingeniously exploited: by offering "reasonable" definitions, rather than rigorous formulations, of basic principles, and by maintaining flexibility in their selection and order of presentation, Perle is able to restrict the complexity and verbiage of his text to a minimum, and to achieve a continuous, unencumbered contact with the music itself that is of particular value in an introductory work. In accordance with this intention, he is in many cases led to leave general conclusions as well as the more subtle ramifications of his observations unstated; the observant reader will, however, often be able to infer these for himself from the copious examples, whereas fuller explanation might have tended to divert attention from the main focus on specific instances of procedure.

The sectional organization is similarly designed to aid the reader in linking contemporary practices with those already familiar to him from tradition. "Tonality, Atonality, Dodecaphony", the opening chapter, describes the atonal "situation" both as it grew out of tonality and in terms of its particular conditions, and also demonstrates the special relevance of the twelve-tone system to these conditions. Here, also, the minimal assumptions of Schoenberg's twelve-tone procedure are sketched, as are those of the Hauer "trope" system (which by virtue of its exclusive specification of segmental content rather than order, has been of particular importance to Perle in developing his own harmonic technique).

The second chapter, "'Free' Atonality", stresses the ambiguity and dependence on purely local association that characterizes this most problematic body of music, and traces several approaches to the problem, particularly that of the single "basic cell". This idea carries over into the following chapter, "Non-Dodecaphonic Serial Composition", in which the techniques of Roslavetz and Scriabin (prototypes more of Hauer's than of Schoenberg's ideas) are treated along with a discussion of Schoenberg's Opus 23 and instances of serial practice in Bartók and pre-Canticum Stravinsky.

In the two chapters that follow, "Motivic Functions of the Set" and "Simultaneity", an examination is made of various approaches taken within the framework of twelve-tone composition to such problems as motivic identification and organization, relation of foreground and background, linear and contrapuntal variation, and chord construction and association. A departure from the informality of the overall style is the section on "Symmetrical Adjacency Relationships", which is a good exposition of Perle's own "twelve-tone modal system". Another such departure is the section devoted to a simple arithmetical tabulation of the total number of different chords obtainable from the twelve-tone pitch material.

Chapter vi, "Structural Functions of the Set", presents instances of overall formal structures involving association with traditional procedures (in Schoenberg's Opus 33A), as well as organizations deriving from set structure itself (the Webern Symphony and Milton Babbitt's *Three Compositions for Piano*, I). Most of the basic twelve-tone properties exploited in the "classical" literature are, in these last three chapters, either identified specifically, or are inferable from more general procedural descriptions; in every case, they are directly associated with passages in which they function as articulative devices. The distinction of linear, vertical, and macroformal considerations results in the separation of each discussion of a single concept into several carefully cross-referenced parts, according to its relevance to the discussion at hand. Thus one finds segmentation first described (p. 70) as ". . . a procedure that permits a great variety of linear elements to be derived from the set without a concomitant weakening of its integrative function. . . . Of more significance . . . is the fact that such procedures suggest a special type of set structure whose transformations and transpositions may be interrelated through segments of common pitch content. . . . Invariant segmental content is a means of delimiting the range of variational procedures and therefore of maintaining the integrity of the set as an organizing principle in spite of the linear revision." Later (p. 94), segmental invariance is considered in its harmonic aspect, and is found to be "particularly useful as a means of reducing and simplifying the harmonic formations generated by the verticalization of set-statements." The emphasis in all these assertions is plainly on function, and the actual nature of the phenomena, either concretely or as part of an integral group of operations, is observable from the examples given, although the wider formal implications of even such assertions as the above are not enlarged upon or demonstrated; however, the examples also reveal enough local evidence of the correspondences in question to enable the reader to infer their integrative functioning on a macroformal scale.

By means of similarly operational descriptions, one is introduced to such phenomena as set construction from segmental generators (such a set is "a composite structure generated by literal transformations of an elementary motivic unit"—p. 79) and their expansion into derived sets ("each segment of any form of the basic set may function as the generating unit of a 'derived' set"—p. 82); secondary set formation (described specifically on pp. 105ff. as "successive statements of noncorresponding six-note segments that vertically combined would form an aggregate", although the suggestive genesis of this technique in the works of Berg may be inferred from the earlier discussion of the association of "independent" sets in *Lulu* (p. 78), but is not so related in the discussion); and combinatoriality, gradually approached at various points and finally defined on pp. 99ff. The property of intersection, so crucial in much of

Webern[1], is not discussed or illustrated as such even in the section on "octave" relationships, but it arises in connection with the Symphony, Op. 21 ("all the inversional relationships being based on a single axis of symmetry, the note A." —p. 131).

In general, there is much to admire in the care and agility with which Perle has undertaken to present these materials in an orderly fashion without resorting to the, perhaps forbidding, rigors of systematization. But inevitably, with a presentational method which, although far from arbitrary in a "musical" sense, is unavoidably divergent from the formal structure on which the concepts depend for ultimate coherence, certain difficulties arise. It is, indeed, demonstrative of Perle's superior command of his subject that so few do occur, and none of these is of a kind likely to give much comfort to either simplistic academicians or mystical parametrists. As one consequence of the sectional division, for example, whose considerable virtue, already noted, is that greatest emphasis is placed on the musical object, some fundamental concepts appear rather late in the book that are actually necessary to a full understanding of many ideas earlier introduced. One of these is the concept of twelve-tone inversion as the complementation of pitch class numbers mod. 12, a basic distinction between the operations of this permutational system and those of traditional tonality, in which inversion has a different signification[2]. But in the book, this concept first appears on p. 146 (of a total of 149 pages of text), and there in connection with rhythmic, rather than pitch inversion. The "working definition" originally given, in a footnote (p. 3), does not actually specify this condition, referring only to "melodic, [rather than] harmonic inversion, since the latter concerns only

---

[1] See Milton Babbitt, "Twelve-Tone Invariants as Compositional Determinants", *Musical Quarterly,* April 1960, pp. 254-256.

[2] Babbitt (op. cit., pp. 247-248) distinguishes a "combinational" system such as the traditional tonal system from the "permutational" twelve-tone system in terms of the relation of the "referential norm" of the system to the collection of available elements. If, from these elements, a sub-collection is chosen as a referential norm, this norm is "distinguishable by content alone. But if the referential norm is the totality of elements, there is but one such norm in terms of content" so that operations such as transposition or inversion which, in a combinational system "result in the adjoining of pitches which are not present in the original collection, and thus [establish] a new collection", result, in a permutational system whose only norm is the ordering imposed on the totality of elements, "only in a permutation of the elements." See particularly pp. 253-254 for a discussion of inversion as a "permutation of pitch class numbers . . . which results from the substitution of complementary pitch numbers in S."

the octave position—not specified by the set—of each note" (for this use of "octave position", see Babbitt, op. cit., p. 248). But "melodic inversion", even where "octave position" is not specified, might, in the widespread confusion surrounding this question, still be taken for "contour inversion", in which, literally, octave position need not be precisely specified. The later description of the "P" and "I" operations in connection with "free" atonality as denoting the "transformations of an unordered set where it is employed as an invertible structure" does not clarify the matter.

Again, in a work which will be for many a stepping stone to the more advanced theoretical literature, one wishes there had been some discussion of so seemingly simple a terminological problem as the choice of transposition numbers for set forms; however supposedly trivial, such a discussion might have provided valuable insight into Perle's own basic approach to the system, and prepared the reader for the difference between Perle's usage for the R and RI forms and that of others, including Babbitt. Here, Perle merely assigns the t of an S ("P" in his terminology) to its literal pitch retrograde (which is thus labeled "R_o"); similarly his "RI" is that form "obtained by reading [the t_oI form] backward" (p. 7). Babbitt, however, notates transposition according to the initial pitch class number of each permutational form, using $S_{o,o}$ as the referential point in all cases. Avoidance of confusion, however, is plainly not the only issue here; more importantly, a fundamental outlook seems to be involved that surely warranted fuller explanation of the choice. For pitch order, as Perle himself evidently acknowledges (pp. 3-5), is less a determinant aspect of set identity than is intervallic ordering. From this point of view, the pitch order retrograde relation of S to the form "obtained by reading S backwards" is not as strong an association as that between S and RI; as Babbitt points out[3], the RI operation results in an exact retrograde of all the *intervals* of S, whereas the exact pitch retrograde R yields an RI intervallic relation to S (see example below, bearing in mind that I refers to a *complementation* of the intervals); thus the RI form may be said to be, of all set forms, closest to S (and R closest to I).

[3] *Op. cit.*, p. 258

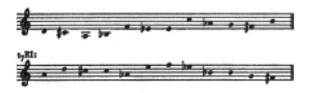

Example: exact interval retrogression of RI relative to S

Another hazard of the informal approach is that definitions may occasionally be incomplete enough to verge on the misleading. On the crucial subject of combinatoriality, the statement occurs that the aggregate formed by two combinatorially related hexachords, "having no derivation other than the set . . . is a corollary of the horizontal structure of the set, whose ordering it reveals" (p. 100). But, as Michael Kassler has demonstrated[4], there is no certain way, without invoking contextual criteria such as registral, timbral, dynamic, etc. treatment in the compositional presentation of such an aggregate, to ascertain from it the ordering of its component hexachords[5]. Later (p. 102), Perle refers to segmental invariance as "the converse of combinatoriality", although segmental invariance is the general principle of which combinatoriality is the extension, a relationship not fully implied by the statement. Another possible misunderstanding arises in connection with the set of the first of Babbitt's Three Compositions for Piano, which is described as fulfilling only "the minimum requirements for an all-combinatorial set" (p. 103). Since the criterion for all-combinatoriality is segmental content alone, the observation is literally correct, but it is perhaps to be feared that the reader may assume the all-interval construction of this particular set to be one of the "minimum requirements."

Unquestionably, the analytic approaches taken to the music itself are among the strongest assets of the book. The inclusion of "free" atonal music is especially courageous, and Perle's treatment of its problems is refreshingly frank. He is particularly successful in making the reader aware of the difficulties

---

[4] *The Decision of Arnold Schoenberg's Twelve-Note-Class System and Related Systems,* Princeton, New Jersey, Princeton University, 1961. See especially Chapter 5/4, "Essential ambiguity and combinatoriality"; and Chapter 7, "Polylynear twelve-note-class composition".
[5] Beyond the trivial fact that order number 6 of one of the hexachords will not be stated prior to the statement of order number 5 in the other.

encountered when large-scale works are to be constructed according to units of association that are either so minimal as to tend toward overgeneralization, or, where larger referential units are involved, require completely literal reiteration in order to retain their associative properties. The assumption that the "basic cell" is the most consistent principle in atonal music is sound as far as it goes; it serves particularly well to explain Webern's procedures which, unlike those of Schoenberg, always tend toward a symmetry of micro- and macroform down to the smallest possible referential unit. Perle significantly points out that, given such a tendency, Webern's "extreme brevity is not an idiosyncratic feature but a necessary and logical consequence of the multiplicity of function of every single element." But in stressing the absence of generalized procedures other than the "basic cell", and also the consequent lack of correspondence among works, Perle, it seems to me, has somewhat oversimplified the case. Granted the obscurity of many of the connective procedures, it might still have been advantageous to discuss more extensively some of the basic problems underlying this obscurity, to make it clear that this is problematic, rather than arbitrary music. Even from the examples, some of these general problems—as well as some of the subtler approaches devised by Schoenberg toward meeting them—become apparent on careful inspection.

The first example given of the "basic cell" in Schoenberg is the opening of Opus 23, No. 1, in which, as it is pointed out, the three-note motive generates all the linear events of the first four measures. However, an examination of the entire first section of this piece reveals both a deeper ambiguity and a subtler structural intent; one could, as well, consider as the primary generators the harmonic intervals of tritone and fifth. Indeed, the two ideas seem to interrelate quite closely, since with too few exceptions to be considered significant, every simultaneity in the first twelve measures is either a verticalization of the basic cell (which occurs at important initiative points: first sonorities, mm. 1 and 4, both phrase beginnings), or contains a tritone or a fifth; the three seem to be treated in a hierarchic order of activity to stability, with the basic-cell chord and the chords containing tritones "resolving", at phrase endings (mm. 3, 6, 12), to those in which fifths predominate (complementary intervals being taken as equivalent). This, much more than the basic cell alone, serves also to explain the linear motion, which is expanded by mm. 5 and 6 to include linearizations of fifths. The harmonic tendency of the first measure, basic cell to fifth, is also realized on a sectional scale: the last simultaneities as well as the last linear phrase ending in m. 12 are clearly fifth-dominated. The strength of these associations is evident in m. 13, where the introduction of new (but still derived) intervallic characteristics effects the important articulations along with the obvious rhythmic and textual factors. The residual ambiguity, given these strong associative devices, is, then, still more puzzling, and would have been worth more discussion in the book; why, for example, when all motivic generators, associative, harmonic, rhythmic, registral, etc. procedures are taken into account, do we still feel at a loss to understand how—or, more precisely from a composer's standpoint, why—this particular structure was arrived at? Both similar structural connections and instances of a more generalized procedure within this area than Perle comments upon may be found in other examples in this section, notably the two drawn from *Erwartung*. Without minimizing the formidable extent to which this work is "refractory to analysis" (p. 24), it seems somewhat arbitrary to describe the quoted passages as consisting of "a basic cell . . . combined with independent details" in which "repeated formations of fixed pitch content . . . have only a temporary and local importance . . . and usually occur as brief ostinati in combination with 'free' elements" (p. 19). But in the example (mm. 1-4, given as Ex. 17 on p. 20), the four-note chord shape selected at five places by Perle as the basic cell actually arises from a more fundamental three-note unit, whose transpositions lead immediately to additional associations exploited consistently in the passage (note particularly the formation G♯-B-C♯ in the upper part, which is extended to the F-E♭-F-D of m.3, and the D-E-G-E of the vocal line, m.4, and which becomes a primary recurrent and developmental factor in the course of the work).

The unit itself (first stated as D-G-G♯) is prominent both melodically and harmonically throughout the passage, but also undergoes transformations of a type used extensively by Schoenberg in his atonal music as a generalized technique to generate expanded associations while retaining essential identification with the basic cell. Thus this unit may be read as 5 and 1 semitones, successively (reading from the lowest to the middle to the highest note of the minimal registral representation—in which form the cell is compositionally first presented), with an "over-all" span of 6 semitones. If the 5 is inverted to 7, retaining both pitch and interval identity, and the interval from "middle" to "highest" pitch is again 1, intervallic consistency among the parts is maintained, although the over-all span now produces a new available interval, 8. (This technique may be observed in Perle's examples from Opus 11 and Opus 23 as well.) This association is first introduced obliquely, through the adjoining of statements of the basic unit (the B♭-D-E♭ of the upper part on the first beat of m.1); the B♭-D correspondence then introduces the "derived" form of the basic cell (the "inversion" of B♭-D-E♭), holding the D and G of the initial statement fixed in register, with the "new" D♯, which by registral association links with the derived form G-G♯-D♯, in which two "common tones" are also held fixed. The system of associations is further expanded in the "parallel fourth" triplets in the bass (second half of m. 2), where the basic cell pattern appears to break on the last two beats but is actually "converted" as above (significantly, the two "derived" forms explicitly here are B♭-D-E♭ and G-D-E♭; see also, in m. 3, the overlapping bass pattern D-D♭-A♭-C, in which the two forms are dovetailed linearly). Incidentally, the third of the four-note chords adduced by Perle depends on the association of the upper-voice B♯ on the fourth beat of m.2 with the G-C♯-F♯ on the third beat, wheras in context this B♯ seems clearly to associate instead with the B in the bass and the ornamented F in the middle voice (third beat), forming a basic cell: B-F-B♯.

Other connective means exploited in this brief example are the consistent association of pitch groups (B♭-D occurs on the first beat, m. 1; last beat, m. 1 to first beat, m. 2; third and fourth beats, m. 2; second eighth-note beat, m. 4; and between the voice and the tremolo, m. 4); and registral correspondences (note the three statements of the pitch complex C-A-B-C whose similitude is sonically emphasized by the retention of the lowest register C—also the lowest sustained pitch in the entire quoted passage). This degree of interrelationship among "independent" elements suggests a kind of structural consciousness on Schoenberg's part that, despite its admitted complexity, warrants more mention than the simple noting of "free" or "variable" details.

In the sections on pre-twelve-tone serial usages, a discussion of the relation of serial to non-serial passages (especially in Opus 23, Nos. 2 and 3), and of the coincidence or noncoincidence of serial passages with important formal articulations might have better drawn together the many perceptive descriptive observations. Also, the suggestiveness of some of these passages as "serial solutions" is striking, particularly the special kind of linearization found in the second half of Opus 23, No. 1, where rather than a series of simultaneities, discrete voices of a contrapuntal complex are "strung out" successively. Perle's statement here (p. 43) that these primary linear formations, "because of their length and complexity . . . appear only in their prime aspect" is incorrect, since in mm. 28-31 the formation derived from the "upper voice" of mm. 1-3 is presented first in prime, then retrograde order: G♭-E♭-D-F-D♯-E-G-E-E♭-F-D-E♭-G♭. Another interesting idea is the presentation of the "set" of Opus 23, No. 2, in "two linear patterns" (p. 45). The particular attack points of the bass pattern coincide with pitches of the upper pattern that, thus isolated, form still another pattern related (D-G-C♯) to the lower voice (C♯-A♭-A) in the same way as the basic cell of *Erwartung* and its "derived" form. These attack points also make explicit the important "major-minor third" relationship. In the second phrase, the two simultaneous attack points involve major-minor thirds, as do the two semitonally related "major thirds" (E-A♭, F-A) of the bass part; at the same time, the two "voices" are, at these points, inversionally related. Perle's examples of the later partitioning of this set similarly reveal Schoenberg's awareness, at this early stage, of set properties that were fully developed only in his very latest works.

Among the twelve-tone examples, the instance of the set as "thematic", from the Schoenberg Piano Concerto (mm. 1-8) is, in the extraction of elements for the "accompaniment" that either associate with segments of other set forms or isolate significant fragments of S, far more subtly "thematic" than is indicated. Here, wherever the set order is "violated", the first criterion above accounts for the successions of elements not adjacent in S, as follows: in m. 1, (3, 4, 5) of S; in m. 2, (5, 0, 2) of S = (2, 3, 4) of t_{10}S; in m. 3, (1, 2, 3) of S; then, in the "melody", in mm. 4-5 (A♭-D♭-A) = (0, 1, 2) of t_5I (the combinatorial I, also implied by the A♭ in the right-hand part of m. 3, and the C♯-A of the left-hand part, mm. 3-4). The juxtaposition, in mm. 7 and 8 of

B-G-E♭-B♭-D-F-E-C (S: 10-11-0-1-2-3-4-5) projects the pitch content of the segment of t_5I between order numbers 4 and 11; the following G♯-C♯, 0-1 of t_5I, and the A-F♯, complete the full statement of t_5I (the repetition of B and G adjoins all pitches of t_5I H_1) within the framework of a statement of S. This emphasis of segments in common between set forms[6] is in fact a more significantly "thematic" use of set formation than the simple differentiation of elements explicitly described in the text, and is fundamental to much of Schoenberg's later work.

Finally, the example given of the extraction of "varied linear formations" by the "employment of the melodically extraneous notes in the 'background'," is the "recapitulation" of the "A" section of the second movement of the Schoenberg Fourth Quartet. Perle states that "since the notes of the set are not in general functionally differentiated, and since there is no all-embracing principle of harmonic propriety as in tonal music, there are no a priori criteria to govern the manner in which 'theme' and accompaniment are to be derived from the set." This raises a number of interesting questions, into which lack of space precludes inquiry here; it is worth observing, however, that the motivic aspect of tonal music is, in some respects, as problematic as the "harmonic" aspect of twelve-tone music, in the sense that the systematic constraints of the tonal system do not completely specify a hierarchy of linear events, just as those of the twelve-tone system do not specify "principles of correspondence" for simultaneity. Both problems admit of solution according to the ways in which individual composers have chosen to interpret and exploit the properties inherent in the "systematic" dimension, horizontal or vertical succession, as the case may be. Thus, although a priori criteria are lacking, it is evident that the set structures and "principles of correspondence" devised by Schoenberg for the perhaps "unprogressive" purposes of constructing genuine analogues to Classical forms (and the subtlety of his means, the extent to which he approached this goal, are truly unique among the musical phenomena of the twentieth century), are equally susceptible of generalization and subsumption into more "purely serial" purposes. It is this, of

---

[6] Called "nesting" by David Lewin: see his "A Theory of Segmental Association in Twelve-Tone Music", published in the Fall 1962 issue of *Perspectives of New Music*, where the technique is generalized as well as investigated with particular regard to the Violin Concerto and Phantasy.

course, that explains why, although Webern was the only early twelve-tone composer "motivated, like Babbitt, 'by the desire for a completely autonomous conception of the twelve-tone system'" (p. 140), it is Schoenberg's procedure—not combinatoriality alone, but the entire complex of means for formal articulation through set structure—that has proven most fertile. An examination of the Fourth Quartet example along with the original "A" section (mm. 285-302) which it "recapitulates" reveals an interplay of contour, set form, permutations of pitch content that establish hierarchic degrees of similitude to referential elements, and a veritable polyphony of noncorresponding set and linear operations (inversionally related linear passages derive from sets in R, RI, or P relation, pitch Rs are derived from RI-related sets, etc.). Rhythmic "squareness" is, in this context, hardly a deficiency, but rather a powerful associative device making possible the coherence of such a wide range of interconnections[7].

I have isolated these examples, and dwelt on them in such detail, mainly to demonstrate the astonishing range and number of provocative issues that are raised in these few brief chapters. If it might be wished that Perle had still further capitalized on his method and drawn upon his fund of experience and knowledge to discuss some of the more special and subtle, but powerfully suggestive and potentially limitless, aspects of the music he introduces, the source of such a wish is in the enthusiasm and appetite for closer and fuller examination of the subject that the book, as it stands, arouses. From the considerable discussion and interest it has already occasioned among serious students of contemporary music since its publication, it seems likely that Perle's stated hope, that "as a result of [his] efforts the composition of twelve-tone music shall have become more difficult", will be realized, but that these efforts will as well result in the elevation of both the teaching and the general professional discussion of twelve-tone and atonal music to a new level of discipline and relevance.

---

[7] See Babbitt, "Set Structure as a Compositional Determinant", *Journal of Music Theory,* April, 1961, pp. 82 and 89, for the relation of Schoenberg's rhythm to pitch structure.

Author's Note, 2003: I wrote this review of George Perle's book in July 1962 at the invitation of *The Musical Quarterly;* however, the Editor of the *Quarterly* (Paul Henry Lang) found the text unacceptably "Babbittonian", and excessive in its extensive treatment of a subject of so little interest to the readers of the *Quarterly* — all of this in a communication addressed not to me but as an internal memo to the Asoociate Editor of the *Quarterly,* Nathan Broder, who somehow managed to neglect to remove it, still in its own separate carefully addressed envelope, from the folds of my rejected manuscript, returned to me with another letter, written according to instructions also contained in Professor Lang's memo, expressing the *Quarterly's* gratitude but regret that my text was just a tad too long for its format, and so would not be published therein. The memo lay upturned on the table at my elbow as Professor Lang and I sat beside one another at the next meeting of the New York Music Critics' Circle, but I couldn't tell if he noticed, and he never mentioned it.

— *BAB*

GODFREY WINHAM'S *Composition for Orchestra*

J.K. RANDALL

Ex. 1

I.

Example 1 is one form of that two-dimensional "array" upon which
Godfrey Winham's *Composition for Orchestra* (1961-62) is based.
Since the second of the piece's two movements may profitably be
viewed as deriving from the curious relations among dyadic
components of "chords" of Ex. 1; and since the opening passage of the
second movement—a passage which I shall discuss in some
detail—explicitly presents the "chords" of Ex. 1 as successions of
dyads; I should like first of all to discuss the dyadic properties of
Ex. 1 with a view toward indicating why its *dyadic* properties
should be singled out, how these properties relate to several
operations (on array-forms) which are exhibited in the piece
(particularly switching of "voices", transposition, and inversion),
and why these properties might suggest not only modes of
progression to quite different arrays but also means whereby such
modes of progression might be composed-out. (It is, above all, in the
composing-out of even the most obvious features of ingeniously
derived pitch-relations that *Composition for Orchestra* seems to me
most ingenious: especially so, considering the fanciness of the
relations and the apparent simplicity of the composing-out.) My
discussion will rely heavily on things pointed out to me by the
composer himself—though he need not, of course, be held
accountable for its virtues.

Each "voice" in the B-part of Ex. 1 is identical, in unordered pitch content, to the corresponding voice in the A-part. But while voices 1 and 2 of B are related, respectively, to voices 1 and 2 of A by inversion; voice 3 of B is related to voice 4 of A by inversion, and similarly for 4 of B and 3 of A. Voices 1 and 4 of A are identical by transposition, as are voices 1 and 3 of B; and, while these voices of B and those voices of A are related by inversion, the interval of transposition is not the same for the A-pair and the B-pair; and, while the ordered set of "vertical" dyads formed by these voices of B exhibits successive half-step transpositions, as does the set formed by those voices of A, the half steps are all "up" within A and all "down" within B.

The set of vertical dyads formed by voices 1 and 2 of B has no dyad in common with the set formed by voices 1 and 2 of A; but the set formed by voices 3 and 4 of B is identical to the set formed by voices 3 and 4 of A—yet this pair of (identical) sets has a simple property shared by the other pair of (non-identical) sets: each of the four sets contains a dyad whose immediate successor is a half-step transposition of that dyad. The dyad-transposition in voices 1 and 2 of B occurs from the first dyad to the second; the same is true for voices 1 and 2 of A. The second and third dyads of voices 3 and 4 in A and B are related in the same way. Yet identity of *directed* transposition distance occurs *within,* not between, A and B.

The flanking "chords" of A are related by inversion, as are the flanking chords of B. The middle chords of A and B are their own inversions; but the middle chord of A is its own cycle-of-fifths equivalent as well.

Since each voice in Ex. 1 contains just three distinct pitchclasses; and since the three distinct p.c.'s of any one voice exhaust a three-note segment of the chromatic scale; and since *no* p.c. occurs in more than one voice; it follows that there must be exactly four transpositions at which the total inversion of Ex. 1 will exhibit, in its four voices, the same four three-note collections as Ex. 1. Of these, Ex. 2 is unique in that it may be partitioned into the same set of "vertical" dyads as Ex. 1, and yet has no "chord" in common with Ex. 1.

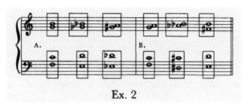

Ex. 2

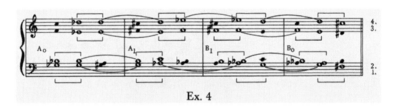

Ex. 3

Ex. 4

In the second movement of *Composition for Orchestra*, another transposition of Ex. 1 occurs: the transposition "up" one half step. The insertion of this transposition (A1 and B1 of Ex. 3) between A and B of Ex. 1 (shown now as A_0 and B_0 of Ex. 3) brings out one of its relations to Ex. 1. In A_0, three of the four voices move *up* one half step from the first chord to the second; similarly, from the second chord to the third. In B_0, three voices move *down* from the first chord to the second; similarly, from the second chord to the third. The succession A_0-A_1 is a succession by total transposition *up* one half step; and the succession B_1-B_0 is a succession by total transposition *down* one half step. This relation is bolstered (see Ex. 4) by another uniformity that holds between certain dyads which are themselves transposed (in some given pair of voices) one half step; the first dyad formed by voices 1 and 2 in A_0—a dyad which is then transposed one half step—and the first dyad to be transposed in the *other* two voices comprise, together, a tetrachord of the form 0358 (i.e. a "minor seventh" chord), as do their transpositions (consequently) in those pairs of voices in A_0; and tetrachords of *that form* result in B_0 from the pairing of initial "transposed" dyads of voices *2 and 3* with those of voices *1 and 4* (and from the pairing of their transpositions). It should be noted that one effect of singling out the 0358 tetrachords in A_0 is an implicit partitioning of A_0 into that particular set of dyads indicated by circles in A of Ex. 2; typically, however, the effect on B_0—where other pairings of voices are involved—is quite different.

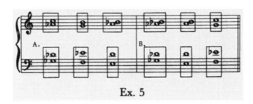

Ex. 5

Ex. 6

It follows from the discussion of Exx. 3 and 4 that Ex. 5 exhibits the dyadically relevant transposition of the total inversion of the A_1-B_1 segment of Ex. 3; and that Ex. 6—in which Ex. 2 has been inserted between A and B of Ex. 5—exhibits the relevant continuity from its first to its second A-segment, and from its first to its second B-segment. Ex. 6, in its entirety, is a total inversion of Ex. 3.

[Example 7, which follows, gives my piano reduction of mm. 1-55 of mvmt. II.]

Ex. 7

Ex. 7 (cont.)

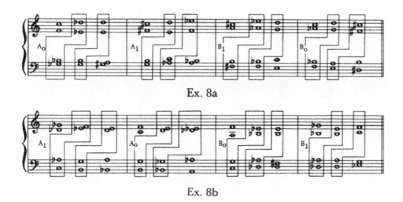

Ex. 8a

Ex. 8b

In Ex. 8a, the voices in the B-half of Ex. 4 have been switched to bring the component dyads of the 0358 tetrachords into the same "voice" and "chord" positions that their analogues in the A-half occupy. In Ex. 8b, the voices of Ex. 6 are switched in a way that yields a total correspondence, by dyadic complementation, to Ex. 8a. [Ex. 8a is the basis for mm. 1-2 of the second movement; and Ex. 8b, for mm. 147-169. Another quarter of the movement is based upon cycle-of-fifths equivalents of Ex. 8a and Ex. 8b.] While Exx. 4 and 6 are *inversionally congruent* to each other, Exx. 8a and 8b are *simply congruent* (in the sense that wherever, within Ex. 8a, two entries represent the same pitchclass, the analogous entries within Ex. 8b also represent some single pitchclass—and vice versa.) (Congruence can, of course, be obtained under transposition and cycle-of-fifths equivalence as well as under inversion; and the various kinds of congruence are also of interest as partial determinants for successions of musical events whose pitch aspects are *not* directly related by transposition, inversion, or cycle-of-fifths equivalence.)

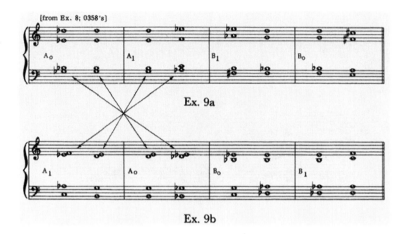

Ex. 9a

Ex. 9b

In Ex. 9, the 0358 tetrachords encircled in Exx. 8a and 8b have been extracted and rewritten as "chords," in order to make apparent the p.c. identities (in retrograde order of "chords") which hold between the 0358's of Ex. 8a and Ex. 8b *in their A-parts only.* The operations upon 8a and 8b which will be presented in Exx. 10 and 11—whose results are the basis (assuming the cycle-of-fifths operations) of one-half of the second movement—will supply, among other things, the missing 0358-correspondents for the B-parts of Exx. 8a and 8b.

Ex. 10a

A₀ [from Ex. 8a]

Ex. 10b

A₁ [from Ex. 8b]

Ex. 10c

1. A₀ [from Ex. 8a]

2.

3.

4.

5. (A₁)

See B₀ and B₁ in Ex. 9b

Ex. 10d

1. A₁ [from Ex. 8b]

2.

3.

4.

5. (A₀)

See B₁ and B₀ in Ex. 9a

In Ex. 10a, a "dyad-sequence" is derived from A₀ of Ex. 8a by means of uniform "arpeggiation" of its three chords into component dyads. The wiggly line separating the two halves of the sequence emphasizes the flanking positions, in each half, of a "transposed" dyad. Ex. 10b is derived from A₁ of Ex. 8b in exactly the same way. [To save space, I am not showing the results of performing this and subsequent operations on the *second* A-parts of Exx. 8a and 8b—which simply correspond at each stage (by half-step transposition) to results shown for the *first* A-parts.] Staff 1 of Ex. 10c presents a *different* (though similarly derived) dyad-sequence for A₀ of Ex. 8a which exhibits some remarkable resemblances to Ex. 10a. The *simultaneities* in 1 consist exclusively of p.c.'s which were immediately *consecutive* in a "voice" of Ex. 10a; and, as in the case of 10a, each half of 1 is flanked by a "transposed" dyad. If we now switch the upper and lower voices of 1 and switch the halves as well, we arrive at 2—which happens to be a *literal transposition* ("down" a minor third) *of Ex. 10a,* and which nevertheless retains the relation to 10a that held in the case of 1. In 3, each dyad in 2 is uniformly "arpeggiated" into its component p.c.'s; and the *hexachords* thus obtained are vertically combined in 4, the result being a sequence of 03 dyads. *These same hexachords* could, of course, have been derived *from 1* by arpeggiating each of its dyads "upward": so that 4 may be regarded impartially as a derivate of A_0 in Ex. 8a or as a derivate, by an analogous route, of a *transposition* ("down" a minor third) of A_0 in Ex. 8a. Notice that 0358 tetrachords are formed, in 4, by the first pair of dyads and by the last pair (see 5: the 0358 tetrachord F-A-C-D is formed by the last pair of dyads in the 03-sequence (not shown) derived from the *second* A-part of Ex. 8a); and that the specific transpositions of 0358's which appear in 5 of 10c are the missing correspondents for the B-parts of Ex. 9b.

Ex. 10d is related to Ex. 10b exactly as Ex. 10c is related to Ex. 10a; and supplies the 0358-correspondents for the B-parts of Ex. 9a.

Ex. 11a   [from Ex. 8a]

Ex. 11b   [from Ex. 8b]

Ex. 11c

Ex. 11d

See A₁ and A₀ in Ex. 9b

See A₀ and A₁ in Ex. 9a

Ex. 11e

Ex. 11f

Ex. 11 performs, upon *B-parts* of Exx. 8a and 8b, operations performed upon A-parts in Ex. 10—but with less elegance: notice that 1 in 11c and 1 in 11d originate solely as transpositions of 11a and 11b respectively; and that, to the *right* of the wiggly lines in 11c.1 and 11d.1, the "direction" of arpeggiation must be *reversed* in deriving the corresponding 2 in order to guarantee a 03-sequence in the corresponding 3. However, 11c.4, 11d.4, 11e, and 11f offer compensation.

The discussion which follows is devoted almost entirely to just one aspect of mm. 1-34 of the second movement: the *registral enclosure* of dyads by other dyads in certain tetrachordal contexts. The passage is based upon a dyad-sequence corresponding to Ex. 8a, and includes the beginning of a passage based upon the 03-sequence derived from Ex. 8a. I shall try to convey the impression that more than one coherent process is at work in mm. 1-34, and that the subsequent applications of inversional and cycle-of-fifths operations to Ex. 8a, and to its 03-sequence, may be relevant to these processes.

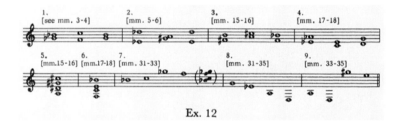

Ex. 12

In the dyad-sequence 1 of Ex. 12, the dyads G♭-B♭ and G-B are both registrally enclosed by the dyad F-C. The sequence is its own retrograde inversion; and hence, the *tetrachord* formed by the first and second dyads is the inversion—and the *registral* inversion—of the tetrachord formed by the second and third dyads. In 2, while an RI-relation holds in the same sense, and while the inversionally related tetrachords are of the same form (namely, 0157 and 0267) as their analogues in 1, it is now the first and third dyads which enclose the second; so that, with respect to order-positions within three-member dyad-sequences, "enclosing-positions" in 2 correspond to "enclosed-positions" in 1, and vice versa. At the same time, the intervals of simultaneity in 1 become the intervals (some by complementation) of succession in single voices of 2, and vice versa—in clear anticipation of mm. 31ff. (See Ex. 10.)

The dyad-sequences 3 and 4 stand in a rather complex relation to 1 and 2; but the complexities are of a kind already suggested by relations within and between 1 and 2. The entire six-member sequence 1-2 was *not* its own RI; but 1 *was* its own RI, as was 2. In 3 and 4 the situation is reversed: while neither 3 nor 4 is its own RI the entire six-member sequence 3-4 *is* its own RI. Within 1 and within 2, each member of the sequence either enclosed or was enclosed by its successor; the enclosing and enclosed *positions* were exchanged in 2 as compared to 1; and, since 1 and 2 were registrally disjunct, no member of either sequence enclosed (or was enclosed by) any member of the other sequence (see mm. 3-10). By exact reversal: within 3 and within 4, *no* member of the sequence either encloses or is enclosed by its successor—and hence there are no "enclosing" or "enclosed" positions to be exchanged from 3 to 4; yet, since each member of 3 encloses *every* member of 4 (see mm. 15-18), the "enclosing-function" of the entire three-member sequence is reversed from 3 to 4.

The simultaneities 5 and 6 are the only tetrachords of the form 0157 or 0267 which appear in mm. 15-18; and although 5 is *identical,* in p.c. content, to the first two dyads of 2, the enclosing and enclosed dyad-forms are those of 1 (namely, 04 and 07) but with 07 complemented as in 2. (Notice that 04 was *not* complemented in 2.) Thus, the pairs of p.c.'s which were registrally disjunct in 2 (namely, E♭-A♭ and A-C♯) take on, in 5, the enclosing-enclosed relation. From 5 to 6, the enclosing and enclosed dyad-forms are exchanged.

In 7—and here we have arrived at the passage which is based upon Ex. 10c.4—the 04 dyad G♭-B♭ is complemented (and this is the *first* complementation of a 04 dyad in the context of 0157 or 0267 tetrachords); and the 05 dyad C-F, whose complement in 1 *enclosed* the complement of B♭-G♭, is thereby *enclosed by* B♭-G♭. In 8 and 9, a feature thus far unique to 2 (and its half-step transposition) is reincorporated: the registrally (and timbrally) *disjunct* dyads are of the forms 04 and 05—except that 05 is recomplemented into its original 07 version; so that, while the p.c. content of 9 is identical to that of the *second* two-member segment of 2, it is the *enclosed* and *enclosing* dyad forms of 1 which are now registrally disjunct.

Enclosing-relations between component dyads of 0358 tetrachords are similarly transformed during the course of this section. However, in approaching this transformation, we must keep in mind two distinctions between 0358 tetrachords and 0157 tetrachords: the former are their own inversions, while the latter are not; and the former can be partitioned—in two distinct ways—into a pair of identical dyad-forms, while the latter cannot be so partitioned at all.

Ex. 13

Just as a 07 dyad was introduced in the dyad-sequence of Ex. 12.1 as an enclosing-dyad and subsequently complemented and enclosed, so is a 07 dyad introduced in Ex. 13.1 as an enclosing dyad—and subsequently (in Ex. 13.2) complemented and enclosed in this sense: although the enclosure-relations throughout 1 and 2 reflect a partitioning of each 0358 tetrachord into pairs of identical dyad-forms, the "0" and "5" components of the tetrachords always enclose the "3" and "8" components in 1 but are always enclosed by the "3" and "8" components in 2—and the "0" and "5" components (which form the 07 dyads in 1) form 05 dyads in 2. The retention of 05 dyads as *enclosed* dyads throughout 1 and 2 is also directly symptomatic of the relations which hold between the A-part of Ex. 1 and the B-part of Ex. 1 (with respect to identities of pitchclass content in identical voices of A and B as opposed to the *non*-identical pairings of voices required to produce identical tetrachord forms throughout Ex. 4), as well as between the uniform arpeggiation (Ex. 10c.3) of the dyad sequence (Ex. 10a) of A parts of Ex. 8a required to produce the 03-sequence of Ex. 10c.4 and the *non*-uniform arpeggiation (Ex. 11c.2) of the dyad sequence (Ex. 11a) of B-parts of Ex. 8a required to produce the 03-sequence of Ex. 11c.3. These relations provide the occasion for mm. 11-14 (a passage which would be gratuitous with respect to Ex. 8a alone); and the distinction between re-pairing (in which *all four* voices are involved) and registral switching (which is required for the *inner* voices only) is reflected rhythmically in the second half of this passage.

The change back to an enclosing dyad of the form 07 (mm. 23-27) is, like its mm. 11-15 analogue, transitional—but in a more ramified sense. The succession from the B_0-part of Ex. 8a to its A_0-derived 03-sequence (cf. Ex. 10c.4) does not call for any intervening tetra-chord B♭-D♭-E♭-G♭ (see 5); yet, the appearance of this tetrachord in mm. 23-27—apart from the obvious pitch-relevance to an impending recurrence of an A_0 derived section (see 3 and 5)—serves to connect the specific relations of dyadic enclosure in 1 and 2 with those in 6 and 7. The tetrachord in 6 is again of the form 0358; but here, for the first time in the movement, a 0358 tetrachord is so distributed registrally that one 07 dyad encloses another—and, as a result, the dyad consisting of the "0" and "3" components of a 0358 tetrachord now lies, for the first time, registrally *above* the dyad consisting of the "5" and "8" components. This registral disjunction is immediately converted (in 7) into registral enclosure *of* a 03 dyad *by* the complement of a 03 dyad: so that the enclosure-relations which held for a 05 dyad in 5 (and in 3) now hold in 7 for a 03 dyad. Thus, the local connection from a 05-enclosure of a 05 (m. 22) to a 07-enclosure of a 07 (m. 27) by way of a 07-enclosure of a 05 (m. 23) which happens to be identical to the first chord of m. 3, can reasonably be viewed as an elegant by-product of a more complex process which covers both a much longer time-span and a much larger range of pitch-events within (and subsequent to) the passage in question.

The retrograde inversion of 7 which appears in 8 (in the form in which it serves as a tetrachordal elision between the A_0-derived section and the A_1-derived section) reflects, among many things, the transference of RI-relations (observed in 1 through 4 of Ex. 12) to the o3-sequence in a manner already suggested by Ex. 12. But any further discussion of mm. 31ff. could hardly avoid reference to the composing-out, *within* the passage, of the double (i.e. transposed and untransposed; see Ex. 10) origin of the o3-sequence.

Author's Note (2003):
Lee Blasius, in his monograph *The Music Theory of Godfrey Winham* (Princeton University Press, 1997), which is based upon his study of Godfrey's notebooks, offers a probing appreciation of this remarkable musical mind, snuffed out too soon by cancer.

Benjamin Boretz

from THE NATION (etc.) 1962-1968:

I: 1962-63

Author's Note:

From 1962 to 1970 I was Music Critic for THE NATION magazine; by the end I had written about 90 columns reporting on the birth pangs and death throes of a variety of musical cultures in New York and elsewhere in America and Europe — most every brand of musical life seemed then struggling with fundamental issues of emergence, or survival — even the ones which seemed most settled in unresistant entropic pacificity. All through this labor I had the unflinching support — encouragement really — of THE NATION's editors, especially the principal Editor, Carey McWilliams, and my boss, Books and the Arts Editor Robert Hatch, both of whose old-fashioned practices of journalistic integrity kept me on the job and blissfully (miraculously) unthreatened for the eight years I worked with them. A substantial collection of the pieces is published in another OPEN SPACE book *(Music Columns from The Nation, 1962-1968,* selected and introduced by Elaine Barkin). Collected here and in three other places in this volume are some pieces omitted from that collection, along with a few texts published during those years in other magazines of general circulation.

-- BAB, 2/03

THE NATION:

March 31, 1962

MUSIC

Benjamin Boretz

SELF-CONSCIOUS "profundity" and the search for a special "American" sensibility that engaged many of our composers before the war seems, in retrospect, to have led to a rather sad displacement of some good creative impulses. One gets the impression that a great deal of this music was composed under the assumption that a distinctive and "important" manner of expression is a principal necessary condition of musical significance and originality. Consequently, not much attention seems to have been paid to the necessities of finding solutions to the internal problems of continuity and style, and this, ironically, delayed for a long time the development of a school of American composition that could be taken seriously as such.

There is nothing particularly American, of course, about this category confusion. European works like the symphonies of Sibelius and Vaughan Williams wear a mask of overt profundity that seems to have convinced a large fraction of the musical world to identify them as cosmically serious productions on the order of iconic masters (the Beethoven/Brahms pedestal) rather than locating them within the literature of cul-tural-token masterpieces — those symbolically reassuring, excellently composed and nicely calculated concert-hall entertainments — with which they probably have more relevant artistic kinship.

But the long European tradition of high-art musical craft prevents such silliness from fundamentally diverting the main currents of artistic development there, as seems to have happened for a time in America. And a European composer competently educated in the tradition could command enough technical polish to disguise beneath an appearance of structural coherence the dependence of his music on purely external expressive gestures.

Thus the "Jewish" music of Ernest Bloch, which became an important example for "American" music during Bloch's residence here, always maintains a connective tissue of sound, sustained or in motion, whose qualities derive most overtly from Wagner and Debussy. This forms a continuous background against which melodic and rhythmic events can rhapsodize without evident constraining formality. (Bloch's pupil Roger Sessions successfully detached this idea from its picturesque ethnic context and made it the basis for his own densely luxuriant expansiveness.) Bloch also found a harmonic and melodic vocabulary of open-sounding intervals that were both coloristically appropriate and able to create an effect of consistent internal continuity.

Some of the textures and harmonic resonances that these tactics generate are arresting in themselves: there is often in Bloch a granitic harshness that has for some people the flavor of Old Testament prophecy—although it is rather what one might have expected when these intervals—fifths and fourths—are piled up in extreme instrumental registers through an entire orchestral fabric. But in works like the *Three Jewish Poems* of 1915, these connective and sonorous ideas are simply used as "characteristic" sounds within conventional and loosely organized formal patterns—"meditative" ideas built rhapsodically to "ecstatic" climaxes—and the ultimate effect is of a one-dimensional music that despite its intense surface activity is fundamentally static. As for the "Jewishness" of the *Three Poems*, they could as easily pass for normal Impressionist *chinoiserie*—like that of Puccini's *Turandot*, for instance.

In Aaron Copland's Piano Variations, on the other hand, the austere sensibility comes directly from the interior, from the restrictive, unornamented treatment of limited materials (hence the frequent comparisons to skyscrapers?). Everything in the Variations is single-minded: through a kind of serial procedure, every event is propagated from the opening sequence of four notes, and nearly everything in the entire piece happens in the extreme foreground; there are no subtle shifts in juxtaposed motion, or layers of differentiated sonority, or variably subordinated configurations. The range of piano sonority is also spectacularly narrow; almost every note is detached, propellant, percussive. The Variations' extreme tension is generated through continuous expository assertion, undiverted by developmental inflection, increasingly stretching attention in unresolved expectancy of a point of expansion or relief to frame or background the relentless action. What is internally a highly formalized and almost rigidly structured music is thus experienced as volcanic outpouring of pure energy.

In this original form, the Variations is enormously powerful music, and, historically, almost sui generis. But Copland's transcription for orchestra (made in 1957) nearly obliterates the qualities that uniquely identify this piece. Somehow, in the orchestral context of multiple voices and tone-colors, the singleness of the piano version emerges as thinness, an effect which is actually emphasized by some of the ingenious devices by which Copland draws varieties of sonority from his sparse materials. The sense of limitation, of the strain of the performer's task, that are integral to the original are not restated in orchestral terms, but are just lost in the literalness of the translation. It is especially surprising that Copland should have mistakenly equated the sound of orchestral percussion instruments with the clang of percussive piano sound. The most disappointing moment comes near the end, where a passage that Copland obviously now regards as pure rhythmic energy, despite the specific and meaningful pitches in the original, is orchestrated for unpitched percussion alone. At this point, whatever drama was generated in the earlier music dissolves in the flatness of the resultant sonority.

ROY HARRIS's music is probably the most extreme recent instance of the strange disconnection between a "Great American Composer" image and an oddly amateur-seeming awkwardness in his command of some basic crafts of music fabrication — a peculiar competence gap which seems in no way to diminish the immediate and considerable expressive impact of his most ambitious music on a considerable body of listeners. Thus the prestige enjoyed by, in particular, Harris's Third Symphony is both surprising and understandable; for this work projects qualities of ideas of line and temporality that are both strikingly original and strongly suggestive of interesting formal possibilities: super-long melodic lines in even notes that expand texturally climactic points without overt rhythmic change (at the opening of the symphony); the

section of strangely long tenaciously sustained chords punctured by searing sharp rhythmic profiles in clashing timbres following an unfathomable pseudofugue (for some reason, this lurid high-theater effect is almost indiscernible in Leonard Bernstein's otherwise definitive recording).

Despite all this suggestiveness, though, Harris's ideas are rarely sufficiently realized in the unfolding of his music. On a large timescale, the music projects, like a compositional aesthetic, a sense of sheer extent rather than one of significant continuity — but then, too often the individual sounds articulating local ideas also project a shaky sense of relevance. I find a much more masterful use of such materials in the music of William Schuman (long-note melodies, such as in his Third String Quartet, and sustained-vs.-punctuated textures in *Judith*), where the placement and juxtaposition of notes seems skillful, inventive, and hangs together cogently, if not perhaps with much substantive depth. A more evolved compositional context for such inventions is their absorption into the recent compositional practices of Elliott Carter, forming, notably, the textural essence of the slow movement of his First String Quartet.

Accompanying the Harris Third on the Columbia recording is Leonard Bernstein's *Jeremiah* Symphony, an adolescent crowdpleaser that has a little bit of everybody's favorite music — from Mozart to Mahler to Copland to, indeed, Harris — and is greatly inferior, as cheap theater, to its Broadway littermate "On the Town" (composed at around the same time).

George Perle's String Quartet, just released by CRI — in radical contrast to some of the above — concentrates on the discovery of original coherences from within the context of contemporary stylistic diction, particularly in the realm of harmonic progression. This music's insistence that such coherence must arise from a consistent harmonic language, rather than surface sonic attractions or sheer forward momentum, results in a surface of stark simplicity, in which melodic and rhythmic motion are essential components of the underlying harmony. The extreme integrity of Perle's way of composing exposes its unsolved problems as well: in the String Quartet the continual articulating pauses between phrases eventually break the form into isolated fragments; without the emollient of purely connective tissue, the thread of sense is occasionally lost.

But it is the very "inwardness" of this music that makes it really impressive; it seems addressed not to an audience so much as to a purely musical task in which its listeners can become involved: it is that authentic reaching for primal relationships which ultimately,

and unfailingly, engages my interest and sympathy.

RECORDS

Bernstein: *Jeremiah* Symphony. Jennie Tourel, mezzo-soprano; New York Philharmonic, Leonard Bernstein, cond. Columbia MS 6506.

Bloch: *Three Jewish Poems.* Hartford Symphony Orchestra, Fritz Mahler, cond. Vanguard VSD 2085.

Copland: Orchestral Variations. Hartford Symphony, Fritz Mahler, cond. Vanguard VSD 2085.

Piano Variations. William Masselos, piano. Columbia MS 6168.

Harris: Third Symphony. New York Philharmonic, Leonard Bernstein, cond. Columbia MS 6506.

Perle: String Quartet. Beaux-Arts String Trio, Walter Trampler, viola. CRI 148.

Virtual Conversation 1, 2003:

[JKR] Top of the Line : Roy Harris' Sym 7 & Wm Schmn's Vln Conc.

[BAB]: I'd add the Harris 1936 Piano Quintet heard in 2001 at the Copland-Sessions Concerts commemorative celebration at Carnegie Recital Hall.

THE NATION:
April 21, 1962

MUSIC

Benjamin Boretz

SO MUCH music by young American composers is being performed this season that a whole new generation appears suddenly to have emerged. Actually, this is an illusion on the order of a newspaper crime wave, but there has been an unusually good opportunity recently to assess the direction and quality of the work of composers under thirty-five. The surprising discovery one makes is not that much of the music is of poor quality, or cynical, or both—a similarly indiscriminate selection of music from any time would show similar defects—but rather that there are more than a few composers in the younger group whose works are already considerably accomplished and mature in their engagement with the exigencies of serious composition.

Whatever their individual successes, composers have become self-consciously interested to compose sounds into coherent "total structures", in which every event is conceived as an articulation of a specific idea rather than a colorful local stimulant. A measure of the prevalence of the tendency toward such "interiorization" is the extent to which even music that centers around an external idea of presentation—such as an instrumental combination or a combination of words and music—is developed according to structural possibilities suggested by that medium, which thus acts as an integral part of the conception rather than as just "color". Both Yehudi Wyner's *Sections* for violin and piano, performed on the March 23 concert of the International Society for Contemporary Music, and Salvatore Martirano's *0 0 0 0 That Shakespeherian Rag* for chorus and instruments, performed on the March 25 concert of the Princeton Chamber Choir conducted by Thomas Hilbish, take their formal departures on these conceptual terms. Despite its small scale, *Sections,* like Wyner's earlier *Concert Duo* for the same combination, is an ambitious attempt to integrate materials from a very wide stylistic and expressive range into a dramatic unity. Although I miss, in *Sections,* some of the boldness and textural intensity of the Duo, whose pulsating first movement with its single-note rhythmic insistence and growing figurational excitement still makes an extraordinary impression, the recent work is far more refined and selective in its choice of materials and careful in their working out. Thus the opening movement is a splendidly simple statement of an idea of instrumental opposition: the piano opens with an abrupt staccato idea that is answered and opposed throughout by a continuous legato line in the violin, all projected with vividly particularized pitches. The second movement camps on the rhythmic idea that ends the first, and subjects it to a development in both instruments that finally dissolves into a passage for violin with the piano as an accompaniment.

Wyner's deliberate eclecticism demands, however, a constant vigilance of taste and judgment in the selection of materials, and his music sometimes lapses; the second part of the Duo especially struggles with the sentimentality of its basic material. Although *Sections* mostly avoids this kind of difficulty, there are disturbing incongruities in the later parts, particularly the over-repeated five-note figure of the piano "accompaniment" referred to above, and the literal rhythms of the following violin solo. But Wyner's effort to find a common ground for the whole range of musical styles is absorbing and potentially liberating, notwithstanding the sometimes diversionary reflections of middle-period Schoenberg and Berg, and Elliott Carter. The increasing sureness and refinement revealed in *Sections* encourages the hope that he may succeed.

MARTIRANO's setting of four passages from Shakespeare comedies has a direct presentational relation to the words that reminds one, on a much more complicated level, of a Renaissance madrigal. Every aspect of its organization, beyond its twelve-tone underpinning, seems to have been suggested by the interaction of the medium (small mixed chorus and seven instruments) and the words. There is considerable sonorous and rhythmic ingenuity in both the choral and instrumental writing, particularly with regard to contrapuntal word-fragmentation and the exchanges of function between instruments and voices. The materials in some sections arise directly from a word-painting idea such as the staccato trumpet for the fairies' chorus, and the arching groan of the men's voices on the word "snoring", which is very much like the snoring of the soldiers in the second act of Berg's *Wozzeck*. But the very vividness of some of the individual effects is a hindrance to the achievement of a fully realized continuous form. The result is more theatrical, finally, than dramatic, as though the flashes of instrumental and vocal image (rather tentatively projected in this performance) were not conceived in their own terms, but in relation to events on an imaginary stage. It is this confusion that seems to have led Martirano astray here, because his other works are remarkable precisely for their naturalness of continuity and genuine invention.

DIAMETRIC to the "characteristic" ideas of the Wyner and Martirano pieces—the integration of strongly contrasting elements—the Cantata III (on Yeats's "Leda and the Swan") by Peter Westergaard, performed on the March 23 ISCM concert, explores the possibilities of creating a differentiated form from the most severely restricted and tightly controlled materials. The work consists of only two basic elements, both derived from the same twelve-tone idea: the slowly unfolding three-note segments of the introduction that return in varying forms between the vocal sections whose materials are in turn suggested by the relationships among the segments; and, in the quick, beating vocal sections themselves, the simultaneous combination of parallel forms of the row in contrast to the single-line exposition of introduction and interludes. The instrumentation of marimba, vibraphone, clarinet and viola, is itself highly restricted, but is handled with impressive sonority and control; one wonders if the omission of a brass instrument is a reflection of the dramatic action, which takes place in mid-air. Every dimension of the Cantata is subject to a clear and audible regulation that is totally "musical" and gives a wonderful sense of lucidity, honesty and closeness to the poetry that more pretentiously "expressive" music often fails to achieve. The performance by Shirley Sudock, so-prano, with an ensemble conducted by Gustav Meier was as finely wrought as the work itself.

The Cantata by Malcolm Peyton (on the Princeton Choir concert), to texts from Joyce's *Chamber Music,* is plainly Stravinskian, specifically from the Stravinsky of the period between the Mass and the *Shakespeare Songs.* However, it is unlike the usual emulation of the master in that Peyton has gone to the root of Stravinsky's technique, rather than only to its surface, and worked with the materials as Stravinsky himself does, thus achieving, rather than borrowing, similar results. In this, Peyton is aided by a superior ear for instrumental sonority and for the integration of instruments, voices and the sounds of poetic syllables. On this occasion, he was also aided by the distinguished presence of Bethany Beardslee as the soprano soloist.

The associativities of Richard Hoffman's Variations for piano (on the ISCM concert, played by Howard Lebow) are of a more academic kind, distinctly Schoenbergian to be sure, but recalling the superficially square rhythms and phrase-structures that are not the most edifying aspects of Schoenberg's work. The twelve-tone aspect of the Variations is a little too unmistakable, and the method of "variation" itself is somewhat archaic in its rigor, especially in rhythm and sectional structure. As a result, it is a little harder than it ought to be to recognize that the work is carefully and conscientiously constructed, and contains several passages of considerable interest. In more recent works (the Variations date from 1957) Hoffman appears to have freed himself from the overpowering shadow of Schoenberg and the constriction it evidently imposed on his considerable compositional faculties.

Benjamin Boretz

American music*

Anyone who has been aware of the post-war developments of music in both Europe and the United States must face with a certain dismay the task of conveying an adequate image of contemporary American music to readers whose primary musical orientation is necessarily that of the present generation of European composers. For the disparities between the concurrent compositional environments in America and Europe are not only, to begin with, founded on those vast differences in intellectual inclination and methodology that have decisively determined the respective directions of our philosophical thought, as well as the relations of the principles and consequences of that thought to the formative artistic developments of our composers, but also derive their current extremity from our extensive progressions along so-determined lines, from an initial point of shared tradition and thus common concern for its legacy of perplexing problems and powerful resources, to a point at which our foundational definitions, and our conceptual and empirical assumptions and objectives seem no longer to possess enough common reference to be even minimally adequate for effectual intercommunication.

Such a critic, then, is faced with the formidable communicative impasse that persists between a European avant-garde whose motivating predilections have engendered an increasingly pervasive consensus in compositional method and perceptual surface, and the diversity and independence that characterizes the desire and direction of American avant-garde music. And whereas many European composers today seem primarily concerned with "freedom" and thus seek to achieve the maximum ambiguation of elements and phraseologies, more American composers seem to be seeking maximum constraint, maximal definition of as many elements as possible in order to enable the widest possible extension of their range of control over situations confronting them with ever more complexity, subtlety, and ramification, to struggle to achieve what Milton Babbitt has called "maximum multiplicity of function". Indeed, to these composers, the European "freedom" with its "latitude of meaning" seems to entail

---

* written for a symposium on "America" in the French journal *Cimaise* (July-October 1964), where it appeared alongside a translation into French. It was an attempt to offer an access to current American music in the face of the largely rejectionist attitudes toward it of the European elites.

an undesirably restricting limitation on the range of relationships that can be brought under the composer's significant command, on what, in the meaningful sense of the word, can be "expressed". It is not only verbal responsibility but also an insistence on perceptual verifiability that leads them to regard as either trivial or meaningless a statement such as that made recently by a young European composer to "explain" and applaud current European works, that "widely divergent techniques produce similar musical results today": for how can one distinguish as techniques, and especially as divergent ones, methods that have no significant perceptual consequences on the works they presumably have generated?

On the other hand, it might seem that the appearance of certain common locutions, often derived from scientific disciplines, would ameliorate this disparity, but the severe disjunction in their signification and usage actually heightens the communicative difficulty manifoldly. Thus, whereas one finds European musicians invoking the terminology and symbology of mathematics and science either as suggestive imagery or as arbitrarily translated bases for the structuring of musical elements, American composers are interested in statements derived from those disciplines mainly insofar as they are not only subject to criteria of verbal cognitivity but have precise correlative analogues in musical structures and, indeed, serve as determinate descriptive statements about musical works.

For the essentially revolutionary attribute of contemporary avant-garde American music is precisely its acceptance of the full implications of twentieth-century thought, of the new creative exigencies entailed in entering the contemporary intellectual mainstream. Consequently, science and mathematics are not regarded by these American composers as objects for mere totemic adulation but as immensely suggestive and familiar tools for the development of relational structure. They find their methodological locus in such statements as that of the great mathematician-philosopher Hermann Weyl that "the human mind senses its full power to fly, through the use of the symbol, beyond the boundaries of what is attainable through intuition... here is manifested the delight, not in the step-by-step opening-up of the infinite, but in the rational subjugation of the unbounded." And they take seriously the relation of theory and practice described by the logician Carl Hempel in which "any theory may be conceived of as consisting of an uninterpreted, deductively developed system and of an interpretation which confers empirical import on the terms of the latter... an adequate empirical interpretation turns a theoretical system into a testable theory." In the face of the common metaphysical impasse, they have preferred, rather than plunge into nihilistic despair or pathetic nostalgia, to choose to take advantage of the formidable responsibilities it has imposed to extend the scope of knowledge and control as far as possible over the most complex possible situations. In this way, their music has a cultural function at least as central to our century's predominant concerns as was the exploration of the individual consciousness to those of the last. Even Schoenberg, who developed the new structural tools capable of generalization into a musical language of the unprecedented efficiency required to permit the current explorations into complexity, remained nostalgic in his musical intentions and tried to find significant parallels with the qualities of the older music by means of the new syntax. Stravinsky, too, whose "objective" surface and technique of "composing with intervals" brings him closer than anyone but Schoenberg to the newest music, has always retained a direct presentational and associative relation with older musical times and functions. Varèse's more overt scientism is only a direct transferral into contemporary terms of romantic sensibility, a surface evocation of a mystique of science rather than a formal manifestation of its significance and discoveries. And among American composers, Roger Sessions's adherence to the image of the "long line" and symphonic scope, and even Elliott Carter's retention of the "large gesture" indicates the persistence of this nostalgia. On the other hand, one of the most conspicuous attributes pervasive in the newest American music is a predilection for a "cool" — almost a classic talky-"pop", or post-bop cool "jazz" — surface, whose profundities and subtleties take place inside, without heavy self-proclamation or coercive manipulation. As in Joyce, and for the same reason, the apparent nonchalance of that kind of surface provides a bright reflective medium for lightning fluctuations and myriad levels of reference and signification, and nonchalant-seeming "jokes" and "puns" — in the Joycean spirit — themselves are likely to be vital associative links in the relational chain, whereas big gestures and important self-declarations are just too inhibiting to the elastic freedom and range this music needs to accomplish its essential work. These "vernacular" qualities are as intrinsic to the music of John Cage and Morton Feldman as of that of Milton Babbitt, Mel Powell, Donald Martino, Kenneth Gaburo or Salvatore Martirano.

Obviously, such predilections have made the availability of the electronic medium increasingly valuable for American composers, particularly those whose compositional ideas demand the precise and effective control it enables in the temporal domain, permitting exploration of complex rhythmic situations that lie well within the bounds of human perception but would be far beyond the capabilities of even the most accomplished human performers;

"new sound" is, to these composers, of no intrinsic interest, except as an articulative timbral resource. Thus, the composer who has most fully envisioned this world of responsibilities and resources and most wholeheartedly accepted its consequences as well as its advantages, Milton Babbitt, was able to find a sound image through which his structural ideas could be definitively projected only with the unimpeded elasticity of electronics; in any event, it was not until the appearance of his *Vision and Prayer* for soprano with accompaniment produced on the RCA Music Synthesizer that his breakthrough into a radical new sonic-intellectual space has become apparent, and the qualities of the entire chain of compositional solutions he has propounded since 1947, in works like the *Three Compositions for Piano*, the *Compositions* for four and twelve instruments, and the song cycle *Du*, can finally be apprehended by way of a retrospective realization of what their qualities should have been under proper, but then unrealizable, performance conditions.

At the same time, there are those among this enormously diverse group in whose works the nostalgic gestures of dramatized expressivity themselves are subsumed as generative, deep-structural properties, rather than as primarily a rhetoric, an ironic manipulation of normative procedure—as they are in Liszt or Wagner. When Elliott Carter wrote of the composer's need to find "new forms" for the "new materials" he obviously referred to his own discovery of the significant new continuity that could be generated through the superposition of highly differentiated traditional musical "gestures"—modes of articulation, timbral properties, contour and dynamic configurations—as fixed elements in a constantly shifting scheme of "contrapuntal" relationship that radically retains the complete sonorous independence of each element in a texture. But Carter's remark also defines the relation to tradition of this entire avant-garde, in its very diversity; it was, in fact, Carter's own First String Quartet of 1951 that first demonstrated to the American musical world that an American music founded on a searching re-evaluation of traditional assumptions on a new level of structural cogency and originality could be drawn from the central issues of Western musical tradition which had devolved upon American composers through the profound moral and intellectual influence of the presence in our midst of Schoenberg and Stravinsky themselves. And that he drew this insight implicitly from a creative "reading" of the music of Charles Ives—from which many American composers have drawn dramatically divergent inspirations—is particularly provocative in our music-conceptual landscape.

The consequences of Carter's discoveries surfaced, in fact, with explosive suddenness and profusion in the period following the emergence of his First String Quartet; its intense emanation was immediately evident in completely different ways in such works as the String Quartet of Arthur Berger, a composer whose remarkable aural imagination had perceived and explored the then hidden connections between Stravinsky and Webern as long before as 1940; the *piece in two parts for six players* of Stefan Wolpe, with its "serialism" that counterposes—in place of twelve-tone progression by orderings within the total pitch range—a distinct mode of generating highly ramified expansions from a highly restricted initial cell; the *Dimensions* of Ralph Shapey, with its successive juxtapositions of stark, rigid, intensely pressurized unchanging configurations; the *Three Movements for Orchestra* of George Perle, who has drawn unique personal conclusions from the harmonic problems (as he sees them) of twelve-tone-systematic music, rounding its jagged rejectionist edges, and expressively colorizing its militant self-saturation; and the paradoxically original phenomenon of Seymour Shifrin's *Lament for Oedipus*, in which the shadow of Carter's assault on traditional continuity has engendered a rediscovery from a totally "inside-music" point of view of the potentiality for new coherences to be found within a "neoclassic" framework—to name only an obvious few of the composers who share in common a preoccupation with the deeper relationships of compositional procedures to perceptual resultants.

It seems, even, that the very — perhaps onerous — responsibilities imposed by such a double-edged engagement with tradition, comprising both rebellion and renewal, have been largely instrumental in engendering that very independence and diversity the desire for which, as was noted at the start of this discussion, so sharply distinguishes the American avant-garde from those who assert the artistic "exhaustion" of such "traditional" modes of expression as the twelve-tone—or any other determinacy-rooted—compositional procedures. Presumably, this disillusion has prompted their withdrawal into minimal or communalized responsibility for their compositions; but to those American composers whose desire is to be able to take maximum individual responsibility for what they compose, such a withdrawal seems incomprehensibly abject in the face of all the original, disparate, intricate worlds still unexplored and possible within—for example—the twelve-tone system, which still seems progressively to reveal that its possibilities have only begun to be discovered. It is, indeed, almost impossible for a member of the American musical community to take the stance of artistic disillusion seriously while finding among his colleagues so much fertility and individuality. So much, indeed, that any single discussion remains painfully inadequate as anything more than a sketch of the most general qualities of a generalized point of view. And even within that modest limit, one is confounded by the unavoidable emptiness of descriptions of any musical phenomena, relations, or ideas in the absence of the opportunity for an empirical demonstration of their nature. But in the hope that such an opportunity may soon arise, and that through it some reasonable avenue of communication between our mutually isolated musical cultures may be opened, it has still seemed worthwhile at least to offer, amid this symposium on perhaps more widely available manifestations of American intellectual activity, some indication of the significant implications our new music may have for the future of this activity as a whole.

THE NATION:
October 5, 1963

MUSIC

Benjamin Boretz

European Report II

After having been so pessimistic about European music in my last column, it seems only fair to devote some space to a more enlivening aspect of the situation over there. But—in truth—most of the memorably original and imaginative (as distinct from just professionally competent) phenomena I encountered in and around musical events in Europe were not in their specifically musical aspects, but in such auxiliary realms as operatic staging and scenic design—particularly, in some of the productions created by Wolfgang and Wieland Wagner for this summer's Wagner repertory at Bayreuth.

I was prepared to find the musical standards there also quite high, since I had heard superior orchestral ensemble and vocal-instrumental coordination on recent Bayreuth recordings. On the strength of these I hopefully engaged myself to spend eight days immersed in the soggy Bavarian gemüt that prevails in the Stadt Bayreuth itself, but the performances I heard turned out to be disappointingly variable, never approaching the tight discipline of either the German or Italian companies of, say, the Vienna Staatsoper, and occasionally even sagging within reach of the wobblier moments at our own treasurable but wobble-prone Metropolitan.

The qualities of the stage direction, however, derived from the extraordinary awareness displayed by both of Wagner's grandsons of the functional relationship between events and appearances on stage and those in the scores. In particular, their approaches were guided by the realization that the pace of the musical and dramatic action must be carefully coordinated with stage movement to bring out the complementary properties of all dimensions as a formal totality. Wagner was, of course, not only quite in earnest, but deeply resourceful in devising the correlated analogical structures that make up the different domains of his *Gesamtkunstwerk*—which, it clearly appeared at Bayreuth, had specific meaning to him as a set of formal problems requiring rational and empirically valid solutions, rather than solely as a suggestive or propagandistic slogan. In short, the Wagners direct Wagner as if they believed that he knew what he was doing, and the results are far beyond anything conjured by the convetional directors who seem to imagine that the only way to prevent the "slow" pace from putting everybody to sleep, and the ludicrous mythology from embarrassing them, is to provide diversion with lots of rapid movement and naturalistic stage business that really only manage to caricature and actually exaggerate the slowness and incongruity.

Thus, Wolfgang's production of *Das Rheingold* paralleled the very special harmonic imagery and rhythm of the work with changing patterns of figures on stage (mostly in various representations of a basic sword shape) and a palpably structural rhythm of color change using degrees of monochrome, as well as consistently identified color elements, to build a formal gestalt. The suspended, ring-shaped saucer on, under and around which the action took place, was not only obviously appropriate symbologically, but also changed shape, from a smooth, full circle to segmented parts, in a rather broad image of the overall musical design. The rest of the *Ring*, however, was on a considerably lower level, as the gravity tended to become stasis and the naturalistic "relief" too veristic.

The most interesting productions were *Die Meistersinger* and *Tristan and Isolde*, directed by Wieland, who approaches the operas' structures without the literal mirror symmetries of Wolfgang, and poses instead precarious contrapuntal balances between elements that are astonishing when they succeed: the third-act collapse of Tristan, with the sudden coincidence of orchestral tremolo,

Tristan's body trembling and bent, and the wavering shape of the vocal line, instantiated the kind of total impact that musical-dramatic form can, optimally, achieve.

On the other hand, there is a certain unmistakable tendency toward chic and pretension in Wieland's work; *Tristan*'s single "abstract" fin-shape set was a hint of this, although it did serve as a unifying shape for first-act sail, second-act tower, third-act rock, and general yin-yang symbol. But the *Meistersinger* production came dangerously close to preciosity despite its daring inspiration of turning Wagner's quite unfunny comedy into a spoof of itself where it is least supposed to be comic. It was a delightfully mischievous idea, almost realized—finally defeated, in fact, only by unself-critical moments like the overdone caricature of the Meistersinger procession and, in fact, by the imbalances created by the director's spoofs being so much better than Wagner's own. The one incomprehensible gaffe was the decision to throw away the most inspired stroke of staging built into the whole opera—the suddenly quiet aftermath of the contrapuntal imbroglio at the end of Act II. Here, keeping the whole crowd on the stage for nearsighted low-comedy byplay with the night watchman, was just incongruous, especially against the drastic orchestral emptiness. But these flaws still did not diminish the invention exhibited in the

Dürer colors and tableaux, and the Breughel crowd configurations, however lightly they may have glossed the deeper structural issues of the opera.

Perhaps it is simply symptomatic of the current state of music in Europe that the conductors involved either ignored or actually opposed the efforts of the Wagners to maintain a lively and intelligent approach to a tradition that by its very nature is prone to sanctimonious immobility. But a highly encouraging sign that the Wagners' insight into Wagner's work may be genuine and have genuine artistic implications is the rumour that the Bayreuth repertory is about to be expanded by the works of other, recent, composers—not those which would probably be acceptable to Wagnerian "traditionalists" on the basis of their mimetic reproductions of Wagner's work, but major landmarks of post-Wagnerian invention: Hindemith's *Mathis der Maler,* Berg's *Lulu,* Schoenberg's *Moses and Aron*—works which continue the essential Wagner tradition by exploring and posing serious hypotheses regarding the problems and possibilities of music-dramatic composition to which the self-demanding efforts of Wagner's own life-work were directed.

MUSIC

Benjamin Boretz

The New York Philharmonic Orchestra is the iconic institution in our public musical culture, the focal point for the public's image of all 'serious' music. Its dominance stems from some particular features of the American musical culture: New York has, since the war, become the unchallenged musical center, as Boston was during the interwar period; and the nineteenth-century orientation of our public attitudes toward music centers on the symphony orchestra as the supposedly highest—and for many listeners the exclusive—medium for serious musical expression. Therefore, what the Philharmonic does, in terms of programming or policy, is likely to be significant both as an indication and as a positive force in determining the direction of the entire range of American concert activity.

The extent of this remarkable domination of concert music derives from the graphic immediacy with which the orchestral situation dramatizes the assertion of individual will that was so prevalent in nineteenth-century literature. There

was then, and clearly there remains, something absorbing in the confrontation of a motley and inchoate horde of instruments and players by a small insignificant man in evening dress—conductor or soloist—who imposes on them all a unified and coherently sonorous image.

Those nineteenth-century composers for whom the vision of a universal audience seemed an all-compelling possibility saw in the potency with which this situation could focus hundreds of attentions on a concert stage a unique resource for projecting their important compositional ideas. The optimism that this idea inspired early in the century is particularly evident in Berlioz, who devoted almost his entire composing career to the orchestra, and whose famous giganticism was a remarkable attempt to translate the qualities of individual virtuosity into a mass-communicative framework. (One wonders, indeed, whether the large orchestra could ever have attained such currency under conditions of efficient modern communication—where volume and massiveness have no crucial bearing on communicative range.)

But even during Berlioz's time, the Faustian snare built into the Romantic supposition became evident: for however profound or original any of the *grandes machines musicales* may have been as compositions, as bearers of musical values to the large audience, they seemed to engender only a kind of 'music-appreciation' listening in which it was possible to derive sensations of musical experience without experiencing any particular musical events. Music presented as a spectacle could evidently succeed entirely as such, but to assume that concurrent musical specifics would somehow also be transmitted was a sadly naive miscalculation.

Still, the transcendental chimera continued to preoccupy composers, and some delusive extremes of length and volume were reached before the crisp sanity of Debussy, the precise economy of Stravinsky, the willful self-restraint of Schoenberg re-established a line of fruitful development by consolidating the enormous creative discoveries of nineteenth-century music while avoiding the destructiveness of its extra-musical consequences. At that moment, however, there arose a sharp and decisive division between composition and performance, as a result of the natural refusal by performers to surrender, for however pressing a musical purpose, a self-expressive independence that could not be maintained through music whose surface offered no license to inflated sensibility. Thus, in the public view as well, 'great' music remained inextricably associated with 'big' music. The prevalence of this attitude is perhaps most strikingly revealed by the Hollywood movies about musicians that proliferated in the thirties and forties, in which the great musical moments are never at recitals or during performances of late Beethoven quartets, but in those strange Hollywood concertos that, by stringing together bunches of cadenza-flourish clichés without much attempt at actual coherence, were a far more devastating parody of Romantic nostalgia than the wildest flight of dada ever conceived.

Thus the Philharmonic, when it engaged a music director who had established his reputation as, above all, a superb theatre man, was only recognizing, with admirable prescience and candor, that a modern symphony orchestra's success and growth depend on a reversal of the traditional function between music and its presentation. Indeed, Leonard Bernstein's unique contribution in every sphere of his manifold activity has been the transformation of musical ideas and materials into effective theatre. His own Broadway shows, even, have effectively diverted the development of our popular musical theatre toward a high-powered New Wave intensity and tricky local stage- and music-crafty sophistication, away from the straighter verbal-musical imaginative craft of the earlier days of Kern, Berlin, Gershwin, Rodgers,

Weill and company.

By bringing such theatrical gifts to his conducting and program-making for the Philharmonic, Bernstein has perfectly fulfilled the necessities created by the growth of a mass musical culture, and the spectacular box-office and television popularity of the Philharmonic under his direction, both here and in Europe, testify to his success. In his performances, he has demonstrated a superb sense for projecting those moments that can be made to proclaim unmistakably their expression of great and noble thoughts, further heightened by virtually choreographic acting-out on the podium (a trademark Bernstein practice). Even though New York has witnessed such performances ever since his City Symphony days, it is still impressive to see the consummate skill with which the conjurer of musical visions, like a benevolent Cipolla, instills in his audiences the sense of having personally experienced the blinding flash of genius.

These qualities of Bernstein's performing persona converged almost quintessentially in the opening concert of the present season, devoted entirely to a performance of Mahler's Second Symphony, a work with which Bernstein has identified himself since his earliest apprenticeship days. In a way, this is an ideal vehicle for pure orchestral theatre. It presents itself as a loosely bound succession of portentous 'characteristic' gestures, none of which is individually very remarkable or original in itself (most seem to poach their solemnity from the redolence of familiar master-sources, as the Fifth and Ninth Symphonies of Beethoven, or Wagner's *Siegfried Idyll*), in a framework that is all 'bigness'—in contrasts, volumes, line and section lengths, and mass restatements. On this occasion, from a purely musical point of view, Bernstein's playing of the second movement was a marvelously penetrating exploration of the special qualities latent in its sequences of outwardly innocuous phrase shapes; at such times, there is no doubt about his inherent awesome musical gifts. But elsewhere, the performance was mostly a comprehensive exploitation of the potential for sheer display enabled by Mahler's unrestrained outpouring of extravagant rhetorical gestures.

In the realm of programming, the most interesting prospect of this season is the series devoted to the *"avant-garde"*. Bernstein has been an active and enthusiastic advocate for 'American' music of the interwar period. So it is at first puzzling that in this purported representation of postwar music the principal emphasis is on 'far-out' European composers, along with a few Americans, including John Cage and Morton Feldman, whose music has had a significant impact in Europe, on composers as well as listeners. Theatrical considerations, however, provide an obvious connecting link: Copland's 'Western' ballets, Harris's scenic symphonies, Schuman's modern-dance psychodramas, whatever their individual musical qualities, all have conspicuous theatrical surfaces that easily enable a transition to the purer, less stage-bound theatre of Cage and the Darmstadt masters. From the Philharmonic's point of view, this collection has the advantage of offering all the old-time aura of mystical expression in a totally new way, without imposing strenuous new executional difficulties—so the image of radical daring is achieved without the necessity of a lot of extra rehearsals. Of the three 'straight' composers represented on the series, one (Stefan Wolpe) is closer than any other recent 'difficult' composer to the purely gestural approach; his symphony is in any case to be conducted by Stefan Bauer-Mengelberg as a special (and formidable) project. The other two, Mario Davidovsky and Edgard Varèse, are to be represented by electronic-vs.-live-performer pieces that have the automatic situational appeal of virtual-human vs. virtual-machine—the machine doing the uncanny, the human the impossible—surefire, if generic, theatre, no matter the musical complexity or creative depth of the works on their own terms.

Evidently, it becomes increasingly necessary for an institution like the Philharmonic to indulge in such flummery in order to sustain the interest of an audience that may have already inflated beyond the limits to which serious music can legitimately hope to reach on its own, relevant, terms. The move of the orchestra to Philharmonic Hall, a tourist attraction in itself, further complicates the situation. But if the Philharmonic's aim is supposed to be the progressive development of authentic musical awareness in its public, it is discouraging that its *"avant-garde"* festival reveals only a remarkable opacity to so much of the contemporary American compositional ferment—especially since it is likely to be accepted in most quarters as a generous and accurate representation of the whole spectrum of new musical inventions. All this, I suppose, is only another indication of how far "symphonic culture"—the public's music—has diverged from the real thing, which now appears to have permanently defected to the more intimately scaled, more insularly populated, music-performance spaces in our city.

CONVERTIBLE COUNTERPOINT IN THE STRICT STYLE (1906)

By Serge Ivanovitch Taneiev. Translated by G. Ackley Brower.

BRUCE HUMPHRIES, BOSTON, 1962. 355p.

Reviewer J . K . Randall

Sources of quotations:

1   B. V. Asafiev, *Russian Music from the beginning of the Nine-teenth Century (Academia Press, Moscow-Leningrad, 1930). Translation by Alfred J. Swan published for the American Council of Learned Societies by J. W. Edwards, Ann Arbor, 1953.*

2   *Joseph Freeman, Soviet Music. In: Voices of October, by Freeman, Kunitz, and Lozowick (Vanguard Press, New York, 1930).*

3   *Serge Koussevitsky. In: Convertible Counterpoint, Taneiev, 7-8.*

4   *Andrey Olkhovsky, Music under the Soviets (1954) (Prager, New York, 1955).*

5   *N. A. Rimsky-Korsakov, My Musical Life (Knopf, New York, 1942). Translated by Judah A. Joffe.*

6   *Leonid Sabaneiev, Modern Russian Composers (International Publishers, New York, 1927). Translated by Judah A. Joffe.*

7   *Igor Stravinsky and Robert Craft, Memories and Commentaries (Doubleday, Garden City, 1960) 60-61.*

8   *S. I. Taneiev, Convertible Counterpoint in the Strict Style (1906), "Introduction" only.*

9   *V. 0. K. S., 1: 11-12 (1930) and 11:6, 10-12 (1931). (Published in English, French, and German by the Soviet Union, Society for Cultural Relations with Foreign Countries, Moscow.)*

1.

Taneiev of the eighties had been a man of glaringly conservative opinions in musical art. Towards Glazunov's early appearances he had shown deep distrust; Borodin he had considered a clever dilettante and no more; and Moussorgsky had merely made him laugh. Probably he had placed no high estimate on Cui, either, or on me.

His opinion concerning Balakirev is unknown to me; but I do know of his clash with Balakirev at a rehearsal of the concert during the festivities in connection with the unveiling of a monument to Glinka at Smolensk. At the rehearsal of the concert he publicly declared to Balakirev: "Mili Alekseyevich. We are dissatisfied with you."

--Rimsky-Korsakov, 383

Alone of all Russian composers, Taneiev was celibate and tee-totaler; so that it became a matter of course, and all his intimate friends no longer paid any attention to it.

--Sabaneiev (Paris, 1927), 28

Honest, upright, and straightforward, Taneiev always spoke sharply and frankly.

--Rimsky-Korsakov, 383

Intimately bound up with the cultured classes, Russian music was hard hit by the Revolution. Russian musicians were bewildered; many of them fled abroad, including singers like Chaliapin, pianists like Borovski and Orlov, conductors like Koussevitsky and composers like Stravinski, Metner and Rachmaninov. From the viewpoint of Soviet musical criticism, this flight brought a certain sterility into the work of the composers who abandoned Russia. An example of such criticism may be obtained in English in Leonid Sabaneyev's Modern Russian Composers. Sabaneyev is himself a Russian composer and musical critic who has been intimately connected with Russian music, both before and after the Revolution. Until 1926 he was president of the Association of Contemporary Music in Moscow. He is quoted extensively here as typifying the new attitude of mind which the Revolution has created in Soviet musical circles.

--Freeman (New York City, 1930), 294

At the end of the first and the beginning of the second decade of the present century, there came to the fore two very talented ideologists of modernism, V. G. Karatyguin and L. L. Sabaneiev, the former in St. Petersburg, the latter in Moscow. Sabaneiev (b. 1881) was a pupil of Taneiev and traces of the "Taneiev yeast" remained with him for ever, in spite of the fact that his tastes and his sharp paradoxical thinking soon distracted him from the views of his teacher. A brilliant writer, a master of biting, but well-aimed characterizations, Sabaneiev distinguished himself first as a propagandist of Scriabin, and later, by his analytical and historical works -- far from irrefutable, but steeped in striking finds of a juggling critical mind (the book on Scriabin, articles and reminiscences of him, a history of Russian music, and a Universal history of music, an aesthetic investigation "The Music of Speech," etc.). A combination of polemical ardor with a malicious irony -- such was the characteristic trait that helped Sabaneiev to disintegrate not only strange convictions, but also his own, and that led to his sacrificing his very thorough and positively firm knowledge, to bons mots and a swankyism of speech. Taneiev also possessed irony, but in Sabaneiev's mouth it often turned into an aesthetic game and a lowering of values. And, along with this, the same man could build up on a strictly rational basis such highly disciplined works as "Rhythm" (1917, in the first issue of Melos).

--*Asafiev (U.S.S.R., 1930), 274*

Already in his declining years, Taneiev resolved to study the contemporary with the same painstaking and persistence characteristic of him as in former times he had studied the old Flemings and Bach.

A certain kind of mathematic quality played a great part in his musical ideas. He loved bizarre tonal half-ornaments, half-problems. He loved the wise and ingenious concatenations of the separate voices. He was fond of overcoming tonal matter with human wisdom, setting for the latter a series of conditions with the proviso of preserving beauty and clarity. Many years he devoted to the unriddling of old contrapuntal "secrets" of the ancient masters, all those secrets of "mirror canons," "riddle canons" and all the other tricks and magic miracles with which those queer semi-mathematicians, semi-chess players and semi-musicians had delighted themselves and others. He believed that there was some rational "Path" in all this. And he proved to be right. In his magnum opus on counterpoint of which we have already spoken, all those secrets have been solved, revealed, reduced to simple calculations, and, in passing, a great mass of new and still more ingenious possibilities have been discovered. The pure infatuation of the chess player used to seize Taneiev whenever he entered this world of musical tricks. To him music connoted a combination of orderliness, mind, and withal some feeling, even though devoid of earthly passion and "blood," yet, in its own way, very very intense.

Before setting out to compose, Taneiev would prepare a special copy book and jot down in it the various themes that came to his mind. Then he wrote various exercises in contrapuntal style on these themes and only after having "mastered the material," as he put it, would he set to work.

After Taneiev's death there was found among his papers a mass of perfectly finished compositions which he, at the time, had not wanted to publish. Three completed symphonies, six quartettes, a mass of minor compositions -- all this had not satisfied him and he had never even mentioned them.

--Sabaneiev (Paris, 1927), 28-35

COMPLEX COUNTERPOINT IS DIVIDED INTO CATEGORIES ACCORDING TO THE METHODS BY WHICH DERIVATIVE COMBINATIONS ARE OBTAINED.

THE TERM "COMPLEX" IS USED FOR THAT KIND OF COUNTERPOINT IN WHICH AN ORIGINAL COMBINATION OF MELODIES YIELDS ONE OR MORE DERIVATIVES. THE TERM DOES NOT REFER TO THE COMPLEXITY THAT RESULTS FROM THE UNION OF MANY VOICES, NOR TO THE COMPLEXITY OF THEIR MELODIC OR RHYTHMIC FEATURES. THE ESSENTIAL MARK OF COMPLEX COUNTERPOINT IS THE POSSIBILITY OF OBTAINING FROM AN ORIGINAL COMBINATION OF MELODIES A NEW ONE, THE DERIVATIVE.

THE TONAL SYSTEM MADE POSSIBLE THE WRITING OF WORKS OF LARGE DIMENSIONS THAT POSSESSED ALL THE QUALITIES OF EFFECTIVE STRUCTURAL STYLE AND THAT DID NOT HAVE TO BE REINFORCED BY TEXTS OR BY IMITATIVE FORMS PER SE, BUT CONTAINED WITHIN THEMSELVES THE NECESSITY FOR THE LATTER.

THE MUSIC OF TODAY IS ESSENTIALLY CONTRAPUNTAL.

BEETHOVEN, WHO IN HIS LATER WORKS REVERTED TO THE TECHNICAL METHODS OF THE OLD CONTRAPUNTALISTS, SETS THE BEST EXAMPLE FOR COMPOSERS OF THE FUTURE.

AS FOR THE MUSIC OF TODAY, THE HARMONY THAT HAS GRADUALLY LOST ITS VIRILITY WOULD BE GREATLY BENEFITED BY THE STRENGTH THAT THE CONTRAPUNTAL FORMS CAN INFUSE.

THE STUDY OF FREE COUNTERPOINT IS THEREFORE INDISPENSABLE FOR THE TECHNICAL TRAINING OF COMPOSERS, BUT BECAUSE OF ITS MELODIC AND HARMONIC INTRICACY IT CANNOT BE STUDIED FIRST. THE FOUNDATION MUST BE LAID BY COUNTERPOINT OF THE STRICT STYLE, MORE ACCESSIBLE BECAUSE OF ITS SIMPLICITY.

IN MULTI-VOICE MUSIC MELODIC AND HARMONIC ELEMENTS ARE SUBJECT TO THE INFLUENCES OF THE TIME AND TO THE NATIONALITY AND INDIVIDUALITY OF COMPOSERS. BUT THE FORMS OF IMITATION, CANON AND COMPLEX COUNTERPOINT -- EITHER AS ACTUALITIES OR POSSIBILITIES -- ARE UNIVERSALLY VALID; THEY ARE INDEPENDENT OF SUCH CONDITIONS, CAPABLE OF ENTERING INTO THE PLAN OF ANY HARMONIC SYSTEM AND ADAPTABLE TO ANY MELODIC IDIOM. THE OUTSTANDING MERIT OF THE FLEMISH COMPOSERS WAS THAT THEY INVENTED THESE FORMS AND FROM THEM DEVELOPED A FLEXIBLE AND EFFICIENT SYSTEM OF TECHNICAL PROCEDURE.

THE ART OF COUNTERPOINT HAS PASSED THROUGH TWO ERAS: THAT OF THE STRICT STYLE, WHICH ATTAINED ITS HIGHEST DEVELOPMENT IN THE SIXTEENTH CENTURY (PALESTRINA AND ORLANDO LASSO), AND THE PERIOD OF THE FREE STYLE, OF WHICH THE CROWNING ACHIEVEMENTS ARE FOUND IN THE WORKS OF BACH AND HANDEL.

HARMONY OF THE STRICT STYLE IS NOT SUBORDINATED TO THE REQUIREMENTS OF OUR MODERN TONAL SYSTEM, IN WHICH A SERIES OF CHORDS IS GROUPED AROUND A CENTRAL TONIC CHORD.

IN THE HARMONY OF THE STRICT STYLE THERE IS NO SUCH DEPENDENCE OF SOME PARTS UPON OTHERS, OR OF WHAT MAY BE CALLED HARMONIC ACTION AT A DISTANCE.

KEY-CONTINUITY MAY BE ENTIRELY ABSENT, AND ANY CHORD MAY FOLLOW ANY OTHER, ON A STRICTLY DIATONIC BASIS.

THE NEW HARMONY, AS IT NOW STANDS AND WHICH FETIS CALLED "OMNITONAL," IS INIMICAL TO THE LOGIC OF TONALITY AND FORM.

NEITHER DID THE HARMONY OF THE STRICT STYLE, IN WHICH ANY CHORD COULD FOLLOW ANY OTHER, THOUGH ON A DIATONIC BASIS, EXHIBIT THE CHARACTERISTICS OF TONALITY AND FORM AS NOW UNDERSTOOD.

APPLYING THE PRINCIPLE THAT BY THE USE OF CHROMATIC PROGRESSION ANY CHORD MAY FOLLOW ANY OTHER, AND PUSHING IT TOO FAR, IS LIKELY TO COMPROMISE KEY-RELATIONSHIP AND TO EXCLUDE THOSE FACTORS BY WHICH THE SMALLER UNITS OF FORM ARE GROUPED AND AMALGAMATED INTO ONE ORGANIC WHOLE....WORKS ARE WRITTEN NOT AS CONSISTENT ORGANISMS BUT AS FORMLESS MASSES OF MECHANICALLY ASSOCIATED PARTS, ANY OF WHICH MIGHT BE REPLACED BY OTHERS.

THE CHIEF DIFFERENCE BETWEEN THE OLD AND THE NEW IS THAT THE DIATONIC BASIS IS REPLACED BY THE CHROMATIC.

--Taneiev (Moscow, 1906), 19-20

Both Scriabin and Rachmaninov were pupils of Taneiev -- two antipodes.

ROSLAVETZ

The contemporary linear-polyphonic culture, an intensive study of the systems of scales, the dynamic doctrines about the process of the formation of music; the definition of the role of melody, as an organizing foundation; the victory of constructivism, as the dominating principle of composition over a mechanical imitation of schemes -- all this points to the very deep insight of Taneiev and the solidity of the theses posed by him. Taneiev's ear could reject the extreme aspects of modernism and impede him in a calm and objective evaluation of contemporary phenomena, but his lucid mind directed him and led him forward. In his domain Taneiev was ahead of Scriabin and is still in many ways ahead of our whole epoch.

The pupils of Taneiev, acquiring from him their technique, remain true to themselves, while the pupils of Rimsky-Korsakov absorb his manner of composing. Taneiev's method becomes dialectically alive, non-personal, and independent of the conservative tastes of its author. The method of Rimsky-Korsakov fades out after the death of the composer, and the disappearance of his personal attraction, and turns into "deductive stipulations," derived from the creative experience of one local school -- stipulations that run counter to the living current of musical actuality.

Thus beginning with the early years of the new century and especially after the first revolution, which stirred up the thought of the public in all corners of Russia, we can observe a great rise of the musico-intellectual wave.

Somewhat apart, in view of its sharp antagonism to contemporary currents, stood the output of Roslavetz.

Roslavetz was, and has remained quite aloof from modernism.

--Asafiev (U.S.S.R., 1930), 175-308

NIKOLAI ROSLAVETZ (born 1880)

At the time when Skriabin lived and worked, when the modernistic group was making its victorious march upon the stronghold of Russian music, in the period of the casting down of old canons, the first compositions of Roslavetz appeared. They were coloured in ultra-modernistic hues with bold complex harmonies in which musicians could at first hearing discover nothing but wild cacophony. At that time his work met with no sympathy, and somehow he became part of no composers' group of the musical world of the time.

But his rise at that time was nevertheless interesting. That pre-war era bearing the motto "Fight against the old musical foundations," and possessing a strong revolutionary colouring in a musical sense, differed exceedingly from the inventive impulses of the former romanticism of the Russian National School of Borodin, Moussorgsky, Balakirev, and Rimsky-Korsakov. The former innovations were naive and arbitrary, asserted in the name of the freedom of creative art, and overthrowing the old canons and rules merely in order to establish the complete power and arbitrary will of creative genius; in their stead. In the epoch of which we speak, we observe something else. The innovations both of Skriabin and those grouped around him (among whom Roslavetz doubtless occupies a formal place) were quite different. Old canons were overthrown only in order to set up, in their stead, new rules, new theoretical foundations, just as strong and categorical if not still more rigid. Skriabin's harmonic tonal system of which we have spoken bears within it all the external and internal earmarks of a sustained specifically "severe style."

--Sabaneiev (Paris, 1927), 201-202

Though he used a different type of material, Roslavetz fundamentally sought the same as Schoenberg -- the precise laws of a severe logic of sounds.

As is demonstrated by the first violin sonata (1913), and then by a number of other works, Roslavetz already then set up, in a far-sighted and daring manner, the problem of constructivism that we are at present so much concerned with. It was necessary to speak of his works at that time using a terminology that has now become elementary, as: the organizational principle, a strictly constructive system, and a business-like accuracy in mastering the material.

--Asafiev (U.S.S.R., 1930), 262

The style of his art has remained almost unchanged even after the great upheavals which have occurred in the world and Russia since 1914. It is difficult to differentiate even the style of his early Violin Sonata written in 1911 in the era of Skriabin's predominance.

His fame began only after the Revolution; previous to that his compositions never found even a comparatively decent performer owing to their difficulty and unusual language.

But in spite of his theoretic premises that the most complex music is within the grasp of the workingman, if it but "organizes tonal matter" well, Roslavetz finally had to make a number of concessions, and his revolutionary compositions, written for workmen's clubs, differ strongly in style from his "serious" compositions.

--Sabaneiev (Paris, 1927), 205-207

It goes without saying, of course, that such extreme experiments as the Violin Concerto by N. Roslavetz (1927), an enthusiastic adherent of atonality, are completely banished from the Soviet composer's general practice.

--Olkhovsky (U.S.A., 1954), 185

Nicolai Alexandrovich Roslavetz (b. 1881) studied at the Moscow Conservatory.

--Asafiev (U.S.S.R., 1930), 321

BOLYESLAV YAVORSKI (born 1880) AND HIS PUPILS

There is almost cause to leave B. Yavorski out of the list of Russian composers, for he composes so little and is so capricious and bizarre, hardly ever publishing his works.

The contrasting traits of a medieval alchemist like Agrippa of black magic fame and a meister-singer are interwoven in him with those of a modern scientific investigator and theoretician.

But one thing is indubitable, among modern Russian musicians B. Yavorski is one of the most curious and interesting personalities not only as a composer but as a great influence upon the musical world, as an original, whimsical thinker, occasionally revealing half-insane symptoms, queer madness and almost fanatic dogmatism bizarrely combining to form a musical Cagliostro of contemporary Russia.

Nearly all composers of the younger generation have in one way or another, indirectly or directly gone through his hands, nearly all of them have tasted of this knowledge which, according to Yavorski's audacious confidence, was to crowd out all the old withered theories and take their place.

I shall not undertake a discussion and exposition of this theory, since its very vagueness makes an exposition of it exceedingly difficult. Being original in whatever he undertook, Yavorski did not publish his theory but handed it down merely by word of mouth as a 'sacred tradition,' excepting only for a few articles of aphoristic character in which the propositions of his theory were given as the fruits of a higher perception requiring no proofs.

--Sabaneiev (Paris, 1927), 208-209

ROSLAVETZ

If, in addition, we may remind the reader that in the atmosphere of that same epoch there was begotten the strictly rational system of B. L. Yavorsky, representing a clearcut doctrine of a modal gravitation, a modal rhythm and structure of musical speech, and that even the visionary and irrationalist Scriabin offered in his music a logical system, of a combination of sounds, it will not appear too exaggerated to say that in the rationalistic tendencies of the Moscow musical culture of the pre-revolutionary epoch a firm basis was set for its further organizationally powerful evolution. All this is a clear consequence of the Taneiev 'enlightened absolutism,' and, of course, Taneiev himself up to his death (1915), irrespective of his taste, sympathies and antipathies, was a source of a great cultural revolution in Russian music, the last word of which has not nearly been spoken.

--Asafiev (U.S.S.R., 1930), 262-263

SERGE TANEIEV (1856-1915)

Taneiev was not only a great Russian composer, whose true worth has begun to loom clear only since his death, but for the Russian musical world he was something infinitely greater, the teacher of several musical generations, and the living and shining ideal of the musician as a priest of pure art. He was an idealistic personality as a man, and all those who in any way came in contact with him, carried away memories not only of a serious, profound and original composer, "a Russian Brahms," but also in a higher degree of a pure, honest, and ideal human being, so typically Russian that he could not have been duplicated in other surroundings or in another nation.

Recognized as the moral and scientific musical authority, recognized as a theoretician, as a teacher, and above all as an "ethical personality," Taneiev at the same time had the queer fate of witnessing the gradual annihilation of his authority as a composer and his recognition in this field. He died a lone death, a man out of fashion, against a background of unfolding new events, in the era of the victorious march of militant modernism that swept away all traditions.

There have remained as a monument of his researches, two great works of scientific music, unparalleled in wealth of contents even on a European scale, let alone in Russia, where at the time, they were absolutely unique. These are Counterpoint of Rigid Writing, published by Belaiev in 1907, and the Canon* still unpublished.

--Sabaneiev (Paris, 1927), 19-37

*This great treatise was published in Moscow in 1909.

--Koussevitsky

In the field of musical ethnography and the research of folk music scholars worked, though sporadically, almost without interruption, which cannot be said of either the history or the theory work. In the latter domain it will always be the book of Taneiev on Counterpoint in the strict style (1906) -- already mentioned -- that will remain the most important work.

With this work of Taneiev's Russian theoretical musicology acquired a firm footing.

Taneiev's pupil B. L. Yavorsky erected, in the first decade of the twentieth century, a clear-cut system of composition, the basic principles of which gave a tremendous impetus to the whole of modern Russian musicology.

--Asafiev (U.S.S.R., 1930), 273

4.

The demands of life lead the Moscow creative musical culture more and more on to the wide and happy path of mass composing: that domain where the emotional loading of music is conditioned by extra-subjective factors and directed at an appeal to the new audiences, uninitiated in the finesses of the music of declining romanticism (I mean the individualistic romanticism). On this path there naturally arise attempts to unite composers not on a platform of common tendencies of taste, but a unified ideological platform. Such is the All-Russian Association of Proletarian Musicians.

--Asafiev (U.S.S.R., 1930), 264

The Association of Proletarian Musicians formed itself in 1923. The first period of its activities (1923-1927) is characterized by the exposure of the bourgeois reactionary essence of the then dominating in music groups; by the explanation with the aid of Marxist methodology of a great number of important phenomena in the history of the music; by the reflection in musical compositions of the main stages of the worker and peasant struggle.

In 1925-1927 a marked revival of musical reaction takes place. Many concerts, bearing a religious and mystical character, are organized, an enlarged activity begins in respect of publication and propaganda of decadent and urbanistic music of Western and Russian composers, as well as of fox-trots, produced by "nepman" composers, and of vulgar "gypsy" ballads and boisterous songs etc.

-- V.O.K.S. (Moscow), 11:10-12 (1931), 40

Twelve years have passed since Taneiev's death and his creative art is gradually and persistently gaining recognition, making a path for itself, as the creative work of the great Russian classic. Serious programmes are no longer made up in Russia without Taneiev's compositions, his quartettes are becoming an indispensable part of the quartette repertory, his songs invariably figure on the programmes. Soon there will come the time for the rehabilitation of his symphonic and oratoric works as well, perhaps the most valuable things he left. The recognition of Taneiev moves slowly, just as his creative work moved, but it moves steadily.

--*Sabaneiev (Paris, 1927), 38*

(A Note on the Author) Andrey Vasilyevice Olkhovsky, born **1900**; musicologist, composer and pedagogue. Received his musical education in Kharkov and Leningrad. For sixteen years taught history and theory of music in Leningrad, Kharkov and (from 1934 to 1942) in the Kiev Conservatory, where he was head of the Department of History and Theory of Music. Left the Soviet Union in 1942; has lived in the U.S.A. since 1949.

--*Olkhovsky (U. S. A., 1954), vi*

But already in 1928 a deep change begins in the musical life of the USSR. Militant reaction on the musical front-line is opposed by the strengthened proletarian musical movement. Under the guidance of the APM begins a hard struggle for the exposure of the church religious musical group, which held in its hands the musical theatres, schools and publishing offices.

As a result of this the Moscow Conservatory (now the Higher Musical School in the name of Felix Kohn), which until then was the fortress of musical reaction, the centre of dull academism, laboriously isolating itself from Soviet life, begins since 1928 a determined reconstruction of its work. The character and composition of its pupils changes. Proletarisation of the Conservatory is going on. A musical workers' faculty, to which musically gifted young workers and peasants come from all the corners of the Union is founded. During a short time of study from their midst a number of talented composers, performers, theoreticians, conductors, mass instructors have arisen. A fundamental reconstruction of the Conservatory takes place; its general principles, its syllabuses are changed and brought into accordance with the needs of the education of proletarian musical cadres. Besides highly qualified performers, pedagogues and composers, the Conservatory educates now the so needed by our country cadres of teachers and instructors for mass musical self-activity. A differentiation has taken place in the ranks of old Conservatory professors: the majority of these old specialists is now standing face to socialist construction.

A similar reconstruction is taking place in the Leningrad Conservatory.

The Musical Publishing House which was in the past a centre of propaganda for decadent modern music on one hand and for pseudo-revolutionary "pot-boiling" on the other changes the direction of its work most decisively. Alongside of the publication of the rich heritage of classic music, a vast propaganda of proletarian music and of the works of "fellow-traveller" composers is going on. For the first time in musical publishing practice mass proletarian songs are published in millions of copies.

In 1929 the proletarian musical movement, which started as a small but steeled in the class struggle on the musical frontline group, begins to turn into a mass movement. The less infected by bourgeois influences composers, who formerly kept in their thematics at a distance of Soviet life, joined it also and now put their creative work to the service of cultural revolution, of the struggle for socialism.

Struggling for 'large-scale bolshevist art,' the APM develops a vast mass activity. The APM sets itself three tasks: to eliminate the decadent bourgeois music from the workers' everyday musical life, to introduce in the wide proletarian midst all that is best in the rich musical heritage of the past, to introduce mass proletarian songs among the toiling millions.

At present hundreds of workers' musical societies have joined the proletarian musical movement, have joined the ranks of the APM. In the foremost ranks of the movement we see the biggest factories of Moscow and Leningrad -- the 'Electrofactory,' the 'Hammer and Sickle' (steel works), the 'Red Knight' (rubber factory), the 'Red Putilovets,' the 'Marty Works,' etc.

Workers' RAPM groups from former narrow study circles turn into a militant active of the proletarian musical movement, fighting for cultural revolution. Their musical activities they include in the general struggle for the fulfilling of the Party's general line, of the Five-Year Plan in four years.

Closely connected with this practical work and struggle of these groups are there [sic.] theoretical studies; they study the fundamental problems of the movement, the works of both proletarian and classic composers; they conduct creative work seeking composers among the workers etc. The groups name musical worker correspondents for the RAPM press and for the local factory press, they publish special wall-papers, devoted to musical problems; they organize collective visits to the opera and concerts, with subsequent critical discussions of the music heard.

Of late we are witnessing a change in the composition of these groups. Foremost shock workers begin to acquire a majority among their membership, the percentage of Party

and YCL members among them is also rising.
Another important circumstance is that
foremost active workers rise from the ranks
to leading posts on the musical front-line.

-- *V.O.K.S. (Moscow), 11:10-12 (1931), 40-45*

After the Revolution musical journalism began to develop rapidly and definite groups
formed around the musical journals. Thus,
several numbers of the monthly 'Towards New
Shores' came out under the editorship of
the well-known critic and theoretician V.
Belaiev, with a strong contributing staff
-- Derzhanovsky, Miaskovsky, Sabaneiev and
others, who later rallied around a monthly
called 'Musical Culture,'of which only four
numbers appeared under the editorship of
the composer N.A. Roslavetz.

-- *V.O.K. S. (Moscow), 1:11-12 (1930), 54*

At present Roslavetz is trying to make his music respond to the new
(Bolshevist) culture and embark upon the ways of a composer for the
masses (the cantata October and many other works).

--*Asafiev (U.S.S.R., 1930), 321*

Then there is Mosolov, a composer who is well
known in European and American modernistic circles
who was at one time the secretary of the International
Association of Modern Composers. There is something
not quite clear about Mosolov's career, particularly his
long residence in Central Asia.

During the 1920's a bitter struggle was going on between Russian creative thought, which was then reviving after many years of quiescence (the years of the
First World War, of the Revolution and of the period of
'war communism') and the art policy of the Soviet
power which was attempting to impose on art the

aims and methods of a "proletarian" culture which was gradually coming into existence.

The major protagonists in this struggle were first, the Association of Contemporary Music (ASM) in which all active composers were united and which aimed at the preservation of the national artistic heritage and at the inclusion of Russian music in the sphere of contemporary European creative aims and problems; and second, the Russian Association of Proletarian Musicians (RAPM), an organization directly inspired by the Propaganda Section of the Central Committee of the Communist Party with the aim of disrupting the activity of ASM, "Kindling the class struggle on the music front," and disseminating the concept of 'proletarian music.' RAPM's membership consisted chiefly of Komsomol members at the Moscow Conservatory.

--Olkhovsky (U.S.A., 1954), 148-188

The shock workers of the Electrofactory have finished the factory's Five-Year Plan in two years and a half, but they have not yet finished with their victories. Neither has their shockworking press finished with its victories. Together with the total aggregate of shock workers, under the guidance of the factory's Party organizations, and leaning upon the shock worker correspondent, it has achieved and will achieve yet not a few glorious bolshevist victories.

HOW I WORKED AT THE ELECTROFACTORY by I. Selvinsky

There were crises and sudden changes in the creative work of every poet. Yet never did they acquire that catastrophic acuteness which is peculiar to the creative work of a Soviet poet.

I had reached the limit in the expression of my intellectual's impenitence, groundlessness, solitude, and individualism.

I had nothing more to say.

I could only repeat myself, i.e., decay.

At that time revolution entered upon the second year of the Five-Year-Plan.

I left my writing, as ship-mates leave their parents' house, to come back as skippers with beards. I joined the tremendous storm life on board of one of the best ships of the revolution -- the Electrofactory.

My aim was to enter into the thick of the factory proletariat to catch its revolutionary enthusiasm, its bolshevist shock nature, to become its poet.

After having for a long time weighed all pros and contras I entered the transformer department as a welder.

However, it certainly not imported to me that I had become a regular welder, but that, being a welder, I had the possibility to see the factory from inside in its human figures.

My social work at the factory was rather varied: I was the artistic director of a circle, I worked in the factory press, made speeches in the red corners during the lunch pause, was an active member of the Party cabinet, etc.

All this was necessary. Yet not this, certainly, was being expected of me. The factory public, represented by its active workers, paid great attention to my poetic work. Those active workers noted my failures and my successes.

This, in connection with the slogans which I composed at the factory's bid, with regard to the struggle for the quality of production, the following notice of the

Party Committee, summing up the workers' impression, appeared in the factory newspaper:

About comrade Selvinsky's slogans.

It is six months already since Ilya Selvinsky works at the Electrofactory. Judging after the verses and slogans which he has written during that time, Selvinsky endeavoured to join the ranks of the shock workers of the Electrofactory and to reflect in his work our struggle for the speed. We must say straight out, however, that this was difficult to him. Most of the lines he wrote were weak and ineffective.

The slogans in verse which are published today certainly signify a serious change. Those lines are what the Electrofactory people expected of the poet. The further successes of the poet Selvinsky will to a considerable extent depend from the degree to which the Electrofactory public will be able to support him.

Three months later I finished roughly my poem 'The Electrofactory Newspaper' and read it at a meeting of the active factory workers.

The assembly expressed their opinion with a straightforwardness peculiar to the Electrofactory and with the absence of any conciliability and any intriguing.

Resolution passed by the workers and employees of the Electrofactory after the reading of Ilya Selvinsky's poem: 'The Electrofactory Newspaper':

6. In summing up, we once more emphasize the very important agitational significance of the poem and note with regard to further prospects of comrade Selvinsky's work that a whole series of the factory's problems -- in particular the rebuilding of human material -- has not been put by him and, if it had been put, could not have been solved by means of the witty but schematic form of a newspaper.

We expect of comrade Selvinsky new accomplishments in other, more deepened kinds of work devoted to the analysis of the new mankind -- the bolshevist worker, the Komsomol shock worker, the active working woman.

President of the meeting Lebedeva

Secretary Kotomin

Here I palpably felt, for the first time, the growth of socialism; here I found that practical fulcrum resting upon which I began to see the world from a new point of view.

ILYA SELVINSKY AND HIS POETRY by M. Mir

Among the so-called 'fellow-travellers' that are closest allied to the proletarian poetry, one of the first places incontestably belongs to Ilya Selvinsky, one of the founders of the erstwhile literary group of 'constructivists.' The latter, one of the most talented among the literary circles of recent years, which kept in contact with the proletarian literature, was dissolved by its founders, and the most prominent of its founders, like Selvinsky and Lugovskoy, have definitely become identified with proletarian poetry.

Of course, in the 'Electrofactory Newspaper' Selvinsky does not discard completely that constructivist formalism, that tonal poetry which consists in employing the local image, the artificial rhyme, and the superficial imitative rhythm, to portray merely the outward form of things and events. But, on the whole, in the general ensemble of his poems, which form the 'Electrofactory Newspaper,' Selvinsky has seized and reproduced, in a most life-like manner, the social substance of the daily life of the works, which are one of the outposts of the

Soviet proletariat in its daily fight for socialism.

-- *V.O.K.S. (Moscow), 11:6 (1931), 60-66*

Even more mysterious is the fate of one of the most active Russian disciples of Schoenberg, the author of works of the greatest interest for string ensembles, particularly quartets, a man who at one time (1922) was the director of the Kharkov Conservatory: Nikolai Roslavetz, who since the twenties has completely disappeared from musical life and perhaps from life altogether.

--*Olkhovsky (U.S.A., 1954), 188-189*

Arensky had been friendly, interested, and helpful to me, however, and in spite of Rimsky, I always liked him and at least one of his works — the famous piano trio. He meant something to me also by the mere fact of his being a direct personal link with Tchaikovsky .

SERGE TANEYEV

R.C. And Serge Taneyev?

I.S. I saw Taneyev from time to time -- as often, that is, as he came to St. Petersburg; for he too was a Muscovite. He was a Tchaikovsky disciple also, and he sometimes took Tchaikovsky's classes for him at the Moscow Conservatory. Taneyev was a good teacher, and his treatise on counterpoint -- one of the best books of its kind -- was highly valued by me in my youth. I could respect Taneyev as a composer, especially for certain passages in his opera The Oresteia, and I admired him greatly as a pianist. But the same hostility prevailed on the Rimsky-Korsakov side, and poor Taneyev was very unjustly treated in St. Petersburg. I might add that Taneyev was held in some awe by us for an extra-musical reason: he was widely acknowledged to be the best friend of the Countess Tolstoy.

ANATOL LIADOV

R.C. What were your relations with Anatol Liadov -- especially after you had accepted the Firebird commission he had failed to fulfill ?

I.S. Liadov was a darling man, as sweet and charming as his Musical Snuff Box. We called him 'the blacksmith,' but I can't think why, unless it was because

A NOTE ON DISCOURSE AND
CONTEMPORARY MUSICAL THOUGHT

(for the International Musicological Society, Salzburg, August 1964)

BENJAMIN BORETZ

IT MAY be taken as an encouraging symptom of concern for the contemporary history of music that attempts are increasingly being made by musicians in non-compositional fields to explicate what are presumed to be its attributes and to assert what are regarded as the special problems arising from them. But this welcome involvement by those who cannot rely on the communion of shared compositional experience to compensate for the multitude of cognitive and communicative difficulties in which the explication of twentieth-century musical phenomena is entangled makes especially crucial the assurance that the underlying conceptual and constructive bases of the phenomena under discussion are precisely and unambiguously understood—or at least that such an understanding is or can be made generally available. Such a requirement obviously presupposes a different shared experience with regard to contemporary music, a shared use of a vocabulary and syntax appropriate to and capable of expressing precisely the inflections of the qualities of contemporary musical thought. For one can surely begin, with one's colleagues in any musical domain, with the agreement that the contemporary musical situation is a unique one, and not only requires unique compositional solutions, but also engenders a unique consciousness about the fundamental implications of every aspect of musical perception, structure, and relationship. And this, in turn, manifestly necessitates the development of equally unique and particular modes of examining and characterizing—and thus of thinking, talking, and theorizing—about everything that has been traditionally regarded or that we wish to regard as a musical phenomenon or object. Otherwise, one runs afoul of all the artificial impasses invariably presented as insurmountable paradoxes (and thus, presumably, normative deficiencies) of twentieth-century music in so much scholarly—not to mention journalistic—writing on contemporary musical problems. However legitimately such conclusions may still arise under adequate methodological and conceptual conditions, they have up to now most frequently resulted from an initial premise that the problems of contemporary music as well as those general musical problems that arise in the course of the development of twentieth-century musical thought are worth comprehending or considering only as they correspond to conventional assumptions and yield to traditional explicative methods. Yet to some composers it has often appeared, conversely, that the definitional necessities encountered in the course of dealing with immediate compositional problems themselves raise direct and serious questions regarding the adequacy of these conventional modes of approach in explaining any musical phenomenon. This, surely, is not now and has long not been exclusively a concern of composers; but it is particularly interesting to see that any attempt to explicate traditional music on more fundamental grounds—such as Schenker's—draws its principal support and sympathy from composers even despite any aspects of explicit normative hostility to twentieth-century music it may also include.[1]

Thus, while a simply schematic description of superficial exterior patterns could never have been regarded as a satisfactory characterization of musical works, individually or collectively, it could be merely ignored as innocuous at a time when traditional practice was supposed to provide a universal, unambiguous context for the definition of function. Today, composers are rather too directly confronted with the problems of contextual definition not to insist that such descriptions are trivial and incomplete, and hence fatally misleading. The kinds of statements that they do find relevant to their own activity are those that, on the one hand, attempt to describe the terms on which individual compositions approach the creation of contextual coherence, and how, toward this end, the relational and hierarchical function of each element is defined—from which the "system", be it only the system of a single work, can be inferred—or, on the other hand, those that

---

[1] See also Ernst Krenek's description of his encounter with Ernst Kurth's *Lineare Kontrapunkte* in "A Composer's Influences", *Perspectives,* Vol. 3 No. 1, pp. 36-37.

generalize from such observations fundamental perceptual principles of the kind that have made it possible to subsume vast and enormously diverse collections of sonic phenomena under the single category of "composed music", distinguishable as such from all other actual or possible conjunctions of sounds, however "musical" or "nonmusical" externally. The scarcity of such statements, or even of evident attempts to make them outside the compositional domain, is too obvious and constant an aspect of all of our daily professional lives to require further documentation here.

But without such fundamental methodological tools, it becomes all too easy to fall into the kind of error most frequently associated with uninformed discussions of twelve-tone structure, in which it is assumed that resources fundamental to tonal musical coherence—hierarchization, for example—are absent in the instances—and more fundamentally, are unavailable within the resources—of the newer system. It is precisely *this* sort of egregious misconception, rooted in the ignorance, it must be said, of a considerable body of both musical and music-theoretical literature, that one would hope to avoid by developing standards for verbal responsibility and accuracy in writings about music. For (to repeat what I hope is a familiar homily) music without discriminative—hierarchical—bases is definitionally "random" in that the correlation between its successions of events and any musically relevant syntactical system is indeterminable, so that it would be impossible in any case to infer whether the successions were generated by twelve-tone or any other systematic operations. But this is far from intended as suggesting that the hierarchical question ought not to be raised—on the contrary, it is perhaps the one with which contemporary composers are most deeply concerned, and where relevant criticism both from within and without the compositional domain would be most valued. Such criticism, however, must proceed from an awareness not only of what constitutes an interpreted "system" and its relevant musical correlates, but also, explicitly, of those "systematic" respects that both conjoin and differentiate the tonal and twelve-tone systems as bases for pitch-structural coherence: in the first instance, those initial assumptions of pitch identity, interval identity under transposition, and octave equivalence which define the fundamental perceptual referents of operations in both; and in the second instance, the significantly different terms in which these primitives are interpreted and extrapolated from. It is, in fact, precisely this difference that is most significant, and on which discussion ought to be focused, rather than those sweeping, usually erroneous, generalities normally invoked. But such discussion, again, depends for its appearance on a general recognition of the fundamental *shared* assumptions and criteria of the two systems (as well as an adequate systematic understanding of at least one of them!)—in short, an awareness of musical structure at a level of depth all too prevalently unavailable in contemporary forums of musical thought. And further, if one considers the implications for composition and musical comprehension of what first may seem simply, or even trivially, a semantic issue, it appears that the insistence on verbal and methodological responsibility is not simply a display of intellectual virtue or academic respectability, but an integral factor in the composer's entire compositional effort. Even more, it should be obvious that the attempt to create structural coherence in the unique relativistic context of the compositional present links the composer's problem directly to the central concerns of present-day thought, particularly those of linguistic and scientific philosophy, from which he thus is in a position to take advantage of relevant discoveries—assuming, of course, that he possesses appropriate educative equipment to be aware of and critical about their relevance. It is out of such considerations that composers have found methodological and conceptual insights into their own work in the work done in these fields, and that they have borrowed symbological, analytic, and critical tools, experimental methods, and descriptive terminology in their attempt to construct musical syntaxes that can be controlled precisely, verified empirically, and characterized revealingly. Thus the essential relation of theory in this sense to contemporary musical practice is perhaps best to be found in Carl Hempel's description of the theory-practice relation in science (in his *Fundamentals of Concept Formation in Empirical Science*[2]) as a process in which "the constructs used in a theory are introduced jointly, as it were, by setting up a theoretical system formulated in terms of them and by giving this system an experiential interpretation, which in turn confers meaning on the theoretical constructs".

The advantages of such methods over purely intuitive or trial-and-error procedures both in arriving at individual

---

[2]Volume II, No. 7 of the *International Encyclopedia of Unified Science* (University of Chicago Press, 1952), p. 32.

"creative" solutions and in providing a basis for genuine development from solution to solution as well as from one creator's work to another's are obvious (or so at least they seem to composers who have wished to be able to accept musical and intellectual responsibility for their work), and would be trivially beyond question in any field but, unhappily, ours. And it is a measure of just how inadequately the compositional process, as manifested either in contemporary works or in the historical literature, is understood, that the question does indeed arise so frequently and persistently, and in so many guises. Naturally, composers need and expect searchingly critical scrutiny of their music, language, methodology, and approach from their fellow composers and colleagues in other musical disciplines, but they will be able to take this scrutiny seriously only when it begins to reveal an awareness of the terms and objectives of the thought with which it presumes to deal.

[1964]

A REPORT FROM PRINCETON

J.K. RANDALL

E A R L Y I N October 1964, Tobias Robison completed the job of adapting the Music IV computer program, developed at Bell Laboratories by Max Mathews and Joan E. Miller, to the idiosyncrasies of the Princeton University Computer Center's 7094 computer. Inhibited only by our collective dependence upon Toby for our daily bail and upon the generosity of the outside world for the conversion of our digital tapes, we have since that time produced more than a sufficient number of musical tapes to convince ourselves that the potential of this program—in the flexibility with which it can accommodate the special demands of each composer, and with which it can absorb the modifications and expansions to which Toby and Godfrey Winham recurrently subject it—is enormous. Even though our best tapes are more aptly described as not bad than as good, veterans of the R.C.A. Synthesizer and of several tape studios have been known to become wistful upon contemplating the short amount of time required to produce, on tape, a Music IV performance of a composition timbrally and rhythmically quite complex—a performance which makes even a "reasonably good" instrumental performance sound like butchery.

There are currently just five people who are officially involved in the Music IV phase of the music department's computer work: Godfrey Winham, William Gale, Tobias Robison, Hubert S. Howe, and myself.[1] Although Mr. Robison exhibits a nearly professional virtuosity as a programmer, and although Messrs. Howe and Winham are rapidly approaching a similar condition, all five of us are by training and declaration either composers or music theorists, and none of us is (though many of us very recently were) altogether innocent of Fortran and FAP. Nevertheless, our daily work requires the services of other people as well. To me, the most striking political aspect of my own work with Music IV has been, not my sudden exposure to the fruits of engineering and programming, but my sudden dependence upon the independent and not-so-independent work of others: composers and theorists, colleagues and students, professional and semi-professional programmers, musicians and musical dabblers. One of the virtues of a university computer center is that it seems at once to create, because of its numerous functions, an interdependence among people of widely divergent positions, interests, and skills; and to guarantee, by attracting such people to a single place where indispensable machines are being

---

[1] The salaries of Messrs. Winham, Gale, Robison, and Howe are being paid under the terms of a grant from the Rockefeller Foundation.

maintained and operated, that the needed exchanges of information will actually take place.

Our work with Music IV has quite naturally led us along the familiar paths of investigating musical perception—with the familiar result that some of us have come to feel that "perception" is a mis-loaded term for what needs looking into. This feeling is partly the product of a distaste for musical theories which have attempted to pin on to musical or pseudomusical extracts, as attributes of the extracts, such qualities as octave equivalence, root-definition, tonicity, consonance, dissonance, etc.; theories which too nearly discount the possibility that "perceiving" music is (and ought to be) a process of inventing structures out of aural impressions derived not merely from "perceived sound" but from sound perceived in whatever way best appeases our lust for inventing structures. My reason for accepting a premise, say, of octave-equivalence should be quite strictly that I am able to make more sense out of certain pieces (such as works of Mozart or Schoenberg) by acceptance than by non-acceptance; but such acceptance is purely provisional—and provisional even within the context of my knowledge of Mozart's and Schoenberg's works—and carries with it not only my freedom but my obligation to reject this premise in dealing with music for which non-acceptance leads me to invent, for that music, structures which I noticeably prefer over those to which acceptance leads me. Not only would I tend to view honestly and intelligently confirmed or disconfirmed rumors that x out of 1,000 students of comparative literature (or filling-station attendants, or physicists, or musicians, or Fiji Islanders) agree that such-and-such was so about some octaves in a perception test as discountable for musical inquiry: I would seriously attempt to view *my own* responses to such pseudo-musical extracts as discountable for *my own* musical inquiries. (The inducing of such an attitude seems to me one of the few legitimate objectives of the subject conventionally miscalled "Ear"-Training.) Perception tests now constructible by electronic means can easily persuade us to renew our wanderings, with such ideas as "timbre", "loudness", etc., among familiar kinds of foolishness about The Ear and The Way Things Sound. To carefully establish that the overwhelming majority of listeners adjudge some tone to be clearly louder than some other is one thing; to claim that the point is binding for music is to overlook the fact that, for a variety of good reasons, we choose every day in the week to perceive as roughly equal in loudness (or on occasion perhaps as just *incommensurate* in loudness) in a particular piece events which we would probably find very unequal in loudness were they presented to us as an anthology of extracts: and we do this, I hope, whenever we come to believe that such "corrections" of our "perceptions" enable us to make more sense out of a piece. The familiarly large variety of ways in which one may painlessly *choose* to hear (or not to hear) the loudness- and timbral-relations among string sections and solo strings, muted and unmuted, pizzicato and variously bowed, offers a good illustration of the futility of "establishing" something about "perceiving" such relations. In similar dependence upon musical context, we may choose to hear, say, some low-register flute tone as being roughly the same in timbre as some high-register flute tone, or as radically different from that high-register flute tone; or, more interestingly, we may choose to regard a difference (that we choose to hear) as a difference in loudness rather than as a difference in timbre; or we may even suspend judgment altogether: that is, we may decide that "different in loudness" and "different in timbre" are, for discussing some piece, *not useful terms.* Such an outcome should not surprise anyone who has learned to decide that "more dissonant than" may not be a useful term in describing a piece by Webern and that "completing the aggregate" may not be useful for Beethoven. But it should be remembered that such an outcome is not a fact about What We Hear, but rather a fact about what we choose to take seriously in this or that musical composition. And I would *not* take seriously some "fact" about a piece which I felt unable to incorporate into any structure which I might take seriously as a structure for that piece; and I would feel rather silly were I to bother to insist that a fact of this kind is, after all, a fact. For tactical reasons, I would prefer to put irrelevant truths on a par with subtle falsehood—particularly since the road to the latter is so often paved with the former.

The above opinions have at least one refreshing consequence: in using electronic media for psycho-acoustical research, rather than leaning on the distinction between perception-tests (anthologies of extracts) and compositions we tend to lean on the distinction between bad compositions (anthologies of extracts) and good compositions, and to regard the latter as a more basic instrument of research than the former. The following table gives a fair summary of some of the composer-provided input for a Music IV realization of a piece of my own—a realization which did much to lead me to conclusions I had already arrived at. (See next page.) The range of pitches used in the piece extends from about two octaves below middle-C to about two-and-one-half octaves above middle-C. Each of the three waveforms is used throughout this range. Similarly, the first two of the five rise and decay patterns, as well as vibrato, flutter-tonguing, and the three durations, are used throughout this range. The duration .428 occurs only during the first sixth and last sixth of the piece, while the duration .232 and the last of the five rise and decay patterns occur only during the intervening two-thirds. (During the inner two-thirds, sine wave tones proceed at 7/6 the tempo defined by the other tones;

during the outer sixths, at 5/9 that tempo.) The other things shown in the table occur frequently throughout the piece. (I think that it would be possible to decompose this piece into a set of perception tests such that most of the distinctions indicated in the table would be recognized by trained musicians having some previous exposure to electronic sound. I leave the reactions of Fiji Islanders, physicists, and filling-station attendants to the appropriate authorities.)

INPUT-TABLE

Waveforms:
  A. perverted open G-string spectrum of violin
  B. simplified clarinettish spectrum
  C. sine wave
Rise and decay patterns:
  a) applied only to waveform A.: rise, 1/200 sec; (peak *input*-amplitude always c. 500 units); decay thereafter; both exponential
  b) only to B.: 1/ 20 sec exp rise; linear decay thereafter
  c) only to C.:
          1. 1/10 sec bulging rise & decay, steady (at c. 200) between
          2. 1/200 sec bulge, 1/10 sec decay to half, lin decay thereafter
          3. approximate retrograde of 2.

Vibrato (applied only to A. and B.):
  a) to A.:   1. width of 6% of center frequency, 3% on each side; speed of 20 complete shakes per second
              2. none
  b) to B.: same as to A.

Flutter-tonguing (applied only to A. and B.):
  a) to A.:   1. 20 attacks per second
      '   2. none
  b) to B.: same as to A.
Durations:
  1) for A. and B.: always .273 seconds
  2) for C.: always either .232 seconds or .428 seconds

Notes in the upper part of the pitch-range having the first of the five rise and decay patterns sound, in a non-pitch and non-durational sense, very different from notes in the lower part of the pitch-range having the fourth of the five rise and decay patterns: this is hardly surprising in view of the sharply contrasting waveforms to which the two patterns are applied. What is perhaps surprising is that the difference does not seem to me to have, as a noticeable component, a difference in loudness— notwithstanding the fact that I can, if I choose, hear the former kind of tone as louder than the latter. For reasons which are probably rather complicated and rather closely related to the way in which I choose to hear the composition, I somehow absorb the difference in loudness merely as one dimension of a several-dimensioned difference in timbre—much as we might absorb a loudness difference between a muted and an unmuted string. And the longer I become accustomed to absorbing the loudness difference in this way, the more I find my perception of a loudness difference recapturable only with effort (where the "effort" takes on the unpleasant quality of being an effort to dissolve the composition as a musical structure in order to rehabilitate it as an errant Seashore test).

The introduction of vibrato (which is both "too wide" and "too fast") and flutter-tonguing (which is "too fast") on some tones but not on others ramifies the "perception" problem still further. In comparing two tones (in this piece) identical to one another except for some difference in the vibrato-domain, for example, I find it just as illuminating to say that the two have "the same timbre" modified by a vibrato difference as I would find it to say that the sine wave tones and the G-string tones have "the same timbre" modified by a spectrum difference. However, I am equally unwilling to say just that the two tones are "different in timbre", since I am too specifically aware of the presence and absence of vibrato. The important point here is that I think I resolve—or refrain from resolving—any issues of timbral or loudness perception (which arise in following a composition) along whatever lines seem to me advantageous in making sense out of the composition. If this point has any general validity, then a psycho-acoustical investigation into, for example, The Determinants of Timbral Perception, would seem to resemble a wild goose chase. Lest such a conclusion seem unprecedented, let us recall that there have been times when (and are still places where) relative degrees of dissonance have been seen as psycho-acoustical facts about intervals *in the abstract,* rather than as an analytical idea (derivable from more fundamental peculiarities of the system of tonality) which we are free to discard in the presence of any composition which renders it analytically useless.

An acceptance of views roughly like these does not, however, enforce a prohibition on the straightforward perception-test: on the contrary, it suggests two musically relevant ways of listening to such tests. The more obvious, though less conventional, way is to hear the test-events in full awareness that the test, which isn't (and wasn't meant to be) a composition at all, is among other things a bad composition: that is, each event not only has its aural context just as surely as does an extract from *The Ring,* but the context is such that our lust to invent structures will be spiked (not suspended, spiked; no one can simply take in a sound "in no context", and awareness of some—any—context is the psychological equivalent of inventing some structure (however subconsciously, faintly or inappropriately) of which the given test-event is a part; and only a trained musician can develop the ability to at least partially recognize his lusts and wherein they are being spiked, and thereby develop any hope of assessing a test-event in a civilized manner). The less obvious way is the more conventional, though its particulars are conventionally understood in a degree that has made such tests useless: we may attempt to hear the test-events not within the context of the test but rather within the context of a remembered or imagined composition (or set of compositions). Bill Gale produced last year a series of test-tapes whose aim was to establish an acceptable electronic substitute for those slippery musical shades (of vaguely remembered unidentified sets of instrumental compositions) which are sometimes referred to as "normal vibrato", "normal amplitude modulation ... choral tone", etc. I have myself run a few tests on timbre and pitch—but in the context of (remembered) unsatisfactory realizations of pieces of my own. Loudness tests made by Hubert S. Howe and rise-shape tests made by Godfrey Winham were likewise suggested by unsatisfactory (remembered) electronic realizations of original compositions, but were tests demanding the first rather than the second way of listening. My own view of these tests is that their real value lies in their potential for uncovering, in connection with actual or imaginable compositional problems, ways of producing a relevant degree or kind of articulation—a matter which I take more seriously than the pursuit of That Sound I Want or That Really Musical-Sounding Sound.

Since the immediate predecessor of Music IV has been discussed rather thoroughly in accessible journals,[2] and since the stickier technical principles (as contrasted with some of the specifics of the two programs) underlying Music III and Music IV are the same, I would like to discuss several of Music IV's fringe benefits. A successful Music IV run automatically produces, in addition to a digital tape indicating voltages to be impressed on a musical tape, two printed versions of the "score" for the piece, test, or whatever. The first of these versions is merely a reprint of the numerically coded score, if any, which the composer fed to the machine in the first place. The second version shows the results of the machine's execution of any computational instructions which the composer may have included with, or supplied instead of, a numerically coded score. These computational instructions may be, in coded form,

[2] James C. Tenney's excellent article in JMT has been especially useful to us in our struggles with the computer-oriented Music IV manual. (Tenney also gives a short list of canonical writings about Bell's music programs: to his list, I would add the Music IV Manual itself written by Max Mathews and Joan E. Miller since Tenney's article appeared.)

anything from "make a gradual ritard from a tempo of dotted-eighth = 65.7 in the middle of measure 17 to a tempo of halfnote = 13.1 at the end of measure 88 and then immediately switch to a tempo of sixteenth = 8059", through "multiply the amplitudes of all notes below middle C by 1.5", to "generate, as 4-part note-against-note counterpoint (in which each 'part' states one trichord), all trichordal partitions of the 9-note collection X which involve only the trichords 017 and 035 in the individual parts and only the trichords 014 and 047 as simultaneities". This second version is perhaps more interesting than the first, since it represents the machine's final opinion about what it then proceeded to put on the digital tape.

In addition to writing the output routines which enable our 7094 to write information on the digital tape in exactly the manner that the converter expects, Toby Robison has written routines which cause the computer to print two additional versions of the "score" which are indispensable for test-runs. One version simply reproduces, in the form of octal numbers, each of the numbers on the digital tape. These are the numbers which indicate the voltages to be impressed on a musical tape at intervals of 1/10,000 of a second, and which therefore don't "look like" a score at all; on the other hand, they do happen to represent a faithful copy of what the machine is doing to the tape, and are therefore a court of last appeal. The other version is less precise but much prettier: it represents the numbers on the digital tape in wave form. (There is some local sentiment in favor of interpreting printed waveform output as our central artistic objective and the eventual musical tape as a sideline exhibition of programming and engineering prowess.)

Even though these last two forms of printout are not feasible for more than a second or so of sound (because of the amount of paper and print-ing-time that would be required for such representations of even a short piece of music—not to mention the amounts of time that nobody would waste trying to read such representations), the mere fact that the computer can, as an integral part of any run, print a score or set of scores fulfilling the composer's particular specifications raises, for each run, the question as to what form of score would provide the most useful printed record of a piece which is, on the same run, coming out as sound anyway. Insofar as we think of a score as any set of instructions which, upon execution, will produce a duplicate of the digital tape, the question is of no interest except as a question of programming technique, since any score (after the tape is produced) will probably serve mainly as a slow-motion camera for those who persist in wondering what happened. However, the exigencies of composing enforce a less carefree view of printed instructions. Several years ago I worked out, in some detail, a complete schematic score for the short piece previously discussed, which

I then gave up on when I became convinced that I would not be able to hit upon a combination of instruments capable of making just the distinctions I wanted and also capable of excluding distinctions I didn't want. The score was "complete" in the sense that all pitches in the piece had been assigned to attack positions; and "schematic" in the sense that each note was either red or green and either bracketed or not—with reds, greens, brackets, and unbrackets left musically uninterpreted. This score has proved to be unusually appropriate for realization through Music IV. Not only does Music IV, like any other mode of electronic sound-production, open up a variety of possible interpretations of such uninterpreted notations as I have described; but it often reduces the problem of realizing *alternative* interpretations to a problem of retyping a few instructions or inserting a simple Fortran subroutine. (General "corrections" of tempo, loudness level, degrees of waveform contrast, width or speed of vibrato, etc., may realistically be viewed as the easiest cases, in Music IV, of realizing alternatives.) This is equally true whether these "alternative interpretations" are to be realized separately—in the form of different versions of the "same" piece—or in some sequence within a single version of the piece. A player in a string quartet would have good reason to regard such an instruction as "now play an exact retrograde inversion, at transposition 8, of what you played in the opening 43 measures" as material for PERSPECTIVES rather than as an acceptable substitute for measures 44 through 86 of his part. The 7094, in executing a Music IV program, has no such preferences: as a result, a "score" may be written in Music IV which looks more like what would normally be considered an analysis of the piece than like a specification of its pitches, durations, dynamics, and so forth. It seems to me clear that a score which took full advantage of this opportunity to feed the 7094 a set of instructions, however complicated, which reflected as strongly as possible whatever the composer viewed as the most significant structure of the eventual taped sound would be a more useful document than a mere record of note-specifications. In Music IV, I could, for example, build into a set of Fortran subroutines not only such instructions as "treat as green and unbracketed any note which is imbedded in such-and-such a kind of passage in such-and-such a way", and "treat green as meaning, initially, a wide fast vibrato without amplitude modulation; and unbracketed as meaning, initially, the harmonic spectrum herewith enclosed; and treat green as meaning, in subsequent occurrences, less vibrato and more amplitude modulation than for the previous occurrence of green; and unbracketed as meaning, in subsequent occurrences . . ."; but also a more fundamental set of instructions which would reflect the reasoning behind the greens and unbrackets, and at the same time produce and cause the execution of their interpretations. At the very least, such a score would have the virtue of exposing and documenting frivolity of intent. (In unwitting anticipation of the notational ca-pacities of Music IV, Hubert S. Howe produced last year a series of Fortran programs for generating and analysing two-dimensional pitch-class configurations which are basic to my own compositional procedures. (I had described these configurations and procedures in an unpublished monograph [written during the winter of 1961-62] called "Pitch-Time Correlation".) Mr. Howe, like Eric Regener (currently a graduate composer at Princeton), has also written similar programs of a more general applicability.)[3] Viewed in this way, Music IV opens up the possibility of writing scores which *are* scores in the sense that a re-run of the same deck of punched cards would result in a duplication of the original tape, and which are yet couched in largely generative and analytical statements. Aside from the sense in which I find this resource of Music IV just plain appealing, I find it particularly appealing in the face of the considerable likelihood that all of us, after perhaps ten more years or so of experience with a rapidly expanding technology of sound-production and with a slowly developing judgment in assessing musical systems and compositional procedures, can achieve at least two things: some better ideas for electronically realizing our old pieces, and some new insights into our old systems and procedures.

I would like to offer a concluding innuendo about the improvement of old procedures:

The term "composer" is being used with suggestive regularity in the real world (as in these occasionally distinguished pages) to denote a tape handler or data-processor who, although "expert" in "the field", is musically a dabbler. This linguistic peccadillo would be unworthy of comment—(musical composition has, after all, survived the far graver threats posed by live performance)—were it not for the fact that com-posers themselves, in their desire to avoid profiting from experience, too hastily and too thoughtlessly discount the likelihood that "findings" developed by musical dabblers represent answers to questions which shouldn't have been asked but which look enough like questions which should have been asked that we may in the long run be willing to overlook the discrepancy on the grounds that dabblers boost sales and science is science. We cannot correct this situation by sitting on our thumbs wait-ing for the dabblers to fork over: surely the reverent anxiety amid which we solicit, ingest, and disseminate their "findings" nurtures more needs

---

[3] Mr. Howe, together with Mr. Alexander M. Jones of the Princeton University Computer Center staff, is the co-author of an unpublished manual describing the input language currently in use in the musicological phase of the music department's computer work—a language which Mr. Jones invented. Mr. Regener has written an unpublished monograph describing an alternative input language of his own; this language is characterized by the greater fidelity with which it preserves certain properties of written musical notation.

for what they have found than findings for what we need. To any composer who feels inconvenienced by his scientific and mathematical ineptitude, I recommend the following status game: disregarding that mote in your eye, take a good look at (and cherish) the irrepressible musical ineptitude of those dabblers who have revealed findings in recent soft-cover publications; then set your own house in order.

Jan. 1, 1965

from THE NATION (etc.)
1962-1968:

II: Music on Records, 1963-67

NATION: 2.2.63

`   6.22.64

               12.14.64: Records of the Year

               4.26.65

               10.25.65

               10.11.65: Some 20th-Century Classics

HARPER'S: Fall 1967

THE NATION:

RECORDINGS

Benjamin Boretz

2.2.63

SCHUBERT: *Die Schöne Müllerin.* Dietrich Fischer-Dieskau, baritone. Gerald Moore, piano. Angel (S) 3628. _____Aksel Schiötz, tenor. Gerald Moore, piano. Danish Odeon MOAK1. *Die Winterreise.* Hans Hotter, baritone.Erik Werba, piano. Deutsche Grammophon (S) 138 778/9.

The recordings of Schubert's *Die Winterreise* by Hans Hotter and that of *Die Schöne Müllerin* by Dietrich Fischer-Dieskau are both symptomatic of the disdain exhibited by many performers toward the most obvious and essential structural properties of the music they perform. They evidently prefer instead to substitute some completely external interpretive idea which is not only invariably far less interesting than the composer's, but also gives rise to continual conflicts between the directions implied by the musical elements and those imposed in the "interpretation". Moreover, where songs are concerned, the presence of a text seems to increase the temptation to ignore the demands of musical coherence, in favor of a supposedly "dramatic" projection of qualities that can be conjured from the words alone.

Thus Hotter approaches the *Winterreise* cycle as, simply, a collection of twenty-four separate songs connected by a sad story, and shows no awareness of the network of subtle interrelations that binds them together into a formal totality. The most glaring evidence of this is his blithe destruction of Schubert's carefully constructed tonal curve by the arbitrary key-transpositions of the songs purely for vocal convenience. The effect of this on the cycle is analogous to what would happen to the integrity of a symphony if one of its movements were to be transposed, or if perhaps just one or two sections within a single movement were conveniently relocated to make them more playable.

Other aspects of the performance are consistent with this level of intelligence: each song is tackled with a kind of exaggerated gesturing that might perhaps be appropriate on the scale of a Wagner opera, where an entire phrase sometimes functions as the smallest perceptible unit of inflection, but is incongruous in the context of this vocal chamber music. In these Schubert songs, a single phrase is as large a unit in relation to the whole as an entire scene is to an opera, and its articulation must be equivalently detailed and sensitive. Hotter's bullish performance flattens the motion within each song, so that it becomes the mere statement of a single idea rather than a fully traversed and developed form. Similarly, the multitude of graduations of quality among the songs is simplified into two general categories: "dramatic", which mostly signifies considerable uncertainty about pitch, especially at faster tempos; and "simple", where the vocal qualities at least tend to be restrained. The equal importance of the piano part is also ignored, but in this case the pianist (Erik Werba) seems too intimidated or too weak to produce even a reasonably clear background. As with other recent Deutsche Grammophon releases, the recorded sound is hazy, and the surfaces are not quiet.

By comparison with Hotter, Fischer-Dieskau's *Schöne Müllerin* is a model of musicianship, principally by virtue of the frequent projection of significant details (especially by the pianist, Gerald Moore), and by the fact that the gamut of vocal qualities, which goes from whispering to shouting, occasionally also includes "singing" as one of its intermediate stages. But the absence of any deep awareness of the nature of the music is equally plain, if differently and less objectionably manifested. Again, the fundamental tonal structure, which is so deliberately simple in the *Schöne Müllerin* that its relevance to the "folkishness" of the songs seems unmistakable, is arbitrarily disarranged; and even though the incongruities here are not so great as in Hotter's case, such a crucial long-range association as the repetition, in the final two songs,

of the relationship between the tonality of the first and second is painfully absent. But the most pervasive misunderstanding is the shaping of each song according to Fischer-Dieskau's reading of the Müller poems. His interpretation, in every case, results in accentuations, phrasings and emphases that differ from Schubert's — and Schubert's intent is fully revealed in the songs themselves, first of all by the musical structure and secondarily by the special relationships between both the piano and vocal parts and the words of the text.

The incomparable superiority of a performance generated by an awareness of these considerations, a superiority not only in terms of musical distinction but also in the heightening of purely verbal qualities, is impressively demonstrated in Aksel Schiötz's recording, made just after World War II. Schiötz traces the line and phrase inflections with such precision and delicacy that he achieves a sense of complete formal statement despite the quite narrow range of dynamics, vocal timbres and rhythmic differentiation that he actually employs. Fischer-Dieskau, on the other hand, for all his vocal acting, insistent stressing of high points, exaggerated tempos and aggressive rhythmic propulsion, seems to cover much less ground, and finally must rely on frank literary pretentiousness (he includes readings of Müller's prologue and epilogue, which have no significance whatever for the music) in order to provide even the semblance of artistic "profundity".

6.22.64

BACH: The Musical Offering. The Wiener Solisten, Wilfred Böttcher, cond. Bach Guild BG(S) 5070. Cantatas Nos. 43 ("Gott fähret auf mit Jauchzen"), 182 ("Himmelskönig, sei will kommen"), 80 ("Ein' feste Burg"), 87 ("Bisher habt ihr nichts gebeten"). Soloists, Heinrich Schütz Chorale; Pforzheini Chamber Orchestra, Fritz Werner, cond. Epic BC 1276; BC 1257.

Webern's instrumentation of the sixpart Ricercar from the Musical Offering ought to be required listening for anyone attempting to perform any part of the work, or to "realize" the sections where no instrumentation was specified by Bach. Had the Wiener Solisten done so, they might have been discouraged from playing everything in parallel legato "lines" that blur all the essential articulations of Bach's keyboard-oriented polyphony, inanely lining out the "main theme" whenever it appears, and interpolating occasional arbitrary hesitations into the prevailing metronomic thump as a substitute for rhythmic inflection. The real trouble caused by such performances is their plausible appearance of textural "fidelity": each line in Bach's bare open-score notation for the two Ricercars is quite literally followed through as an instrumental "part"; and since the playing itself is reasonably competent in instrumentalism and ensemble integration, the actually radical distortion of the musical context is hidden from the innocent listener, whose incapacity to detect such deficiencies is reinforced by the prevalence of this practice in most Bach performances.

The Werner-Epic Cantata series is a happy exception, however, and seems to be continuing on the same level of judicious performance and selection that was noted here previously. Of the present group, the least successful is "Ein' feste Burg", mostly because of a persistent fuzziness in the choral texture and rhythm; but No. 43, which I had not heard before, was a particular discovery as one of those wonderful late Bach works where a structure of marvelous inflections is hung on threads of the simplest external continuity.

BRAHMS: Symphonies Nos. I-IV; *Academic Festival* and *Tragic* Overtures: Variations on a Theme of Haydn. L'Orchestre de la Suisse Romande, Ernest Ansermet, cond. London CSA 2402.

This album does as little for one's estimation of Ansermet's conductorial competence as most of his recent pseudo-profound writings have done for his eminence as a musical thinker. Ansermet's beat in these works is as weak and unvaried as that of a pit-band conductor, and his way of dividing measures is manifestly contrary to the demands of the scores in an astonishing number of instances. But what is most striking in these performances is his unfailing instinct for choosing the precise tempo at which nothing seems to "go", for placing accents where they are most obtrusively inappropriate, for slithering past the most broadly demarcated articulations, and for muffing even the most elementary formal transitions. The result is a trivialization of the music to a degree that one would not have imagined possible — there are moments in the Brahms Symphonies that might be mistaken for badly orchestrated Délibes, which is perhaps a more considerable tour de force than I appreciate. The orchestra also fails to play in tune, together, or at a controlled volume level with enough consistency to reassure one about its status as a professional ensemble.

BRAHMS: Alto Rhapsody; Song of Destiny. MAHLER: Songs of a Wayfarer. Mildred Miller, mezzo-soprano. Columbia MS 6488.
HAYDN: Symphonies Nos. 88 and 100. Columbia MS6486.
BRUCKNER: Symphony No. 7. Columbia M2S 690.
All with Columbia Symphony Orchestra, Bruno Walter, cond.

The most remarkable impression that emerges from the totality of Walter's last recordings is of his ability to impose upon a pickup group of Hollywood musicians the precise individual sound qualities with which he conceived each of the works he performed.

Thus, even though the Brahms performances suppress much of the inner detail of rhythm and polyphony from which the real strength of Brahms's developments arises, in favor of a long Wagnerian line (which makes the Alto Rhapsody seem like Brahms's *Liebestod*, a parallel that Walter probably intended), the beautiful singing and playing project the authentic sound and shape of the phrases, if not all their essential content. And the Haydn Symphonies have the true gutty sound of the old Vienna Philharmonic: a more highly clotted and viscous sonority than that of the best American orchestras, such as Cleveland and Chicago, but still clear and articulate, so that sonorous masses mesh accurately despite the leisurely pace at which they often approach. The Haydn performances of Walter's last period also seem rather less tampered with than his earlier attempts, but his lifelong proclivity for imposing extreme dynamic contrasts, extended retards, broad sonority and phrasing, and "expressive" exaggerations on Haydn's deceptively straightforward continuities overstuffs the context and blunts its deft and subtle inflective edge.

In Bruckner and Mahler, however, Walter's conducting is entirely on the terms of the works themselves; the Bruckner Seventh is perhaps somewhat less transparent and refined than in other performances, but Walter sustains its continuously progressive unfolding as long as anyone could, with particular impressiveness in the seamless entrances and exits, and the unforced "arrivals" at dynamic and sonorous climaxes. As far as the *Songs of a Wayfarer* are concerned, they have the characteristic quality of most of Walter's Mahler performances, in which one is aware that however superior in some respects subsequent performances may be, Walter's complete faith in the relevance of every detail and nuance of these highly problematic scores enables him to create a uniquely individual coherence and sound image that is unlikely ever to be duplicated.

DVORAK: String Quartet in C, Op. 61. WOLF: Italienisches Serenade. Juilliard String Quartet, RCA Victor LM/LSC 2524.

The Juilliard Quartet does some of its best recent playing on this record, with a taut, concentrated ensemble that provides a tensile framework within which events can be discerned clearly and connectedly. The Dvorak is an especially impressive achievement, particularly since the Juilliard often tends to tear heedlessly through music that does not offer formidable surface resistance. But the extraordinary originality of the composer's "orchestral" string-quartet writing, in which each instrument is treated like a miniature section, with a characteristically symphonic line of development, seems to have stimulated the players to real heights of interpretive insight, and they project it with breathtaking alertness and comprehension.

The Wolf Italian Serenade, on the other hand, is a curious piece of nineteenth-century neoclassicism that wanders from one ingenious connective detail to another, while remaining essentially featureless, as though no real compositional issues were being raised. The players' responsiveness to every suggestion of a possibly significant event only serves to underline the ultimate futility of the effort.

RECORDS of the YEAR:
12.14.64
BEETHOVEN: Piano Sonatas: in
B-flat, Op. 106 (*"Hammerklavier"*); in
E, Op. 109; in A-flat, Op. 110; in
C-minor, Op. 111. Wilhelm Kempff,
piano. DGG 138944/45.
BRAHMS: Intermezzi, op. 117; Kla-
vierstücke, Op. 118; Klavierstücke,
Op. 119. Wilhelm Kempff, piano.
DGG 138903.

Kempff's awareness of connective formal
ideas, especially in the linear dimension,
gives considerable strength to both his
Brahms and Beethoven playing, which
emerge much more cleanly on records
than "live", although with correspond-
ingly less flexibility. Of the sonatas
heard both at his Carnegie Hall recitals
and on these records, the Hammerkla-
vier, a frequently incoherent disaster
under the punishing physical conditions
of live performance, is firmly, if still
somewhat narrowly, controlled on the re-
cording (although Kempff remains an
incorrigible A-naturalist in the first
movement). But the Op. 109, relatively
undemanding in a purely mechanical
sense, was given a beautifully articulated
performance at Carnegie Hall, of which
the recording seems a close duplication.
In the Brahms works, Kempff avoids the
salon overlay imposed by many pianists
on Brahms's hardheaded ideas, while
maintaining a subtly nuanced and tim-
brally lovely piano sound that is trans-
parently reproduced in the recording.

THE COLUMBIA-PRINCETON
ELECTRONIC MUSIC CENTER:
Babbitt: *Composition for Synthesizer*
(1961); Ussachevsky: *Creation-Prologue*
(1962); Arel: *Stereo Electronic Music* No.
1 (1964); Luening: *Gargoyles* (1962).
Columbia MS 6566.

The Babbitt is a major foundation work
in the electronic medium which estab-
lished, at its first appearance, an entirely
new sense of the potential for significant
compositional development made possible
by electronic resources; more important,
it is a beautiful realization in electronic
terms of the qualities of Babbitt's other
recent work. Vladimir Ussachevsky was
one of the important pioneers of Ameri-
can electronic composition, and remains
one of its most adept and resourceful
practitioners, particularly in finding elec-
tronic equivalents for large-ensemble
music in the traditional sense. Bülent
Arel is the brilliant technician of the
group, a manipulator of electronic re-
sources in tours de force of sheer sonic
exuberance. Mario Davidovsky's work
is a personal synthesis of the "sound"
and "structure" polarities of the elec-
tronic medium which has quickly estab-
lished him as one of the most mature
and developed of our younger professional
composers. Otto Luening, the benevolent
and musically knowing father figure of
the American electronic-music develop-
ment (as he has been of the entire ex-
perimental-music tradition since the
thirties), has a characteristically
witty-wise and occasionally farcical ap-
proach that makes capital of the oddness
of the relationship between traditional
musical qualities and their perceptual
effects in electronic surroundings. This is
a treasurable and probably historic re-
cord.

COPLAND: Piano Sonata (1941); Violin Sonata (1943); Trio *Vitebsk* (1929). Hilde Somer, piano, Carroll Glenn, violin, Charles McCracken, cello. CR1 171.

The Piano Sonata is perhaps the most fully realized work in the "declamatory" instrumental style of the "abstract" post-Piano Variations style; the Violin Sonata, though not the best Copland, is one of those forties works that have a sense of secure self-discovery and full mastery within an individual musical territory; Vitebsk *is a searching prefiguration of the skeletal manner of the Variations, impressive in its gritty toughness and unrelieved expository aggressiveness. Having all three on a single record, well performed, is a compelling attraction.*

MAHLER: Symphony No. 2 in C-minor (*Resurrection*). Jennie Tourel, Lee Venora; New York Philharmonic, Collegiate Chorale, Leonard Bernstein, cond. Columbia M2S 695.

This, at least, is a Mahler symphony whose qualities are precisely what Bernstein conceives them to be, so that his customary flair makes things happen in the right places and most effectively; and his sense for the special sound of the piece is, for once, stunningly projected without hoarse strain or distortion. It might be especially significant to note this recording's superiority to Klemperer's, which succumbs to its own mercilessly analytic exposure of this work's deepseated vulnerabilities.

MENDELSSOHN: Quartets in A-minor and D-major, Op. 13 and 44, No. 1. Juilliard String Quartet. Epic LSC 1287.

As with the Dvorak listed above, the Juilliard's intense, alert playing restores to arresting life some of the most brilliant and original works of the 19th century, too long moldered beyond hearability under the thick fuzz of a parlor Romanticism they never possessed.

POULENC: The Art of Francis Poulenc: Three Songs; Sonata for Two Pianos; Sextet for winds and piano. Jennie Tourel, mezzo-soprano; Leonard Bernstein, piano; Gold and Fizdale, duo-pianists; Philadelphia Woodwind Quintet, Francis Poulenc, piano. Columbia ML 5918/MS 6518.

A definitive representation of the decidedly ephemeral qualities of the last of the drawing-room composers, containing all the Poulenc any record collection will ever need.

SCHUMAN: *A Song of Orpheus* (with Barber: Piano Concerto). Leonard Rose, cello (in the Schuman); John Browning, piano (in the Barber); Cleveland Orchestra, George Szell, cond. Columbia ML 6038/MS 6638.

Song of Orpheus *is a much more authentic and thought-out idea than much of William Schuman's more extravagant music as, say, the rather power-assertive 8th Symphony. Although Orpheus is still a bit abstract and schematically neat (a set of "characteristic" variations according to an a priori formal plan that seems superimposed on the inherent tendencies of the materials), it has many sonically gracious passages and genuinely engaging sounds and tex-*

tures, especially the focal "Orphic" idea of a "singing" (usually cello) sound against a lutelike "plucking" in various orchestral groups.

STRAUSS: *Arabella* (1930-32). Lisa Della Casa, Anneliese Rothenberger, Dietrich Fischer- Dieskau; Munich Opera, Joseph Keilberth, cond. DGG 138883-85.
Die Frau Ohne Schatten (1914-17). Inge Borkh, Ingrid Bjorner, Martha Mödl, Jess Thomas, Dietrich Fischer-Dieskau; Munich Opera, Joseph Keilberth. DGG 138911-14.
Symphonia Domestica (1904). The Cleveland Orchestra, George Szell, cond. Columbia ML6027/MS 6627.

The Strauss Centenary seems a good time to become acquainted with the immense range and extent of Strauss's production. These are all "shadow" works to the towering landmarks of his output: the Frau Ohne Schatten *is on the far slope of the* Salome-Elektra *period, where the sensationalism and dark mysteries have become somewhat routine if no less resourceful;* Arabella *is like a wise old man's remake of* Ariadne *(1911), with a few special qualities of its own, especially in the continuity; the* Symphonia Domestica *has virtually an "and-then-I-wrote" relation to the earlier tone poems, and recapitulates many of their salient characteristics with nice accuracy — this composer always knew not only what he was doing, but precisely what he had done. It must be noted that the two opera performances are unremarkably sung and played, but the Cleveland Orchestra sounds superb in the Symphonia.*

BRAHMS: The Four Symphonies. Berlin Philharmonic; Herbert von Karajan, cond. DGG SKL 133/36.
Symphony No. 3. Cleveland Orchestra, George Szell, cond. ML 6085; MS 6685 (S).

My remarks on the deterioration of the Berlin Philharmonic under Von Karajan, made in connection with its complete recording of the Beethoven Symphonies (*The Nation*, Nov. 9, 1963), were received with outraged incredulity by some readers of this column. But although its playing on these new recordings of the Brahms orchestral music is considerably less discomposed, the basic observation holds, and on essentially the same grounds: the solo and ensemble wind playing is weak in the most fundamental orchestral respects; ensemble attacks and balances are consistently unreliable; there tends to be an unsettling discontinuity of sound-quality at contrasting dynamic levels and textural densities; and Von Karajan's conceptual contribution is mostly conspicuous for capricious changes of tempo that are obtrusively "interpretive" in their confusing disruptions of Brahms's continuity. In particular, the wind playing reveals a really remarkable lack of minimal discipline: each player has developed eccentric timbral mannerisms that are not only irritating in themselves but antithetical to any unitary ensemble (the flute's hooty vibrato and the overtremulous oboe are particularly distracting). The result is that doublings and combined wind passages disintegrate, and dovetailed lines emerge as unrelated successions.

A particular consideration of the Third Symphony, which was also recently recorded by the Cleveland Orchestra under George Szell, is revealing. At the very opening of the first movements, for example, the sonic contrast is unmistakable: Von Karajan's orchestra is heavily overbalanced at the registral extremes; the middle that is so essential in the generation of Brahms's special rhythmic and linear inflections is unclear and undifferentiated; the loud tutti is strained and coarse; and the only dynamic distinction seems to be from very loud to very soft, with minimal connection between the sounds of the one and the other. Where the score indicates (at m. 609) a textural change to *leggiero* in the string and wind figuration, nothing changes: accents are as heavily marked as before, and in general the minimum amount of overall timbral differentiation projects an unarticulated sameness that is only underlined by the fluctuating accelerations (particularly the one that winds up and charges into the beginning of the development) of which none is indicated either explicitly or contextually by the score. And after the typically thin and quavery playing of the crucial horn solo (at m. 101), the hyperaccelerated tempo is drastically decelerated where the score asks for "poco sostenuto".

This exaggeration of large-scale tempo change also destroys the manifold internal rhythmic subtleties whose perception depends to a large extent on a continuously coherent large frame of metrical reference; but even where this is maintained, subtle accentual shifts are dealt with rather perfunctorily (see mm. 168-180 for a particularly scrambled passage). The fortissimo ensemble brass playing (such as at m. 188) is remarkably messy, too, and in general the balance of voices seems continually haphazard — individual sounds are always popping out of the texture, seemingly unwilling to keep their proper places in the ensemble, and constantly threatening to burst the bounds of coherent single-ensemble sound into a crazy quilt of competing timbres.

These problems are even more conspicuous in the third and fourth movements, from the exaggerated hold on the first note of the famous third-movement tune to the senseless acceleration before its repeat, the renewed accelerando at m. 28 in which the basses accelerate a little behind the others, and the ritard before the third statement (at m. 45) — in fact, every reprise of this theme appears to be in a different tempo. . . . The one for solo horn (at m. 98) is perhaps the real nadir, toneless and unarticulated, seeming more like a muted trombone played offstage than the sound that is most central to Brahms's concept of orchestral sonority. And in the last movement, many of the rhythmic complexities are seriously mismanaged; some attacks are so uncoordinated that they take a full eighth-note beat to complete (see m. 90), the crucial triplets are perennially uneven and inaccurate (especially m. 149), and even the final chord seems about to come unhinged with gaps like glaring 'white' spaces appearing in the sonorous fabric.

In the Cleveland recording, on the other hand, the sound-quality and articulative sharpness are immediately striking; there is a remarkable sense of sonic continuity through all the timbral and dynamic changes, in which 'loud' is a relative degree on a continuous scale beginning from 'soft' and not a matter of noise, intensity, or strain toward the limits of sonority. And the sensitivity of the Cleveland ensemble to rhythmic differentiations, the clarity of figurational polyphony and temporal coordination — a precision in which releases are as accurate as attacks so that one is suddenly aware of them as a crucial articulative dimension that hardly seemed to exist before — project a completely different world of music making. Moreover, it is precisely in the individual distinction and remarkable ensemble of its wind playing that the Cleveland Orchestra must be considered the superior of other functioning ensembles. In this sense, perhaps, comparisons are almost invidious, but all the more significant for the perceptive listener. Notice in the two recordings, for example, the woodwind doubling and counterpointing in the second theme of the first movement, especially the sparkle of the Cleveland ensemble staccatos next to the Berlin thud; the precisely intoned and phrased Cleveland unisons at mm. 55-58 that realize the Brahmsian concept of orchestral chamber music; instead of Von Karajan's hurtling accelerations, Szell's coherent progression into and through the development; the cascading dovetailed woodwind arpeggios, like a continuous thread of sonority at m. 160 in the Cleveland recording, and the lucidity of the ensemble playing that follows; and the wonderful fast and total cutoffs from loud tutti attacks (and string pizzicatos) that leave some real articulative space (a full quarter-note space of silence at m. 194 in contrast to the persistent sonic overhang in the Berlin performance). In the second movement, compare the Cleveland horn's entrance into the ensemble with the sense of its imposition onto it in the Berlin recording, and the beautiful solo wind playing, and the sense that each "entrance" is merely the point at which an already present instrument begins as well as the way the tempo is sustained, held and controlled throughout, so that the big rhythmic change where the woodwinds and strings are antiphonally counter-poised (m. 41) makes a real relational point next to the preceding accentuations. In the third movement, the triplet figuration is part of the foreground sound that binds all the timbral changes together; and the triplets in the last movement as well are suddenly clear as part of the same idea (because accurately played), so that the building down at the *diminuendo* coda (which also takes place through triplet figuration) becomes a genuine resolution of the entire work's structural issues. However, my one reservation about the Cleveland performance arises at this point: the overemphasis of the third in the final sonority seems to me a strangely perverse denial of the chain of thought and association out of which it arises after so much lucidity and care.

SCHUMANN: Symphony No. 2; *Genoveva* Overture. Berlin Philharmonic; Rafael Kubelik, cond. DGG 138955 (S).

Schumann's Second Symphony, that most complex, difficult, subtle and fully realized of his large orchestral works, is conceived by Kubelik with a massive simplicity that blurs almost all its small-scale inflections, leaving the work to project only its broadest and least interesting level. In this sense, Kubelik's is less than half a performance; his insensitivity to dynamic variation is extreme: he hears throughout only two elements, a top, "main" line to which

everything else that happens is "accompaniment"; and he encourages some brass-band playing in the finale that brings to the fore the Teutonic tendencies in Schumann that one would most like to forget. Aside from the (anticipated) bad oboe playing in the slow movement solo, Kubelik is efficient enough in eliciting what he conceives, but he has simply not discovered what makes this piece worth playing. The *Genoveva* overture is chiefly remarkable for one of those wonderful Schumann introductions that are so much more promising than the movement they deliver.

10.25.65

BELLINI: *Norma*. Joan Sutherland, Marilyn Horne, John Alexander. London Symphony Orch. and Chorus; Richard Bonynge, cond. RCA Victor LSC 6166.

VERDI: *La Forza del Destino*. Leontyne Price, Richard Tucker, Robert Merrill, Shirley Verrett, Giorgio Tozzi, Ezio Flagello. RCA Italiana Orch. and Chorus; Thomas Schippers, cond. RCA Victor LSC 6413.

Macbeth. Birgit Nilsson, Giuseppe Taddei. l'Accademia di Santa Cecilia, Rome; Thomas Schippers, cond. London OSA. 1380.

Rigoletto. Anna Moffo, Robert Merrill, Alfredo Kraus, Rosalind Elias, Ezio Flagello. RCA Italiana Orchestra and Chorus; Georg Solti, cond. RCA Victor LSC 7027.

The Victor *Rigoletto* reveals, primarily, the continuing destruction of Anna Moffo's once brilliant vocal quality. Here again, the overuse and overprojection required of singers on the international opera circuit appear as the inevitable killer of any genuinely individual vocal sound. Instead, what pass for "qualities" in the coarse vastness of the opera houses are such exaggerated mannerisms as Birgit Nilsson's "metallism", Leontyne Price's off-center fuzziness, or Joan Sutherland's muscular chirp. In Sutherland's case, her métier is actually rather appropriate for the special requirements of *Norma,* which otherwise deserves much more attention to detail and phrasing than can be discerned in the present recording. Among the others, *Macbeth* is somewhat primitive if frequently striking Verdi, *La Forza del Destino* is mature middle-period Verdi con tutte le forze, and *Rigoletto*, helped by Solti's intelligent control, is ever more unmistakably the classic essay in masterly music-dramatic timing. On the other hand, the performances directed by Mr. Schippers testify mainly to Verdi's astonishing ingenuity in guaranteeing striking dramatic results even under the shabby routine of careless opera-house tradition.

BLITZSTEIN: *The Cradle Will Rock.* Gershon Kingsley, musical director. MGM SE 4289.

Although I find little in this work beyond a rather less inventive and sophisticated Depression musical, its re-recording will undoubtedly exert a powerful nostalgic pull on those for whom it will recall the do-it-yourself atmosphere of theatre, art and music of the WPA days, and even more especially on those for whom the hope of a real "serious music for all the people" is a sadly lost — or still envisioned — artistic millenium. For anyone interested in American music as a whole, it is a fascinating insight into a direction that was taken quite seriously in the prewar period by some of our most celebrated composers. Apart from these considerations, though, what remains to be noted are mainly cartoon-stereotyped characters and musical ideas, all considerably stripped down from the sharply contoured Kurt Weill works of which the *Cradle* obviously hoped to be an American extension. But it seems to have been dwarfed in every such respect even by Weill's own later Broadway works. Still, the "message" must have been, then as now, unmistakable.

WAGNER: *Götterdämmerung*. Birgit Nilsson, Wolfgang Windgassen, Gottlob Frick, Dietrich Fischer-Dieskau, Christa Ludwig. Vienna Philharmonic Orchestra; Georg Solti, cond. London OSA 1604.

Like the recent *Siegfried* recorded by London, the present performance is especially distinguished by the superior orchestral resources, under Solti's generally intelligent control and care for total sound and pace as well as detail. And again, the vocal performances are on the highest level currently available in opera houses — higher, in fact, since recordings can utilize first-rate singers even for minor roles. The result is a total performance on a level far superior, for example, to the *Ring* that I heard at Bayreuth two summers ago. The sound, too, seems even cleaner and more effectively projected at extremes of intensity and density than in the earlier *Siegfried.*

All this is particularly impressive in view of the special interpretive conditions confronted in *Götterdämmerung.* Of all the *Ring*, it is the most multilaterally ramified (naturally enough, since there converge in it the dramatic-musical threads of each of the more singly developed earlier parts). In one sense, the variety thus generated presents less of an articulative problem than do the longspanned unitary textures of some of the others. On the other hand, the total time span of *Götterdämmerung* is commensurately (though not literally) extended to connect the time sense in each section with its generative origins (for Wagner was completely serious in regarding the Ring as a single four-evening work!), so that the individual sections present an at least equally difficult task in the realization of their organic unity.

BERLIOZ: *Romeo and Juliet.* Gladys Swarthout, John Carris, Nicola Moscona, NBC Symphony; Arturo Toscanini, cond. RCA Victor LM 7034. *Romeo and Juliet.* Rosalind Elias, Cesare Valletti, Giorgio Tozzi. New England Conservatory Chorus; Boston Symphony Orchestra; Charles Munch, cond. RCA Victor LD 6098.

Berlioz was the 19th-century Varèse, and his absolutely original sonic vision was most fully and multi-dimensionally realized in *Romeo and Juliet.* On this level, it seems to me that Berlioz still awaits his conductor; neither Munch's fondling nor Toscanini's crackling efficiency really explores much of what one can "hear" from even a superficial reading of the score: the violin line at the opening of "Romeo Alone", for example, requires an awareness of the inflective sense of every turn in its fantastically complex course to guide its coherent articulation. But Munch's indiscriminate hesitation on every note and Toscanini's brisk observance of exact noted durations are equally inadequate to project either this or its development in the passages — through the end of the Love Scene — that follow.

On the whole, however, the complexity of the score gives the contemporary sound resources on the Munch recording the decided advantage, although the neatness of the playing that Toscanini evokes at great heights of speed and complexity (aside from the "live"-performance *accoutrements* of audience coughs, conductorial vocalism and instrumental *gaffes)* is rather more attractive than Munch's somewhat messy, blurred outlines.

BRUCKNER: Symphony No. 4. Philharmonia Orchestra; Otto Klemperer, cond. Angel 36245.
DVORAK: Symphony No. 9 ("From the New World"). Philharmonia Orchestra; Otto Klemperer, cond. Angel 36246.
Klemperer's integrative gifts achieve spectacular results in music like Bruckner's, where long, and not always equally weighted, spans threaten to wander into perceptual randomness. In particular, the "white" registration of Bruckner's organ-derived orchestration is beautifully realized in this recording, and the larger time units in which essential rhythmic shapes are projected — overlying point-to-point literal reiteration — are immediately and continuously evident. Thus the pacing and dovetailing in both phrasing and instrumental entrances in the slow movement are an especial discovery. Still, this is perhaps the least exploratory of Bruckner's symphonies, and the merely "charac-

teristic" quality of its turns of harmony and sonority often seems more decorative than relationally significant. There remains a considerable subtlety in the movement-to-movement association that is made remarkably apparent in this performance and may be sufficient reward to listeners patient enough to wait for them during the long stretches of internal inactivity.

The Dvorak "New World" Symphony represents, along with the recent recording of the Tchaikowsky Fifth Symphony, Klemperer's most significant contribution to a seriously misunderstood domain of the music literature. For these performances make profound structural sense out of pieces that are usually exploited entirely for their local prettiness, brilliance or orchestral opulence. The real originality of Dvorak's vivid orchestral sonorities is in their primary function as formal articulants; and they 'sound' even more stunning when their formal impact is realized. In this light, the way Klemperer evolves a dynamic curve to which every nuance of harmonic, linear and timbral inflection contributes should give a new dimension to most listeners' concepts of orchestral virtuosity.

SOME 20th-CENTURY CLASSICS:

10.11.65

STRAVINSKY: *Apollo* (1928) Columbia Symphony; *Orpheus* (1946) Chicago Symphony Orchestra, Igor Stravinsky, cond. Columbia MS. 6646.

These two works are among the most specially treasured by "inside" Stravinskyans: unsensational in surface, but spectacular in the subtlety and richness of their details and formal designs, especially in the direction of the restraint and precision that are so powerful in Stravinsky's recent music. In *Apollo*, this is centrally evident in the incredible variety of sonority drawn from the string ensemble, and in the unique phraseology generated by a stunning revaluation of the formal meaning of a "lyrical" continuity. And in *Orpheus,* the selection of timbres around the initial harp sound (a process that actually "happens" as the harp is gradually surrounded and submerged by the mounting overlap of pitches sustained from its own steadily unfolding line) creates sonorities that resonate through later works from *Agon* to *Movements* and beyond. Here, too, a filmic intercutting (it becomes a "dissolve" in the slower tempo at either end, the most wonderfully "deliberate" passage in all of Stravinsky's even-note continuities) is the articulative basis for a total time-sense that, even for Stravinsky, is singularly original — especially as he hears it on these extraordinary recordings. Indeed, this soon-to-be nonagenarian remains his own discerning interpreter; the *Apollo* he conducts, for example, is a revelation in the replacement of the "sweetness" of every other performance by an "edge" and muscularity that is most belligerently un-*Siegfried-Idyll*-like. The playing by the Columbia Symphony strings is precise enough, though not as clean or unforced as the Chicago Orchestra's performance of *Orpheus,* which is as close to ideal for the sonority of the piece as one need imagine.

BARTÓK: The Six String Quartets. The Juilliard String Quartet. Columbia DL 317/ D3S 717.

The string quartets remain *the* Bartók literature, the source of almost everything original and significant in his compositional thought. Even the First Quartet is in striking contrast to the superficially "moderne" music Bartók was producing in other media at about the same time. Indeed, the First is already quite clearly the work of a serious and probing deployer of notes, especially in terms of linear interrelations — the special "counterpoint" of the traditional string-quartet texture — although the resultant harmony seems to discover rather too little ramification for all the complicated activity out of which it arises.

But one is also ever more aware, and particularly in these most important works, of all the inconsistencies and limitations of scope and depth that diminish Bartók's size among the 20th-century musical visionaries. In particular there remains an occasionally disturbing eclecticism, the sudden appearances of familiar sounds unsubsumed within an overall context — the Liszt added-sixth chords in the First Quartet, or the hurdy-gurdy music in No 5.

Of the other quartets, the Second also predates Bartók's rather late-developing compositional maturity. Nevertheless, it explores the dissociation and merging of (in the first movement) simultaneously and (in the second) successively occurring planes of texture, rhythm, tempo and register, with some arresting results, if still an ultimate sense of overall incompleteness and conceptual uncertainty.

The Third and Fourth Quartets, on the other hand, reveal a sustained compositional intensity that creates, out of an amalgam of "heard" string-quartet contexts from Beethoven to Webern, an articulative universe of its own and is the focal achievement that really justifies the continued currency of the entire set. The Third's remarkable idea of sonority and organization is apparent from the outset; perhaps for the first time in Bartók's work, the event-succession seems totally generated out of a comprehensive internal procedure, and the result is an immediately fascinating web

of association in a palpable totality. In this context, all of Bartók's prodigious inventiveness in string-quartet sonority focuses on the articulation of important relationships, and this functionality gives the famous "effects" their real brilliance.

The Fourth is a "fourth quartet" in the Schoenberg sense amid Bartók's work, the locus classicus for any observations about his attempt to reconstruct a new syntactical coherence by nontonal means. It is, surely, the most concentrated and directed of all Bartók's works, certainly the one that most rewards repeated and attentive listening — particularly to progressive expansion of the interval-spans that form the melodic core of each successive movement, and the descending curve that ends with the return to the interval vocabulary of the opening.

The last two quartets appear to retrench from the resourcefulness and control evident in the Third and Fourth (whose qualities, in fact, seem to have undergone no real further development in any of Bartók's later music). Instead, there is often a facile effectiveness, an apparent willingness to settle for the association that arose most immediately and improvisatorily. The Fifth is thus a somewhat diluted restatement of elements of the Fourth, while the Sixth takes the direction of a kind of wandering lyricism that, for all the external ingenuity of its progressively fuller harmonization of a "basic line", fails to convey any powerfully motivating structural concern.

The Juilliard Quartet first recorded these works some sixteen years ago, and the superiority of those performances has never been challenged. The group has by now discovered in the quartets a range of variety and nuance that considerably modifies the unrelieved aggressiveness of the earlier approach. At the same time, the Juilliard has acquired a security in every detail of the scores that results in a level of mechanical ensemble hardly ever encountered even in the most familiar traditional literature, and marred only by an occasional want of timbral finesse. Given the excellence of the recorded sound as well, there would seem to be no further need to look for a definitive recording of the Bartók quartets. For this reason, one especially regrets the substitution in the new album of some really pretentiously silly program notes for the uniquely illuminating, actually path-breaking remarks that were included with the old set.

Virtual Conversation 2: [JKR, 2003:] 4 Darkhorse Candidates:

Alexei Haieff: Piano Concerto
Roger Goeb: Woodwind Quintet # 1
Walter Piston: Sonata for Violin and Piano
Nikolai Lopatnikoff: Sonata for Violin and Piano

Harper's, 1966
STRAVINSKY: Stravinsky Conducts *Perséphone.* Vera Zorina as Perséphone; The Columbia Symphony Orchestra; Igor Stravinsky, cond. Columbia MS6919.

André Gide's *Perséphone,* with its vacuous mythos and relentless verbal liquidity, along with the *vapeurs mystiques* of Ida Rubenstein's *métier* of melodramatic recitation, presented an obviously maximal challenge to Stravinsky's normally transcendent capacity to transform what appear to be extremely adverse contextual contingencies into the vividly defined elements of powerful new musical inventions. But where the worlds of such as Pergolesi, Diaghilev, Billy Rose, Barnum and Bailey, Tchaikowsky, Hogarth, and Woody Herman were all appropriated with aplomb and panache into Stravinsky's syntactical synthesizer, where they were processed through 'appropriate' analogies which elevated them to spectacular heights of artistic consequence, the literary-theatrical fluff of the Parisian salon world remains, in *Perséphone,* unamenable to Stravinsky's multiple ingenuities, and persists in diffusing the many strokes of brilliance in sonority, texture, and continuity with which he invested it. For the subtle variation in phraseology and articulation within each section, and the macro-scale differentiation in sonority and configuration between the first-act 'upper-world' (strings, percussion) and the second-act 'underworld' (low woodwinds and brass), followed by the gradual and breathtaking retransformation by the second into the first as Perséphone 'ascends', are among Stravinsky's music-theatrical *trouvailles*. But the accompanying *mélange* of pitch- and duration-uncontrolled spoken recitation, the dramatically and verbally ambiguous solo tenor role, the decorative balletic interspersions (the first performance was mimed as well!) and the pervasive choral wallpaper, creates a terminally encumbered presentational environment.

This new recording perhaps underlines the ultimate softheadedness of *Perséphone's* conception with the extreme elasticity and precision of articulation that Stravinsky almost belligerently evokes from his players — every unit of the stringtrill burr in the first part stands out as a distinct articulate entity; and the choral phraseology is so clearly demarcated that its occasional aimlessness, stagnation, and event- emptiness are sharply extruded. Vera Zorina makes all the right lugubrious vocal noises as Perséphone, but Michele Molese as Eumolpus is occasionally short of phrase and hazy of pitch. The chorus and orchestra seem to be doing what Stravinsky wanted.

THREE LECTURES TO SCIENTISTS

J. K. RANDALL

I

Theories of Musical Structure as a Source for Problems in Psycho-acoustical Research

[Read to the Acoustical Society of America, Boston, 6/3/66.]

LET us explore for a moment some paradoxical consequences of the view that a piece of music—whatever else it may or may not be besides—can be viewed as an anthology of sound-events each of which can be psycho-acoustically investigated on its own; and that the scientific investigation of the perception of such sound-events has nothing in particular to do with the artistic capacities of the investigator. Even at the risk of having to disinter it first, I would like to cast doubt upon this view—not because I suspect that psycho-acousticians are too prone to graze in the pastures of art, but because I suspect that their own work suffers a severe malnutrition resulting from their not being too fussy about what they eat when they do graze there.

A psycho-acoustical investigation of a sound-event (or sequence or combination of sound-events) is normally carried out utilizing not only the usual variety of washed and unwashed auditors, but also a variety of sound-event contexts in which the test-event is imbedded. For example, a typical event in a perception test will be designed to elicit from an auditor a statement that two sounds are roughly the same in some clearly (or not-so-clearly) defined respect or that, in this respect, one is more this or that than the other. Now since the scientist is well aware that responses to any one event may depend in part upon the exact context provided by the sequence of events which constitutes the test as a whole, he is properly concerned to build any central event into a variety of contexts; and hence he is properly concerned to develop some contexts for this event which, in his judgment, might tend to suggest one response and others which might tend to suggest another, perhaps even an opposite, response. It would seem then that a scientist framing a perception test is required not merely to know a great deal about the interactions of the various perceivable aspects (durational, intervallic, etc.) of sound-sequences upon one another in influencing whatever may be "perceived" about some individual elements or elements within those sequences; he is required also to exercise no little skill in inventing sequences which will possess the double virtue of introducing a relevant variety of influences without at the same time introducing influences whose operation the scientist may be unaware of. (With luck, of course, his evaluation of responses to his test might lead him to discover these unintended influences. But luck is apt to be fickle: it seems at least equally probable that, were the responses nicely uniform, the case would be prematurely closed.)

At the risk of sounding faintly socratic, I would like to ask by what name we traditionally refer to someone who exercises no little skill in inventing sound-sequences which reflect the kinds of knowledge and possess the kinds of virtue just described. At the least, we call him a composer; and we call his inventions compositions. Yet it is essential to the scientist's alleged artistic non-involvement that he modestly insist upon a radical distinction in kind between the humble perception test and the lofty realm of musical composition, a distinction which is alleged to thrive upon the fact that perception tests traditionally (and intentionally) lack artistic merit. But mere lack of artistic merit is insufficient. The "clean" psycho-acoustician's claim of artistic noninvolvement rests additionally upon our ability to view his "artistically" worthless sequences of sound-events as *non*compositions *rather* than as *bad* compositions: for if his noncompositions carry with them that power to elicit misguided responses to individual component elements in anything like the degree to which *bad* compositions so notoriously do (as any composition teacher who has on occasion been frustrated in his attempt to identify "the trouble" with some dismal undergraduate concatenation of notes can testify), then it would be more germane—indeed, it would be essential—to the scientist's purposes simply to classify his traditionally artistically worthless sound-sequences as *bad* compositions, admit that his artistic non-involvement is a myth, and proceed to improve his compositional technique. It seems to follow that the "clean" psycho-acoustician must stake his professional life upon his (or someone's) providing a satisfactory answer to this double-barreled question: What is a *non*composition? *And* wherein lies its safeguard against our shredding its scientific insulation by mistakenly or unwittingly listening to it as if it were simply a bad composition? I can't answer this question. But more importantly, I can't imagine how it could be answered by anyone who was not invoking rather elaborate techniques of specifically contextual (i.e., specifically musical) analysis: how else could we be sure that our "noncompositions" really *lacked* some all-too-suggestive qualities of (good or bad) compositions than by thoroughly investigating at least the qualities of compositions? And since any technique of organizing sound—however inadequate when unsupported by other techniques—is likely to enter into full-fledged musical composition from time to time and to be extensively explored there and to become willy-nilly a technique of musical organization, how can the "clean" psycho-acoustician eventually construct "clean" sound-sequences (i.e., noncompositions) without mastering the compositional technique of utilizing only those techniques of musical organization which serve his nonmusical purposes while eschewing all those which might get in their way? that is, without becoming not merely a composer, but a spartanly disciplined composer to boot?

Thus we have arrived at the following dilemma: Either the distinction between noncompositions and bad compositions is tenuous, in which case there is no such thing as "clean" psycho-acoustics; or there is indeed such a distinction, in which case the psycho-acoustician must master whatever compositional techniques are appropriate to the production of noncompositions, and hence in which case there is no such thing as "clean" psycho-acoustics.

If my reasoning has been more or less correct thus far, then I hope it is clear that I do not wish to say to psycho-acousticians: Quit grazing in my pasture. On the contrary, I want to say something like this: Inasmuch as you must graze in my pasture whether you mean to or not, please examine the terrain at least well enough to be confident that you are munching on what grows there rather than on what no one has bothered to remove yet. Now just how well is well enough?

In working with electronic sounds—especially with unfamiliar ones—it is a matter of everyday musical experience that compositional possibilities (that is, relevant musical contexts) for some sound may emerge only gradually: concomitantly, my very awareness of certain properties of the sound may emerge only gradually, and it is precisely my proceeding to exploit the sound in a variety of musical contexts that brings these properties to the fore. The essential point of this musical experience for psycho-acoustics is this: only after a certain amount of compositional exploitation is anyone in a very good position to know what to test.

Now perhaps it seems to the psycho-acoustician that there are a sufficient number of purely routine questions which must be asked about any sound-event, and which require virtually no special musical insight to formulate. But I think it perfectly realistic to say that the more adept someone becomes at specifically musical analysis, the more he justifiably tends to doubt the utility, and sometimes even the meaningfulness, of those allegedly "routine" questions.

Let me illustrate by invoking a very familiar musical example about which I will ask a couple of very elementary and routine psycho-acoustical questions. Notice as we proceed how heavily what we "do" hear comes to depend upon what we can hear if we try, and upon what we think we ought to hear in pursuit of whatever we think constitutes a coherent musical structure.

Look now at Chopin's Prelude No. 10 in E flat, mm. 9-16. The second half of this passage exhibits relations traditionally called enharmonic equivalences. In this case at least three major-minor scales are simultaneously, though perhaps over different time-spans in different registers at different structural layers, relevant for intervallic measurements: the major-minor scales whose tonics are, respectively, E flat, G, and B flat. (That this succession of local tonic notes spells out the tonic triad of the piece as a whole is something that a trained musician would notice on first hearing.) Pitch-classes 6 and 7 (counting here all C's, B sharps, and D double-flats, or whatever, as pitch-class zero; up through all B's, C flats, or whatever, as pitch-class eleven) are both contained in all three of the scales I mentioned. Only in the G scale, however, is the scalar interval from 6 to 7 *nonzero*. In this scale the pitch classes 6 and 7 are distinct, consecutive scale-steps—which is to say that they delimit an interval of *one* scalar unit. In the E flat or B flat scale, by contrast, 6 and 7 are simply alternative versions of the same scalestep—which is to say that they delimit an interval of zero scalar units even though they delimit, as always, a chromatic interval of one unit.

Now let me ask my very elementary and routine psycho-acoustical question about a particular place in this passage: Are the intervals G over C and G flat over C flat identical in size?

One defensible answer would be the following: At the most local level, yes. At the two-measure level, no: the C flat-G flat functions as C flat-F sharp and therefore is chromatically the same in size but scalarly different. In relation to the impending tonicization of B flat: perhaps. In general: the musical coherence of the passage subsists in part on the various functions of the dyad C flat-G flat, each of which induces a different scalar measurement. But presumably my elementary and routine psycho-acoustical question envisioned nothing more challenging to the auditor than unadorned chromatic measurement.

In other words, we have brought to light a sense in which my elementary and routine psycho-acoustical question—which merely asked for a comparison of the sizes of two intervals—contained a hidden assumption that any trained musician knows to be false in the context of the music we all know best: namely, the assumption that an auditor will at least refrain from measuring a single interval along incompatible scales simultaneously. It turns out that the structure of tonal music has been inducing just such precise simultaneous aural measurements along incompatible scales for at least two and one-half centuries. And our grasp of this structure would become shaky indeed were we henceforth to decline, in the context of classical tonality, to perform these prodigies of precise aural measurement which trained musicians perform on first hearing with about the degree of effort they expend telling a violin from a cello. (It follows that further musical analysis would be required to evaluate an assertion that the re-attack of G flat over C flat represents a change from a scalar 6th to a scalar 4th; and I would be happy to counterassert, on the basis of musical analysis performed on some other occasion, that such an assertion overdoes a good thing.)

Please notice the implications of this Chopin example (written well over a century ago) for an even more elementary and routine psychoacoustical question such as this: "Are the following two pitches the same or different?"

In the context of the music we all know best, a succession of G flat—F sharp is both an identity of pitch and an inferable scalar descent. Furthermore, a violinist, for example, in playing a succession G flat—F sharp might actually play two noticeably different pitches in order to articulate the local function of each: and yet the harmonic context would undoubtedly require that we interpret these two distinct pitches as representatives of the same pitch. To make matters even worse, the violinist might legitimately play the F sharp slightly higher than the G flat; so that an inferable scalar descent might actually and legitimately be played as an ascent in pitch.

My example raises by implication two rather more general points which seem to me of fundamental importance to psycho-acoustical research: First: Any trained musician *could* hear that Chopin passage in the terms I have indicated whether or not he endorsed my description. Second: Any trained musician *could* edit out from his hearing of that passage at least some of those described characteristics which seemed to him irrelevant or detrimental to his own conception of the significant musical structure of the passage.

Thus far I have spelled out some familiar musical structural conditions under which a clear perception of unmitigated intervallic identity, or of a higher and a lower pitch, might be not just irrelevant but downright misleading. Very similar conditions can be spelled out—and yet only with the aid of specifically musical analysis—for such allegedly bread-and-butter concepts as octave-equivalence, consonance and dissonance, the definition of roots and tonics, etc.; and can serve to make even more palpable the dangers of discounting the possibility (discussed by a recent contributor to *Perspectives*) that "perceiving" music is (and ought to be) a process of inventing structures out of aural impressions derived not merely from "perceived sound" but from sound perceived in whatever way best appeases our desire to invent structures. Nor should we discount the possibility that perceiving just plain sound, musical or otherwise, is similarly permeated by our desire to invent meaningful structures—a possibility which I imagine some psychologists would claim amounts to a virtual certainty.

My reason for believing that psycho-acoustical research should keep in touch with current concerns in composition is partly that musical composition continues to play the central role in defining the current frontiers of the aurally perceptible (and in shaping the modes in which we aurally perceive); and partly that the evolution of new musical systems is sometimes a prerequisite to our understanding old ones—and especially to our understanding that some old musical system was just a musical system rather than the perennial embodiment of the laws of perception. And unquestionably, the flowering of the so-called 12-tone system in our era has given us a new perspective on the system of classical tonality. The realization that such traditional musical concepts as the relative consonance and dissonance of intervals are irrelevant to the analysis of 12-tone music has led composers and musical analysts to re-examine the function of these concepts in their traditional context. What we have sought to define is some ahistorical sense in which these concepts may be said both to cohere and to cohere in such a way as to shed light on the layer-structure peculiar to music in the tonal system.

Even more surprising, perhaps, is the realization that the notion of timbre may be not too much more than one of those leftovers from a dead musical system. In electronic music, where spectra, envelopes, vibratos, and tremolos may be structured over a whole composition with the degree of subtlety and efficacy to which we have become accustomed in the domain of pitch, we must learn to stop hearing vibrato, for example, as a vaguely subliminal way of lushing-up a tone; that is, we must learn to stop mixing together a set of potentially independent musical dimensions into a monolithic dimension within which we can continue to get off easy by discriminating among "mellow timbres," "nasal timbres," and other similar bushel-basket catches. In the presence of music so structured, the perception of "timbre" must be viewed not as a difficult psycho-acoustical problem, but as a sloppy habit.[1]

The psycho-acoustician of the future who insists on asking questions about "timbre" in electronic music may be in the same awkward position as the legendary psycho-acoustician who tested perceptions of various "pitchvolurations" in music for conventional instruments—pitch-voluration being that monolithic bushel-basket dimension (of questionable utility) whose independent component variables are pitch, loudness, and duration. I do, of course, hope that this legendary psycho-acoustician may have learned something he should have known to begin with: namely, that musical concepts uncritically accepted as perceptual dimensions generate loaded psycho-acoustical questions, no matter how many independent, component variables his view of some dimension may have left room for; and that loaded questions invite careless or recalcitrant answers. As a general rule, it seems to me that tests administered to the musically semi-literate by their peers (or tests which might just as well have been) yield results only for those disciplines which might take an interest, for example, in my impressions of

---

[1]Cf. nos. 2 & 3 of these lectures for less cursory treatments of "timbre" and its alleged components.

what goes on inside a cyclotron; namely, the disciplines of sociology and folk humor.

Once again, let me make it clear that I am not advising scientists to quit meddling with music: on the contrary, it is perfectly clear that the benevolent interest and imaginative work of scientists has opened up vast new territories for composers to explore. But I think it no accident that such work has been done largely by scientists who, as a matter of policy, have collaborated closely with composers and have even taken the risk of committing composition themselves, thereby constantly testing their own familiarity with the musical problems to which they are devoting their professional talents. It seems to me that any psycho-acoustician who forges ahead blithely out of touch with current concerns in musical analysis and musical composition is putting himself in an excellent position to produce silly science, silly music, or silly both.

II

"New Sounds" vs. Musical Articulation

[Read to the Audio Engineers Society, New York City, 10/12/66.]

I have contracted to make some derogatory remarks about the search for allegedly "new" sounds—and I shall try not to disappoint. However, in order to avoid any misunderstanding, I would like first to make some derogatory remarks about the search for allegedly "old" ones; and I would like to approach this essential phase of my discussion indirectly by first describing a malfeasance commonly practised in the analysis of a musical domain somewhat less thorny than the domain of timbre, and then proceeding to illustrate a sense in which similar analyses of the domain of timbre may be similarly malfeasant.

My stalking-horse is in the domain of rhythm.

Suppose we were to analyse the various renditions of three-eighth-note figures in a single performance of Beethoven's Fifth Symphony. And suppose that our analysis were directed toward the resolution of three questions:

No. 1: Are the three eighths within single figures usually rendered as three equal durations?

No. 2: What are the frequency and amounts of deviation from equal duration?

No. 3: Do some patterns of deviation emerge?

(I am resisting the inclusion of an obvious fourth question about uniformity of tempo among the various figures more in the interests of brevity than of adequacy.)

Now suppose that the following were a passable summary of our eventual empirical results:

The three eighths within single figures are but infrequently rendered as three equal durations; the amounts of deviation are usually tiny, although here and there they are quite large; and while certain patterns, especially in the form of gross limitations on kinds of succession and concurrence, do emerge, these patterns are not sufficiently detailed to dispel a somewhat random aura.

(Please notice, as my argument unfolds, that its drift would not clearly be affected were some much fancier-looking empirical results substituted for my very simple-looking ones.)

Next, let us further suppose that analyses of a large number of performances of a large number of familiar pieces yield results of a sufficiently striking similarity to our results for Beethoven's Fifth Symphony to lead us to believe that those first results cannot seriously be interpreted as revealing things peculiar to just Beethoven's Fifth.

And finally, let us suppose that we have arrived at the verge of electronic simulation: our first venture will be to electronically simulate not some specific already-existing performance of Beethoven's Fifth, but just a performance of it which we intend to be a musically acceptable one—that is, an excellent one; after that, the world.

Let me ask two questions which I have been heading toward from the outset.

First: In electronically rendering the very large number of three-eighth figures in Beethoven's Fifth, would it not be a musically sensible extrapolation from our hypothetical sets of empirical data to distribute somewhat randomly selected small amounts of deviation from equal duration somewhat randomly over most of the eighth notes, while at the same time enforcing those gross limitations suggested by our data?

Second and more generally: Would it not be sensible to do this in any electronic sound-generation in which we intend to produce conventionally "musical"-sounding renditions of equal note-value figures?

Notwithstanding the seemingly rhetorical quality of at least the first of these two questions, I think that both questions must be answered: No, these are not musically sensible extrapolations. Or rather: Insofar as they are sensible extrapolations from our hypothetical empirical results, they help expose the musical triviality of our initial three questions. While such questions cannot fairly be said to represent the nadir of musical analysis, they can fairly be said to represent the nadir of cognitive musical analysis. For the moment, let me indicate a major source of their musical inadequacy this way: Quite intricate and elaborate musical analysis is required to discriminate between those tiny deviations which are just deviations and those tiny and not-so-tiny deviations which are part and parcel of the projection of an entire musical structure and which are therefore intimately involved in, and qualified by, a complex developing musical context. Those rubatos don't just occur in x percent of the population: they probably belong right where they are—for instance, right there where that middle-register line joins that upper-register line from a more background layer—and could easily suffer reduction to non-consequence (or worse) if redistributed.

Let us recapitulate, but this time in the domain—or domains—of timbre:

Suppose we were to analyse the various renditions, by the violin, of the note A above middle C at a rather soft dynamic in a single performance of, say, the Kreutzer Sonata. And suppose that our analysis were directed toward the resolution of an analogous three questions:

No. 1: Are the speed and width of vibrato constant within single notes?

No. 2: What are the frequency and amounts of deviation from an average speed and width?

No. 3: Do some patterns of deviation emerge?

(On the model of the rhythmic example, I am resisting the inclusion of a fourth question about uniformity of tempo among vibrato-speeds on different notes.)

And now suppose that, having obtained our empirical results, we extend our investigation to cover many different pitches at various dynamics in a large number of familiar pieces; and we become convinced that our first results revealed nothing peculiar to just the Kreutzer Sonata or even to just violin performances.

And again we arrive at the verge of electronic simulation, armed with our hypothetical sets of empirical results and with my two questions:

First: In rendering vibratos in an acceptable electronic performance of the Kreutzer Sonata, would it not be a musically sensible extrapolation from our hypothetical sets of empirical data to construct a vibrato population reflective of these sets of data in the way that we proposed to construct an eighth-note population reflective of those other sets of data?

Second and more generally: Would it not be sensible to do this in any electronic sound-generation where we intend to produce conventionally "musical"-sounding tone-quality?

If something in the structure of my argument leads you to suppose that I am about to answer these two questions in the same old way and for the same old reason, you are right. I also agree with you in supposing that the same form of argument would lead us to deny much musical relevance to similar approaches to problems of acceptably simulating acceptable spectra with acceptable transients, intermodulations, and so on.

On this basis, it is incumbent upon me to insist that the researcher who advocates as self-evident truth the claim that you can't simulate a violin melody until you can simulate a violin tone is, conceptually if not procedurally, putting the cart before the horse: that violin tone, in any specifically musical use, is at least *no less* than a local open-ended agglomeration of musical developments in progress whose degree of timbral acceptability and whose very timbral identity are, in part, determined by the particular developmental context which that melody provides.

It follows that the only evaluations of timbre we ought to indulge in are contextual ones. No less an authority than Jimmy Durante used to stop the band in the middle of a phrase and call on the trumpet player to repeat his most recent note over and over again—Durante exclaiming the while, "I wanna hear *that note;* that's a *good note!*" Since I have always supposed that Durante's description of that note was intended as a gag, I am sometimes mildly puzzled that no one laughs when a psycho-acoustical researcher renders the same gag by substituting "good sound" or "inherently interesting timbre" for "good note." But—whatever the explanation may be for this collective failure in our senses of humor, I think we should in any case once and for all abandon the metaphysics of "inherently interesting timbres"—especially for laughs—and proceed with the cultivation of, at the worst, more complicated mistakes. If I claim that some timbre—say a raucous electronic buzz or a nicely shaped pear from the stage of the opera house—is a "good" (or "satisfactory," or "interesting," or "sophisticated") timbre, I should mean no more than that this timbre is an integral part of an actual or imaginable musical composition which I would consider to be a "good" composition. And if I deny virtue to that timbre, I should mean no more than that I can imagine no decent composition incorporating it—and if the history of music is any guide, such a judgment would prove to be no more than a tribute to the low quality of my compositional imagination.

A corollary of this contextual view is the obligation to suspect that an inadequacy of some timbre in some particular context is itself a function of the whole context, and hence a structural compositional inadequacy rather than a deficiency inherent in that timbre.

I hope what I wish to say about the search for allegedly "new" sounds is, by this time, predictably brief and anti-climactic:

If "new" sounds are the inferable or extrapolable other side of the coin from "old" sounds—and if the characteristics of the "old" ones are in the process of being discovered on the basis of research whose very questions powerfully suggest antecedently inadequate musical analysis of the old contexts—then the coin itself, both sides, must be a slug.

III

Operations on Waveforms

[Read to the Fall Joint Computer Conference, San Francisco, 11/8/66.]

However useful the concept of "timbre" may be for music in which relations of spectrum, vibrato, tremolo, and so forth, are less elaborately structured compositionally than are relations of pitch and rhythm, new possibilities for articulating musical structure (that have arisen specifically by virtue of the control given us, by electronic media, over each "ingredient" of timbre separately) are rendering this concept, if not useless, then at least misleading and inhibiting both to current research and to current composition. If we contend, for example, that vibrato is a component of timbre; and that to exert beneficent influence upon a timbre, a vibrato must be moderate in speed (say, several cycles per second, not several per minute or several hundred per second) and well within the boundary of the chromatic semi-tone in width, with both speed and width of course somewhat randomized; then we must recognize that such contentions invoke, at least tacitly, our generalized rememberance of what vibrato "sounds like" (or, worse, *ought to* "sound like") in familiar musical contexts—that is, in contexts where vibrato is not among the most highly compositionally structured aspects of sound. I am concerned here not with the demonstrable[2] irrelevance of this generalized remembrance even to those contexts which our remembrance generalizes upon; I am concerned here rather with the musically useful results of considering, say, vibrato as a perceivable, structurable, and electronically controllable musical continuum in its own right: that is, with perceptions which only the music of the future and the very recent past can induce us to make. Please keep in mind that such refinement and extension of our abilities to perceive, and more importantly of the very modes in which we perceive, is one of the more basic and traditional roles of the art of music.

In compositionally exploiting vibrato as such a continuum, let's consider what it would initially seem reasonable to *avoid.* First, I would recommend avoiding techniques which reduce vibrato to the least structurally relevant of its traditional roles: namely, the role of subliminally "lushing-up" tone quality. Second, I would avoid segmenting my continuum on the model of generalized remembrance: identifying a particular segment as the good stuff or the real thing and everything outside that segment as "too" this or "too" that can only stultify my compositional imagination at the outset, and thereby prevent me from ever inducing those very perceptions I ought to be most solicitous about. Instead, I would simply ask myself in moving along this

---

[2]Cf no. 2 of these lectures.

continuum: what kind of musical structures can I imagine that would most strikingly exploit, and thereby make most perceptible to me, the relations I think I ought to be able to hear? My most interesting problems will arise not where I think "normal" passes over into abnormal vibrato; but rather where vibrato itself seems to pass over, first, from a wiggling of pitch into some sort of noise *around* a pitch, and then over into a complex mode of pitch-*production* in which the center frequency, the speed of the vibrato, the difference between the two, the sum of the two, the frequencies which delimit the width of the vibrato, and individual frequencies of the spectrum to which the vibrato is applied, all participate as principal components. And these problems will not necessarily be "resolved" by my determining, democratically or otherwise, just where within my continuum each boundary lies—rather, I would expect that, just as the right musical context could fully articulate, for my perception, one of these boundaries, so some other musical context could either dissolve that boundary or reduce to contextual irrelevance the very terms in which it was defined. In short, these seeming boundaries might well prove to be musical structural relations internal to and dependent upon specific musical contexts—and not psycho-acoustical "facts" about the "materials" of music. And third, I would avoid saturating individual tones with additional, contextually nonsignificant, ingredients, chosen to instrumentalize, i.e., lush-up, electronically generated timbres. Instead, I would devote my attention to musically developing however few or many timbral ingredients a compositional idea may suggest in somewhat the sense that I would try to musically develop basic configurations of pitch and rhythm. The often-deplored uniformity, monotony, or outright nastiness of electronic timbres seems to me more properly analyzed as a failure of some existing electronic compositions adequately to structure and develop their timbral components as elements of the composition rather than as any inherent debility in current technology or any musical dullness "inherent" even in the balder electronic timbres. It is of course simply true that we can produce an electronic tone each of whose components remains uniform from the beginning of the tone to the end; and that a composition which spends 15 or 20 minutes, or even 1 or 2 minutes, celebrating this truth courts triviality. But a composition which meets the threat of triviality with a barrage of irrelevancies is at least as feeble a composition; and perhaps a feebler one, in that it explicitly presents so many things which—specifically by virtue of electronics—could have been musically developed. If I am willing, in instrumental music, to put up with that hopefully rather small percentage of the total sound which *can't* fairly be said to participate constructively in any "local open-ended agglomeration of musical developments in progress"—that is, with these musical irrelevancies which lush-up the tone—this is no reason why I should be willing to put up with them in electronic music where we have become for the first time free to build into individual tones precisely what the musical contexts may suggest *and no more;* that is, free to treat the individual tone as something which need resemble in no degree whatever an extra-structurally prefilled garbage-can.

Now vibrato is just one of the many potentially structurable aspects of sound which have been too often, in effect, written off as ingredients of something more vague. I would like to discuss specifically a few of the characteristics of sets of partials, harmonic and nonharmonic, which composers including myself have tried to release from subliminal influence upon "timbre," and to develop musically as compositional elements.

In the right musical context, it becomes quite easy to perceive and relate sets of partials in the following terms:

1. Registral position: that is, position of any set in the pitch continuum —regardless of the pitches of perceived or unperceived "fundamentals."

2. Intervallic spread: that is, the musical interval defined by the highest and lowest frequencies in any set.

3. Density: that is, the average number of elements in a set which lie within some relevant standard musical interval.

4. Total number of elements in a set.

5. The distribution of relative amplitude over any set.

6. Physical place or places from which any set, or any element of a set, seems to emanate.

This list could obviously be extended; but it is already sufficiently detailed to provide a basis for defining some musical operations on sets of partials—operations many of which may be viewed as attempts to capitalize upon the capacities of electronic media in order to subject to elaborate and continuous musical structuring aspects of sound which the composer for instrumental media cannot risk reliance upon except for rather gross general contrasts and rather subtle local articulations. For example, we know that certain instruments can noticeably transform their tone-qualities in the course of single notes: strings, say, by sliding and tilting the bow; winds, say, by slowly inserting or removing a mute. We know that, in percussion instruments especially, different components of the spectrum fade out at different rates; that most instruments have some junk in the attack; that the component partials, even during "steady state," fluctuate in amplitude; that many instruments can, in a highly limited degree, vary their speeds and widths of vibrato and amplitude modulation; that certain percussion instruments produce sounds which lie in a tantalizing no-man's-land between definite and indefinite pitch; and that the physical positions of several instruments relative to one another can be of structural musical, as well as of acoustical, consequence. But because of the severe limitations imposed upon the compositional exploitation of all these facts of instrumental sound by the physical limitations of instruments and the human body, it is computers, and not conventional instruments, that have the capacity to really capitalize even upon instrumentally-suggested transformations of waveforms[3], whether over the course of a whole composition, from note to note, or within single notes. Partly in this connection I have welcomed the chance offered by computers to try using exclusively sets of partials (harmonic and nonharmonic) derived from one another and pitch-configurations basic to a composition by operations appropriate to that composition; and certain operations have been sufficiently appropriate to a composition I am now working on for me to have incorporated them as alternative branches in a Music IV subroutine. These operations upon sets of partials, in the use of which I lean heavily on the assumption that in the right musical context we can perceive the characteristics I have listed, are the following:

1. Mappings of basic sets of partials onto enlarged and compressed spaces:

(My subroutine does this by preserving the proportions among the component musical intervals of the basic set of partials while gradually changing the intervals themselves. In the continuum thus generated, the basic set itself corresponds to the point of zero enlargement of the total space.)

2. Mappings of basic sets which preserve frequency differences while gradually changing the musical intervals:

(My subroutine does this by adding a constant to each of the partial numbers. In the continuum thus generated, the basic set itself corresponds to the constant zero. I should perhaps here emphasize that the relation between a set of partial-numbers and its corresponding musical intervals and the relation between a set of frequency-numbers and its corresponding musical intervals is one and the same relation: specifically, a given ratio, whether of partial-numbers or frequency-numbers, corresponds to the same musical interval. Hence my subroutine—whose variable arguments are largely operation-codes and musical intervals—treats partial-numbers with impunity as if they were, in effect, frequency numbers.)

3. Mappings of basic sets which exponentiate the partial-numbers by a constant:

(In the continuum thus generated, the basic set itself corresponds to the constant *one*. Since it is not intuitively obvious to me what the musical intervallic result might be of exponentiating partial-numbers by, say, the constant 3.508, the relevant variable argument for this (as for any other) operation in my subroutine is a desired intervallic spread of the result: the subroutine computes whatever mysterious constant it needs to get that intervallic result.)

4. Mappings of basic sets which treat partial-numbers themselves as exponents for a constant base:

---

[3] I ask the reader's indulgence for my continuing to include physical places of origin among the "properties" of a waveform and hence among its transformables.

(This operation is suggested by the rather well known effects of using the twelfth-root of two as a base for integral exponents. However, it should be noticed that this operation has one characteristic which fundamentally distinguishes it from the other operations I have discussed: in the continuum thus generated, the basic set itself does not in general appear at all.)

5. Mappings of basic sets onto their total inversions—intervallic, frequency-differential, or exponential:

(In order to retrieve for me my control over the assorted registral positions of the assorted new spectra generated by sequences and combinations of these operations applied to derived as well as to basic sets of partials, my subroutine accepts a transposition-number as one of its variable arguments: for example, any derived set at transposition zero will have the same weighted center as the set from which it was derived. I hope it is clear without illustration that, because of the sheer messiness of the calculations required, the computer is as necessary in deriving the new sets of partials in the first place as it is in simulating soundwaves resulting from their use. And yet the results of appropriate musical use of these operations seem to me quite readily perceivable as various kinds and degrees of intervallic distortion, while quite distinguishable in musical function from "chords.")[4]

In compositionally using any such derivations as these, we now have, realistically, the chance to structure developments within any single note exclusively in ways that reflect developments, or the principles of development, in a composition as a whole. There is no longer any gross physical limitation upon the particular ways in which, during a single note, one set of partials may become transformed into another; upon the particular rhythms in which structurally relevant chunks of a total spectrum may fade out—whether immediately following the attack or more gradually during an eminently unsteady state; upon the relevant permutations of amplitude-values which any single set of partials occupying an entire note may undergo; upon the range over which speeds and widths of vibrato and amplitude modulation may change during a single note; upon particular ways in which a single note may fluctuate between definite and indefinite pitch; or upon the complexity of arrangement of moving and stationary sources from which various stereophonic sounds seem to emanate.

---

[4]Notice the injustice of claiming any more radical distinction between sets of partials and sets of simultaneous notes (i.e., "chords") in the case, say, of an orchestral performance of a Mozart symphony: it's not that we *can't* hear those individual overtones *if we try*—on the contrary, it's by succeeding in the attempt that we most convincingly reinforce our musically well-founded determination not to. Somehow our musical intelligence persuades us to absorb these overtones as qualifications of fundamentals; much as it persuades us to absorb an assortment of messages traceable to balky (plastic) gut, slithering (plastic) horsehair, dental protruberance, and salivary dispersion as qualifications of attack. In these cases as normally, our ears admirably perceive in modes conducive to musical sense.

If I have repeatedly directed my discussion from electronic possibilities in general toward possibilities for single tones in particular, it is in order to suggest a realistic alternative to the stultifying concept of "timbre": I think that concern with electronic "timbre" should be replaced by, and indeed probably has as its only salvageable inspiration, the compositional exploration of modes of musical development within single tones. The new electronic possibilities may even lead us to the belief that the concept of "timbre" was really never much more than the repository of some notion that individual tones have "moods." We long ago quit talking about "happy melodies" and "pungent harmonies," in favor of contextual musical analysis of developing musical structures of, primarily, pitch and rhythm; and I would hope that we could soon find whatever further excuse we still need to quit talking about "mellow timbres" and "edgy timbres," and "timbres" altogether, in favor of contextual musical analysis of developing structures of vibrato, tremolo, spectral transformation, and all those various dimensions of sound which need no longer languish as inmates of some metaphor.

from THE NATION (etc.), 1962-1968:

III: 1964-65

THE NATION:

March 16, 1964

MUSIC

Benjamin Boretz

The young virtuosos who have been transforming the quality of new-music performance in New York now seem to have produced a striking transformation in musical life as well. For the flair and enthusiasm with which they devour the most complex mechanical and musical intricacies have generated an atmosphere of great performance excitement around difficult music, which has thereby become the focal repertory for a kind of musical off-Broadway. Like its theatrical counterpart, this activity draws a steadily growing public composed largely of professionals and intellectuals in other fields who are evidently prepared to present themselves, at places strung out geographically from the New School to Carnegie Recital Hall to Hunter College to the 92nd St. Y to Columbia's McMillan Theatre, to attend concerts composed entirely of twentieth-century music, for which their approval seems to vary in direct proportion to its manifest boldness. The result, of course, has been a proliferation of such events, and a tendency to search for music presenting the farthest-out surface complexities. But, far more important, all this activity has provided a basis for a con-

temporary performance practice, whereby listeners and musicians can experience and become reliably aware of what is happening in the compositional world, and perhaps even more significantly, the great classics of the twenties and thirties are finally being heard within an appropriate sonic and presentational environment.

Thus Schoenberg's protest that his music was "not modern, but only badly played" appears to have been more than a bitter joke. As long as performers addressed all twentieth-century music as equally 'modern', their performances necessarily insured its impenetrability to their audiences, regardless of how much time elapsed after its composition or how frequently it was performed. Given the pervasiveness of this practice, it was obviously impossible for the cycle of disconnection between people and their contemporary music to be broken within the mainstream music-making world. Significantly, the new approaches have been developed mainly by composer-performers, joined by those New York studio musicians who are the world's best sight readers and most intrepid instrumental adventurers.

Naturally, players whose training and experience orient them toward certain habits and attitudes as non-negotiable norms are going to misconstrue a context in which different norms are operative. Indeed, the greater the surface resemblances among fundamentally divergent musics, the more disinforming the consequences of misrepresentation. And even the highest level of conventional virtuosity and literal accuracy will not overcome the alienating awkwardness that playing from 'outside' the music being played produces: every wide-spaced linearity becomes a manic *jeter* or a 'pointillistic' fragmentation of something 'normal', i.e., scalar; every single-pitch attack becomes a traumatically disoriented isolated blip violating a norm of continuous linearities; every extreme dynamic differentiation becomes a jolting accent rather than a meaningful separation of articulative streams; and 'off-beats' are always syncopations, rather than, perhaps, time-creating positions within shifting timespan frames. So every action required by the basic syntactic premises of adventurous contemporary music imposes a severe strain on the conceptual and concentrative powers of the best conventional musicians—not primarily on their technical abilities—and the result is what used to be called 'expressionism' by critics who perhaps understood the mutual alienation they were observing, but chose to represent the (safer) opaque perspective on it.

The intriguing possibility that such 'expressionist' qualities might be extrinsic to even a work so famous for them as Schoenberg's *Pierrot Lunaire* was advanced, for example, in the performance conducted by Harold Farberman at Carnegie Recital Hall on February 16. Here, that notoriously melodramatic *Sprechstimme* vocalization was, in Bethany Beardslee's secure and sonically beautiful performance, a transparently and intimately integrated thread within the music of the total ensemble. What resulted was, really, a remarkable fabric of magically mutated Classical chamber music, in which Robert Helps's sensitively and delicately adjusted piano playing was the alchemical integrator of all the divergent, resistant, disparate vocal and instrumental qualities.

It is the composer Gunther Schuller's Twentieth Century Innovations series, however, which has, for us in New York, principally taken the measure of the inadequacy of conventional performances of classic twentieth-century literature. The performance problems presented by that music are particularly severe, since its composers subsisted within a performance culture which had not yet generated any substantial population of co-creative performers; though Schoenberg did have some colleagues like Edouard Steuermann, Hermann Scherchen, and Hans Rosbaud as sympathetic interpreters, very few others emerged to participate in the creation of a real 'Second Viennese School' performance practice—and Stravinsky's music has had its authentic sonic images resonating in the real world largely through his own performances. But on the other side of the generational divide, younger players who effortlessly execute the extreme articulative demands of their own contemporaries' music seem to be almost as baffled by the essentially tradition-derived qualities of music like Schoenberg's as are their conventional elder colleagues. So Schuller has been almost alone in offering the indispensable examples, demonstrating, work by individual work, that these legendarily intractable pieces are no less playable than, say, Beethoven's *Grosse Fuge*—which is, in a sense, their specific historical inspiration.

This season, thus far, Schuller has offered Schoenberg's Serenade, Webern's Concerto for Nine Instruments, and Berg's Chamber Concerto. None of these performances has been anywhere near perfect; the problems of balance, intonation, and long-range temporal accumulation are simply too formidable to be solved in the absurdly limited rehearsal-time constraints under which this series has to operate. Nevertheless, the essential qualities of continuity, texture, and temporality crucial to the authentic identities of these works are, amazingly, being projected and heard in a midtown New York concert series. It became vivid, for example, how Schoenberg composed highly individualized rhythmic configurations and embedded subtle, non-literal analogies to Classical style in inventing an idea of 'serenade'. For me, this performance peaked in the "Song Without Words", where the precision and alertness of Matthew Raimondi's violin playing fused a myriad of subtle inflections into a radical recasting of a 'Schubert' or 'Mendelssohn' melodic line. Elsewhere, impossible problems, like balancing the thickly textured winds with fine-grained violin and piano sounds, and finding the linking rhythmic and sonorous threads amidst the relentless superabundant polyphonies of Berg's Chamber Concerto, were addressed with Schuller's special kind of cool, rational penetration that seems to ferret out maximal clarity even where impending chaos seems inescapable. In that performance, Paul Jacobs's electronic-music pianism imposed a sharp, lucid directionality on the entire ensemble, while Raimondi's command of the refractory violin solo was much too masterly to have been allowed to be so largely inaudible.

The vital center of the younger-generation experiment in creating a self-generated, composer-oriented new-music performance culture is, undoubtedly, the Group for Contemporary Music's concerts (at McMillan Theatre on the Columbia University campus) of works by middle- and younger-generation American composers. The unique virtuoso of this group is the flutist Harvey Sollberger, who can maintain a continuous articulative coherence while materializing and dematerializing mercurially at wildly divergent registral extremes, making an effortless succession-stream at any speed out of any combination of unlikely inflective changes. Even the Italian flutist Severino Gazzeloni, Sollberger's European counterpart, seems not quite to rise to Sollberger's level of dexterity and sonic distinction.

As an ensemble activity, the Group's most impressive work comes from its unique practice of scheduling and using adequate amounts of rehearsal time. This results not only in stunningly tight ensemble work and intensely secure and responsible individual playing, but also—sometimes—in performances where the absence of the usual residual impediments to transparent projection of sound-image and continuity create an almost bodiless communicative medium between composer and listener. One spectacular beneficiary was Milton Babbitt's Composition for Four Instruments, whose special coherence can only emerge with a degree of precise differentiation, balancing, weighting and connecting of every single sonority that is exponentially beyond the most extreme demands of conventional music. And, also, Lukas Foss's *Echoi,* a work that builds great performance excitement, and projects striking qualities of sound and idea beyond anything else of its compositional genre, when all its elements are as fully articulated and precisely focussed as they were in the Group's performance.

I've mentioned only a small fraction of the events of the last few months. Jim Tenney's Tone Roads at the New School, Max Pollikoff's YMHA series, the Composers' Forums at the Donnell Library, the Ford Foundation commissioning series, the ISCM, the Hunter College Lecture-Concert series, as well as numberless individual events, have generated such a deluge of activity that it hasn't been possible to consider what deeper implications might be involved. Obviously, much of the excitement is skin-deep, aroused by the spectacular novelty and difficulty of the music, and the virtuosic brilliance of its young performers. But anyone who suffered through all those painful events where the intense anticipation generated by a score of a new work was crushed by its massacre in 'live' performance (is there any doubt that the strong attraction of electro-acoustic means of sound production for composers largely originates in these experiences?) will forbear from complaining about an excess of occasions to engage the music they most intensely want to hear and need to know.

MUSIC

Benjamin Boretz

NEW WORKS AND NEW PERFORMANCES II

Perhaps the most conspicuous recognition of the recent new-music performance activity discussed in my last column was the programing by the New York Philharmonic of an *avant-garde* series as the central event of its current season. In effect, this was a characteristic "official" adoption of aspects of the other realm that had attracted enough notoriety and seemed obviously sensational enough to make an appropriate impact on the general audience. But the actual confrontation proved mainly diffuse and confusing to a public that had no previous awareness of any aspect of the milieu out of which the new works arise, and hence was unable to grasp even the purely iconoclastic points being scored. Even more striking was the effect that a similar gap in the experience of the players themselves had on their capacity to perform such new works; the conceptual and mechanical leaps required simply to apprehend the nature of their functions and actions in the new contexts were obviously unattainable, even had the programs been given many times the rehearsal hours normally available to the Philharmonic.

Under these circumstances, the brilliant performances of the Copland Piano Concerto and Varèse's *Déserts* that were included in the series seem especially noteworthy, for both are older works whose performance qualities are clearly related to traditional practice, and in fact respond quite spectacularly to being treated as "modern" extensions thereof. Bernstein's handling of the Copland Concerto was a particular revelation; he managed to produce transparently clean sonorities even in the slow passages that have always sounded blurred because of the multiple doublings of lines that crisscross in the middle of the texture, and he evoked a continuous stream of inventive rhythmic, sonorous and formal ideas in the fast sections, where a fascinating continuity is developed from the juxtapositions and crosscutting in asymmetric lengths of *ostinato* jazz figurations. The result seemed a much more integrally and originally jazz-derived form than anything in, say, Gershwin, and more imaginative and fresh-sounding than any of the twenties-jazz genre outside of Milhaud's *Création du Monde*. Copland's own performance as piano soloist was not only unexpectedly agile and propellent, but produced a curious and hollowly resonant clangor that is obviously the essential sound-image in terms of which all his piano music is composed.

Similarly, the brass playing in *Déserts*—especially as it sounded in the acoustical framework of Philharmonic Hall—projected a "big" proclamatory intensity that is exactly right for Varèse's music, which sounds either blatantly raucous or uncomfortably constrained in the closer and smaller-proportioned chamber-music halls and ensembles. Indeed, given Bernstein's obvious flair and enthusiasm for music of this kind, and the orchestra's evident ability to update its playing (at any rate, its brass, woodwind and percussion playing) if the steps are sufficiently gradual and the effort is convincingly demanded of them, one wonders why works from this literature are not programed more often by the Philharmonic. Such an approach, it seems to me, could well be the salvation of all our major orchestras; I was equally struck by a recent Philadelphia Orchestra performance under Ormandy of Roger Sessions's new Fifth Symphony, which was not only a controlled and coherent presentation of the facts of the work (as compared, for example, with their helpless wandering through Elliott Carter's Variations for Orchestra last year), but contrasted sharply with the sloppiness and coarseness of their performance of the Brahms First Symphony on the same program as well as of much of that orchestra's recent conventional-music playing. It might have proved far more permanently valuable for the Philharmonic to have programed a series of works that could bring both the orchestra and its audience into a closer apprehension of the musical present than to fling them both into a spectacular collision with the most extreme limits of the current *avant-garde* chic—a collision that could only harden their sense of incomprehension and alienation.

As far as the *avant-garde* works themselves were concerned, it should be pointed out that my frequent reservations about music where the composer relinquishes control to the performer or to "chance", have always been concerned with the perceptual qualities of the results rather than with any "moral" objections to the procedures of its composition and performance. In fact, it has mainly seemed odd to me that anyone should have assumed that performers making choices on the spur of the moment are more likely to produce interesting relations, striking ideas or even novel sonorities than composers working deliberatively or even on a trial and error basis; or that the abandonment of existing compositional resources without replacing them by at least equivalently powerful new resources should result in musical enrichment, rather than in the sonic impoverishment which so far has seemed to be a pervasive outcome.

Still, no composer has any obligation to compose in any particular way, or even to be coherent, or intellectually or artistically "responsible"—or, for that matter, to take public credit for his work; the sole question is the sound of what is eventually heard. And, the only legitimate way to discuss such works seems to be in terms of what actual sound was heard at an actual performance. Accordingly, it seems reasonable to consider that each performance defines a particular composition—whatever peculiarities or confusions of nomenclature surround it—and to disregard any considerations of more general "identity" understood in terms of some underlying plan of action or some numerologically dictated event choice. And we can assume that the composer takes responsibility in the usual sense for what is played judging by his acceptance of authorship credit on the program. So—for example—the particular sonic miasma produced by Iannis Xenakis's music, not only in the Philharmonic's pathetic attempt at a performance of his *Pithoprakta,* but also in the probably competent performance of *Achorripsis* heard on Gunther Schuller's series last year, should not be attributed entirely to the arbitrary application of "stochastic" methods, but also on the evident properties of Xenakis's compositional capacities and his musical "ear" that have led him to accept such results.

It must also be assumed that the considerable difference between the light and delicate sonic interactions heard in the perform-ance of Earle Brown's *Times Five* at the Schuller concerts, and the blurred incoherence that emerged from the Philharmonic players as an ostensible performance of his *Available Forms II* (despite the utilization of about twenty times as much timbral variety and ensemble intricacy), as well as the flat uniformity of *Hodograph I* on the Contemporary Music Society's Guggenheim Museum series, had as much to do with qualitative differences among these compositions as with the manifest variations in quality among the performances. But since I had previously heard performances of György Ligeti's *Atmosphères,* I can report that it is possible for it to project some quite atmospheric surface sonorities in the inventive manner of the "new sound" school of electronic-music composition, none of which were even inferable from the Philharmonic performance.

Of all the new works in the Philharmonic's series, however (I exclude Stefan Wolpe's Symphony because only two movements were performed and because the work is straightforward enough so that one could tell it was badly misrepresented on this occasion), the most conventionally attractive sounds were unquestionably those produced by Morton Feldman's *Out of Last Pieces.* Although my own ultimate interest is bound to be limited in any piece whose principal qualities are those of individual sounds rather than the relational resonances among them, the succession of quiet figurational curls in the winds, and gentle sustained sonorities of varying tone-color mixtures could have been listened to for much longer than they were played without the fatigue of *non sequitur* intervening, far beyond other music of its kind.

John Cage's *Atlas Eclipticalis,* on the other hand, cannot be described in such purely musical terms. However lightly Cage plays his psychosocial games, they exert heavy stress on the equilibrium and conviction of players (who can't actually figure out whether they're being performers or being performed), audiences (who can't actually figure out how or whether to be 'listeners'), critics (who can't actually figure out what they're being coopted into delegitimating, especially whether it's them); what's remarkable is how few of those present opted into the performance by either protesting or exiting the hall.

MUSIC

Benjamin Boretz

The Metropolitan Opera season just past was certainly as dismal as it has generally been considered, but this was more noticeable as a matter of degree than in any fundamental respect. For in recent years the impact of the Metropolitan's activities on the awareness of the active musical world has been about as significant as that of Madame Tussaud's on the world of visual art. This nullity might be thought more the Metropolitan's problem than the music world's, but its quasi-official status as the only major opera company in the United States (which, with the forthcoming move to Lincoln Center, becomes almost officially official) has enabled its activities effectively to divorce the whole area of opera from our musical environment and consciousness. And that can scarcely be regarded a matter for purely private concern.

The deprivation has, in fact, been so extreme that by now we are hardly aware of what we are missing. But even a cursory glance at what European audiences have been hearing and taking for granted in their major opera houses, in terms of repertory and originality of production, makes it painfully evident that we are being robbed of about as much essential artistic experience as we would be if, say, all our major museums suddenly stopped exhibiting sculpture. And we are really missing this experience quite completely, for whereas orchestral and chamber music can at least be approximately perceived on recordings, opera must be seen in all its dramatic and visual dimensions to be effectively experienced.

Thus Europeans have, before and since the war, been able to regard such works as Berg's *Wozzeck* and *Lulu,* Hindemith's *Mathis der Maler* and *Cardillac,* Schoenberg's *Moses and Aron,* Stravinsky's *Oedipus* and *Rake's Progress,* Krenek's *Jonny Spielt Auf* and the operas of Strauss, Milhaud and Prokofiev as familiarly, if not necessarily with as much enthusiasm, as the staples of the repertory. Moreover, imaginative and original productions of the classics, such as Wieland Wagner's intensely brilliant Wagner at Bayreuth and elsewhere, Walter Felsenstein's searching re-creations of the classic and modern repertory in Berlin, and Ingmar Bergman's staging of contemporary works like *The Rake's Progress* in Stockholm, are established aspects of the regular European operatic scene. Productions of new operas by living composers are, in this context, a steady and unquestioned function of every major opera company.

We, in contrast, had our first *Wozzeck* at the low-budget New York City Opera some fifty years after its composition. (It penetrated the Met in 1960, in a misconceived and vocally inept performance that was quickly withdrawn; it will return there next season with a more promising cast.) *The Rake's Progress* was composed in California but first performed in Venice—and it was so butchered when it finally reached the Met that it, too, was hastily buried after a barely decent interval. *Lulu* was given its American premiere only this past summer—but in Santa Fe, not New York. And *Mathis, Cardillac, Jonny, Moses and Aron* and Milhaud's *Orestie,* among innumerable other twentieth-century notables, have not yet had complete professional performances in the United States.

All this would still not be so critical were it not that, whereas all the leading European composers are active in the operatic realm, and have their works competently and prominently produced, American operatic composition has largely been relegated to the workshop hacks, in the total absence of either context or hope of production. Even when a major American composer does produce an important operatic work, whose production is likely to create new awareness and interest and stimulate serious new activity, it, too, is left to Europe. While

Roger Sessions's *Montezuma* was becoming a significant operatic event in its Berlin production, and Ernst Krenek's new opera is scheduled for performance in Hamburg in June, the Metropolitan is content to console itself with Menotti's trouble-free *Last Savage.*

What we do get is principally a parade of the more or less spectacular vocal acrobats of the international circuit (most of whose voices have long since been destroyed by overuse) in assiduous explorations of the best-known workhorses in the most conventional performance styles—all carried off with varying degrees of shabbiness in discipline, ensemble and visual appearance. Occasionally, in the name of an original and imaginative production, we are treated to such apparitions as Franco Zeffirelli's recent *Falstaff,* with its third-hand imitation and boffo vulgarization of Wieland Wagner's low-comedy *Meistersinger* style. And when the confluence of singers comes off, as in this season's *Otello* with McCracken, Corelli and Tebaldi, it is almost in spite of the surroundings and atmosphere at the Metropolitan that the image of a masterpiece emerges.

Aside from the prevailing dullness of one season, however, or even the barrenness of our entire operatic culture, the most disturbing aspect of the current situation is the quality and character of the Met's present management. Unlike our other major performance organizations, the Met has never indulged in any euphemistic pretensions about cultural or artistic responsibility; it has always been frankly a public institution run as a private club whose chief steward, lately Rudolf Bing, serves up new productions only on special order of members who are prepared to pay for them. But Mr. Bing has, I believe, reached an entirely new level of cynicism with his recent reply to the criticisms leveled at the Met's repertory and performance standards by the New York critics. Essentially, Mr. Bing's contention is that since everything the Met does is designed solely to maintain financial equilibrium by filling the house every night and presenting the sort of thing that will guarantee the continued interest and patronage of his moneyed box holders, the critics, whose concerns are peripheral to these essential objectives, and who have no responsibility for the company's solvency, are simply incompetent a priori to evaluate its activities. Nowhere in this extraordinary document (published in full in the *Saturday Review* and in part in one of Harold C. Schonberg's Sunday *Times* columns) is any real attempt made to justify the company's policy on artistic grounds, only on those of financial expediency, popular support and precedent—and surely nothing is easier to justify on the basis of precedent than eternal redundancy... In Mr. Bing's view, moreover, everything unconventional or experimental can conveniently be left to the New York City Opera, a position that completely disregards the fact that that institution lacks the resources, prestige or directorial ability to undertake this responsibility in more than its current desultory fashion.

The depressing attitude of this position for the future of opera in America is, unfortunately, unmistakably borne out in the announced program for the new Metropolitan Opera House in Lincoln Center. For one thing—perhaps most significant because of its permanence—the blueprints for the physical plant itself include no provision for sound equipment, complex stage manipulation or any resources of even the kind that would be needed to perform adequately a 30-year-old work such as *Moses and Aron,* let alone anything new or experimental. This, in turn, is no more than a concrete manifestation of the approach that, in choosing a work to commission for the opening of the new house, overlooks both the many American composers whose originality in other media would seem to hold exciting possibilities for opera, and those few who, like Hugo Weisgall and Ernst Krenek, have also given serious thought to the question of a contemporary combination of music and drama. Instead, we are given Samuel Barber again, who has already proved his acceptability to the Met by way of the low-intensity blandness of *Vanessa,* and who, with all due regard for his unquestioned super-professionalism and limitless facility, hardly seems likely to produce anything less predictably routine now than he has for the last twenty years.

Still, as long as Mr. Bing can plead poverty and dependence on the whims of private donors, it will hardly be possible to bring effective pressure to bear on him and his colleagues to accept the responsibilities of their public trust. Furthermore, our opera and concert audiences have not been well enough trained musically by their schooling to demand—or even to know that it is possible to demand—anything better than what they are given. Under these conditions, perhaps the only salvation for opera in America would be to call Mr. Bing's bluff by officially subsidizing his company, by providing him with the means specifically to carry out the essential functions he now neglects for, presumably, practical reasons alone. Such functions are, after all, educative in the deepest sense, and their fulfillment cannot but result in the ultimate development of a more demanding and enlightened audience. And it seems to me that the channeling of public resources and effort into a medium that could generate a vast new creative development in which, for once, a wide audience could participate from its inception, is a cultural investment so potentially lucrative that we can scarcely afford to ignore it.

THE NATION:
June 21, 1965

MUSIC

Benjamin Boretz

THE B.B.C. IN NEW YORK

If the significant public value of musical events can be measured as the product of an audience's extent, the intensity and interest with which it comes prepared to listen, and the level of musical awareness represented among its members, then the response to the programs of 20th-century music played at Carnegie Hall last month by the B.B.C. Orchestra suggested some interesting hypotheses about the true facts of public musical life. The six closely spaced programs devoted to music composed since 1900 were given at the extreme end of a vastly expanded concert season by an orchestra of no particular local cachet, featuring no conducting celebrities beyond an *avant-garde* composer (Pierre Boulez) and the resident director (Antal Dorati), and offering no internationally glamorous soloists or any traditionally popular program material. These conditions seemed almost purposely designed to test every principle of concert-hall self-preservation that is conveniently invoked to justify the timid behavior of our own musical institutions, but the B.B.C. concerts attracted an alert, purposeful and respectable-sized audience that seemed to fill the hall far more significantly than do those masses of diffident tourists who regularly populate Philharmonic Hall. On these terms, a series such as the B.B.C.'s contains the promise of incomparably greater public "success" both as an individual event and in its permanent effect on musical culture, than do all those indistinguishable Philharmonic rituals where the noncontact between the attendant crowds and the programs offered is extreme.

As far as the B.B.C. concerts themselves were concerned, greatest interest was focused on Boulez's conducting of the 20th-century "classics" for which he has acquired an elevated reputation in Europe, and on the new works included in the programs, particularly Boulez's own *Doubles,* Roberto Gerhard's Concerto for Orchestra, and Aaron Copland's *Music for a Great City.* Considering Boulez's internationalism (he lives in Germany, teaches in Switzerland, and regularly conducts in Holland and England) and his compositional orientation, the unmistakable association of his conducting with the French conservatory tradition was somewhat startling. But all the fastidious attention to balance and to the articulation of detail that characterizes the best French operatic conducting is evident in Boulez's approach, neatly mapped onto the 20th-century literature.

The most interesting of Boulez's performances were of works whose overall continuity is self-evident, but which respond to the clarification of textural and rhythmic detail by a lucid projection of each event's precise significance in creating the total sense; the Three Fragments from Berg's *Wozzeck* (with Heather Harper as soloist) and the Schoenberg Five Pieces for Orchestra, Op. 16, were particularly successful in this regard. But the Webern Six Pieces, Op. 6 and Variations for Orchestra, Op. 31 (a major work whose single previous New York performance was on Jacques Monod's little Town Hall series in 1956) were also accurate and controlled, if less spectacularly clarified. On the other hand, in works whose large-scale succession depends for its articulation on the precise building of a succession of highly concentrated individual events—notably the Stravinsky Symphonies of Wind Instruments and Four Etudes—Boulez was considerably less successful in differentiating essential rhythmic and linear shapes and thus in maintaining a sense of continuous development.

Of the new works, it was difficult to judge Boulez's *Doubles* on the basis of an apparently inadequate performance. What emerged was surprising in its conventionally "busy" texture and unexploratory sonority despite the evident presence of locally striking ideas

of rhythmic and linear combination such as one would expect to follow from the *Marteau sans Maître,* the *Mallarmé Improvisations* and the Third Piano Sonata. Compared with the manifest sonorous brilliance of those works, the disappointing drabness of *Doubles* on this occasion throws particular suspicion on the performance, but it also seems possible that the heavy metaphysical drift of some of Boulez's recent writings reflects into his compositional thought as well.

Gerhard's Concerto, played on one of Dorati's concerts, was considerably less problematic in its predictable amalgam of virtuoso orchestral gestures from the current European vocabulary which, however, it asserts less colorfully and ingeniously than do earlier works of the same title by Lutoslawski and Petrassi. Copland's *Music,* originally the score for the movie *Something Wild,* is full of bright sounds and ideas recalling the pre-*Connotations* period, and continually reminds one of his consummate mastery over certain kinds of material—particularly that unique sound which he calls "glassy", and which generates the best moments in *Connotations* as well. But after the rather full development in the first two movements, the succession of passages becomes a little too obviously a series of fragmentary "cues" to project a globally realized composition on the level of the Piano Variations or *Connotations.*

It was a particularly happy idea to use regular B.B.C. soloists rather than more prestigious ringers to provide a cohesive and adequately rehearsed image of the B.B.C.'s musical life. John Ogdon's extraordinary piano playing is already well known here; the Tippett and Bartók concertos on these concerts exploited his capacity to articulate evenly limitless quantities of notes, although they do not impose any equivalent musical demands.

The cello playing of young Jacqueline Du Pré in the Elgar Cello Concerto was a genuine discovery for its virtuosity over a broad sonorous and technical range that resembles Zara Nelsova's. But again, the work was an unfortunate choice, especially since it represented a remarkably inventive and perceptive compositional mind—perhaps the best England has produced—by a singularly diffuse and idealess bit of professional routine.

TWENTIETH CENTURY HARMONY: CREATIVE ASPECTS AND PRACTICE by Vincent Persichetti
W. W. NORTON AND CO., 1961. 287p., $5.45.

REVIEWER J. K. Randall

Vincent Persichetti and the W. W. Norton Company have issued a grab-bag of Mr. Persichetti's recipes for short-order cookery under the label "Twentieth-Century Harmony". By Mr. Persichetti's own admission, the book may be used as a "text" in "advanced" harmony courses.

The relevance of Mr. Persichetti's recipes to the music of this century is forcefully suggested by the fact that not a single one of them is attributed to any particular composer or group of composers. Indeed, not a single piece of music, or a single composer or group of composers, is mentioned so much as once in the entire body of the text. All references to pieces of music are appended to the various chapters of the text in the form of lists, whose frivolity is apparent in the captions which head them, in the kind of citation which they include, and in their scarcely credible omissions. In the earlier chapters the captions are quite specific: "Two-part writing in a two-voice work" (first item: Bela Bartók, 44 Violin Duets), "Two-part writing in a work of more than two voices", "Pentatonic writing", "Whole-tone writing", "Various kinds of seventh and ninth chords", "Fifteenth and seventeenth chords", etc. In general, the citations under these headings refer to a particular spot in a piece. For example, we may verify that somewhere in the second movement of Bartók's 1st Quartet the first violin plays a whole-tone scale; or that the first nine attacks of Debussy's Prelude 5 (Vol. I) state five different pitches (caption: "Pentatonic writing"). In such references, Mr. Persichetti is concerned exclusively with the presence of some collection of pitches for which he has a name. Later on, the captions become more whimsical: "Harmony with characteristic doubling, spacing, or omission", "Irregular harmonic rhythm", "Passages featuring repeated notes or chords", "Passages with characteristic dynamics and rests", "Works containing contrasting techniques", "Passages containing various kinds of harmonic textures", "Unique thematic ideas", etc. It should be stressed that throughout the book these captions are the sum total of Mr. Persichetti's comments upon the lists of works which they head. Equally symptomatic of the educational value of these lists is the absence of Debussy's name from the lists headed "Real parallel harmony" and "Tonal parallel harmony"; of *Le Sacre du Printemps* from the lists headed "Examples of pedals" and "Examples of ostinatos"; and of any reference to a twelvetone work of

Schoenberg, Berg, or Webern from the lists following the subchapter entitled "Serial Harmony". On the other hand, Schoenberg's Violin Concerto is listed elsewhere under the heading "Chromatic harmony with chromatic melody": the reference is to p. 33 of the piano reduction. I submit that the advanced student might even survive exposure to the first page and that the advanced student who reads music might risk a peek at the orchestral score. (Curiously, although Mr. Persichetti professes to regard harmony and its instrumental setting as inseparable, his lists repeatedly cite the piano reductions of works for which the orchestral scores have long been available.) The very next work in the same list is Scriabine's 9th Sonata. The fact that the Schoenberg and Scriabine works are both based upon rather specific principles of pitch organization, and that these principles are radically different for the two works, does not interest Mr. Persichetti. The main thing is that both pieces splatter sharps and flats all over the place.

A sampling of Mr. Persichetti's recipes cannot fully portray the dense musical and linguistic fog which seals off the world of the text from the world of the lists:

> Pizzicato strings define uncertain passing tones in woodwind voices, and a harp may underline obscure rhythms in lagging strings. (p.27)

> Chords by fourths are used as "dominants" in cadences of any harmonic idiom. (p.101)

> Ornamental tones increase harmonic circulation in passages of clusters. (p.132)

> The harmonic ambiguity or sudden unison allows for the entrance of any texture. (p.273)

> The versatile ornamental tone also provides textural means for entering any harmonic region. (p.273)

Mr. Persichetti courageously demonstrates his hundreds of recipes with the assistance of musical fragments concocted for the occasion, I can only assume, by Mr. Persichetti himself. In this attempt to compose-out a half-century, Mr. Persichetti has exceeded his capacity.

Although the few theoretical ideas which do seep through the prevailing shroud of obscurity[*] are in large part already familiar from Hindemith's Craft of Musical Composition, Howard Hanson's Harmonic Materials of Modern Music, and from the most benighted

---

[*] W.W. Norton's editors were gratuitously tolerant in committing to the printer such expressions as "ease of readability", "played on a medium", "when color gradations of the ninth formations are made part of the composer's aural apparatus", etc.

traditions of chord-pushing pedagogy, no credit is given to any of these sources. Indeed, no book about contemporary music, nor any article, nor any book or article about any musical subject whatever, is cited at any point in Mr. Persichetti's book.

Of the following, however, Mr. Persichetti is undoubtedly the sole proprietor:

> Dynamics have a rhythm that is projected by means of piano, forte, crescendo, diminuendo, sforzando, and subito directions of accentuation. (p.226)

In short, dynamics have a rhythm that is projected by means of dynamics. The book abounds in such tail-chasers. On p. 265 we have this one: "When a melodic set includes one or more identical notes, doubling of chord members produces colorful serial doublings". Mr. Persichetti gives no example of a set with one identical note, although presumably even in this case doubling would produce doubling. Less original, but of some sociological interest, is Mr. Persichetti's impression, as of 1961, that the twelve-tone system is a "contrapuntal principle" best dealt with in a "treatise on counterpoint". (p. 262) In accord with his cover-all-exits approach to controversy, Mr. Persichetti does concede in the next paragraph that "when harmony is regulated by a horizontal, unifying idea (twelve-tone or not), the texture may be serial; this kind of writing creates harmony of extraordinary compactness through the manifold variations of the motif relationships". The clause preceding the semicolon means that serial principles produce a serial texture—with the term "texture" enjoying syntactical rather than semantical status. Here and throughout the book Mr. Persichetti stands unwaveringly on guard against any unseemly emphasis upon those techniques of twentieth-century composition usually associated with that number of notes which is greater than eleven but less than thirteen. Although Mr. Persichetti hazards an excursion into serial cookery on page 263, he serializes only seven notes and thus emerges with his virginity intact.

In view of Mr. Persichetti's notion that whatever can be done at all can be combined with everything else, he naturally neglects to point out that much of the best-known music of the twentieth century—specifically, works of Bartók, Copland, Debussy, Hindemith, Satie, Schoenberg, Scriabine, Stravinsky, and Webern; not to mention Boulez, Cage, Carter and Stockhausen (all cited in Mr. Persichetti's lists)—has been consciously and often explicitly produced to elucidate "new" or "extended" premises conceived as antidotes to allegedly outworn traditions or inadequate alternatives. Mr. Persichetti's version of the history of the past six decades appears on p. 11: "Composers have, in their music, coordinated the various musical resources of the early part of the century". (This is Mr. Persichetti's only hint that the twentieth century may have "parts".) Now surely any composer who has "coordinated the various musical resources" exhibited in the works of Satie, Scriabine, and Webern deserves, at the least, to be mentioned by name. Or on second thought, if by "coordinated" Mr. Persichetti means "joined by a sudden unison" or a "versatile ornamental tone"; and by "musical resources", scales and chords; then perhaps we should allow the identity of that composer to remain an open secret between the author and the advanced student.

Author's Note (2003):

Sure. Stupidities abound. (Par for the course, in those days.) Musical insensitivity, however, does not. And I do wonder: What's so bad, after all, about presenting a bunch of weirdchords and advising us to do what we want with them?

So what was the problem?

Vincent Persichetti was an able composer, a gentleman, and a supportive teacher with reputedly spectacular skills. He, if not his book, deserves better than this uppity snotwad.

The problem was a pervasive culture: a plethora of musicians — composers, performers, teachers, unbudgeably indifferent or hostile to "modern music" (whose rapsheet featured the all-brain no-heart complaint) — among whom any attempt at cogent thought about music (especially, cogent thought toward urgently needed new foundations) was not merely unnecessary [— as in: "brains is no substitute for talent, my dear"; or: "well, she *talks* a good game, but ...."] but outright disrespectful [— as in:""*real*"music (= the speaker's own inviolable biases) is far *beyond* ...."]. If you don't know already, thinking won't get you there. And if you do know, what's to think about? Just do it. (In that environment [: think Cleveland OH, 1940; or Harvard Univ., 1955], the breathy brainlessness of a sentence became a guarantor of its musical uplift.)

{Summertime, Tanglewood USA or:}
SIGHTREADING AS A WAY OF LIFE

I. *How it Grows on You*

WITHIN the world of musical per-formance there is a tradition which esteems correct playing as an indis-pensable part of reasonably projecting a musical structure. The typical believer in this tradition is on extreme occasions less put off by mere wrong notes, wrong rhythms, and wrong entrances than by correct playing which manages to project no discernible musical structure at all. (He even doubts that the term "correct" is appropriate in this connection.) At low ebb, he will characterize such correct playing as "professional sightreading" meaning, if I understand his phrase, not so much that the number of man-hours spent in rehearsal was nonpositive as that too many of the performers involved apparently had yet to catch their first glimpse of any musical structure which they might be doing in.

Perhaps such feelings about the proper relation of the performer toward the piece he performs are immune to correction. Or perhaps they are immune only to correction through rational persuasion; and perhaps no Kafka is required to anticipate the profoundly correctional influence which might be transmitted (if the setting were right) through a daily routine in whose clutches even the most gifted and conscientious performer could develop good reason to settle for professional sightreading not merely as the only target within range, but as a target far enough away to make any more distant target seem provision-ally nonexistent.

Imagine our typical believer — at an age when he is more likely to try in a euphoria of generous enthusiasm to live up to the demands made upon him by his profession than he is to worry too much about the implications for his profession (and for himself) of the purposes and attitudes which are reflected in these demands — absorbed into a well-publicized, prestigious, ad-vanced eight-week educational enterprise run by the Musical Director of one of the most durable institutions in show-business and staffed by professional musicians of national and international reputation; then imagine the crisis of pro-fessional conscience which his euphoria might enable him to bypass under conditions where the following schedule represents the educational experiences he will enjoy, as an active participant, during a single average week:

Monday
9:30-12:00. Orchestra rehearsal.
(1:00-3:00. Attend a lecture.)
8:00 p.m. Chamber music concert of pieces rehearsed during the previous week.

Tuesday
8:00-11:00. First rehearsals of three cont-emporary works to be performed one week hence.
9:30-12:00. Orchestra rehearsal.
1:30-3:30. Second rehearsal of a 20-minute contemporary chamber work to be performed Thursday night.
3:45-5:45. Third rehearsal of a 30-minute contemporary chamber concerto to be performed on Sunday.

Wednesday
11:30-12:30. Orchestra rehearsal.
1:30-3:30. Second and last scheduled rehearsal of one of the three works rehearsed yesterday morning at 8:00.
4:00 p.m. Chamber music concert.
8:00 p.m. Orchestra concert.

Thursday

10:00-12:30. Third and last scheduled rehearsal of the work rehearsed at 1:30 on Tuesday.

1:30-3:30. Second rehearsal of a contemporary chamber work to be performed next Wednesday. (The first rehearsal took place several weeks ago.)

3:45-5:45. Second rehearsal of a 15-minute contemporary work for large wind ensemble to be performed next Wednesday.

8:00 p.m. Chamber music concert.

Friday

10:45-12:30. Section rehearsal.

3:45-5:45. Second rehearsal of a 10-minute contemporary work to be performed early next week.

Saturday

9:00-10:45. Section rehearsal.

3:45-5:45. Fourth and last scheduled rehearsal of the work rehearsed at 3:45 on Tuesday.

Sunday

10:30 a.m. Concert.

1:00-2:30. Dress rehearsal for tonight's concert.

4:30-6:00. Dress rehearsal continued.

8:00 p.m. First concert in a five-night Festival of Contemporary American Music.

This posted schedule (sprinkled among the fourteen posted mimeographed multicolumned pages — of which I retain copies — comprising the total schedule for this single average week) accounts for only forty-five hours of our believer's time: in addition, he may wish to study the scores and practice his parts for the dozen or so pieces in which he is currently involved (there will be other pieces other weeks); he may wish to participate in an unscheduled rehearsal of one of the works in trouble — about a dozen or so; and he may wish to review standard repertoire for his impending audition with the Boston Symphony Orchestra.

(That the concert performances of music old and new thus prepared at Tanglewood last August were invariably better than the first rehearsals is no small tribute to the quantity and quality of the talents which this kind of enterprise so frantically wastes.)

As our believer retreats to a noisy corner at 1:45 p.m. on Friday to spend an hour and a half practicing the four or so hours of music for which he is currently responsible, the dulled sense of panic which keeps him awake may yet drive home loud and clear the sustaining motto for such seasons: You may not be able to play it well, but you'll damn well play it. (The show must go on, so to speak.) And with this revelation, the psychological foundation has been laid for a revised professional credo which he will feel uneasy about at first, but which he may — as the years pass and his own artistic vision ripens — come to embrace as impassively as any veteran of a major symphony orchestra: In one of these contemporary pieces, if you play right notes and wrong notes, right rhythms and wrong rhythms, right entrances and wrong entrances, *with no change of facial expression or tone-quality,* nobody will know the difference; and after you've pulled it off for ten or twenty years, *you won't know the difference yourself.* (It goes without saying that the difference will remain unnoticed by those apprentices in loose journalism whose narcotic if inessential fictions are so randomly embalmed on the Public Entertainments page.)

Although some performers (not to mention most composers) regard the practitioner of the revised credo with distaste, I must admit that their distaste seems sometimes to engulf too modest an object: the revised credo is but one of many anaesthetics in short supply at those outposts where music masquerades as just another highcultural excrescence on the underbelly of show-business.

II. How to Cure it

The suggestions for a four-week summertime conference which follow are based in part on an assumption that the objectives of the Fromm-sponsored Festival of Contemporary American Music are at odds with the tactic of infiltrating show-business; and hence that any failure to assimilate the forms and conditions of show-business need not be taken as a flaw in either the objectives or the suggestions. (I believe that my suggestions are realistic: partly because so many of them aren't much more than adaptations of things I have seen happen at the Fromm Seminars in the late fifties, at the Bennington Composers' Conference last August, and even off-stage at Tanglewood.) Such a conference would be able to approximate the concentrations of talent and leisure which would be needed both to make intelligible to the participants some of the legitimate grounds for differences of attitude toward problems of composition and performance and to examine with care a few specific well worked out instances of alternative attitudes toward both kinds of problem.

A conference might be organized as follows:

Participants

1. A director (assisted by a liaison person and a secretary).
2. Two or three "established" composers.
3. A conductor experienced in conducting contemporary music, and at least one young "apprentice" conductor.
4. Four or five articulate Fromm-commissioned nonestablished composers. (Commissions should be awarded at least a year and a half in advance of the conference.)
5. Twelve to twenty-four young performers, plus a few established veterans known to be untainted by the revised professional credo.
6. A small corps of interested and qualified resident observers. (Problems of housing, feeding, etc., could best be solved by reproducing as faithfully as possible the living conditions which prevailed at the Bennington Composers' Conference last August.)

Schedule of Leisure and Events

Wednesday of each week would be set aside as "fallout" day, devoted to collective retrospection, revision, filling-in, and catching-up.

Evenings would be used, at the discretion of the participants, in whatever ways might best serve to further or to escape from the business in hand; there need be no rule against putting on whatever formal or impromptu concerts the current condition of the conference might inspire.

Saturday morning of each of the first three weeks would be used for a mandatory griping session; on the final Saturday morning, dissatisfied participants should be asked to submit their written evaluations of the conference to its director within a short time.

All Saturday afternoons and Sundays would be reserved for cumulative nonmusical activities.

The first week would be the week during which the senior composers, conductor, and performers would "set the tone" for the conference; seminars and rehearsals would be devoted to a work by each of the senior composers (which might be chosen, perhaps, by the commissioned composers) and to at least one work by a nonresident composer which the senior composers considered a contemporary classic.

The second week would be the week during which the performers would conduct all four of the scheduled seminars (devoted, for example, to characteristics and problems of various instruments and instrumental groups); and during which all the participants would study scores, engage in impromptu seminars and tapeplaying, and do whatever else might seem desirable in preparing for the third and fourth weeks and in improving the tone of the conference.

The third and fourth weeks would be devoted to the commissioned pieces and to one older piece by each of the commissioned composers. Everyone — the commissioned composers in particular — would be expected to serve in a variety of capacities. For example, a composer might be asked to supervise one three-hour rehearsal of his new piece conducted by the senior conductor; to conduct one three-hour rehearsal of his old piece supervised by the senior conductor or a senior performer; to supervise or conduct a rehearsal of another composer's old piece; to give a seminar about his new piece; and to give another seminar about something else. Or a young performer whose services as a performer would not be needed for several days in a row could be asked to conduct or supervise a rehearsal.

During each of the four weeks, seminars would take place at 10:30 a.m.

on Mondays, Tuesdays, Thursdays, and Fridays, and would be attended by all the participants. It might prove advisable to assign primary responsibility for discussion at any one seminar to about six of the participants who acknowledged a particular interest in the scheduled subject. (Well-advertised extracurricular seminars in the rudiments of logic, semantics, and literacy, designed to equip selected representatives of leading institutes of musical research — such as the *New York Times* — with the tools of their trade, could at the discretion of the participants be repeatedly postponed.)

During the first, third, and fourth weeks, rehearsals would take place every Monday, Tuesday, Thursday, and Friday from 2:00 p.m. to 5:00 p.m. Two three-hour rehearsals would always run concurrently, and each would be taped in its entirety. During the third and fourth weeks, each composer's new piece would be rehearsed on two consecutive afternoons; and his old piece might be rehearsed at the *other* rehearsals on the same two afternoons. This scheme would relieve each composer of any obligation to survive all rehearsals of his own music and at the same time guarantee him the satisfaction of being able to attend at least one rehearsal of each work by each of his colleagues. (Each composer would, of course, be given tapes of any rehearsals he regretted having missed.)

This layout of rehearsal time would devote to each piece two three-hour rehearsals: perhaps the first and last of the six hours could be used to go through the piece, for better or for worse, from beginning to end; but the remaining four hours ought to be used to work up a few short passages to perfection: it is essential that performers and composers alike be granted this much chance to do something right.

Since the conference would not be

expected to provide the commissioned composers with complete performances of either their new or their old works, such performances — scheduled for the academic year *following* the conference — should be arranged during the planning of the conference.

Just selecting the participants for the conference would require consultation with the numerous performing groups now attached to various universities, colleges, and conservatories all over the United States; and these consultations should in part be directed toward securing performances on a number of representative campuses. A given work might be taken on tour by a single group, or performed on each of several campuses by the locally resident group. I think that the attractions of the proliferated premiere compare favorably with the attractions of a single summer-time premiere in the mountains: although both summertime and mountains are ideal for professional conferences, neither seems unarguably relevant as the convenient way to reach a representative segment of the right public.

(I should think that by the summer of 1970 it might become useful to have four conferences running more or less concurrently at otherwise abandoned small-college campuses in, say, Vermont or Massachusetts, northern Michigan, Colorado, and northern California or Oregon.)

For the participating performer, the benefits of such conferences would hardly be confined to his performance of new music: if the musical callousness bred by the revised professional credo has conferred upon standard repertoire (which highcultural show business still claims to preserve and disseminate) no noticeable benefits, then we can reasonably hope that the attitudes reflected in such conferences would inflict upon it no noticeable damage.

Only reticence in the presence of persistent claims prevents me from suggesting that in some year each conference be extended by one month to provide time enough for the participating composers and performers to work together intelligently on a movement from a Beethoven quartet.

JKR

THE ACOUSTICAL FOUNDATIONS OF MUSIC. By John Backus
New York: Norton, 1969. 312 pp.

THE STRENGTH of Mr. Backus's book lies in its orderly arrangement of a wide-ranging selection from familiar materials considered by acousticians to be "foundational" with respect to music, and in its level and pace of exposition. Its major weakness lies in its conceptual and methodological inadequacies which vitiate the "foundational" claim that for Mr. Backus is central to his own motivations in writing the book. I will try to get at the trouble by examining a particular subchapter (pp. 138-140, "Theories of Consonance") in which an embodiment of this claim most unmistakably emerges.

This subchapter reports that "the whole subject of consonance and dissonance, like so many in the field of musical acoustics, is quite unsettled." It briefly surveys a few psychoacoustical (but no music-analytic) theories on the subject, as well as a few of the apparent discrepancies among test responses reported by different investigators. It even endorses the likelihood that "a good deal of our feeling as to what constitutes consonance is a matter of musical training." Yet this very subchapter opens with the assurance that "it is agreed" that consonant intervals "exist." (By what ontology a "feeling" about a thing, and moreover a feeling which is probably "a matter of training", may be said to "exist" as a property of the thing, is not explained. Nor is it explained why the division of the entire gamut of tempered intervals into exactly two mutually exclusive domains on the basis of "our feelings" should be allowed to evade the author's elsewhere-applied censure as "arbitrary emotional classification.") Whether or not this reported agreement (but about what?) obtains among psychoacousticians, among musicians the whole subject has of course taken a rather different turn. Thus, at least one well-known music-analytic viewpoint treats the terms "consonant" and "dissonant" as useful chiefly in analyzing certain pieces of music for which the major and minor triads, construed as referential intervallic structures, can serve as analytically useful constructs. Within the context of such analyses, an interval is (by definition) consonant wherever it is interpreted as representing a single major or minor triad, and dissonant wherever it is interpreted otherwise. (Within such analyses, although certain intervals will be dissonant in every occurrence, no interval need always be consonant.) In short, this viewpoint relativizes the concepts of consonance and dissonance to a particular music-analytic conceptual framework (useful for much pre-20th-century music, useless for much 20th-century music), and thereby renders their usefulness for any particular piece of music dependent upon our adjudging that framework applicable to that piece, rather than upon our "feelings" (if any) about intervals outside the context of works of music.

The "Theories of Consonance" subchapter culminates in the following side-swipe at the old notion that different emotive qualities may be associated with different musical "keys": "In the tempered scale, any given interval is exactly the same as every other interval of the same kind. It follows that, except for their height in the pitch-scale, all intervals will sound alike. As a consequence, the practice of ascribing certain "key colors" or certain psychological moods to different music keys has no basis in fact." In these three sentences, confusion and non-sequitur run rampant. By the most charitable reading I can come up with, the drift of the first of these sentences could be construed either as "In the tempered scale, any two pitch-pairs belonging to the same interval class exhibit the same frequency-ratio"; or alternatively as "In the tempered scale, any two pitch-pairs belonging to the same interval class exhibit to perception exactly the same span". Unfortunately, the assertion in the second quoted sentence not only fails to "follow" from an interval-to-frequency or an interval-to-span correlation (or from both in conjunction), it fails even to be the case—as the author himself suggests in an implicit retraction no later than the sentence immediately following the quoted three (in a reference to the timbral differences between open and stopped strings). The third sentence introduces still further surprises: precisely how it is that a sentence (namely, the second) whose only salvageable segment is devoted to specifying a perceptible difference (namely, difference in pitch-level) lays the groundwork from which absence of "basis in fact" follows "as a consequence," is not explained. Throughout the quoted passage, a tendency to offer equivalence from a clearly (or not so clearly) delimited point of view as a "demonstration" of equivalence from a different or more comprehensive point of view seems to be a central weakness.

I should emphasize that I have no quarrel with the eventual punch-line which states that "Arbitrary emotional classifications of this kind are of no more help to music than are astrology or numerology." Indeed, the words "are of no more help to music" are more crucial than might at first appear: even those classifications which do rest "on a factual basis" need still pass the test of operational relevance to each discourse employing them. Thus, even if we were to consider difference in pitchlevel (together with all the differences in relative overtone-strengths normally associated with difference in pitch-level) an acceptable "factual basis" for difference in emotive response, we still might find the fickle metaphors in which such responses are usually preserved superfluous in discussing any particular piece of music which had elicited them. But these are methodological considerations which are not yet commonly faced by musical acousticians.

Now certainly the information Mr. Backus has gathered concerning the physics of sound-propagation, the construction of musical instruments, auditorium and room acoustics, the electronic production of sound, and the physiology of hearing, is on the face of it potentially more musically relevant stuff than "arbitrary emotional classifications, astrology, or numerology." But to suggest, as Mr. Backus does on the last page of his book, that these "various pieces of knowledge, miscellaneous facts, and scraps of theory" constitute—in however underdeveloped a present form—"the science of music," is a little bit like suggesting, at remote remove from all coherent ideas about disease and cure, that some handy anthology of information about toe-nail parings, mattresses, and sunshine somehow constitutes—even in rudiment or in outline—"the science of medicine." And Mr. Backus's few explicit attempts to weld his "pieces" and "scraps" together into coherent ideas about music merely engulf the reader in that miasma of conceptual and methodological confusion where the alleged discipline of psycho-acoustics traditionally finds itself at home.

J. K. Randall
Princeton University

from THE NATION (etc.), 1962-1968:

IV: 1966-67

THE NATION:

January 24, 1966

MUSIC

Benjamin Boretz

The current New York concert season has been remarkable chiefly for the number of events that have sharply revealed the deep separation in our musical "two cultures", between the public musical life and the state of the musical culture it supposedly represents. At first glance, the observation seems paradoxical: this has been the season in which the activity of music's "inner" world, represented mainly by the many contemporary-music performance groups, has become an established "presence" on the New York scene partly through its steady increase, but even more because of the secure base it has found within the educational community (Columbia, Rutgers, New School, 92nd Street Y, etc.). At the same time, too, the 'big' musical world has made some conspicuous gestures toward 20th-century music; most notably those connected with Leonard Bernstein's return to the Philharmonic after a year's absence. But it was, precisely, the contrast with the reality and stability of a seriously functioning new-music world that most clearly exposes the shallowness and ignorance underlying these gestures.

It was possible, for example, for William Steinberg and the Pittsburgh Symphony to play in Carnegie Hall the first all-Schoenberg orchestral program given in New York (regarding which the *New York Times,* whose music section perhaps represents still a third musical culture, ran the extraordinary headline, "Steinberg Leads Modern Works"). But this kind of event seems almost a cliché to anyone in the least acquainted with the other domain, or even with conventional European orchestra and opera-house activity, and it comes long after both the publication and recording of complete Schoenberg editions have been begun. Furthermore, the quality of execution, which was in fact on a level usually associated with first performances of new works, could hardly have seemed tolerable to anyone familiar with the incomparably superior standard available no farther away than the little Recital Hall next door, or the nearest Columbia recording.

A considerably more spectacular, or at least maudlin, gesture has been Leonard Bernstein's publicly expressed anxiety over the state of the symphony in the 20th century, and the pessimistic conclusions about the present and future of orchestral composition (though not orchestral performance) to be inferred from it. The basis for his reflections is being presented in a comprehensive survey, over a few Philharmonic seasons, entitled

"Symphonic Forms In the Twentieth Century." Out of this will undoubtedly come the judgment that the orchestra, far from being annihilated by the poverty of 20th-century symphonic writing, is now relieved of its unbecoming and painful responsibility to represent the musical present, and can enter a glorious twilight as a museum of comfortable sounds.

It is an obvious absurdity, of course, to equate the condition of 20th-century orchestral composition with that of "the symphony". For not only has the idea of the symphony lost any force as a categorical distinction in modern orchestral music, but it appears only rarely as a designate in the orchestral works of the most advanced 20th-century composers. Those who have cultivated it have been, for the most part, relatively retrospective, with not much impact on the development of seriously contemporary orchestral ideas or sound qualities. But having set up such an equation, Mr. Bernstein in his programs appears to exclude such infrequent works as do in fact represent serious thought about the contemporary possibilities of symphonic form. Stravinsky is unmentioned in the Philharmonic program book's note on the series, and primary figures like Schoenberg, Hindemith, Sessions and Carter are mentioned only as future possibilities.

What does emerge in Mr. Bernstein's series is rather more Mahler than he usually performs on three consecutive weeks, and a festival of such antediluvian creampuffs as the complete works of Sibelius, and docile monsters by Vaughan Williams, Nielsen, Prokofiev and Shostakovich, along with a few prewar and recent American works.

The programs I have heard so far included the tiny chamber-music Webern Symphony next to the Mahler Seventh (at the opposite extreme), and Ives's least interesting but easiest symphony, his Third, along with the demanding Mahler Ninth, which was in fact played with impressive restraint and control. But the naive attempt to smooth Webern's carefully isolated pitch events into Schubertian phrases, and the painful technical problems encountered, especially by the Philharmonic's horn player, were in vivid contrast to the standards of interpretation and execution that have become routine for the performance of this work in the chamber-music domain.

Yet one remembers when, with no publicity to speak of, the Philharmonic was actually the principal source for first hearings of advanced music—*Wozzeck* had its first American performance here under Mitropoulos, who also performed the major orchestral works of Schoenberg long before they were available on records. And when one recalls that the Philharmonic's own Chamber Ensemble, which in many ways anticipated the recent new-music groups, was still functioning in the early fifties, it appears that the present radical discontinuity in the musical world is actually a product of the last ten years, a bizarre corollary both of the phenomenal popular success of concert music in America and the vitality of our compositional activity.

In the new-music world itself this season, interest has focused on the work of the new Rockefeller-supported group in residence at Rutgers, under the direction of Arthur Weisberg. Predictably, given the known superiority of most of the players, and Weisberg's customary conductorial approach, the performances have generally been reliable; but the problem of establishing their individuality in an already crowded field can be seen in the ambiguity of the group's programing. Thus, even the titles of its two New York series display uncertainty; the Hunter College concerts are being presented as "The Twentieth Century: The First Sixty-Five Years", which surely represents the ultimate in non-commitment, while the idea of calling the Carnegie Recital Hall programs "From Hindemith to Stockhausen" (leaving out, I presume, Stravinsky, Schoenberg, Bartók et al, and anyone under 38) seems particularly obtuse for an American ensemble.

But obtuseness, apparently, has been the order of the season: it was last fall that the death of Varèse was considered newsworthy enough only for the deepest inside pages of our newspapers, while the Ford Foundation's orchestral program (see *The Nation*, November 15, 1965) was proclaimed widely as the salvation of American musical culture. And in December, the New York Music Critics' Circle finally disbanded on the grounds that the major critics could not spare time from "important" concert activity to hear any new works, and that new music was in any case being played in such quantity as to make further encouragement by the Critics' Circle Awards unnecessary. In short, this season has been a time when one wondered whether a serious musician could any longer pretend to recognize in the public world of music some significant aspect of his own concerns.

Virtual Conversation 3:

[JKR, 2003]: No way Vghn Wms' 4th, Sibelius' 7th, & Shostakovich's 10th are creampuffs.

[BAB, 2003]:
Standoff: Right, no way Vaughan Williams' 4th rates as a creampuff, but it's still not very believable to me, stlll seems like a fairly crude slumming excursion into the "other"- genre of "barbaric" modern music.
Guilty as charged: Back then I didn't really get the deep subterranean energies of Sibelius, just as I couldn't really bond with the more expansive temporalities of Bruckner.
Not Guilty: At the time I had not yet heard Shostakovich's 10th; what I was was a recovering Sh.-addict rebounding from my feckless teen obsessions, more aware of the maudlin extravagances I used to respond to than of the fierce far-out intensities I might have noticed had I been receptive.

THE NATION:

August 18, 1966

MUSIC

Benjamin Boretz

In the four years since the inauguration of Philharmonic Hall, public musical life in New York has come to be dominated, psychologically if not statistically, by the pattern of events at Lincoln Center. This is particularly evident in the prevalence of the 'Festival' strategy, generated by the need to produce large audiences with which to fill expensive and oversized new auditoriums, of inflating the intrinsic appeal of an event by the creation of an associated 'occasion'—an 'inauguration', 'commemoration', or 'series'. This tendency has done a great deal to exaggerate even further the disparity between large- and small-scaled performance activity; the sheer mass of these portmanteau-events has virtually obliterated public awareness of, for example, individual recitals by any but the most prestigious international celebrities, at the Horowitz-Rubinstein level of renown. At the same time, there has been an accompanying change in the audience from a specifically 'musical' orientation to one oriented to 'entertainment' generically. As a result, the traditional area of regular music making, which formerly sustained the continuity of performance, is the really neglected aspect

of musical activity—far more so than events at the 'specialist' extreme, which seem to retain their audiences of musical colleagues and, recently, extra-musical aficionados as well. The attrition of the mainstream recital world increases as the performers who inhabit it persist in offering the same type of obligatory necrophilic program, whose irrelevance is even more sharply exposed in this age of superabundant recordings of the historic literature.

As the public relevance of recitals has thus diminished, their importance to the creative musical world has almost disappeared; for the conservatory education that prepares an instrumentalist for the nonexistent recital vocation is totally inimical not only to his development of an exploratory or serious repertory whether traditional or contemporary, but also to serious (as distinct from spectacular, decorative, or atmospheric) interpretive approaches. But whatever marginal professional existence such a performer can achieve depends entirely on his manager's ability to arrange concert tours in the American provinces, where even the slightly 'esoteric' programs are regarded as naked threats to the management's solvency and to the audience's sanity. As a result, the typical recital performer is not equipped, motivated or managerially permitted to revitalize his repertory or to collaborate—or even come into relevant contact—with those other young musicians, performers as well as composers, whose direct involvement in contemporary phenomena has begun to generate a new tradition for musical activity at all levels of performance.

But those of us who avoid egregious warhorses at one extreme, and seek frontier developments at the other, are likely to contribute to this malaise by disregarding those few promising efforts to reinvent the recital medium. There are performers—some of whom are also active in 'specialist' projects—whose musical value is most effectively projected through their personal implementation of the recital framework. The pianist Charles Rosen, the violinist Paul Zukofsky, the soprano Bethany Beardslee and her pianist partner Robert Helps are, as I've noted here before, performers whose instrumental (or vocal) personalities and interpretive ideas are individual and wide-ranging enough to sustain interest over a program of works drawn from anywhere in the existing literature, historical as well as contemporary. In this respect their concerts run counter to the 'specialist' events with their increasingly narrow focus on contemporary music, and even contemporary music of some particular, if loose, stylistic orientation. But these performers seem to exist in a vacuum; the concert managers who make up the bulk of New York recital audiences ignore them, and the new-music public stays aware out of an indiscriminate dismissal of anything 'traditional'. The press, too, contributes to this miasma by maintaining a strictly impartial indifference to all recital activity— although it would seem that from their point of view the discovery of a new first-rate performer or piece would be 'news'.

During the season just past, at least two such opportunities for discovery were on the schedule of Carnegie Recital Hall, in the recitals of Paul Jacobs as harpsichordist and of Samuel Rhodes as solo violist. Apart from the extraordinary work of Fernando Valenti (harpsichord) and Walter Trampler (viola) these are instruments rarely played as media for serious solo playing, so both these debuts were, from a music-cultural standpoint, newsworthy. Paul Jacobs is familiar to new-music (and New York Philharmonic) audiences as a pianist and musician of substantial executive and interpretive qualities; the transference of his skills to the harpsichord (previously encountered in ensemble performances of Milton Babbitt's Composition for Tenor and Six Instruments and Elliott Carter's Double Concerto) produces a rhythmic precision, timbral delicacy, and mechanical fluency that create a completely new sense of the range of this instrument's resources. His performance of Carter's Sonata for flute, oboe, cello, and harpsichord (with Thomas Nyfenger, George Haas and Robert Sylvester) was especially revelatory of the work's special ensemble and rhythmic qualities, deriving from the extension of harpsichord sonority and attack through the entire ensemble texture, eliciting from these performers a precision and specificity of balance and articulation that I haven't heard in any previous performance.

Jacobs's programming was in itself a sophisticated—and exploratory—event. Opening with the Bach Four Duets, whose virtual absence of surface color, and its interior of involuted relational ideas make it quintessentially 'musician's music', was instantly intriguing; and the subsequent performance of Haydn's A-flat Sonata-Divertimento revealed a remarkable work that was unknown even to most of the professionals in the audience. While the other music on the program was more conventionally recitalistic, Jacobs's spectacular riffing on the complex pyrotechnics of Bach's F-minor Toccata, and the precisely judged sonorities, balances and phrasing of his performance of DeFalla's Harpsichord Concerto fused transcendent instrumental authority with far-out musical savoir-faire such as to dispatch all previous standards for concert harpsichordism.

Samuel Rhodes's recital introduced a violist in the superior tradition of Trampler and Abram Loft. His capacity to draw a continuous amplitude of sound from the viola under however ferocious technical and musical demands aligns him, more than Trampler, with a tradition of string playing that has almost disappeared. But there is also a level of musical cultivation and awareness that is even more exceptional in a musician of this old-school virtuosity. Throughout this recital one was aware of innumerable details of special perception and care, along with a large-scale command of direction and succession: the precise matching of viola and piano trills in the opening Bach G-major Sonata, the continuousness of the Stravinsky solo Élégie, and especially the security of the maximal complexities of pitch, rhythm, and registral imagery projected in the Brahms E-flat Sonata, Op. 120 (better known in its version for clarinet).

The vital center of this concert, however, was the first performance of a stunning new work by Claudio Spies, his *Viopiacem* for viola and keyboard instruments. Like his *Tempi* for fourteen instruments (played on a Fromm Foundation concert last year), *Viopiacem* is full of imaginative ideas about sonority, registration, continuity, and—especially—the possibilities of multiple articulations of the same segments of (musical) time and space, where the extension of the viola-keyboard dialogue to piano and harpsichord, first alternately and then simultaneously, is a richly and deeply embedded musical image rather than just a presentational novelty. And the intelligence and refinement of the performance corresponded exactly to the most conspicuous qualities of Spies's own compositional thought.

Apart from such exceptional events, the performance of contemporary music has depended primarily on those composer- and university-oriented groups that have been less the example they originally hoped to provide and more the permanent center for their kind of activity. Accordingly, the Group for Contemporary Music at Columbia undertook a major expansion of its work by presenting a fully staged performance of *Mr. and Mrs. Discobbolos,* Peter Westergaard's new opera. *Discobbolos* is what results when a compositional sophisticate, with equal awareness of the possibilities of verbal-musical playfulness, intrudes on the supposedly exclusive domain of the opera specialists— Westergaard's sense of what might constitute a lively and effective music-theatric fusion seems so obviously right on that it's hard to understand the persistence of heavy dramas, flamboyant vocalisms, symbolic jokes that are not dramatic, melodic, or funny, in much of what gets performed as 'new opera' within the Lincoln Center culture. *Discobbolos* is an opera in the Stravinskian mold, with that kind of verbal-rhythmic vocal line contouring within stable, slowly changing macro-events; a work, that is, of counter-pointed 'intervals' of pitch, attack, and (dramatic) event-

unfolding that creates a multi-dimensional richness on the foundation of the purely verbal triologue of Edward Lear's text.

A different sort of local operatic premiere was the Juilliard School Opera Workshop production of Roger Sessions's *The Trial of Lucullus* and Hugo Weisgall's *Purgatory*—a kind of penance, really, since *Lucullus* was composed twenty, and *Purgatory* thirty years ago. Typically, these first New York performances were student productions, but the sets designed by Ming Cho Lee and the staging by Ian Strasfogel rose to a high artistic level in their imaginative solutions in every dimension (except lighting) to the intractable problems posed by the radio-script character of the scene succession of *Lucullus*, and its analogues in the musical *sequitur.*

Purgatory's performance was altogether less satisfactory; compared with other of Weisgall's many operas, it comes off as rather tenuous, even tame, and its presentation was often unable to rise to any adequate level of conviction. But, again, a work of such manifestly serious compositional and dramatic thinking should be available to us as a necessary piece of our musical self-awareness. That we are constantly deprived of knowing such works—even that they exist—is a discouraging consequence of our acquiescence in the work of the compulsive mass-audience-builders who administer whatever is left of our musical culture.

New Music, Old Words

by Benjamin Boretz[*]

Stravinsky: The Composer and His Works, by Eric Walter White. University of California Press, $18.

I Am a Composer, by Arthur Honegger. Translated from the French by Wilson 0. Clough in collaboration with Allan Arthur Willman. St. Martin's Press, $4.95.

For almost sixty years, the public image of the "modern" composer has been virtually localized in the name and figure of Stravinsky. The extent of his predominance is overwhelming; compare, for example, the almost total public nonconsciousness of such masters as Schoenberg and Webern, whose gigantic imprint on the music of the immediate past and present is equally unmistakable. Yet it has been Stravinsky's flair for self-presentation, his association with the ballet, his status as the promulgator of the world's champion music scandal, and not inconsiderably his incredibly lively and extended longevity rather than any attachment to, or even awareness of, his music that have accounted for his great réclame.

The biographer-exegete who wishes to convey the qualities of Stravinsky's career is therefore confronted by a complex situation. For, to begin with, the indifference and, frequently, antipathy with which almost every new Stravinsky composition since *Firebird* has been received and the absence from the "regular" concert repertory of any Stravinsky work composed after the *Sacre du Printemps* impose formidable burdens of conceptual insight and perceptual evocation on any attempt at verbal description. The problems inherent in a large-scale synthesis for nonspecialist readers are proportionately staggering.

And even the task of describing Stravinsky's work in terms of

Harper's, February 1967

its position within the musical world presents a difficult problem. For the multiplicity of significances his work has assumed, and the variety of pretexts for sometimes violently antipathetic musical positions that it has successively—and often simultaneously—provided, are surely unparalleled elsewhere in contemporary creative thought.

There has been, for example, the Stravinsky of the neoclassic ideologues, whose flag is that "pandiatonic" surface of his music from the Octet to *The Rake's Progress*—the Stravinsky of Nadia Boulanger, and many of her American students. At the same time, there has been the far more essential Stravinsky of the profound reexamination of tradition, from the tradition of Russian music to that of tonality to that classicized in the works of Schoenberg and Webern—a Stravinsky who complements Schoenberg in creating a new, multidimensional musical syntax whose implications are wholly independent of any surface "manner." And there is, too, the Stravinsky whose utterances and performances have revolutionized the composer's relation to public and performer, whose insistence on the self-sufficiency of a musical object has created an atmosphere in which music can be discussed and presented as a product of the same creative rationality that explores and expands the range of human capacity in all its dimensions.

Nor can one fully measure Stravinsky's presence in the musical scene without considering the ironies of his later years as a remarkable anachronism whose newest works still make "advanced" discoveries as provocative as any in our time. But Stravinsky is the sole survivor—by almost a quarter-century—of the last compositional generation for whom the avenues of public prominence were still available, and he has spent that quartercentury in bewildered isolation from his colleagues, unable to perceive the value and relevance or even, one fears, the existence of the new musical vitality emerging in the American university, where his work, in its entire range, is as powerful a generative force as ever.

I have mentioned these essential dimensions of Stravinsky's musical biography because none of them appears in Eric Walter White's book. Instead, we are yet again presented, *in extenso,* with the record jacket Stravinsky of our, and perhaps even Mr. White's, infancy. It is an account whose significant *moments critiques* find Stravinsky in the company of certain contemporaries just before composing certain works, and whose denouements are the degree of public and journalistic success achieved at first and subsequent performances—surely, of all historical documentation, the least relevant. Musical "explanations" consist of simple quotes of Stravinsky's own literary conceits, without any description of how they generate and are reflected in a unique context of articulation and continuity; these alternate with note-to-note detail (trivial to the musician, incomprehensible to the layman, especially since no score references are given for the examples) and outrageous simplicisms and flat-footed assertions of approbation or reservation.

Virtually all the documentation in the book is from published, readily available sources, especially Stravinsky's own widely read books, without special commentary or even apparent organization. And otherwise, it contains a quite complete list of Stravinsky's works with their performance specifications (immensely useful to librarians of performance organizations) and reprints of some interesting journalistic documents. But where the eternal presence of so many "false Stravinskys"— including some of his own progeneration—has created a desperate need for a truly "inside" view of the sense of his life and work, White's book, for all its impressive bulk and detail, leaves the inquiring reader as "outside" as ever.

Arthur Honegger presents a diametrically opposite biographical problem; on the evidence of *I Am a Composer,* a book of dialogues and monologues, as well as of his compositional work, he was a composer of frequently remarkable music whose musical concepts were, however, like the conventional one-dimensional formulations of journalism, hard to elucidate because of their persistent banality. Thus, given the opportunity to range over any musical idea, and given a medium through which to address a literate public, Honegger chose to be concerned with details of notation, complaints about the economic and social condition of composers, depressing forecasts of the concurrent collapse of society and music, and anecdotal descriptions of his collaborations with important French poets, notably Apollinaire, Gide, Claudel, and Valéry. His description of his musical submission to Claudel's ideas ("Thus the whole musical atmosphere was created and the score prescribed, so that the composer had only to submit to its guidance. ... It was sufficient to hear Claudel read ... his own text ... with such plastic force ... that the whole musical pattern emerged") is particularly revealing in contrast with Stravinsky's complete domination of every articulative situation into which his music enters. Here, as elsewhere, Honegger reveals a sad, fundamental uncertainty about his own work that perhaps explains its tendency to project the most available, secure gestures of musical grandeur. But perhaps the melancholy portrait that emerges will remain valuable as a genre-picture of the frustration of a whole generation of compositional *petits-maîtres* who, in the first half of this century, found themselves stranded without a *métier.*

THE NATION:
January 23, 1967

MUSIC

Benjamin Boretz

The interest of our mass-circulation journals in the views and activities of composers is so sporadic that the appearance of an extensive interview with the Italian composer, Luciano Berio, on the occasion of the first performance of his opera *Passaggio* at the Juilliard School *(The New York Times,* January 8), was a notable and welcome event. But its very rarity heightened one's concern for the content of Berio's remarks, in the prevailing vacuum of public awareness not only of what composers actually do represent nowadays but of what music represents altogether. I found particularly unfortunate the attribution to Berio of the remarks that "in tonal music there were predetermined forms; now we invent forms every time. In tonal music there was a hierarchy, with melody first, then harmony, and finally rhythm taking their places. Now there are no such components—no melody as such." The inapplicability of these remarks should be self-evident: "Predetermined form" is surely the least significant aspect of meaningful creative work in any language, at any time, tonal or otherwise, musical or otherwise. The absence of "such components" as "melody" which is simply an exposed surface of pitch relation; "harmony"—the sonorities resulting from simultaneous conjunctions of pitches; and "rhythm"—the quality of event-change over time, however asserted, is — thus — definitionally impossible.

But what is really troubling about these statements by an authentically distinguished composer is their implications for public consciousness not only of traditional music but of non-traditional contemporary composition as well. And this is especially unfortunate at a time when such serious work tends to be widely associated with all "modernism", however primitive, in the general category of *"avant-garde".* So much simplistic musical "extremism", whether of the "right" (in the manner of, say, Samuel Barber's *Antony and Cleopatra*) or of the "left" (the know-nothing or -as-little-as-possible *avant-garde*) is in reality traceable to a lack of awareness of the enormous range of qualities and ideas that music has already engendered. Here, perhaps, a failure of education may be crucial; and those who regard the increasing orientation of composers to the university as an anti-creative "narrowing" of outlook might consider how unlikely it would be for a historically informed composer to remark, as Berio was quoted, that "tonality can still work [sic]...for moments of escapism, like with jazz. But for serious art, absolutely NO!"

Yet I wonder how many readers of the *Times* felt quite sure that some similar statement would readily be made by, let us say, any average "committed" twelve-tone composer; even though, in fact, any real understanding of the bases of twelve-tone coherence — or of any coherent musical syntax, actual or potential — would be the surest possible guarantee against the currency of such beliefs. And Luciano Berio is, actually, among the most perceptive and intellectually responsible composers within the current European *avant-garde*, who also makes such "ideologically" reasonable statements as that "control is the *sine qua non* of composition", and that "there is a . . . global type of thinking today, a concern with musical processes that has nothing to do with geography", although the latter remark is illustrated only by the mention of three *European* composers from the local Darmstadt "inner circle" (Stockhausen, Boulez, Pousseur) who are "not compatriots", being German, French, and Belgian; but there's no hint of even the existence of any American or Asian or even Eastern European compositional activity which might actually internationalize this "global" phenomenon. This kind of parochialism, whether naive or "political", is another symptom of the conceptual crudity that plagues any effort to represent music, past, present and potential,

with any reasonable sense of its true range of subtlety, complexity, profundity, or diversity.

One of the contributory aspects to an environment in which attitudes such as those expressed by Berio can flourish has been the deep general unawareness of the existence and nature of a substantial and abundant 20th-century musical tradition. So it was particularly gratifying to hear, on the same weekend as the publication of the Berio interview, the Philharmonic's performance of the Schoenberg Violin Concerto, a music that seems to me one of the most deeply engaging, complex and original compositional inventions of any time. On this occasion, Zvi Zeitlin's playing the solo part, still prodigiously difficult in its demands on the outer limits of contemporary violinistic capacity, was especially impressive, in both its technical and musical adequacy. The articulation of pitch, duration and phrase, in the solo part, was invariably clear and precise, despite the somewhat small sonorous and dynamic range of Mr. Zeitlin's playing. And wherever the soloist was responsible for generating the entire coherence of a passage (as in the two solo cadenzas in the outer movements), the results were remarkable — the multiple-stopped trills and chords of the last-movement cadenza, the multiply articulated arpeggios of the first movement cadenza, and the simultaneous, bowed-plucked attacks were real feats of violinism and musicianship, far beyond any performances I had heard before.

Moreover, after hearing these qualities in the performance, it was revealing to read in Zeitlin's program note that "thinking people, who fully accept the need for some preparatory study of Shakespeare, Joyce, Thomas Mann, or the Talmud, reject, on first hearing, music that needs equal conditioning. They are reluctant to apply the principles of one area of human endeavor to another." I wonder what the implications of such a remark are for the attitudes professed by Luciano Berio in his public discourse.

I should not, however, minimize the orchestra's contribution to this performance; its playing, under Leonard Bernstein, seemed the product of careful and conscientious preparation. The crucial requirements of ensemble accuracy in reproducing the pitches and durations indicated in the score were in large part realized, far beyond their performances earlier this year of Schoenberg's *Survivor from Warsaw* and Second Chamber Symphony. Thus that there remained such problems as the misrepresentation or even near-absence of dynamic differentiation, and a general uncertainty of the shaping of events and successions, seems less noteworthy at this point than that the totality constituted probably the most competent performance of a

Schoenberg orchestral work in New York since Hans Rosbaud's visit to the Philharmonic in 1961.

A still more remarkable event, under the present musical conditions, was the performance by the Opera Company of Boston of Schoenberg's opera *Moses and Aron*, another monument of the 20th-century tradition which, incredibly, was receiving its first American performance. This alone would have guaranteed to the Opera Company of Boston the distinction of presenting the most significant American operatic event since *Wozzeck* at the City Center and *The Rake's Progress* at the Metropolitan in 1952 (unless inaugurations of buildings are seen as more significant musical events than performances of works).

For *Moses and Aron* represents the ultimate development of the concepts of dramatic-verbal-musical structure that were crucial for Schoenberg throughout his compositional life from his earliest songs to the first works in which his real originality was manifest (the *Book of the Hanging Gardens* and *Pierrot Lunaire*) to the furthest extended explorations of structural ideas *(Erwartung, Der Jakobsleiter, Die Glückliche Hand, A Survivor from Warsaw,* etc.). And this ultimacy obviously precludes any attempt at even minimal exegesis here—except to point out that, as one might expect, the work is "operatic" in the deepest of senses—is in fact generated out of a deep reconsideration of whatever is constitutive of operatic continuity. This becomes especially evident, in the manner in which the extraordinary diversity of resources and media—and the sense-perceptual contexts associated with each—all contribute to a unitary "dramatic" unfolding, not in trivial synchronism but in a fantastically complex counterpoint of rates and qualities of unfolding in its multiple projective domains.

In a direct sense, *Moses and Aron* is also an ultimized realization of the potential of German Expressionist theatre, a musical and dramatic purification of its resources that reconceives characteristic "devices" as the generators and projectors of a unitary structural continuity. Thus the constant interplay of two "dramatic" levels—the verbal, intimate and "abstract" dialogues of Moses and Aaron, on the one hand, and the externalized pure action of the massed crowds on the other—is realized through an extraordinary development of a single set of presentational qualities — orchestral, vocal and visual — for each scene.

The "expressionist" idea of the unseen murmuring chorus whose location (the spatial sense of the source of sound) constantly shifts to represent the "burning bush" idea—a great stroke of musical theatre in itself—is immediately juxtaposed with the chamber-music, recitative quality of the Moses-Aaron dialogue. The continuity of ideas thus created, each sharply characterized by "profiles", relates *Moses* to the heart of the operatic tradition from the upper-lower world juxtaposition of Monteverdi's *Orfeo* to the outdoor-indoor, natural-supernatural musical correlates in Mozart's *Don Giovanni*, to the merging and interdevelopment of a multitude of such identities in Wagner.

But beyond the virtue of the mere fact of the presentation, the Boston company's performance was extraordinary in the ingenuity and discipline of many aspects of the production. Throughout, the accuracy of the chorus, which is virtually an ensemble soloist, and frequently an ensemble of differentiated ensemble soloists, was phenomenal, and perhaps contributed more than any other factor to the projection of the special sonic-articulative qualities of the work. Above all, however, the settings and the stage direction by Sarah Caldwell—under the most inadequate conceivable of physical conditions in an old movie theatre—were the uniquely imaginative and original aspects of the production, brilliantly "effective", yet at almost every point deriving evidently from an awareness of what was going on, musically and dramatically, in the work.

The transformation of a ridiculously shallow stage by vertical, lateral and even circular extensions (the orchestral ensemble was entirely surrounded by stage aprons), and the sense of relations of space, volume and (visual) speed and shape of events were strokes of authentic genius that make most of the presentations by the financially affluent but conceptually indigent New York companies seem quite shameful. Miss Caldwell must immediately be given an adequate orchestra, an authoritative conductor, and all the funds, stage resources, electronic equipment and mechanical devices she requires. At the very least, the old Metropolitan ought to be rebuilt to her specifications and turned over to her. For her work (beginning more than ten years ago with the first, and thus far only, American performance of Hindemith's *Mathis der Maler,* and continuing with Berg's *Lulu,* which has not yet appeared at the Metropolitan or the New York City Opera, and Nono's *Intolleranza* of last year) has been the only vital sign exhibited by American operatic activity (excepting individual productions in Santa Fe and Washington). Even if all the compositional activity in America is worth only 50,000 matching-grant dollars to the National Endowment for the Arts, it still seems possible that our national reputation for operatic incompetence might appear deserving of the rectification uniquely available through activities such as Miss Caldwell's.

[from the Music Educators Journal, November 1968, Volume 55, Number 3. The assigned, and welcomed, topic is my title; the subtitle and intro were created, with my acquiescence, by the editor.]

ELECTRONIC MUSIC AND MUSICAL TRADITION
[editor's subtitle:] A DIALECTICAL FANTASIA

[editor's intro:] The reader faces this one article as he would face the most inscrutable piece of electronic music. He may comprehend on many levels by analyzing its intricate arguments, by absorbing the illusion of its rhetoric, or, perhaps most profitably, by letting it launch his mind into new consciousness.

Suppose that we felt in some way puzzled, or even put off, by piano music. We might ask an avowed composer thereof to help us out by discussing its relation (or lack of relation) to other, more anciently accepted kinds of music—that is, to musical tradition. Our composer would face at the outset a serious strategical difficulty, upon whose resolution the drift and cogency of his subsequent remarks would depend. He would have to decide whether his purposes would better be served by repudiating the very term "piano music" as a classification that, while undeniably reflective of gross and evident resemblances (namely, identity of instrumentation), implicitly butchers a host of more profound, more subtle, and more interesting resemblances and differences (namely, of musical substance) among compositions however similar or dissimilar in their instrumentation; or, alternatively, by accepting the term as at least provisionally useful in circumscribing some interesting idiosyncracies of musical substance. In short, we would have to decide at the outset whether to approach piano music as *music* that just happens to be for the piano, or alternatively as a world in itself—much as *I* will have to decide whether to approach electronic music as *music* that just happens to be electronic. In developing his strategy, our composer might be tempted to espouse any one (though hopefully not all) of the following rather incompatible opinions:

I. The term "piano music" should be scrapped as insufficiently reflective of the changes the piano itself has historically undergone: that is, the term, rather than reflecting gross and evident resemblances, reflects gross and evident ignorance of existing differences. Nor does the trend of the evolution of the piano mesh with the evolution of musical ideas. Bach's *Well-Tempered Clavier* was not composed for the modern piano. Yet we may argue that the fugues in particular receive their most adequate projection precisely on the *modern* piano, which resonates all "parts" together (as did older keyboard instruments, insofar as they resonated anything at all) and at the same time offers the subtlest dynamic shadings within any general dynamic level (as older keyboard instruments assuredly did not)—shadings upon which the continuity of "inner" parts intimately depends. And although the piano works of Chopin and Liszt seem to require the modern piano even more than do the *Well-Tempered* fugues, the piano works of Satie and Webern seem to require it even less.

Someone in my position might wax even more understandably cantankerous about the way the term "electronic music" can on occasion reflect gross and evident ignorance of gross and evident existing differences at every level of the phenomenon thus classified: at the level of the composer's degree of involvement, where electronic weaponry is being used in some quarters (I think of the well-known experiments of Lejaren Hiller) to make all specific compositional decisions (whose rendition as sound is in several instances given over to conventional nonelectronic instruments), but in other quarters to carry out compositional decisions made down to the most minute detail by the composer himself; at the level of sound-production, where the particular electronic mode may involve the equipment of the classical tape studio, or a special sound-synthesizing machine, or a digital computer, or some refinement of one or combination of several of these; and at the level of social consumption, where electronically generated sound may be exclusively stored on tape for delivery through playback, or may be delivered in the flesh by machines used as instruments played by visible performers (and in either case may be combined with "live" or taped conventional instrumental sound electronically transformed or in the raw). Nor do these manifold differences in electronic mode themselves offer a useful guide to differences in musical substance. Something actually done in a tape studio might well be done next time on a computer.

II. The term "piano music" should be scrapped as pointing toward resemblances and differences that are too often trivial by comparison with structural musical, or even compositional procedural, resemblances and differences more clearly elicited in disregard of the boundary the term defines. In treating a late Beethoven piano sonata, or the Schoenberg *Suite*, Op. 25, for example, more interesting resemblances are often to be found with works of the same composer from roughly the same period for whatever instrumentation than with works, even works by the same composer, that happen to be for the same instrument; and more interesting differences, differences independent of purely sonic contrasts among instrumental media, are often to be found with works that happen to be for a variety of instrumentations. In short, sheer sonic resemblance or difference of media, while indeed a resemblance or a difference, is a poor guide to the more interesting resemblances and differences of musical substance.

To anyone who suspects that at least part of what he is puzzled or put off by in electronic music is its sheer sonic novelty, I would suggest the following instructive aural exercise:

Listen a number of times to the first of Mario Davidovsky's *Synchronisms* for conventional instruments and electronically generated sound. (The CRI recording (CRI S204) offers a typically matchless performance by Harvey Sollberger, for whom the piece was written.) Concentrate at first on the flute part, hearing the electronic sounds in a supportive role. (During predominantly or solely electronic passages, try to hear structural analogies with flute passages.)

After getting a general sense of the piece from this particular point of view, try hearing the following kinds of monophonic connection for which exclusively flute figures will serve provisionally as our model structures in hearing the unfolding of the piece:

(1) Predominantly flute figures. Notice the many cases in which several electronic sounds enter into the figure as plausible sonic extensions of contrasts within the flute part itself: particularly contrasts of mode of attack (untongued versus hole-popped) and of mode of sustaining ("normal" versus flutter-tongued).

(2) Exclusively flute phrases and figures whose immediate continuations are, or which are themselves immediate continuations of, exclusively electronic phrases and figures. Notice in particular the clear analogies of registral contour and rhythm and, in a few cases, the actual sonic match. And notice the more frequent cases in which the sonic relation between flute and electronic sound is simply a more elaborate development of the kind of relation just mentioned under "1" above.

(3) Predominantly electronic figures. Notice how several flute sounds may be dropped in on exactly the same basis as electronic sounds are dropped into predominantly flute figures.

(4) Exclusively electronic phrases and figures. Notice that these now offer no difficulty at all, and hardly even require more than an appropriate reapplication of the concepts that guided us through the previous steps of our exercise.

Having developed an ear for these kinds of monophonic connection, we may approach the polyphony with some confidence. Most significantly we are prepared to grasp one of the central means by which polyphony is generated throughout the piece—a means forecast by the appearance of its first electronic sound as the culmination of a flute figure, which is then continued in different ways by flute and tape at the same time: polyphony recurrently branches off from monophonic interactions between flute and tape (and recurrently converges into monophonic connections that branch off again).

A principal virtue of this exercise, ostensibly designed to reduce the obstacle of sonic novelty, is its concentration on matters of structural continuity within the piece. Success in integrating individual sonic events, however novel initially, into a coherent and interesting continuity is equivalent to success in hearing as in composing; just as failure in integrating individual sonic events, however familiar, is equivalent to failure.

Perhaps surprisingly, considering the size of its instrumental ensemble, we might even more easily impose such an exercise upon Henri Pousseur's *Rimes pour differentes sources sonores* (RCA Victrola VIC S1239), long stretches of which overtly maintain a surface monophony. Nor will such exercises in monophonic hearing leave us totally unprepared to follow the surface continuity in numerous purely electronic pieces.

Quite otherwise is the situation with the electronic works of Milton Babbitt, whose dense polyphony comprises not merely a counterpoint among concurrent individual strands of sound events, but also counterpoints within each strand of different aspects of the sound events of that strand. Unfortunately, I can think of no exercise useful in approaching these works (*Composition for Synthesizer, Ensembles for Synthesizer, Vision and Prayer,* and *Philomel*—the last two as yet unreleased by the recording companies), which constitute the most impressive body of electronic music to date, short of a thorough musical education in the works principally of the best-known 18th-, 19th-, and 20th-century composers—an education against which the current market in 18th-, 19th-, and 20th-century harmony and form-and-analysis manuals erects a formidable barrier.

> III. The term "piano music" is all right so long as it stands more or less on a par with *a very large number* of other terms (such as "clarinet music", "string quartet music", "electronic music", and "band music") but inadmissible as one (however small) half of a world whose other (however large) half is called "nonpiano music". (This attitude seems most consistent with a feeling that such terms, however handy across the counter or by mail, are neither notably useful nor notably noxious in discussing matters of musical substance.)

While a hypothetical dichotomy between piano and nonpiano music may seem *récherché* even as an idea worth rejecting, the analogous dichotomy between electronic and nonelectronic music seems to cut something of a figure both explicitly in common parlance and implicitly in the title of this article.

Fortunately, our successfully consummated aural exercise seems to have sprung us from this trap.

> IV. Piano music raises an interesting set of problems inseparable from the idiosyncrasies of the piano; these problems, however, associate only loosely or superficially with problems of musical substance and therefore tend to arise mostly for composers and for them mostly as obstacles or stimulants to musical ideas in themselves not peculiarly bound to the piano. The Chopin nocturnes come immediately to mind. Think of the many cases of ornate right-hand *cantabile* whose contour and rhythm seem so inseparable from an instrument each of whose sounds is but the reverberation of an almost instantaneous attack and release. Yet we would probably be overdoing it if we were to insist that such passages represent a "uniquely piano-kind of melody"; it seems more judicious to speak of a new wrinkle on a more general musical idea, with the new wrinkle being unquestionably a response to the idiosyncrasies of the piano —just as the new wrinkles in the Paganini caprices are to those of the violin.

We have already encountered many a new *electronic* wrinkle during our aural exercise, in which we followed extensions of flute-structures into another sonic domain; and we might now inquire to what extent the chosen specifics of that new sonic domain constitute a response to the idiosyncrasies of the classical tape studio.

At this point we must recognize some basic likelihoods in the composer's response to a particular electronic apparatus. Notwithstanding the bromide that *all* sounds are *in principle* available electronically, the practical day-to-day fact has been that some sounds are more available than others—because of the design of this or that set of electronic components, because of the computer programs currently at hand, because of limitations in current knowledge or current budget, and so on. And since the tape studio, for example, has made eminently available a whole range of sounds not normally associated with any conventional instruments, we should not be surprised to discover within the repertoire of tape-studio music a number of pieces that seem in at least this negative sense "idiomatic" to the tape studio. Notable among these are all those pieces in which the organization of discrete pitches plays only a minor role, and whose musical structure is in the exceptional case commensurately novel. Nor is it surprising that exploitation of the readily and widely available has been the frequent precursor of (or surrogate for) the slow and painstaking conquest of the unavailable; or that such exploitation may have nurtured the impression that electronic sound is "inherently" one kind of thing rather than another—or at least that the computer has a "computer sound", the tape studio a "tape-studio sound", the RCA synthesizer a "synthesizer sound", and so on. But these are impressions that undoubtedly will be dispelled every year or two for many years to come as the repertoire of electronic music grows and as the traffic across alleged boundaries becomes sufficiently heavy and notorious to obliterate them without a trace. It is no longer easy, after all, to suppose that piano music is "inherently" Chopinesque.

V. Piano music may profitably be viewed as a musical world distinct from the world of nonpiano music. The special combination of capacities and incapacities exhibited by the piano suggests, or in any case has historically elicited, concepts of musical structure whose most significant exploration is embodied entirely in compositions for piano. Think of the 1ˢᵗ and 24ᵗʰ Chopin etudes. True, these are pieces in the tonal system, and pieces that exploit the tonal system elegantly and ingeniously. But might we not insist that this surface continuity of resonating cascades of arpeggiation is, in its redefinition of what constitutes sufficiently developed and interesting detail, at least as profoundly different from any nonpiano tonal piece as, say, an aria by Verdi is from an aria by Bach? But for the existence of electronic music, we might make a similarly strong case for profundity of piano-orientation in some recent "inside-the-piano" pieces. (I think immediately of the middle movement of a work written by Frederick Rzewski about ten years ago.) Yet the very pieces I would be most tempted to invoke in this connection are among those I would most confidently invoke in showing some obvious profound connections between instrumental and electronic music: specifically, between instrumental music and those exceptional cases of nonpitch-oriented, tape-studio music whose novel music structure we have already injudiciously described as a response to the "idiosyncrasies" of the tape studio. Indeed, in our concern with the composer's response to an instrument or apparatus, we have neglected to mention the response of instruments and apparatus to the demands of composers: after all, pianos, like electronic media and Wagner tubas, are themselves in part responses.

Our aural exercise may have been useful in leading us from the purely instrumental to the purely electronic in a case where the relation of the two could hardly be ignored. We may even concede that such an exercise provides a sort of prenatal conditioning for the inevitable moment at which the umbilical cord must be cut. But isn't Vladimir Ussachevsky's *Of Wood and Brass* (or for that matter Davidovsky's own *Electronic Study No. 2*) at least as different from *Synchronism No. 1* as the 1ˢᵗ Chopin etude is from the 1ˢᵗ Chopin nocturne? Do not the kinds of musical structure adumbrated by such profoundly "nonpitch" pieces stand in sharp contrast to all musical structures in which pitch organization plays the central, or at least a central, role? Or are such structures more profitably viewed as new wrinkles on the phraseology and textures of older 20ᵗʰ-century instrumental music — specifically, upon the varieties of phraseology and texture to be found in the works of Schoenberg, Webern, and Varèse?

Perhaps such questions lead us away from what seems to many composers a more important matter: namely, the interaction in their continuing work of their own images of desirable musical structures and the continually expanding availability of hitherto peripheral aspects of sound for elaborate structuring. This interaction on the one hand continually modifies and transforms these images; and on the other hand continually stimulates and redirects the expansion, and in the process stimulates and redirects the development of the electronic media themselves.

It is this interaction that most forcefully suggests that we may eventually wish to make a stronger case for the uniqueness of electronic music than for the uniqueness of piano music. Indeed, in dedicated anticipation of such a judgment, many composers of electronic music (both in their capacities as composers and in their capacities as publicists) regard radical novelty in their own work and in the work of others as a moral imperative. Leaving aside the question whether such radical novelty is on occasion more evident in the packaging than in the product, we should at least point out the inverted form of slavery to the nonelectronic past the pursuit of radical electronic novelty entails: such pursuit is explicitly conditioned and circumscribed by the past, but takes place exclusively beyond rather than exclusively within the boundary.

Yet the genuinely unlimited horizon the digital computer in particular has opened for electronic sound-generation suggests that our eventual case for the uniqueness of electronic music may turn out weaker, not stronger, than our case for the uniqueness of piano music. The conquest of the unavailable is yielding not just new sounds and new ideas about new sounds but also new ideas about old sounds, new ideas about old ideas, and the means for implementing all kinds of ideas. In the upshot, the term "electronic music" may convey not a special kind of music, but rather the most general set of musical conditions, under which the musical imagination is liberated from all those mechanical and physiological impediments that in the past have contributed both positively and negatively to the development of musical ideas. By this view, the term "electronic music" might insensibly wither away to be replaced simply by the term "music". And such a view would undoubtedly bring with it new insights into the virtues and limitations of the more specialized musics for conventional instruments.

We have thus far developed some reasons to suppose that the utility of the widely acceptable and traditional classification "piano music" depends not only upon what we believe about existing music for the piano, but more generally upon what kind of thing we think important, wish to understand or demonstrate or sell, or just happen to be interested in. Furthermore, we have managed to suggest quite a variety of notions about its utility that become attractive the more we focus on this rather than that set of pieces, on this rather than that composer, on this rather than that historical era, or on this rather than that kind of problem. And our discussion thus far has been chiefly about piano music, which we are as a matter of fact probably neither puzzled nor put off by, and whose distinguished membership in our musical tradition probably very few of us doubt. We must now notice that all this preliminary ado about piano music indicates among other things that our musical tradition (of which piano music is presumably only one small part) must at the very least be a rather knotty tangle, which could comfortably accommodate a few more or a few less strands without perceptibly ruffling its texture.

Since we are having so much trouble with terms like "piano music" and "electronic music", let's try working from the other end of our title by getting a better grip on the term "musical tradition".

I. Musical tradition is the sum of all things musical.

[This one has the disadvantage of rendering superfluous all articles whose titles or subject matter take the form "X-Music and Musical Tradition". Attention shifts to the question whether x-music is a thing musical, a question that this one provides no means to discuss apart from an auxiliary discriminative definition of "things musical", a definition that would be indistinguishable from a narrower definition of "musical tradition" and hence a replacement for this one. This one is, in short, vacuous.]

II. Musical tradition is the sum of those things musical that have stood the test of time.

[This one is disingenuous, since it seems to imply that some transpersonal, transtemporal agency called "time" designs, administers, and keeps score for a test that can, in fact, only be designed, administered, and scored by us individually or collectively in the service of our own individual and collective present purposes.

Rebuttal: Wrong. The "test of time" is the continuing accretion of such individual and collective judgments, an accretion to which we may of course contribute but over whose general drift any "present purpose" can exert only a limited and fleeting control.

Counter-rebuttal: Evasion. The sole repositories of that accretion are individual present heads who can only see it as they choose to see it. The fact that each head may see it differently signifies not "limited and fleeting control" but rather the absence of any "it".

Re-rebuttal: But what if they see it the same? A high degree of uniformity among judgments from different heads is the assumed precondition for identifying tradition just as for identifying fact.

Answer: If it seems to you or to me that they do indeed see it the same, then you or I would have reason to conclude that either they share present purposes, or else seeing it that way suits a variety of purposes. And in either case, your or my purposes might on occasion be well-served by speaking to them as if it were simply that way, rather than by constant grammatically tortured reference to whatever set of purposes is suited by seeing it that way. The explicit spelling out of purposes becomes a convenience—indeed a prerequisite for communication—precisely when those other circumstances arise in which we see it differently. And not seldom we discover for the first time our own purposes in seeing it as we do when some new purposes—our own or someone else's—impel us, however provisionally, to see it otherwise.]

III. The past, like the present, is an agglomerate of small and large, individual and collective endorsements, conformities, indifferences, disconnections, and confrontations. Tradition, far from being a known existent thing, is a concept that we continuously invent, and whose application we continuously augment and revamp, in order to organize this agglomerate in our own minds for our own individual and collective purposes, depending upon what we wish to understand or advocate. Four examples follow below:

Musical tradition is whichever way of slicing the past makes what's happening now look

        (1) grisly.
        (2) good.
        (3) like a continuation.
        (4) like a revolution.

[These are familiar enough, with "1" being the model stance for clobbering the present and "4" for clobbering the past. To the extent that we tend to dismiss such views as mere ax-grinders, we may be making a serious mistake: these views have the virtue of dramatizing in full detail the purposes that inform them and hence make their internal relevancies and irrelevancies easier to assess. They also may induce in us a more thorough analysis of our own purposes in slicing the past and thereby dissolve any latent assumption that one may slice the past "impartially". The upshot of thus clarifying our own purposes will hopefully be the propounding of new points of view productive of more interesting and more satisfying ways of slicing the past.]

A final example similar to the immediately preceding four is provided by those definitions of "musical tradition" that familiarly arise unbidden from advocacy of future direction. (Lest a misunderstanding arise at this point, allow me to emphasize that I am *not* trying to suggest that "illicit" advocacy can "distort" our view of what our musical tradition "really" is. Indeed, I disclaim all knowledge of what anything "really" is. On the contrary: since "tradition" is a concept with which someone tries to sort out the past in a particular way and for some particular purpose, and since concern with future direction seems to me a legitimate purpose, I see no reason why the particular purpose at issue should not from time to time be the purpose of advocating some future direction.) Confronted by such advocacy, I would not say, "Your particular concept of musical tradition is vitiated by intentional orientation toward your vision of a desirable future." Rather, I would try to assess the scope and quality of the vision both in its capacity as a proposed future and in its capacity as an interpreted past. If the future proposed looked good; and if the past as interpreted looked coherent, elegantly detailed, agreeably documented, and interesting; and if the two were of one piece; then I should be hard pressed to find any fault in the advocate.

Still, I should take care to recognize the presence of advocacy. And particularly inasmuch as the electronic musical past comprises as yet hardly more than two decades, I would tend to suppose that most statements about what electronic music "is" are largely informed by advocacy of future direction, and therefore impose upon us a duty to assess the advocated future. Although I myself am not usually eager to advocate a future direction for someone else's music, I should nevertheless probably have offered at least two more versions of musical tradition:

> Musical tradition is whichever way of slicing the future makes the past look like
>> (5) prelude.
>> (6) a waste of time.

Not only the future, but even one's own composing, can provide insights into the past.

With apologies to anyone who may already have achieved these same insights by another route, I would like to describe a particular problem I faced during the three years I devoted to composing *Lyric Variations for Violin and Computer* (scheduled for release on the Vanguard "Cardinal" label).

The piece is twenty minutes long and consists of five minutes of pre-recorded several-track violin, followed by five minutes of computer, followed by ten minutes of violin and computer together. Such a layout sets up a very special and obvious problem at the beginning of that sixth minute: not only must the computer enter persuasively at that moment even though the violin has managed well enough without it for a rather long time; but it must then proceed to behave itself in a way that will make plausible a five-minute dereliction of the violin. (Getting the violin back in at the beginning of the eleventh minute was no soft touch either.) These problems were exacerbated by my determination to restrict the opening five minutes for violin largely to the more familiar kinds of violin-playing, and the next five minutes for computer largely to sound-events quite unreminiscent of any kinds of violin-playing.

In contemplating the dispiriting insertions and joints I had tried and discarded at that sixth minute, it grew upon me that this kind of thing had all been faced and solved before: specifically, in the Classical piano concerto.

Consider the magnitude of the sonic irrelevancies that might seem almost guaranteed to disrupt any attempt to weave the orchestra together with a mechanical contraption that may have its own special charms but that unfortunately can't do that rather pervasive and elementary musical thing every string and wind will be doing all the time: namely, keep a tone alive.

Now think of the last Mozart piano concerto, K. 595 in B♭. The same ingredients of disaster are all there:
(1) An initial decision to use both the piano and the orchestra for long stretches alone.
(2) An initial decision to give free rein to their grossly disparate idiosyncrasies, and the consequent reduction of sonic matching to a minor role.
(3) An initial decision to begin the piece with a long passage for orchestra alone and then to bring the piano in alone, and the consequent impossibility of cushioning the shock by separating the piano-sonority out from an initial tutti-sonority gradually over a period of time.

Then consider how we might construe the actual design of this orchestral opening as a cushion against that very shock a purely orchestral opening might seem to guarantee. First of all, the orchestral opening seems to make a virtue of necessity: gross sonic disparity *within* the passage is not merely cultivated, but is even reinforced at the outset by gross disparity of musical substance in the antiphony of strings and winds. Yet already within the first sixteen measures a path toward reconciliation of strings and winds is traced out. First, the registral course of the string melody responds to the registral layout of the triad arpeggiated by the winds; and then the dotted rhythm initially special to the wind interpolations is generated within the string melody at two successive registral peaks. This dotted rhythm now becomes the explicit common denominator in an antiphony that is therefore now sonic only, and that even occurs within the strings as well as between strings and winds. Furthermore, the previously stark antiphony is itself reduced to the milder antiphony of entrances only, with everybody sustaining and continuing thereafter. And all of these features of the dotted-rhythm "antiphony" are relevant as intermediate stages between the stark antiphony of the beginning and the tutti cadence—winds and strings doing the same kinds of thing (and even the same things) simultaneously—that now immediately follows.

The dovetailing of violin and flute figures to form a single melodic line, which next follows against an accompaniment in which the other winds join with the strings, may easily be construed as the next ramification in the continuity of antiphonal processes we have been describing—a ramification that initiates a new path along which sonic and other disparities are again gradually reconciled and reconstituted as the piece unfolds. And if the ultimate antiphony of the solo piano entrance will first of all embellish each of the opening half-notes of the originally orchestral tune with rhythmically compressed inversions of the melodic figure, which follows there as before; and if the strings then replace the winds for the antiphonal interpolations just as the piano has replaced the strings for the "theme"; we may surely recognize the symptoms of continuation of the process of development initiated within the purely orchestral opening itself. (The tone of this achievement is somehow inadequately captured by the usual observation that the piano enters with a reexposition of the first theme.)

I have offered the above personal anecdote partly to plug my composition and partly to illuminate my closing remark:

To contend that the past is dead is to advocate that we kill some part of our own imagination.

[jkr]

NELSON GOODMAN'S *LANGUAGES OF ART,* FROM A MUSICAL POINT OF VIEW

Benjamin Boretz

(For the Sixty-Sixth Annual Meeting of the American Philosophical Association, Eastern Division, on December 29, 1969, at a symposium devoted to Nelson Goodman's Languages of Art.*)*

To many of us in music, the virtues of a confluence of rational inquiry and art have long been evident, if rarely exhibited. So the existence of a book explicitly devoted to the epistemology of art by the author of *The Structure of Appearance* seems to us not only an imposing benefice, but an entirely appropriate one as well. We do not, moreover, share the surprise of some of Professor Goodman's philosophical colleagues that he, in particular, should have become engaged in such an enterprise; for, from our vantage point, Goodman's contribution to the metalanguages of art had already seemed a considerable one, long before the publication of his most recent book. And that it was an indirect contribution, a use to which his work was put rather than one it specifically proposed, in no way diminished for us the scope and explicitness of that contribution's significance to our art-theoretical concerns. Thus, before turning to the matter of *Languages of Art* directly, it might be useful to elaborate briefly on the nature of this antecedent contribution, so that the Goodmanian influence on the music-conceptual scheme out of which my remarks about *Languages of Art* emerge will be apparent.

Quine has pointed out that "the less a science has advanced, the more its terminology tends to rest on an uncritical assumption of mutual understanding". Given this observation, it is hardly surprising that the customary inadequacy of meta-artistic communication has resulted in the usual, though erroneous, attributions of cognitive indeterminateness to the manifestations of the object-domains of art themselves, an attribution which is evident in the prevalent practice, in the philosophy and theory of art, of identifying as the salient aspects of art almost anything other than the contextually observable properties of those manifestations.

Here another remark of Quine comes to mind: that "what counts as observation sentences for a community of specialists would not always so count for a larger community". The converse of this sentence is, of course, frequently also true, for many other domains as well as for art; but the particular failure of nonartists to recognize, and of artists to explicate, the intersubjectivity of the entities the observation of which constitutes the contemplation of something *as* a work of art of a particular kind, has made this fact a particular burden to the theory of art, as it is not in science, linguistics, or mathematics, in all of which the authority of competence is assertible in a metalanguage that is culture-wide recognizable.

But it is the explicative theory of art—not the theory of structure which may be understood as what is unfolded by a set of perceptual data selected and contemplated in a certain way which we may call "making a musical (or visual-artistic, or literary) structure of that data"—that has been in the primitive state characterized in Quine's remark. And therefore, those of us who have observed the cognitivity of music as a highly developed medium of thought within its empirical object-language have attended with increasing urgency to contemporary epistemology, philosophy of science, philosophical linguistics, and the study of formal and interpreted systems, to derive an explicative theory of music that might do justice to what may be called the "empirical theory of music" of which it would be a model.

Now the special character of art entities as entities has lent a particular art-explicative relevance to the literatures of nominalistic epistemology and rational reconstruction, quite apart from the positions in specifically intraphilosophical controversy they represent. Such relevance resides in particular in what Quine concedes to rational reconstruction: that "imaginative construction can afford hints of actual psychological processes". And since "actual psychological processes" are all there are in the entification of things as works of art, such reconstructions have obvious epistemic value in these cases. The nonimperativeness of the construal of any slice of sensory experience as determining an art entity and the determinacy of the entities derived from such a construal, as well as the variability of that determinacy with respect to the supposedly "same" entities within the range delimited by the "field"-term involved, are all aspects of artistic cognition that correlate with the methodological attitude toward entification adopted in Goodman's epistemological investigations.

Thus the replacement of the Given by the Chosen, or at least by the choosable-in-principle, is an indispensable practical concept in the perception and composition of art entities. What this concept enables, principally, is the awareness that the structure, or the identity, of a work of art is in the mind's eye or ear of the perceiver. And this consequence of Goodman's earlier epistemology is significant in that of *Languages of Art* as well; for example, in the explication of the dependence of representation on what Goodman calls the "non-innocent eye". But a further consequence of this dependence, namely the necessary presence, in the cognition of something as an art entity, of a *theory,* however internalized, of that entity's structure, is not explicitly engaged in the book; and this is a matter to which much of the sequel will be addressed.

The kind of analysis undertaken in connection with such constructional systems as those of Carnap's *Aufbau* and *The Structure of Appearance* also represents an intensely practical matter for art, since the very identity of an art entity is a theoretical construct quite remote from the pragmatics of object-identification in the physical world. Art entities, in fact, may be said to *have identity as entities of their types* just by virtue of being identifiable as interpretations of a general notion of *entityhood within that type*. Therefore, the extent to which they can be determinately recognized as *particular* entities of their types depends first of all on the *generality* of the concept of entityhood they are regarded as interpreting. And secondly, the degree of their particularity depends on the number of intervening concepts that can be, or that are, invoked between the atomic and the global levels, concepts which distinguish and order subentities as the ultimate determinants of the global structure. Thus the salient characteristic of an art entity may, most generally, be considered to be its "coherence"; and the *extent* of its coherence, and hence of its particularity as a work of art, may be considered to reside in the degree and nature of determinate complexity exhibited in the ordered structure of subentities of which it is a resultant.

Moreover, in speaking of artworks as such we denote entities which, though they are *inferred from* observable characteristics of particular slices of the physical-entity world, *are not* themselves, as art entities, *composed of* those slices. Rather, these art entities are, so to speak, purely phenomenal things, intersubjective in the sense of thoughts rather than in that of sounds and sights. Now here I may appear, contrary to my assurances, to be raising strictly philosophical issues of the nature of reality; but I don't believe so. For I mean to suggest that art entities are purely phenomenal not in the *pre-objective* sense that has vexed constructional systems with the problems of abstraction from particulars or of concretion from qualities, but rather in a *post-objective* sense, as constructions placed on intersubjective aspects of entities that have been *previously* identified as concrete, *however* that prior identification is understood. The component elements of such constructions are indeed *qualia,* which are indeed *with* one another in concreta, in Goodman's senses. But as qualia they are retreads of previously identified qualities, and the entities they determine are not concreta at all, but structures of selected, discriminated, and quantized relations of qualia *in* ordered successions of distinct concreta. In this sense, our phenomenalistic constructions of works of art would begin where Carnap's and Goodman's constructions of the world would terminate, had they been completed.

Sounds, then, are not part of music, however essential they are to its transmission. And neither are paint, pigment, or canvas parts of paintings, nor masses of bronze parts of sculptures, nor pages and letters parts of poems. Sounds, in fact, are not even what musical notation specifies, a matter which Goodman seemingly overlooks in his discussion of such notation in *Languages of Art.* What scores do specify is information about music-structural components, such as pitches, relative attack-times, relative durations, and whatever other quale-categorical information is functionally relevant. Thus it may be said that the notations of scores determine their interpreting musical works, and the performances thereof, to varying degrees and in varying respects, depending on the identity of the functioning quale-categories and on quantization thresholds that are functional within each category.

So the varying determinacies of score-notations with respect to various quale-categories at different music-historical junctures, which Goodman engages in his chapter on music in *Languages of Art,* simply correspond to the degrees of structural functionality that are at maximum assignable to those categories in those compositions, at least on the evidence of their scores. "Precision" of notation is, of course, relative to inferred "thresholds"; and a piece whose pitch notation specifies only "relative height" may be one where pitch-relational characteristics function only to within "higher-than" determinations. Thus such a notation would constrain the appropriate interpretations just to within the "higher-than" boundary criterion without any lack of music-structural "precision". For *any* interpretation conforming to such a criterion contains precisely "the" correct pitch-structural information for that piece.

Now this means that our present pitch notation is not necessarily *more precise* relative to the piece it notates than, say, that of pre-Gregorian chant, but only that what counts as compliance to it of interpreting sounds may be inferred as being more highly constrained with respect to their pitch components, and thus that our music *may* be interpreted as invoking *discriminable* pitch differences more *determinately* than just in terms of "higher than".

But even so, what will count as compliance to even a supposedly "precisely" notated score is relative to a theory of the structure of the work with reference to which the score-performance relation is evaluated. It is in the nonrecognition of this music-structural theory-dependence of compliance that I think Goodman goes wrong in his explication of musical notation. For whatever the *notation* involved, a listener to early church music conditioned to more precisely quantized pitch-functional music such as our own might infer that he was hearing *two different pieces* in successive performances that, under the pitch-quantizational concepts being used by the performers, were also noticeable as being performances of the *same piece*. One reason for this perplexity is, of course, that it is *sound-successions* rather than *notations* that are the real symbolic languages of music; and notes require prior music-structural interpretation to be regarded as *music-determinately* symbolic of sounds.

Thus a listener from an Eastern culture, learning that a given notation represented two attacks of the same pitch, might hear a Western-culturally "correct" realization of that notation as an "incorrect" succession of *two different pitches,* because his background pitch-structural vocabulary was more finely quantized than ours. For pitch-function assignments are *contextual,* and take place within thresholds that in practice enable such apparent anomalies as the assignment of discriminably different pitches to identical pitch functions, and of indiscriminable pitches to different pitch functions, depending on the *structural* context.

Similarly, the difference of a G♯-versus-A♭ notational problem as it arises with respect to a piano score and as it arises in connection with a violin score is not, as Goodman seems to believe, a question about pitch-function difference, but only an observation of the inflectional room left by our traditional quantizations of pitch-functional thresholds. Similar differences *within* a piano-score realization are assigned the status of "out-of-tuneness", which can be determinately distinguished from "wrong-pitchness" only by the operation of a background pitch-function reference.

Thus the notational question raised by Goodman of the relation of "wrong pitches" to "genuine instances of a musical work" is tied to the structural question of what constitutes a "wrong note" with respect to a given work. For the theory of the structure of that work, which is, first of all, requisite to determine what that work's *identity* is, will interpret some wrong notes as wronger than others, disenabling any correlation of "degree of nongenuineness as an instance of a work" with "number of noncompliant sounds presented". To give a crude example, say that one's theory of some work's pitch structure constructs it by means of just three pitch functions, which we may call "high", "middle", and "low". Then the *structural* limits within which notation-determinably wrong notes may still be part of a "wholly correct" performance of *that piece* might be considerably wider than the notationally determined limits; but such structural limits would still be *non-indifferent* to the question of "wrong-note" determination, even after that question had passed out of the range of the notational limits.

Moreover, the compliances determined by a figured-bass notation and a free-cadenza notation are similarly theoretical. By Goodman's purely notational criterion, only a failure to observe actually notated "facts" counts as a "mistake"; but a music-structural theory will extend from what is notated to what is interpolated, and, for any given performance, will determine how what is not specified is constrained by what is specified such that literal compliance to the specified entities is no more or less determinate of "correctness of realization" than is the appropriateness of what is *chosen* to intervene between them.

Thus I would argue that Goodman's avoidance of music-structural questions in talking of musical notation is not so much frivolous as impracticable; and in fact his own discussion does not fail to *be,* however inadvertently, music-theoretical. For what he tells us about the limits of determinability of compliance-classes for John Cage's notations is pure music criticism, since it really tells us what he thinks the ranges of music-structural determinacy in Cage's compositions are likely to be, with determinate consequences for the specific kind and degree of particularity those compositions are likely to exihibit as musical structures.

On the other hand, Goodman's allographic-autographic distinction is obviously useful; indeed, the problem of pure "autographicalness" has already arisen in connection with some forms of electronically performed music, although computer-synthesized electronic performances use a numerical, musically interpretable, allographic notation.

Now if my account of musical structure can be taken as art-typical, it implies that the "actual psychological processes" which Quine allows that rational reconstructions may "hint at" are, in the case of art entities, in fact *crucially determined by* those reconstructions.

The path and content of a hierarchical construction of an art entity, through progressive subentity articulation, determine the content of that entity in the only sense in which it may be said to have a content as a work of art. And the more such a construction proceeds through relational concepts defined in a maximally *open* way, consistent with the retention of the intuitive concepts involved, the more different-appearing things may be subsumed as interpretations of the same concepts, and, hence, the more works may be commensurable at the more levels of their construction. For a perceiver, this engenders the capacity both to "understand" a greater number of more unlike-appearing things as instances of a single art-entity domain, and to regard each such thing as a more individuated thing within its domain.

This consideration engages the most general art-theoretical aspects of *Languages of Art*. For it is crucial to the argument of *Languages of Art,* as to the above remarks, that what the observer brings to his perception of a work in the way of predisposition is a crucial determinant of what he perceives therein. But my remarks raise the additional question whether some aspects *of* what a given perceiver might bring to such a perception might not count toward the *competence* of that perception, as a perception of a, or in particular of that, work of art, and whether some other aspects of what such a perceiver might bring might not count as *irrelevant* thereto. A rough analogy may be the relevance of English-understanding to the perception of an utterance as an English sentence, as against the relevance to that perception of a disposition to regard English utterances as "sad-sounding".

This suggests that some kinds of "non-innocence" may be more sophisticated than others, where art-perceptual competence is concerned; and although Goodman and I seem to agree that relevant non-innocence involves previous experience of artwork perception, I would insist additionally that it also requires that such experience of artworks be *of* them *as* artworks.

Thus, in analyzing ascriptions made to artworks, we might distinguish between those which are relevant to them as artworks and those which are not. The issue is related to that of the interpretability and applicability of theoretical terms. Sometimes, for example, it might seem from the form of an ascriptive discourse that evidence of a certain type—for example, observations on the perceptual data *of* a work *of* art—could influence the determination *of* a truth-value assignment of a given use of a predicating term, when in fact it could not. In other words, we might distinguish terms whose uses *make a difference* to our perception of a thing from a *certain* point of view, from those whose uses matter only in the context of some *other* point of view.

To take a simple example, compare the ascriptions to, say, something identified as "Beethoven's Eighth Symphony" of 'This is sad' and 'This is in F major'. Now it would be as absurd to decide the question "This is in F major" by an audience poll as it would be to decide "This is sad" by surveying the musical data[1]. In which case, then, are we making a statement "about" Beethoven's Eighth Symphony? A popular way to resolve the issue has been to say that

---

[1]Goodman describes me (in his Reply to Benjamin Boretz, *Problems and Projects,* pp. 125-129) as an "ardent formalist" to whom "the actual structure of the work is all that matters". But since what I call "musical structure" is just the coherent juxtaposition of *everything* relevant to the identity of a musical work, I can't see what an "exclusive concern with musical structure" excludes. And I cannot imagine, as a practitioner of music, what significance might be attributed to a property of which it could be said that "works differing widely in detail may have the *same* property of sadness" (emphasis mine); the notion of "details that don't matter" in the ascription of properties to a work would seem to have a legitimate place only in an aesthetics of the immediate, such as is disclaimed by Goodman in the first paragraph of his reply, or in a study of art as inattentively or casually observed. In any case, I would not know how to distinguish "romantic poppycock" (Goodman, *ibid.)* from just plain opacity of reference, and the phrase is certainly not mine. If the matter is one of emphasis, it is no less crucial. For interchangeability under some descriptive guise is not necessarily synonymy, and the distinction is critical, for it has to do with what "makes a difference" to the perception of something as a (particular) work of art. For "differences in detail", which I take to signify specifiable differences in sets of data in any dimension, are determinable, whereas it is precisely the absence of any possibility of musically specific evidential support, pro or con, for the attribution of "sadness" that seems, to me, to place it well out of the domain of matters of musical interest.

Moreover, whatever the temperature of my "formalism", the notion that there is "the" structure of a work to be invoked is manifestly counter-entailed by the kind of Goodmanian theory-dependence that is explicated in my paragraph on Beethoven-vs.-Schoenberg experiences, whose consequence is a virtually limitless relativism constrained only by intersubjectivity and traditions of what is plausibly regarded as "art".

This obviously engages, too, the points made in the second and third paragraphs of Goodman's reply. In addition, I do not anywhere advocate the "direct approach" suggested by his first paragraph, but suggest rather that art-perception, like 'aesthetic perception', is 'post-objective', using qualities perceived 'quasi-analytically' in something identified in a *prior* sense as a physical entity—sound, bronze, inkmark, etc.

Finally, I do not make the error of confusing (perceptual) 'pitch' with (physical) frequency, however intercorrelatable they may be, but rather intend to show the vacuity of *any* notion of 'notation' independent of a theory of its 'linguistic context', a point which Goodman ignores in his reply as in his book.

the referents in the two cases are different, as those of 'book' might be in two possible uses of "This is a weighty book".

But here the problem is deeper; for how is the "this" being *identified* in the first place in the case of "This is sad"? The "book" model breaks down here, for no observation comparable to that which could confirm a porter's report that something was a weighty book could be brought to bear. And to bring the point closer to Goodman's investigations, how does an ascription like "high note" differ from one like "sad piece"? Goodman methodologically equates the "is a red book"—"is a novel" type of disjunction of our earlier example with this latter case: he suggests that "Calling a picture sad and calling it gray are simply different ways of classifying it". But what observational specificity is invoked in declaring a picture "sad"? Not "psychological", since that would have to do with making assignments by observing correlations with other people's assignments, not by observing as they do. I find a clue to this perplexity in our musical example: a "high note" is understandable as a hypostatization of observable relations of "higher than"; whereas "sadder than" is just as inscrutable as "sad". Another clue may be that such predications as "sad", of pieces, are invariably restricted to familiar musical domains, such as tonal pieces, whereas the pieces in unfamiliar domains like, for example, twelve-tone pieces, are more often described as "noisy" or in some other way that simply reports failure to ascribe identity.

The latter case seems to provide the better clue; for I think that the "this"-identification underlying the "This is sad" ascription is just a hidden music-theoretical one of the "This is in F major" type, just as the "picture" referred to in the activity of "calling a picture sad" is in a *prior* sense the picture that was called gray.

Now this means that the *whole* act of identification that underlies a "this-is-sad"-type ascription to works of art is, in fact, located in the data-discriminative domain relevant to the particularization of things as entities of certain types. As predications *in those domains,* the status of such ascriptions is thus as mere "proper names". For they are intelligible only as ascriptions to things to which prior, if hidden, recognition has been given as entities of the structural kind; but as ascriptions with regard to those structures, they are *empty,* in that they make no discernible difference.

Whether these ascriptions are metaphorical or not is, moreover, immaterial in the same sense; as defined predicates, they are systematically indifferent under explication: "higher than" could be called "lower than", as it was by the ancient Greeks, or "greener than", or "greater than", or "left of", without affecting the music-identifying question. The etymologies of metaphors, their "schema-transferring" attributes investigated by Goodman, are *heuristically* useful just to the degree that the transferred term-names can be determinately correlated with observables. Thus Goodman's explication seems essentially to enable the *elimination* of metaphors as special "types" of ascriptions to works of art. And in this light, the only problem with "sad" is that we simply have nothing observational to tie it to in either music or painting, and so it makes no difference to the music- or painting-identity of anything. In use, however, such "proper names" have *negative* value, since they serve to perpetuate the internalization of a perceiver's theoretical scheme and, hence, to minimize his competence. The world of the average listener contains very little music and a great deal of noise, a gap which he tends to cover by the invocation of picturesque placeholding slogans.

But to a more sophisticated observer, the space thus straddled is filled with so many determinate particulars producing such particular identities that the sloganizing terms actually do seem abjectly inapplicable. Like prescientific attributions, to natural phenomena, of anthropomorphic and volitional characteristics, predications like "sad" of art simply symptomatize an underprivileged *stage* of cognition, not a *category* thereof. How cogent, I wonder, would philosophers find the assertion about *The Structure of Appearance* that it was "colorful"?

But to call such predicates "supervenient terms" or "slogans" is only to characterize their inapplicability to art, not to explicate their cognitivity in *any* respect. To understand their cognitive status, however, I believe it is necessary to look to those domains where metaphorical schema transfer is part of the determinate identity of structures, namely, to the arts of language, as exemplified in literary structures. For paintings are represented by predicates like "sad" in literary works as objects are represented by color-patch structures in paintings, not as paintings *are* objects.

This last observation invites a confrontation with Goodman's notion of *representation.* Here again, I think that the epistemological interest of the explication is quite independent of its relevance to art-theoretical concerns. For the problem in ascribing representation to works of art as a primary attribute thereof is not uninterpretability or inapplicability, but grossness. Most of the attributes that distinguish a painting as a *particular* painting lie below the level at which representation is predicable of it; the situation is rather like that of predicating "a gas" of something where what was important was *how* it was a gas, whether it was *helium* or *oxygen,* for example. Hence I suspect that Goodman's principal interest was to explicate representation, rather than paintings. Otherwise I cannot understand why he would take such a complex "fact" about a painting as that it "represents something thus" as virtually "atomic" for it, without investigating what particularizes, determinately, that representation with respect to any other. For to say just that "awayness up" and "awayness forward" are "differently represented" from each other in a given *literature* of paintings is not to characterize what constitute the palpable determinants of even the observation that in a given *single* painting "things receding upward are represented as parallel and things receding forward are represented as convergent". That is, is not the level at which color areas articulate the visual space itself a distinctive determinant—for each single case—of the particular identity which is only loosely classified as "parallelism" or "convergence"?

Music's failure to represent, of course, has happily always been an embarrassment to the art-as-representational thesis. On the other hand, traditional music does reveal, at a comparable level of grossness, an observational characteristic that corresponds to representation in painting; namely, "thematicism". In both cases, it seems to me, such entities as "themes" and "represented things" are best understood as subglobal structural frameworks that enclose complex sets of quale-relations in mnemonically convenient form, as advantageous strategies in the optimal communication of the often highly complex structural identities of the global structures they articulate.

As to the predicate "picture of x", this, like the "theme" of a symphony or the fact that it is in "Sonata Form", can be eliminated altogether as a special stage in the subentity ascension. As part of such an ascension, it is merely a "proper name" for a defined predicate, with more or less heuristic value; as such, it may also function as a conceit, constraining the limits of what would count as an appropriate resultant, much as the "Mickey-Mousing" of literary texts in songs provides such external constraints. But as a significant individuating term for paintings, "picture of x" seems to me only slightly beyond the level of "oil painting", "landscape", "portrait", or "abstraction". Thus, again, I find that Goodman's explication enables rather the *elimination* of a notion than its invocation as a significant factor in the construction of art entities.

What then, do art entities *express?* Ideas of relation, I think, *particular* coherences, in analog form; and what they *exemplify* are their structures. That is, works of art may be regarded as analog models of closed formal-systematic structures whose interpreting entities express the relations of the formal-systematic entities through patterns of relative quantity of perceptual qualities, such qualities being quantitatively articulated by scales of measurement chosen by a perceiver. A "scientist" constructs an experiment to test "his" structure of the world against the measurable facts of observation, on the scales of magnitude relevant to the properties being tested for. The experimental complex is strategically designed to extrude optimally those properties regarded as critical. The composition of works of art may be described as the definition and creation of relational "universes" of elements in whose interrelations are embedded hypothetical properties of relational behavior; hypotheses, that is, of "what can be learned to be observed" on the basis of what has already, by appropriate receptors, been learned to be observed. And, ultimately, it is the reasonable possibility that, from the data he specifies, the relational properties he has embedded will be the "most favorably inferable" things, that justifies the artist's "experiment". In art, of course, all the "measuring instruments" are perceptual, not physical; but their measurements, on the quantizational scales needed to infer all the significatively embedded properties, are as precise and unambiguous as those of the scientist—which is not surprising, since the data relations were designed in the first place to be measured by perceptual instruments.

Moreover, the relation of the "analog" state of non-art-theoretical quality perception to a syntactically and semantically interpreted perception of those qualities as components of art entities seems to me to explicate the relation between what may be termed "aesthetic experience", on the one hand, and "art", on the other. I would liken an "aesthetic experience" to an informal act of "quasianalysis", in which the component qualities of concrete entities rather than their gross entityhood are what is being taken note of. Noticing the sunset *as* a certain confluence of a certain red over a certain spatial extension, etc., is an activity of the "aesthetic" type.

Art, on the other hand, uses these quasi-analytically derived qualities as materials with which to build structures, whose syntactically differentiated and discontinuous elements are semantically interpreted by qualia that are degree-ordered into differentiated and discontinuous *vocabularies*. Here, of course, I am engaging Goodman's explication of the digital-analog relation (157-173), which is for me not only the most enlightening passage of *Languages of Art,* but that which seems most directly to enable the connection of art-entity construction with the constructions of *The Structure of Appearance*. But Goodman does not specify how the connection is to be made, nor does he otherwise take note of it.

The final question that I want to engage with respect to *Languages of Art* is the analogy between verbal and art-symbolic languages proposed by Goodman. Again, we seem to invoke quite disparate desiderata and, accordingly, to arrive at quite different conclusions. Goodman locates the analogy in the problematic area of *reference,* the *aboutness* of language. This assignment seems entirely consistent with his concern, throughout *Languages of Art,* with representation, expression, and the "comprehension of our worlds" to which he refers. He replaces Oscar Wilde's epigram about art and life with a stronger one of his own: "Nature is the product of art and discourse". And throughout the book, the discussion centers on what is *in* works of art, while never once addressing the question of what works of art *are.*

Although he never says so explicitly, I wonder whether, as a nonspecialist, Goodman felt constrained to attempt a cognitive explication of what is commonly *said about* art rather than one of art itself, limiting himself to a rational analysis of popular notions about art, as reflected in traditional aesthetics and the critical and journalistic literature, rather than attempting to explicate the identities of artworks from a rational analysis of their perceptual attributes directly.

In any case, the trouble with regarding works of art as primarily *about* the world is that they are in the first place *of* the world. And in the sense that the world is what communicates through language-dependent perception, art works surely *add themselves to* the world and *use* the *ways* that the world communicates to communicate themselves.

The issue of the languageness of the languages of art clears, moreover, if we turn from the aboutness of language to the special entityness of verbal-linguistic things, which, like art things, are entities just by virtue of being inferred as such from aspects of concreta filtered through a syntax and a semantics. As such, they may be mentally experienced as *thought;* the same, I believe, is true of art entities. And the absence of "aboutness" in the languages of the musical and visual arts, at least, frees them from the constraints of conventional norms of syntactical and lexical formation and association. As a result, they are free to create their own norms contextually from much simpler perceptual-assumptive bases. Hence, for example, works of music are constructable with experiential realism from a general notion of "music" without the *essential* intervention of stages identified as, say, "tonal" or "twelve-tone", which would be analogous to the construction of a particular English utterance wholly from a system that defines "language" in general, without the essential intervention of an English dictionary or grammar.

Thus the structures of the "contextual" arts are like man-made possible "mini-worlds", perceivable and palpable, and yet not constrained by the exigencies and recalcitrances of the physical, constrained only by the bounds of human perceptual and intellectual capacities, which are thereby both demonstrated and expanded. This, it seems to me, is essentially the awareness that the epistemology of *The Structure of Appearance* has contributed to the theory of art, locating the relevant focus of such theory in the activity of entification and particularization by means of conceptually guided systematic construction.

Therefore, that art has fed back into the epistemology of *Languages of Art* mainly in the form of a *referential* theory is something I find deeply perplexing, and which I earnestly hope that Professor Goodman's remarks will help to explain. For even linguistic entities *refer* only by virtue of linguistic interpretation, so that, like art entities, they *are* something before they *do* anything. And I thought it was from Goodman himself that we had learned most lucidly that just *being* something is *doing* plenty already.

COLUMBIA UNIVERSITY, 1969

BENJAMIN BORETZ

(for a meeting of the American Society of University Composers, Dartmouth College, 1970)

Composing with Electronics:
Sensitive Mirrors for Subtle Echoes

The traditional electronic-musical lore treasures at least two distinct genetic myths. One is a rather deterministic story that begins from the development of electronic technology, whose very existence confronts composers with an inexorable compositional imperative: to compose that music, and only that music, which is expressive of and appropriate to the Age of Electronics; in particular, to compose that "kind" of music which, as the myth admonishes us, is uniquely latent in the medium, and so to conjure, as it were, the ghost from the machine.

The second, complementary, myth relates that the electronic musical media themselves developed as a direct consequence of the necessities of compositional progress; such necessities having been already manifest, and clamoring increasingly for recognition, in pre-electronic music of "advanced" persuasion. In this story, the shadows of music's requisite future are unmistakably cast in its past, either through sounds and surfaces already conceived, however subliminally, in proto-electronic terms, or through intricacies of ensemble virtually presuming the mechanics of electronic resources for their adequate effectuation. In such ways, pieces composed for traditional resources were already "straining" the ultimate capacities of their antiquated media to the inevitable disintegrating point. In particular, the music of "total serialism" and that of "total surrealism" were allegedly born yearning for electronic voices.

And so, according to the currently cherished dogmas, either the existence of electronic media conjured into being a certain sort of piece, or a certain kind of piece engendered the invention of electronic media. Now simplemindedness is, I suppose, among the principal qualities required to give myths their mythological power; but whatever their appeal in what is often referred to as the real world, neither of these stories seems especially plausible, in the light of either evidence or experience, though both appear to cover what are undoubtedly true facts of the case. We, in our awarenesses and interests as composers, however, might prefer to espouse some such story as the following: composers have ideas about possible musical images, and seek to ramify and project such ideas along lines that appeal to them, using any resources of ramification and projection, known or inventable, that seem favorably disposed to resonate those ideas. And so electronic media, having become available, suggest the availability of resonating possibilities already latent—to an alertly self-serving hindsight—in previous music.

Now a resource of musical realization, a mode of capturing and reflecting musical imaginings, is of course, in any instance of particular use, ipso facto a "musical idea", and an instrument or medium of projection is similarly a "resource of composition". But since instrumental technology is not, strictly speaking, musical technology, however musically guided any of its origins or applications may be, the instrumental resources envisaged by composers normally lie within the realm of contemporary instrument-technological possibility; thus their particular compositional application is what counts as the "musical technology" in question. It seems reasonable to say, for example, that the violin of Schoenberg, and by extension the orchestra of Schoenberg, are different *instrumental media* from the violin and orchestra of Mozart; and by the same token the question of how (or whether) Mozart would have used electronic means of sound production *had they been available to him* is a pretty empty one.

To us, then, the relation of electronic media and the music composed with them might be regarded not as a simple matter of determinism versus accident, but rather as still another facet of that complex inextricability of "ideas" from their "modes of representation" that is the most familiar and embracing fact of our musical lives.

Thus the question what specifically *compositional issues* are raised by the existence of electronic media might first be answered by the question what *but* compositional issues are raised thereby; further reflection might principally proceed from two observational perches overlooking the total musical landscape: the first providing a broad view of the directions in which compositional ideas have been lately modulating, and of a picture of the "compositional resources"—understood as I have described them above—emergent in recent music; and the second affording a view of which of the features and how much of the scope of recent musical developments may be significantly associated with the existence of electronic media.

What follows, then, is a very bare sketch of some of the configurations that might appear at the horizons of such a reflectively induced music-conceptual vista:

1. The process of compositional development—individual or collective—if it is conceived in accord with real and realistic musical practice rather than historistically—can be seen to result from, or at least to be powerfully assisted by, the practice of conceptually guided *abstraction,* addressed both to the "logic" of musical coherence and to whatever may be inferred as the "structural functions" that determine the identities of existing musical works. What such abstraction consists of essentially is the identification of individual "things" observed in a piece with members of a vocabulary of invented functional concepts, so that those concepts are considered the essential, or underlying, "things" of which the actual sound things are particular nonunique interpretations, or *concretions.* Just so, "triad" is a "functional concept", and "pitch-class C", "pitch-class E", "pitch-class G" are others, of which a particular three-pitch *sound* in a particular place in a particular piece is a particular interpretation. In such an abstracted state, the same principles are available to underlie new interpreting concretions, that is, events in original compositions, so that functions tied to a given set of particulars in one composition may be tied to a dissimilar, even a radically dissimilar, set of particulars in another composition.

2. In default of some acts of abstraction of this sort, even in just hearing music, there would be no structure, or character, for any pieces that was distinguishable from the simple self-identities of the single sounds, however observed, through which that piece unfolded. There would, in effect, be no identity attaching to "the piece" as such, that is, as a *particular* thing among things of a certain *kind.* The piece would itself *be* just a kind of thing, *sui generis,* and thus have no speciality beyond a categorical "difference" from everything else in the world. If we heard pieces that way in fact, we would have no worthwhile use for the word "music" as one with which to identify more than one thing in our world.

So it can be seen that abstraction is the stuff that ideas, musical or otherwise, are made of. The crucial matter for musical abstraction is to preserve with imaginative insight the intuitive essence of the properties being abstracted; and also to so characterize those properties as to suggest a maximum range of possible interpretations, marked by maximal divergence in appearance to any conceivable extremity.

3. Now without being too metaphorical, we could observe that the composers who have in fact penetrated to a particularly deep level of abstraction with respect to existing music have often produced music of especially radical appearance. The observed presence of such radical

divergences from familiar surfaces is the content of what are sometimes called "musical revolutions", or the emergence of what are in effect new musical languages. Notice that the result of viewing the process of compositional development this way is that a new musical language can be asserted to be a determinately intelligible new musical language, and thus to be revolutionary in a determinate and coherent way. Indeed, it is surely the case that to observe how something is revolutionary is equally to observe the substantive content of the fact that it is revolutionary.

4. In our century, the most conspicuous* result of such revolutionary abstraction has been the development of the twelve-tone system. In the course of this development, basic traditional notions, such as pitch identity, interval identity, and octave equivalence, have been transferred literally into the new context, while other, more complicated notions—such as concepts and modes of *reference* which relate the foreground pitch events of a piece to some inferred background pitch collection, and the significance of modes of generation of harmony and counterpoint—have been radically reconstructed in their transference to the twelve-tone context. To take a brief example, consider the notion of interval in twelve-tone music: here the traditional tonal notion of scale-degree relations, were it transferred without reinterpretation, would either seem unintelligible or make the music seem so. We could not, without disaster, use the *same* notion of interval for twelve-tone music as for tonal. But we can use a commensurable, and commonly grounded, notion, if we are able to conceive the scale-degree intervals of tonality as special interpretations of more general interval types, namely the so-called "chromatic" ones (indexed as numbers of *semitones* distant, rather than numbers of scale degrees). In fact, those who do try to describe twelve-tone intervals as though they were scale-degree relations of the un-reinterpreted tonal type generally find the task pretty awkward, and are often led into analytic, if not also compositional, anomalies.

5. A further stage in our reconstructed process of compositional development, proceeding by suggestive analyses of the structures of traditional musical functions, is the exploration of ways to give a high degree of correlation to structures in the distinct domains of musical articulation, while at the same time giving to such structures a high degree of functional independence, such that both the degree of correlation and the degree of independence are noticeably higher than in the existing musical literature. For example, suppose the notion of "counterpoint" abstracted as the projection of a total pitch complex as the apparent resultant of the conjunction of several distinctly unfolded

---

* though not necessarily the only, or the most worthy

pitch paths. Such an abstraction makes conceivable the extension of contrapuntal resources by varying, or multiplying simultaneously, the dimensions through which such pitch-path complexes may be delineated, in addition to the traditional registral one. Such a "composed" mode of projection is what Jim Randall was just now calling a "delivery system". So we find in some recent music distinct pitch counterpoints projected simultaneously by the interdependent operation of register, timbre, dynamics, durational sequences (or time intervals), and attack-style characteristics.

Moreover, if we define the notion of counterpoint at a still deeper level of abstraction, we might describe it as the projection of a complex of elements of a given dimensional type as the conjunction of distinct paths traced among elements of that type by means of identifiable associations and distinctions among elements of other dimensional types. At this stage, we might be able to conceive that a mosaic of paths traced through, for example, a complex of timbres by means of pitch or interval associations, or paths traced through a complex of durations by timbral associations, and so forth, might coherently extend the notion of counterpoint in an intersubjectively meaningful way.

6. Even at so simple a level of abstraction, the character of electronic resources suggests a rich field of potential new dimensions in which to resonate musical structures conceived contrapuntally: for example, spatial location, as front to back, left to right, or any diagonals within; rates and types of reverberation; pitch or amplitude oscillation; spectrum variation—the possibilities are constrained only by the composer's orchestrational technique and projective imagination. Encouraged by the availability of highly flexible resources of electronic realization, however, we can conceive of musical realizations of abstractions of considerably more radical natures, extending presently available notions of musical coherence over things of even more unlikely aspect. To take a simple notion again, what interprets "a pitch" in a given musical structure might range over any band of pitch, any mode of referencing fundamental-partial complexes once it is evident how the essentials of what count as "pitch-relational properties" (beginning with identity, of course) can be preserved; how, that is, the given interpretation—or structured variation of interpretation—is experientially consistent.

Thus if we "know what we mean" by the "pitch" function, the "interval" function, and the "octave" function, we need no longer be restricted to pitches, intervals, and octaves—or, rather, to the sounds that have traditionally interpreted those terms—as the invariable interpretants of those functions. For not only can we quantize the interpretations differently within the traditional domains (as in band of pitch-band of noise association, or non-semitonal octave-subdivisions, or non-standard octaves), we can cross domains entirely, by assigning a set of musical functions and their characterizing relations "normally" associated with a given domain, to elements of a distinct domain. In such a case, I think, we would really be creating essentially *new* auditory-conceptual domains to which the old names—pitch, timbre, and so forth—would no longer be adequate, or even applicable in any intuitively effective sense. But one can grasp something of the scope for imagining strategies and objectives of unfolding unleashed by such a notion by supposing how, say, the kinds of functions assigned to something we normally call "pitch" might, through an appropriately determinate definition and an adequately sophisticated sonic strategy, be assigned to something like what we normally call "timbre." We can, that is, not only imagine how such a conceptual redistribution might be implemented, but how it might be observable as a coherent compositional development despite the most radical departure from what musical "subject matter" might be conceived to be. Such a radical reorientation is, I believe, at the heart of Jim Randall's notions of the compositional suggestiveness of the phonic structure of natural language systems, just as I think many of the steps described above are already taken in music he has recently composed in which "pitches" and "timbres" in variable senses function as differential elements of an unfolding contrapuntal continuity.

7. Now from my characterization of abstraction and its formulation in conceptually guided definition and interpretation as an essential matter for both ear training and compositional revolution-making, I trust it has become obvious in what senses *electronic* media seem to me especially capable of fulfilling a crucial role in the future of composition and audition: in the first place, electronic media are to an unprecedented extent sonic mirrors in which the most wildly speculative notions of how a musical function might be interpreted and expressed can be given voices—and tested for veracity. And in the second place, the rich conceptual and experiential feedback that makes it possible to hear the echoes of such ideas through controllable electronic experimentation seems capable of providing a new impetus of immediacy and suggestiveness to creative speculation and imaginative formulation. For electronics raises the creative potential latent in devising alternative paths of abstraction, and in developing new music-relational types on the skeleta of traditional types, to the level of compositional reality, as the possible content of the possible musical worlds of our own immediate future.

1970

A note on "elide", "elision" :

For many years, and especially while writing <u>Depth of Surface</u>, I misconstrued the bite of this concept. I recall being taught, in highschool Latin class, to pronounce a terminal vowel followed by an initial vowel as a single syllable. The practice was called "elision". So far, so good: in my usage in <u>Depth of Surface</u>, elision will be said to have occurred when the last note of one musical unit serves as the first note of the next. The trouble starts when I speak of what was elided. My dictionary unambiguously identifies the casualty — i.e., the space between — as the what that was omitted, abridged, passed over, deleted, i.e., elided; whereas my usage identifies (incorrectly) the culprits — i.e., the two musical units fastened together tail-to-head — as the whats that were elided. <u>Depth of Surface</u> abides firmly by this (incorrect, but) clear usage. At Ben's suggestion, we tried "fuse" and "fusion" for a while; but I hate the rhythm; so we reverted.

—jkr 07/02

(1971)

J.K.Randall

depth of surface

in Beethoven op.22, III

1.

—(Graceflesh.)—

(Herein, the expression "...is...."

may be profitably construed as

"....may, from the point of view herein emerging,

be profitably construed as....".

IA. The second figure is prefigured in the first.)

IB. From an opening dotted figure which ascends scalarly

through the 3rd from D to F

is derived a turning figure,

whose rhythmic and melodic contour

fleshes a dotted figure which ascends scalarly

through the 3rd from G to Bb.

IC. To this derivative turning figure

is appended an F,

whose accompaniment

restores the configuration

in which the F of the opening figure ended.

ID. Such a peeling off of F

from the opening figure

is prefigured in the configuration

in which the tune's turning figure's fleshing F

concurred with the accompaniment's D-Eb-D neighbornote unit;

which was prefigured in the succession,

within the opening figure,

from D-Eb unaccompanied to F accompanied.

(Before F fleshed, A graces.)

IIA. (—*Within the accompaniment,*

three figures (: a Bb-C-D passingnote unit;

the D-Eb-D neighbornote unit;

a D-C#-D neighbor note unit)

were simultaneously elided.

IIB. *While the accompaniment repeats this simultaneous*
three-figure elision,

the tune starts to climb a 7th-spanning ladder of conjunct 3rds

whose bottom 3rd is the derivative figure's G-Bb

and whose top 3rd is the opening figure's D-F

up one octave,

and will successively elide three figures.—)

IIC. To a repetition of the turning figure

is elided a proliferation,

through turning contour,

of dotted rhythm.

is elided a turningdotted figure.

is elided

an elided twofold presentation

of the opening rhythm

within a single presentation

of the derivative contour.

III. That a scalar ascent from Bb to D should here span

a twofold presentation

<u>1.</u>

1. is prefigured in the accompaniment's twofold presentation

of a scalar ascent from Bb to D—

—at the moment of whose completion,

the turningdotted figure,

picking up and re-attacking Bb over D

> *(—ascending to D over Bb;*
>
> *sending its fleshing part A-Bb down one octave*
>
> *into the accompaniment*
>
> *to become elided back onto the G-Bb 3rd*
>
> *whence it came—),*

2.&3.

2. fastens to the accompanying D-C#-D,

> *by twice-attacked concurrence*
>
> *from registrally above,*

3. what has twice been fastened to it,

> *by elided succession,*
>
> *from registrally below.*

4.5.6.

4a. The attack-points of the opening figure

and of each (unappended) turning figure

spanned the 3rd to the 1st crotchets of their measures.

4b. The turningdotted figure,

matching the duration of the appended turning figure,

spans the 1st to the 3rd.

5a. A repetition followed by an elision

spanned the succession of turning-contour figures,

from appended turning figure

to unappended turning figure

to turningdotted figure.

5b. The turningdotted figure,

the last of the turning-contour figures,

itself spans an elided repetition.

6a. In the turning figure,

the (fleshed) dotted attack-rhythm

spanned the turning contour.

6b. In the turningdotted figure,

the turning contour

spans (an elided twofold presentation of)

the dotted attack-rhythm.

THUS:

—(Thus:

just where registral distributions and metrical boundaries

    are reversed,

the spanning/is-spanned-by relations

        of successional mode to individual figure

        and of opening rhythm to derivative contour

are reversed as well.)—

        <u>In the end is the beginning.</u>

To the elided top of the ladder

    is transferred

the scale-degree functionality of the bottom.

(The bottom is transferred into the accompaniment.)

) Flesh fastened: No grace. (

Looking backward from the top of the ladder,

disjoining

the opening figure's D-to-F pitchclass ascent

from its dotted rhythm

    (—repeating E-nat: completing the dotted rhythm

    without yet completing the scalar ascent—),

        matching

the unfleshed rhythm and metrical distribution

of the appended turning figure

    (—whose 1st-crotchet completion of a (fleshed) dotted rhythm

    was also followed by a 2nd-crotchet F:

    : an F peeled off from the opening figure,

    from the lower two-note first part

    of the opening D-to-F ascent—),

        transferring

the unappended turning figure's 6-7-8 scale-degree ascent

to the opening figure's D-F 3rd

    (—reflecting the bottom of the ladder in the top—),

matching

the duration of the turningdotted figure

(—which also completed a dotted rhythm

before completing its scalar ascent through a 3rd—),

completing

its D-to-F scalar ascent on a 2nd-crotchet F,

—the cadential figure—

refers back

through all intervening derivatives

to the opening figure

and restores to it

what had been peeled off.

The Cadential Figure: —Just here:

where the opening figure's ascending D-F 3rd

has ascended one octave,

the turning figure's ascending G-Bb 3rd

descends one octave

(—with 𝓕 still appended—)

(—with 𝓕's in both octaves appended—)

and becomes descending.

IV. LOOKING BACKWARD AND DOWNWARD

From the Bottom of the Ladder

: While the tune's turning figure's opening-derived dotted scalar
   3rd-ascent

(—gracefleshed—)
                              ,repeated,

puts the tune's second, upper, derived, 3rd onto the bottom of the
   ladder;

(—so put, the tune's ladder's repeated
lower two-note first 3rd-part—)(;)

: the tune's opening figure's scalar 3rd-ascent's unaccompanied
   lower two-note first part,

(—the accompanied other upper one-note last part
                        peeled off;

appended unrepeated to the tune's ladder's repeated
lower two-note first 3rd-part——)(,)

put out of the tune into the accompaniment,

repeats.

In The Middle of the Ladder

: While the tune's turningdotted figure's opening-derivative derived
dotted-repeating scalar 3rd-ascent,

(——fleshed——),

puts the accompaniment's whole repeated scalar 3rd-ascent

out of the accompaniment

up one octave

into the tune;

puts the accompaniment's first, lowest, only, 3rd

onto the middle of the ladder;

: the figure's whole fleshing part

(——the tune's turning figure's scalar 3rd-ascent's peeled off
upper two-note last part——)

is put out of the tune

down one octave

into the accompaniment.

At the Top of the Ladder

: While the tune's cadential figure's opening-derived dotted-
disjoining scalar 3rd-ascent,

(—ungraced; unfleshed—),

puts the tune's opening figure's scalar 3rd-ascent's unaccompanied
lower two-note first part

out of the accompaniment

back into the tune,

(—the peeled off accompanied other
upper one-note last part

(—appended unrepeated
to the tune's ladder's repeated
lower two-note first 3rd-part—)

fastened back onto it—)(,)

& puts the whole 3rd-ascent up one octave;

puts the tune's first, lower, opening, 3rd onto the top of the
ladder;

: the tune's ladder's repeated lower two-note first 3rd-part,

(put out of the tune

down one octave

into the accompaniment),

    (—the tune's turning figure's scalar 3rd-ascent's
peeled off upper two-note last part fastened
back onto it

    (—whence it came—)—)(,)

    (—the tune's opening figure's peeled off accompanied
other upper one-note last part appended

    (—repeated; put up one octave—)—)(,)

descends.

Just here:) CADENTIAL(

: where the tune's ascending D-F

has ascended

within the tune

and remained ascending;

where the tune's ascending G-Bb

has descended

    into the accompaniment

    and become descending;

: the tune's ascending A-Bb

        (—its wandering flesh—)

having descended

    into the accompaniment

    and remained ascending;

ascending back again

    into the tune's octave,

becomes descending.

)—unfastened,

      —becomes a third voice.(

2.

(Graceflesh.)

TUNE UNDER SCRUTINY

(Ladders ascend.)

descend.)

(Tunes ascend ascending ladders.)

descending ladders.)

descend ascending ladders.)

descending ladders.)

TO BE QUIZZED

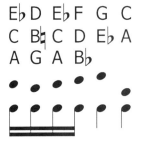

1. flipswitch

2.retro

1+2

2. retro

1. flipswitch

2+1

up the down
up the up

down the down
down the up

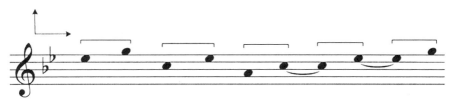

upside frontside
downside backside

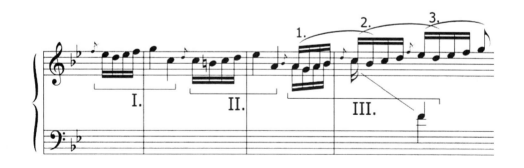

A graces F fleshes A fleshes.

Now F graces.

□A graces before F fleshes. □A fleshes before F graces.

□Before A fleshes A graces. □Before F graces F fleshes.

First A graces twice. □Second A fleshes once.

First F fleshes twice. □Second F graces once.

F graces
> > *D fleshes D graces*
> > > > *B(nat) fleshes B(b) graces*
> > > > > > > > *(G)*

Here, at the lower registral bound,

low G, fleshing,

lies within the gracing-fleshing time-span

and terminates this gracing-fleshing pattern.

𝓕 gr
    𝒟 fl 𝒟 gr
             𝓑 fl
                 (𝒢 fl)

flipswitch + retro
                     (𝒢)
        𝓕 gr
𝒟 gr   𝒟 fl
   𝓑 fl

Here, at the upper registral bound,

high G, neither fleshing nor gracing,

lies beyond

and terminates this gracing-fleshing time-span.

                        BEGINNING TO END

(—Graceflesh.—)

V. A1. In the 1st phrase,

the tune's appended F

lies registrally just below

the ascending ladder

    which it immediately precedes.

A2. In the 2nd phrase,

the bass F

lies registrally just below

the set of ascending and descending ladders

    with which it concurs.

    (—The only part of the tune's descending ladder

    which precedes this F

    is its initial 3rd Eb-G.—)

A3. Toward the end of the 2nd phrase,

the appended middlevoice F

lies registrally just below

the descending ladder

which it immediately succeeds.

(—The only part of the tune's ascending ladder

which does not precede this F

is its terminal 3rd Eb-G.—)

B1. In the 1st phrase,

the initially juxtaposed 3rds (: D-F and G-Bb),

by succeeding themselves in adjacent octaves,

created the ladder and

,between tune and accompaniment,

concurred.

B2. In the 2nd phrase,

whole such ladders

,in adjacent octaves between tune and accompaniment,

will concur.

B3. The tune's first ascending ladder

of three successively elided figures

began

over the accompaniment's repeated simultaneous elision

of three figures.

> > (Of these latter three,
> >
> > one succeeded (by elision) the other two,
> >
> > which concurred.)

B4. The tune's second ascending ladder

of three successively elided figures

will begin

,at the end of the accompaniment's ascending ladder,

by elision

to the tune's descending ladder.

> > (Thus, of these three ladders,
> >
> > one will succeed (by elision) the other two,
> >
> > which will concur.)

TUNE REGRESSES

C1. *The tune's 1st phrase,*

 after juxtaposing the opening figure

 and its most remote derivative

  (: the appended turning figure),

followed

 ,in its second half,

a three-stage path

 ,along a 7th-spanning ladder of conjunct 3rds,

from a less remote derivative

 (: the unappended turning figure)

back towards the opening figure.

REGRESSIVE TUNE PROGRESSING

C2. *The tune's 2nd phrase*

will follow

,but from the outset,

an analogous three-stage path,

again creating a 7th-spanning ladder of conjunct 3rds

—but with the three stages shifted in the "more remote"
direction

: so that the path will begin at the most remote derivative

and end (back towards, but)

not so far back towards(,)

the opening figure.

LADDERS REGRESS

C3. The tune's two 2nd-phrase ladders

will themselves follow a path from "most" to "less" remote:

: from most remote

(back towards, but not all the way)

back towards(,)

the 1st-phrase ladder:

: the first of them deriving from the 1st-phrase ladder

by transposition and temporal re-ordering,

the second

by transposition alone.

LADDERLIKE GRACEFLESH REPORTED
RETROGRESSING REGRESSION
(Enmeshed in the tune's 2nd-phrase ladders,

the ladderlike gracing-fleshing sequence

will reverse their note-by-note temporal order

at the pitchlevel of the tune's 1st-phrase ladder.)

C4. In the tune's 1st-phrase ladder,

the first 3rd carried the (rhythm and) contour of the turning figure;

the middle 3rd retained the contour of the turning figure,
and proliferated through it the rhythm of the opening figure;

the last 3rd retained the rhythm of the opening figure

(and carried its disjoined contour).

)—Thus—(

the first and second 3rds together

proliferated a contour,

the second and third a rhythm:

: so that :

in the ladder's temporal middle,

contents of its temporal extrema

elided.

C5. In the 2nd phrase,

the tune's descending ladder of individually ascending 3rds

will carry the proliferated appended turning figure
        from top to bottom;

and the tune's ascending ladder

will carry the proliferated unappended turning figure
        from bottom to top.

)—Thus—(

,in the temporal middle,

,(: the A-C 3rd, where the ladders themselves will elide),

the contents of the temporal extrema

(in the form of their common unappended turning figure)

will elide.

THUS:

(Thus: *: whereas*

in the tune's 1st-phrase ladder,

proliferation is partial (: of rhythm or contour),

local (: through just part of a ladder),

and occurs within the temporal middle

as the enabling agent of elision;

in the tune's 2nd-phrase ladders,

proliferation is total (: of figure)

and itself globally generates the contents which

,in the temporal middle,

elide.)

NO PROGRESS REPORTED

The conjunct 3rds of the tune's second ascending ladder
will be elided

(by the threefold proliferation of the unappended turning figure)

in the same sense
as were those of the first.

D1. But the individually ascending 3rds of the tune's descending ladder

(created by threefold proliferation of the appended turning figure)

are not susceptible to elision—since the note of conjunction (for each pair of conjunct 3rds) which

,in the ascending first and third ladders (: at the temporal extrema), occupied, and will occupy, the temporal middle,

now occupies, at the temporal middle, the temporal extrema.

D2. Conjunction of 3rds and elision thus divorced, a new kind of commontone linking arises.

Appended crotchets, no longer referring back to ends of previous figures, refer forward to beginnings of next.

And it is to this new kind of commontone linking that elision will be applied

when the appended F of the last appended turning figure joins the middlevoice return to the original pitchlevel of the opening 3rd :

: when the last appended F thus rejoins what the first was peeled off from:

: when the descending ladder of individually ascending 3rds, thus picked up by the descending middle voice,

thus culminates in a descending individual 3rd.

E1. In each phrase

    ,about halfway through,

the tune picks up something unfolded in two parallel phases

    in its first-half accompaniment.

E2. The moment of pickup,

    simultaneous with the completion of the second such phase,

initiates a concurrence

    ,within the tune,

of its own early-presented contents

—a concurrence which culminates in a concurrence

    ,between tune and accompaniment,

of the pitchclass 3rds of the opening and turning figures

    (with the accompaniment's 3rd for the first time descending).

E3. The first half of the 1st-phrase accompaniment unfolds,

    as two pitch-identical units (: Bb-C-D; Bb-C-D),

an ascending 3rd which the tune picks up

,at the moment of completion,

as its own ladder-component 3rd

wherein elision of contents is to occur.

TRIADS IN TUNE FOUND RETROGRESSIVE

E4. The first half of the 2nd-phrase accompaniment unfolds,

as two interval-identical units (:A-C-Eb; C-Eb-Gb),

an ascending ladder which the tune picks up

,at the moment of completion,

as its own content-elided ladder.

E5. (Concurrently,

the tune's three appended turning figures unfold

,in temporally reversed order,

all three (:F-A-C; A-C-Eb; C-Eb-G(flat/nat)) of the
accompaniment's triads.)

E6. But whereas the tune

,at the moment of pickup,

links its two pitch-identical ladders
(—through their temporally inmost common 3rd (:A-C)—)

by elision,

the accompaniment has linked its two interval-identical units
 (—through their common, temporally inmost, 3rd (:C-Eb)—)

by double-commontone re-attack.

—SCHENKER SAYS NO—

—(Thus: just as —and just while—the appended crotchets of the
 tune proceed from commontone re-attack to commontone
 elision with the middlevoice F-Eb-D,

the accompaniment proceeds from double-commontone re-attack to
 double-commontone (:F and Eb) elision with that same
 middle voice,

where the top 3rd (in the form of the passingnote unit Gb-F-Eb)
 of the accompaniment's ladder will overlappingly resolve (in
 the form of the overlapping passingnote unit F-Eb-D) to the
 opening pitchlevel of the D-F 3rd.)—

VI. In the first half of the 1st phrase,

tonic and nontonic harmony alternate

in the rhythm minim, crotchet, minim, crotchet.

The first of the nontonic crotchets

initiates the appended turning figure

with a 3rd-crotchet attack of G over Eb,   whose resolution,

already implicit

in the subsequent 1st crotchet,

becomes explicit

in the tonic 2nd-crotchet attack of F over D

which terminates the appended turning figure

and restores the configuration

in which the opening figure ended.

These two attacked 3rds, G-Eb and F-D,

which bound the appended turning figure,

syncopate

the minim/crotchet unit of tonic/nontonic alternation

against itself.

In the 2nd phrase,

terminating the two parallel phases

of the accompaniment's ladder,

Eb and Gb occur in the old register of Eb and G,

and in 3rd-crotchet syncopation

—but on successive 3rd crotchets :

: and resolve to 2nd-crotchet F and 2nd-crotchet D

—but on successive 2nd crotchets.

The rhythm of pitch change

(: minim/crotchet/minim/crotchet)

by which Gb-Eb thus resolves to F-D

is the old rhythm of tonic/nontonic alternation

shifted to the "3rd-crotchet" metrical position

at which the old resolution

syncopated

the minim/crotchet unit

against itself.

And the middlevoice re-attack of Eb
in the cadence

: not only :

refers back

to the re-attack of E-nat

during the ascent through the D-F 3rd

in the 1st-phrase cadence;   : but also :

confers the minim/crotchet rhythm

identically (and overlappingly)

as an attack-rhythm

upon each of the overlapping units

Gb-F-Eb and F-Eb-D.
[:crotchet/quaver=minim/crotchet?]

(MIDDLING)

(The pairing of D-F with Eb-G

which thus occupies the middle register

at the beginning of the 1st phrase

and the end of the 2nd

occupies the highest register across the phrasebreak,

where the 1st cadential figure's D-F

is succeeded by the Eb-G of the first of the proliferated
turning figures:

—: so that :—

the pairing

which occupies the registral middle

at the temporal extrema

occupies a registral extreme

at the temporal middle.)

Cadential:

1. *The figure now elided to the final Eb-G of the tune's ladders*

> *(: over bass F, appended to Bb-G in the 1st cadence's accompaniment)*

> > *restores A-Bb to G-Bb.*

2. *The registration of A-C*

refers to the A-C 3rd (over bass F)

in which the tune's ladders

were elided   *—in which the two forms*

> *in which the turning figure was proliferated*

> > *were elided.*

3. *The resolution of A-over-bass-F in register to Bb*

> *refers to the 1st cadence's middlevoice resolution*

> > *of that Bb over that F*

> > > *to that A.*

Having descended into the accompaniment

and become descending,

<u>4.&5.</u>

G-Bb has now ascended back again into the tune

4. and, as pitchclass,

again ascends

5.—but, as pitch,

descending then ascending,

then descends

(: so that,

just as dotted rhythm

is completed within the figure before G-Bb scalar pitchclass
ascent,

the registral path for succession of G-Bb figures

is completed within the figure before the figure);

and matches the metrically-positioned 6-7-8 of the 1st cadential
figure,

but on G-A-Bb;

whence it came.
}**The C is overflesh. [Cf. Minore.]**

(Others being underflesh like F (,□making references).)
The scalar pitch-contour gracenote-induced by figure-succession

<u>6.</u>

[Cf. ladder-elision's A-C 3rd.]
[Cf. opening-turning succession.]
6. *has become the scalar pitchclass-contour (:G-A-C-Bb)*
within the figure.

3i.

Allegro con brio

Adagio con molta espressione

Menuetto

3*ii.*

Fine

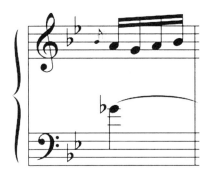

[Commentary by an anonymous scribe:]

1.   2.   2.   1.

3iii.

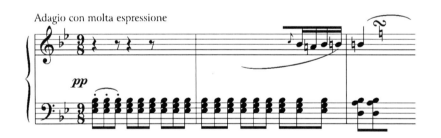

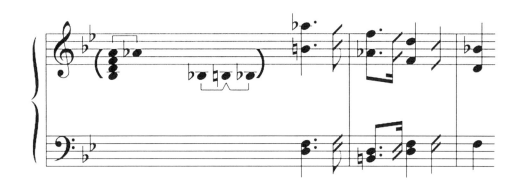

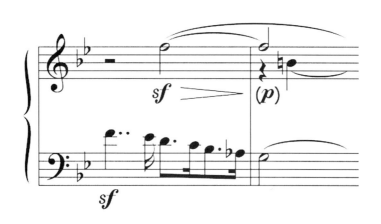

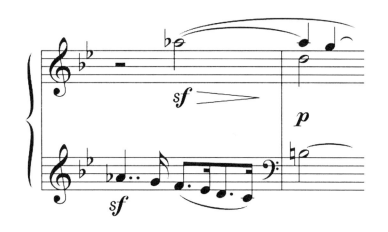

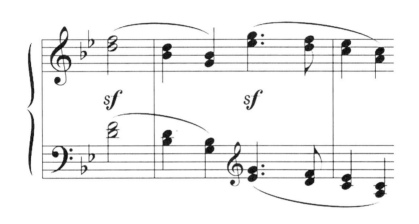

3*iv*.

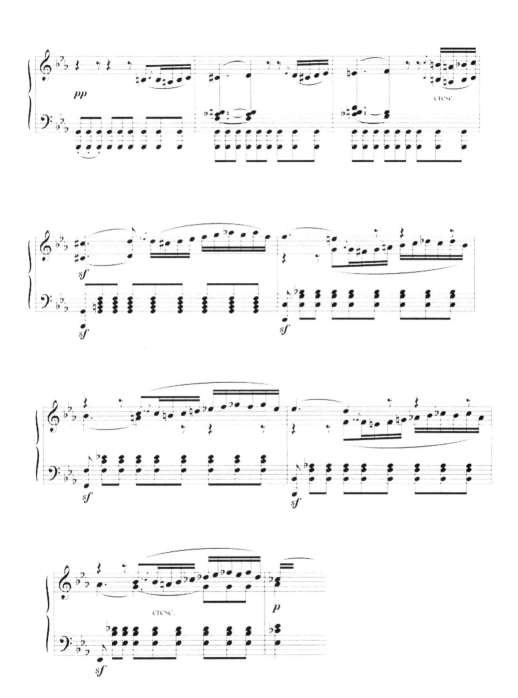

Rondo
Allegretto

written for the E.P. Dutton *Encyclopedia of Twentieth-Century Music,* 1971

Babbitt, Milton (b. Philadelphia, 10 May 1916)

[. . .]The significance of Babbitt's work in the theoretical reconstruction and compositional extension of the 12-tone syntax of Schoenberg and Webern, in the reformulation of the conceptual and empirical basis of musical tradition, and in his articulation of the explicit relation of the study and invention of musical structure to the whole spectrum of contemporary intellectual development, amounts virtually to a second 20th-century musical revolution. Schoenberg, Stravinsky, and Schenker, the principal architects of the first such revolution, reaffirmed, reconstructed, or replaced those musical "universals" on which musical thought had long rested, but which no longer accounted for compositional developments within the same tradition. Babbitt, with all of the developments of 20th-century scientific, philosophical, and linguistic study at his disposal, was the first to recognize the relativistic nature of such constructs as tonal functions and 12-tone relations. From this followed the further recognition that a musical composition might be understood as representing a set of interdependent empirical-rational choices out of a vast domain of possibility (and hence as representing a potential for uniqueness in musical identity far greater than had ever before been envisioned). In being so understood, moreover, a composition could come to be perceived, in a more than metaphorical or honorific way, as a unique and complex instance of rational thought within an empirical domain. Thus for Babbitt the force of any "musical systems" was not as universal constraints for all music, but as alternative theoretical constructs, rooted in a communality of shared empirical principles and assumptions validated by tradition, experience, and experiment.

Under such an interpretation, the invention of musical systems themselves becomes an act of composition rather than its invariant context. Even more significant for the music-conceptual scheme of the newer musical "revolution" is that the absence of universals virtually necessitates the notion of a composition as a "total structure"—that is, as a multiply integrated set of determinate, particular relations among all its discernible components. For since no principles external to the contents of a work can provide it with musical identity, no less comprehensive a notion of musical structure could suffice to account for the unique experiences and qualities associated with particular musical works, even in a superficial sense. Thus some of the most far-reaching and powerful contemporary notions of "musical structure" originated with Babbitt, quite apart from the particular systematic and structural inventions originated in his compositional and theoretical works.

These inventions themselves, of course, are the principal substance of Babbitt's creative accomplishment. But their individual ingenuity, which is their most often acknowledged and most frequently emulated aspect, is perhaps less accountable for the unique character of Babbitt's works than is the depth of creative discovery, examination, and reconstruction of resources of musical coherence, and of unprecedented numbers of levels of musical structure, all of which may be observed in practice to make a significant difference for the special experienced identities of musical works that the totality of his inventions represent. Thus, one may say that not only has Babbitt found unique ways to think about musical things, he has uniquely found musical things to think about, and unique ways to represent his thoughts in both verbal and musical formulations. And perhaps most significant, he has uniquely conceived each aspect of that thought in a context of significant and continuous interconnection with every other aspect of it.

To give even a minimal account of the nature of Babbitt's work, one has to go beyond the mere citation of individual attributes to the demonstration, however sketchy, of the significant interlinking of such attributes into a consequential chain whose totality constitutes a particular musical conception. For convenience in facilitating such a demonstration (i.e., rather than to create or resolve any substantive music-theoretical issues), it seems useful to distinguish three hierarchically connected music-conceptual levels on which Babbitt's inventions can be ranged: the *structure* of a given musical system, the *compositional resources* of that system, and the *realizations* of such resources as individual "compositional ideas" of individual works. In the first instance one is concerned with that collection of functions (e.g., scale-degree, fifth, triad, etc., in the tonal system; set, trichord in the 12-tone system), their relations (e.g., tonic, dominant, dissonance-consonance, etc., in the tonal system; transposition, retrograde inversion, order adjacency in the 12-tone system), and the properties of these relations. These functions constitute a set of dispositions to perceive acoustical events in certain ways as one would use a notion of "English" to hear speech sounds in a particular way and "French" to hear such sounds in a different way. The contents of one such set, then, may be considered to provide a *syntax* in terms of which musical ideas may be articulated; and hence, one may designate this level as the *syntactical* level of musical structure.

The compositional resources of such a syntax may be considered to consist in possibilities of association, connection, differentiation, and dimensionality available through the selective, ordered juxtaposition of particular functions and relations contained in the syntax. Such possibilities, of course, result from the relational properties embedded in the system itself; but they are not themselves part of the system nor is their exploitation in a given composition prescribed or entailed by the system, which is merely a reference for anything which might in fact be present. Familiar examples of such compositional resources are prolongations or triads by arpeggiation or *linearization,* as well as modulations, cadences, or *Ursätze* in tonal music. Finally the utilization of such resources in a particular ordering and by means of particular acoustical events in individual musical works constitutes the level of musical realization, the level at which specific composition and analysis may be said to take place.

For Babbitt, the study of the music of Schoenberg and Webern may well have provided the point of departure for his own original musical constructions. One can imagine how, in the early 1940s, he observed that the compositional connections—harmonic, contrapuntal, and phraseological—in works of Schoenberg and Webern could be regarded as projections of original musical continuities in a traditional sense (hence, as 12-tone *compositions)* through the ingenious exploitation of properties inherent in the structures of the particular 12-tone sets on which those works were based, as they related to the transformational array of sets generated by the structure of the 12-tone system (hence, as *12-tone* compositions).

To take a single example: the observation that the phraseology of the second movement of Webern's Op. 27 is defined by an obvious two-part counterpoint, immediate repetitions of single pitches, and large-scale repetitions of simultaneously attacked pitches is connected with the observation that this pattern is generated by a two-part counterpoint of set forms, such that the particular choice of intervals within the set, transpositional relations of simultaneous sets, and relations of successive transpositions of set pairs all have crucial and interrelated significance in providing the resources for the projected associations. A further observation on the music of Schoenberg reveals the congruence of phraseological and textural articulation with a harmonic association in which completions of 12-pitch-class aggregates in the total texture articulate simultaneous contrapuntal unfoldings of distinct set forms. This procedure, too, is discovered to be possible because of properties intrinsic to the structure of the particular set within the range of relations "prescribed" by the system. For given particular sets, particular intervals of transposition, inversion, and retrogression will make possible counterpoints where presentations of two or more sets simultaneously will result in nonduplications of pitch classes over segments of the sets.

Now both the duplication within a segmented counterpoint in Webern and the nonduplication in Schoenberg are seen to derive from a similar property, that of the *content invariance* of certain segments of sets given the existence of certain interval properties. Thus for example, if the first and second members of a certain set are related by a given interval (say a semitone, as C and D♭), and if there are two other adjacent elements in the set related by the same interval (say, D and E♭), then a transposition of the set by the interval between the first and second semitone-pairs (here two semitones) will result in the appearance of the pitch classes of the second semitone-pair (D and E♭) in the order position of the first semitone pair (i.e., as the first and second elements). Moreover a transposition by the inversion of the same interval (i.e., by 10 semitones) will result in the appearance of the first semitone pair (C and D♭) in the order position of the second pair. This property can be extended to segments of any size, such that the structure of the set can insure that various transpositions will have various degrees of pitch-class duplication or nonduplication, which then become an available resource for compositional articulation. The generalization of this property is greatly assisted by the discovery that the intuitive notion of interval identity is representable, with satisfactory results, as equal differences (i.e., pitches that lie equal numbers of semitones apart are heard as determining equivalent intervals), so that transposition can be represented by the arithmetic operation of addition, applied to numbers representing semitone (-class) relations of pitch (-classes).[1] Thus the powerful resources of mathematics in the investigation of relational properties can be invoked to discover musically intuitive resources of association. Such, and strictly such, is the role of mathematics in Babbitt's musical thought.

Our example proceeds: Just as transposition can be represented as addition of a "constant," so inversion can be represented as complementation or subtraction from a "constant" (i.e., the octave as a

---

[1]Babbitt devised the terms *pitch class* and *interval class* to represent the traditional notions of the functional equivalence of octave-related pitches and intervals.

"quantity" of 12 semitones). And so too can retrogression be represented as order-position complementation (so that a first pitch class of a set appears in the last order position of the retrograde of the set, etc.) and retrograde-inversion as both pitch-class position and order-position complementation (so that the complement of the first pitch class of a set appears in the last order position). And properties of interval invariance under these transformations are also discovered and generalized to reveal the particular relation of set structure to compositional possibility.

Thus emerges a notion of segmental invariance as a compositional resource of 12-tone-systematic music. And the special case of nonduplication of pitches over stretches of set counterpoints is generalized as a notion of combinatoriality. And the prevalence of combinatorial construction as a structural principle of Schoenberg's music is formulated, as is the prevalence of controlled segmental duplication in Webern, giving special musical meaning to the set-shapes and choices of transpositions in the small and the large in their music—thus articulating both significant individuating characteristics for each of the pieces involved and for the "styles" of the two composers and rooting these differences in a common resource of musical relation.

These notions, moreover, are highly suggestive to further development in composition. For example, Schoenberg's simultaneous counterpoints of half-set segments containing no duplications suggests the possibility of connecting successive sets such that the two adjacent halves do not contain any duplications either. Thus is created a new articulative resource, known as secondary set formation (see the first of the *3 Compositions for Piano* for instances of secondary sets). And Webern's notions of duplications, such that his sets tend to be constructed out of internal segments related to each other by the same relations (transposition, inversion, retrograde-inversion, retrogression) as those by which whole sets are related suggests the development of sections of pieces by the extension of parts of sets into locally "whole" sets by means similar to "derived sets" (examples of derived sets may be observed at the openings of the *String Quartet No. 2* and *Composition for 4 Instruments*). And noticing that what is true of elements of sets adjacent in order may be extended to relations of elements not adjacent in order suggests that a "counterpoint" made up from the presentation of a single set by stratification of its elements through different registers can be related to other such "counterpoints" in significant ways through the understanding and control of set structure. Thus are conceived various partitionings of a set in presentation (as for example in the presentation of a set succession

C, D♭, D, E♭, a "correspondence" can be set up by presenting C and D in a low register, D♭ and E♭ in a high one so that the temporal successions C, D♭, D, E♭ is partitioned into two registral successions C D and D♭ E♭, thus giving two significant motivic levels). One way of realizing such a resource of partitioning is that through suggestive presentations of background sets, significant instrumental and registral lines may be generated so as also to present 12-tone sets; thus the notion of set completion, derived initially from Schoenberg's counterpoint, can function on yet another time and function level of musical structure. (See, for example, the set partitionings in the opening bars of *Relata I*.)[2]

The resources of pitch association in music are, of course, realized through time. All musical structure is thus in a fundamental sense rhythmic structure. So the differentia among time intervals may also be structured through a syntax, that is, in a globally consistent way rather than in a locally determined, articulative manner. And similarly the other traditional musical differentia (dynamics, timbres) are also subjectible to structuring in this sense, such that a single succession may represent simultaneously a multiplicity of interrelated functions, a counterpoint of counterpoints in different dimensions, in which a single pitch attack may represent part of a pitch line delineated by time adjacency, as well as parts of different pitch lines delineated by registral adjacency, timbral identity, dynamic identity, etc.

But since durational structure is primarily defined by pitch functions, and since its properties are not inherent in the sense that pitch properties are, one's *durational syntax* is more variable from piece to piece than one's *pitch syntax*. Thus *sets* defined by successions of different-sized bundles of evenly spaced attacks (articulated by phrasing, accentuation, etc.: *3 Compositions for Piano*, 1), or defined by successions of "time intervals" between attacks *(Composition for 4 Instruments)*, or defined by variable articulations of the time contents of a fixed "measure" *(Composition for Tenor and 6 Instruments, All Set, Partitions, opening of Relata 1, and most subsequent compositions)* might function to generate the *durational counterpoint* of a piece.

The complexity and subtlety with which chains of musical reasoning are realized in Babbitt's actual compositions virtually preclude their explicit exemplification to any revealing extent in a limited context such as this.

---

[2] The notion and utilization of sets that represent each interval class as well as each pitch class uniquely is another of Babbitt's inventions (see, for example, *3 Compositions for Piano*).

The notions already mentioned are only a tiny subset of those he has originated and realized musically in a variety of ways so great as to necessitate deep study of many scores for the acquisition of even a superficial sense of their musical scope. Nevertheless a schematic registral representation of the first four "harmonic" (pitch) aggregates of *Partitions for Piano* may prove suggestive (Ex. 1); notice in particular pitch and interval contents of registral lines, dimensions of registral lines in each partition and in each pair of partitions (they all sum to 6 in pairs), contents of total-successional lines, harmonic content of local groups, and registral successions across set-counterpoint boundaries, which by virtue of the contents and dimensions of the individual partitions result in the presentation of a linear aggregate (set) in each registral voice.

AGGREGATES	REGISTERS		NUMBER OF ELEMENTS
I	1	E (E)(E)	1
	2	B (B) (B) D---Bb	3
	3	Eb Ab F#-F(F)C#	5
	4	C G--A (A)	3
II	1	C# F (F)F#G#D#(D#)	5
	2	A G (G) C (C)	3
	3	E	1
	4	Bb D B	3
III	1	A (A) D C	3
	2	F# (F#)C#(C#) Eb E	4
	3	Bb G B	3
	4	F Ab	2
IV	1	B G (G)Bb(Bb)	3
	2	Ab F(F)(F)(F)	2
	3	C D (D D) (D)A(A)(A)	3
	4	E Eb Db Gb	4

Ex. 1.

The compression and ramification in this partial representation of a fragment and the narrow conceptual slice offered in the narrative account preceding may be taken as indicators of the protean scope of Babbitt's work. Even at this early date that work appears to have extended the musical universe in a multitude of directions and respects and has taken it near to the bounds of human conceptual and perceptual capacity, while taking it near as well to the heights of contemporary intellectual accomplishment.

Benjamin Boretz, 1971

PREFACE

(for Perspectives on Contemporary Music Theory, *co-edited by Benjamin Boretz and Edward T. Cone)*

THIS BOOK, the first of several devoted to aspects of contemporary music theory, celebrates in particular the engagement by composers in fundamental music-theoretical explication, although not only composers are represented among its contributors. The recognition of music-theoretical questions as critical compositional ones is not, of course, unique to the twentieth century, nor to composers. But the uniquely explicit, uniquely consequential, and uniquely exposed contemporary involvement of composers in theory as writers and system builders has given the theoretical-compositional connection unprecedentedly wide, if not always benign or even accurate, publicity: we live, as every reader of the public musical print knows, in an age of "theoretical composition". Yet this characterization seems oddly skew to the actual singularities of the contemporary theory-composition relation: it is scarcely that compositions have become in any observable way more "theoretical", but rather that theory has become radically more "compositional". Surely the unique "theoreticalness" of the musical present is not to be found in any of those anciently familiar phenomena of conformity in composition to the supposedly transcendent authority of externally imposed theoretical principles, be they those of a Zarlino, a Fux, a Rameau, a Sechter, a Gédalge, a Hindemith, or a Schillinger. On the contrary, the demand of contemporary composers has been for the formulation of *adequate* theoretical principles, principles in conformity with what they know and need empirically, and capable of accounting for and supporting all the complexity, depth, and scope of what is musically actual, potential, and problematic.

That such a demand should be the particular child of our century is plausible, in view of the musical crisis precipitated by the appearance of extraordinary compositional events following a long habituation to a stable and powerful tradition. For the very inexplicability of these events at the moment of their appearance exposed brutally the inadequate conceptual and empirical scope of existing traditional theory, even in its function as the theory of the existing musical tradition, by revealing its powerlessness to render them explicable, to account for them as departures by extension rather than discontinuity from that tradition. To the composers thus left stranded by what was supposedly the intellectual foundation of the very tradition in which their own compositional thought had matured, and to which it was still committed, the issue must have hardly seemed one of ideological or pedagogical nicety, but of sheer musical survival. The virtually "metaphysical" problem that the failure of their own theory must have represented to them is probably inconceivable to composers of the pluralistic, relativistic 1970s. But surely there has never been a more heartfelt need in the history of music than that of composers like Schoenberg for an adequate theory of musical structure.

Schoenberg in particular, and by his own account, felt himself utterly abandoned to conceptual isolation and empirical self-reliance by the failure of any available account of traditional music to provide a coherent reference for the developments taking place within his own work. And since Schoenberg, like Schenker, had grown up in a world where the precepts of tonality were the only musical "universals", it is natural that his theoretical preoccupation should, like Schenker's, have been the elucidation of still deeper universals which, in being derived from a searching re-examination of the traditionally unimpeachable literature, would serve to "justify" a given compositional context. That this context was tonality, for Schenker, may suggest that, say, Brahms's enthusiasm for his work had a deeper compositional relevance than the mere communing of shared traditionalist prejudices. And that for Schoenberg it was the supposed "motivicism" of all music served his obviously profound need to have the history of music come out "inevitably" his way.

In this, Schoenberg, despite the deterministic surface of his prose, behaved theoretically, as he continued to behave compositionally, in a truly empiricist spirit. To be sure, the effort was metaphysical "justification"; but it was justification sought for the affirmation of what was, rather than its denial, or the legislation of what was to be. Hindemith, by contrast, for all his vaunted practicality, was as a theorist, and ultimately as a composer, a radical idealist rather than an empiricist. For the principles Hindemith derived from his own scrutiny of musical tradition were offered as ideological prescriptives of transcendent authority, immune from empirical correction; and their effect was not explicative or suggestive but imperative, for both composition and evaluation.

In Schoenberg's theoretical quest, moreover, one can discern the spirit of what might be termed the *Bauhaus* mentality, which in turn reflected, however hazily, the philosophical Vienna Circle's ideal of "unified science". For the musical Vienna Circle's aspiration to a reintegration of the shattered musical literature into "one music" again is remote only in verbal surface from the philosophical notions of "one scientific language", of one mode of representation for all cognitive human endeavors, and indeed of the very equivalence of "cognitivity" and "experiencability" that pervades the writings of Schlick, Neurath, Carnap, and Wittgenstein.

This extraordinary correspondence of intellectual developments on either side of a chasm of mutual ignorance, which were yet almost literally opposite sides of a single street, strenuously tempts nostalgic speculation regarding the amount of conceptual anguish Schoenberg might have been spared had he shared the epistemological and methodological discoveries of his Viennese co-habitants. But, in fact, the explicit relation of the study of musical structure to the whole spectrum of contemporary intellectual development was an insight of a later generation of composers. Milton Babbitt, in particular, was the first to suggest that the force of any "musical systems" was not as universal constraints for all music but as alternative theoretical constructs, rooted in a communality of shared empirical principles and assumptions validated by tradition, experience, and experiment. Under such an interpretation, the invention of musical systems is itself seen to be part of the creative resource of composition, rather than its invariant context. And the remarkable structural power of the (Schenker-) tonal and (Schoenberg-) twelve-tone systems, revealed under Babbitt's explicit and implicit analyses of them as empirical-theoretical systems in the classic scientific mold, served not as demonstrations of the universal validity sought for them by Schenker and Schoenberg, but as standards of depth, resource, and relevance against which to assess the music-structural inherences of any hypothesized or presented instances of systematic invention. An even more radical relativism, in which standards of musical cognitivity are still further detached from universals—among others, from those extramusically invoked standards of "unified science" themselves—is suggested in the writings of some younger composers (cf. the essays by Randall and Boretz in the present volume).

Alongside, and often in explicit criticism of, such contextualism, a more strictly "classical" traditionalism has also been developing as a rationalized compositional position. This position, in its contemporary form, was initially inferable from the early, and influential, critiques by Roger Sessions of the writings of Schenker, Schoenberg, and Hindemith. Its individuating characteristic is the conviction that the continuity of compositional tradition depends crucially on the retention of traditional musical appearances in the surfaces of texture, succession, contour, and sonority, and that the continuity of theoretical tradition requires as well the conservation of traditional models and terms. The fuller articulation and ramification of the consequences of such beliefs for composition, performance, analysis, and pedagogy have been undertaken by some of Sessions's younger colleagues, including Arthur Berger, Edward T. Cone, and Peter Westergaard, among those who have contributed extensively to the prose literature (and to the present volume).

There are, moreover, other uniquely twentieth-century modes of theorizing about music, not necessarily concerned with the predominantly "inward" issues that occupy all the multiple facets of what may be considered the "Brahms-Schenker-Schoenberg" tradition. The most spectacular of these modes, undoubtedly, is a "radical historicism" whose origin may be in Wagner's polemical prose (rather than in his musical practice). Such theory tends to view "tradition" as an ideological position, as a set of merely conventional constraints reflecting an exterior *Zeitgeist*. Musical "progress", then, depends not on renewal and reconstruction but on the wholesale replacement of these conventions by alternative constraints equally, but more "relevantly", ideological in their supposed conformity to a contemporary complex of metaphysical, socio-cultural, political, or psychological dynamics. The scope of this tradition is considerable: its fundamental premises are shared by the speculations and proposals regarding inner musical resources and outer musical "functions" emanating from such manifestly divergent composers as Busoni, Varèse, the Futurists, the Dadaists, Ives, Seeger, Cowell, Partch, and, more recently, the exponents of "total serialism", "indeterminacy", "microtonalism",—and the various "temperaments" (cf., in the present volume, the essays by Boulez and Stockhausen). Although much of the literature associated with this mode of theorizing is polemical rather than rationalized, which seems a natural effect of its deterministic, populistic, and speculative biases, it is in fact defensibly "theoretical" in the sense being employed here, for the reflection of its explicit compositional concerns in correlative characteristics of musical surface and structure is undeniable.

Neither these remarks, nor the collection of essays that follows, reflect any effort to survey exhaustively the "tendencies" or the significant instances of this remarkable theoretical output. The principal point we hope to make, beyond the intrinsic intellectual and musical significance of the essays contained herein, is that the vitality and diversity of contemporary music theory is comparable to, and—more pertinently—closely aligned with, that of composition itself. And while much of this theory has revealed, retrospectively as it were, the extent to which our experience of traditional music itself would have been impoverished in the absence of an adequate theoretical-conceptual framework, it has even more crucially revealed how our experience of and within contemporary music would, in such an absence, have been virtually inconceivable.

(with Edward T. Cone)
New York, December 1971

[jacket notes for IMPROVISATION on a poem by e.e.cummings
on CRI]

    My IMPROVISATION should seem very much the poem speaking.
Not something being done with (or to) a text. Nor someone delivering the
poem. (Please read it.) Not vocalisation packaging phonemes as timbre; or
aping the rhythms and contours of "natural" speech either. (Nor like a
Syllable Count.) And certainly not like music going like music goes, fending
off (for both's sake) some debris of what once was language. Nor known
words speaking, except as carriers of a meaningrhythm evolving as the
poem's own vocabulary evolves as the poem speaks: (words in a vocabulary
evolved along some finely erotic edge of what once was mystic; somewhere
i have never travelled). Like rhythms of grammar made flesh. (Nor does
the title report the method of composition.)

                                          —JKR

in Quest
of the Rhythmic Genius

Consider a Stravinsky memorial framed to celebrate his genius as a rhythmic inventor: (Stravinsky's rhythm: a natural perspective from which to memorialize him: it focused his first notoriety, and remained all his life the principal public token of his compositional originality; was it not, too, the immediate locus of that sharp awareness of rhythm as a vital, independent dimension of musical invention and experience which seemed so imminent early in this century, and has become so manifest?)

One would wish, at the outset, to focus on some instances of his singular rhythmic invention: (exemplification is clearly indispensable here: for how eulogize a rhythmic genius except in the presence (at least implied, at least ostensively displayed) of rhythms he may be said to have invented; or, not to put too fine an ontological point on it, the presence of something plausibly isolated as the rhythmic constituent of some passage of his music; or, even, the presence of some passage of his music whose overall identity arises most overtly from its rhythmic characteristic?)

Perplexity, however, unexpectedly intervenes: (is it obvious what to display—*what* to count, that is, *as* a rhythm, or even what *sort* of thing to so count? Does believing "Stravinsky was a great master of rhythmic invention" imply believing that he invented "great rhythms"? And how does singling out his rhythmic invention distinguish him: does it, perhaps incautiously, imply the inferior originality of the rhythms of Bach, Haydn, Mozart, Beethoven, Wagner, Brahms; or does it imply that Stravinsky's music is less remarkable in its non-rhythmic than in its rhythmic aspects? Suppose (after following such a deliberative path past the observation that, clearly, rhythms are "things" in a sense quite different from that in which pitches are, or timbres, or melodies) rhythms come to be regarded as *patterns* of relative duration, determined by the timelengths occupied by discrete subsegments of a timespan totality. Or suppose, rather, that rhythms are understood to be *instances* of such patterns: the timelength pattern exhibited by an (auditory) succession, whatever the (auditory) character of its constituents, is the (musical) rhythm of that succession. It follows, then, that anything auditory that exhibits that timelength pattern embodies that rhythm. And a "great rhythm" will always be recognizable and experienceable as such—and as itself—under all such transformations in embodiment.)

The intuitive uncertainty of this proposition may be resolved by an experiential test: (suppose the chord-repeating opening of the Dance of the Adolescents *(Sacre du Printemps, No. 13)* to be illustrative of a Stravinskyan rhythmic invention. By the proposed characterization, its rhythmic identity should be preservable in a transcription for, say, tom-tom solo. But new difficulties arise as soon as we try to perform the test: what counts as "a transcription of the passage for tom-tom solo," with respect to "preserving the rhythm"? What are the things whose durations project the pattern that is experienced here as "the rhythm": the individual chords (all evenly spaced); the chord-stretches articulated by accents and horn doublings; or? Is, then, the relevant tom-tom transcription: 1. a string of 32 undifferentiated eighth-note-apart attacks; or 2. a string of 6 attacks spaced as are the 6 horn-doubled, accented chords? Perhaps both patterns are crucial "rhythms of the passage"; perhaps only their polyphony can reenact the total rhythmic event. Perhaps the relevant transcription combines 1. and 2.: a tom-tom duet, one of whose parts contains 32 evenly spaced eighth-note-apart attacks, while the other contains 6 attacks spaced as are the 6 horn-doubled, accented chords.)

In performance, how likely does it seem that any Sacre*-innocent listener to any of these versions will experience what "the rhythm at the opening of the Dance of the Adolescents" is meant to signify?* (Would a piano transcription be an improvement; but not an unqualified success? And does the answer suggest that the pitches of the chords, registered as string and horn sounds, bluntly detached by all-downbow articulation, and—even perhaps—set in the context of the preceding and following *Sacre*-stretches—does it suggest that these all figure, to varying degrees, in what is mentally indexed as the "rhythmic feel" of these measures?)

Here, perhaps, a comparative examination of an unquestionable instance of "pure rhythm" could be revealing: (the contents of a recording of African drums in concert qualifies as not only a classic, but an obvious test: what but "pure rhythm" is there to respond to? What experience but a purely rhythmic one is possible? For answer, try a transcription for clavichord, or one for chicken feathers scratching glass: does the response to pure rhythm now seem separable from the responses to drum timbres, pitches, polyphonies of these, or even perhaps extramusical predispositions; if this is an instance of what is meant by "throbbing rhythms", in what sense can it be the *rhythms* which are said to throb?)

Some tentative hypotheses may now emerge: (1. the intuitive content of "a rhythm" seems sometimes to include coincidences of several rhythms simultaneously unfolded; 2. the intuitive sense of "a rhythmic identity" of some stretch of music, its characteristic quality as a rhythmic event, arises not only from the pattern-of-duration complex observed but also, crucially, from the special disposition of that complex relative to significant functional events in other auditory dimensions.)

These may bring the notion of "rhythmic invention" to a broader, if not a sharper, focus: (1. perhaps the rhythmic stratum of a total musical structure is isolable by slicing, out of the totality, just its durational components. Then, the independent disposition of these components in pattern-of-duration complexes might indeed be regarded as the "rhythmic structure" of the whole. Like the pitch structure or the timbral structure, the rhythmic structure, just in that it may be determinately isolated, is externally independent; but its contextual identity, its identity as a particular musical rhythm, is dependent on a specific interaction with all the other functioning strata of the whole.

2. Rhythmic invention, then, involves *both* the projection of a particular "rhythmic structure" *and* a particular association of this structure with a complex of structures in other dimensions of musical perception.)

Which represents progress: (a virtue of the above characterization is that it enables one to account consistently both for the strong intuitive unease felt about the rhythmic identities of the attempted transcriptions (out of context, the "same" rhythms produce different "rhythmic effects"), and the equally strong certainty that the observable rhythms of the original were in fact being transcribed with demonstrably literal veracity (the transcription events match the original events one to one in a determinately consistent way).)

Notice, however, that the proposed characterization conceals an assumption that "durational components" are analogous (in at least their independent isolability) to pitch components, timbral components, et al.: (concede that simple patterns of attack duration are only the most immediate aspect (and often, as in the *Sacre* example, a trivial aspect) of the significant pattern-of-duration totality identified here as "rhythmic structure," and the assumption of parity or analogy is seen to be suspect. For even under the "neutral" definition proposed, a rhythm is always a rhythm *of* something. That is, the "patterns of duration" that have been mentioned are *determined by* the relative times between the initiations of successive things; in music, this priority of determinacy is substantive, and thus a musical duration is necessarily the duration of *something*. And apart from "attacks" (which may be identified with the atomic "sounds" of a musical context), the musical "things" that have durations are determined by functionally guided slicings in the non-rhythmic strata: pitch things, timbre things, registral things, etc., and their complexes (for example, pitch-timbre things). Patterns of durations, moreover, are individually derived from uniform thing-type successions: the *Sacre* example counterpoints a "rhythm of all attacks" with a "rhythm of horn-doubled and accented attacks." "Phrase rhythm" is thus a rhythm of things which are themselves composed of complexes of counterpoints and successions of sub-things, typically in several strata.)

Hence the analogy appears to be unwarranted: (for while durations are independently specifiable, the question which durations it is relevant to specify hangs on a *prior* identification of the things of which they are durations; and these things depend for *their* identification on observed functional activity in dimensions other than that of duration. So the durations in a piece cannot even be identified beyond the one-attack-at-a-time level, along with whatever larger-scale uniformities the attack-scheme projects independently, prior to the determination of a functional basis for events in at least one of those dimensions in which things are to be independently observed, or whose components are crucially involved in the determination of complex events. How could a tremolo unfolding of a single chord be distinguished durationally from a fast alternation of chords, prior to the observational operation of a functional concept of pitch relations? And how could "events" such as phrases, chord successions, etc., be distinguished observationally except by the operation of a theory, however subliminal, of tonal function? And without a whole battery of functional discriminations of dynamics, timbres, registral locations and dispersions, and modes of articulation, how would a listener distinguish the first two attacks of the *Eroica* Symphony as an event from the possible (and possibly corelevant) events comprised of the first 3, 4, 5, 6, 7, 8, 9, or 10 attacks?)

Now, perhaps, a further refinement of the notion of rhythm may be possible: (characterize as "rhythmic structure" the complex of relations observable between "functional extents" (as defined within the functional dimensions of a musical structure) and "time extents"; thus, the variable temporal projection of, say, some basic pitch-functional event in distinct presentations, counterpointed with the variable pitch-functional contents of successive timespans of a given length, might more closely capture what is intuited as the rhythmic nature of a musical structure.)

But notice at the same time that such a characterization of "rhythmic structure" virtually deprives rhythm of its independent status as a musical stratum: (according to the proposed account, the rhythms of a piece cannot be determined prior to a determination of the other-dimensional functional things which *create* those rhythms by virtue of the times they take to occur and to be succeeded. And so rhythm is seen as the secondary creation of other aspects of musical perception, an automatic effect of their significant activity. As such, it seems hardly to qualify as a significant activity in itself, except in its most superficial and immediate manifestation: the successions of single attacks and their independently articulated patterns.)

Thus the net effect of the attempted clarification is to generate still deeper perplexity: (here a concept of rhythmic structure, carefully molded to capture and account for just that which seems intuitively significant in the experience of rhythm in music, has as an apparent consequence the denial of the importance normally and with intuitive rightness ascribed to that experience as a determinant of musical identity; that is, the concept appears to deny the very intuition on which it is principally founded and by which it is principally motivated: the intuition, in fact, whose affirmation is its principal task, and hence whose denial would be its ultimate failure.)

But a question of perspective arises: (for rhythm itself is not necessarily what the proposed concept may be said to have depreciated, but only the independent role of structures of duration. And insofar as such structures have been taken to *be* rhythm in the foregoing, it is this policy which has been called severely into question.)

Once abandon the identification, and the asserted notion of rhythmic structure permits a spectacular rehabilitation of the place of rhythm in musical structure: (to speak of a rhythm is, as noted, to speak of the rhythm of something; from this followed the downfall of purely durational rhythms as significant musical entities.

But equally it follows that to speak of a structure formed within any musical dimension(s) is to speak solely of a rhythmic structure, a structure unfolded in time.

To speak, for example, of the pitch-structural contents of a piece merely as a collection of available functions is to speak of the piece arhythmically. Once speak of a particular succession of partial or whole instances of that collection, and that is talk of the rhythmic structure of pitch relations. To speak of pitch structure only as an ordinal relation of events is to speak of the rhythmic structure of pitch relations in a rather loosely determinate way; speaking of it as a temporally proportionate ordering of those events is talk of rhythm that is relatively more determinate. And to speak of the patterns of duration contours, however inferred, *as* rhythm, is simply to speak of rhythm in a relatively impoverished way: hence the depreciation rightly suffered by such talk in the foregoing.)

Thus, in the denial of the independence of rhythm, its transcendence is affirmed: (the *rhythmic* structure of a piece is, in the current view, simply all of its *musical* structure, subsuming every dimensional and inter-dimensional substructure, *including* as a more or less significant aspect the foreground structure of attack durations.

The theory of rhythm, then, is nothing more or less than the theory of musical structure in its most comprehensive form. Yet the "need" for an independent theory of rhythm can hardly be said to exist; for, since no musical theory can fail to be an at least partial rhythmic theory, every existing musical theory is in fact a contribution to the theory of rhythm. Moreover, there can be no useful *general* theory of rhythmic structure, since the particular disposition of functional events in different strata, over differently overlapping and coinciding spans, is the most individual, the least "systematic", attribute of a composed musical structure.

So, for example, the question "What was Schenker's theory of rhythm?", variably but persistently asked by some of the most enlightened recent musical thinkers, is identifiable simply as the question, "What were Schenker's observations regarding music?". Insofar as Schenker offered remarks about harmony, counterpoint, and the projection of time-ordered pitch-structural events, his work is devoted precisely to the rhythmic analysis of tonal music, failing only to carry it to its most "foreground" stages: a matter of presentation rather than one of principle. Rhythm, in fact, is the one major respect in which Schenker's notions of structural levels and structural voice-leading significantly enrich Rameau's theory of triadic functionality; and it is this rhythmic enrichment that accounts for the great superiority of Schenker's analyses: "structural levels" subdivide given timespans into sub-timespans. These subspans are (in context) precisely determinate as to timelength, as their extent is determinable by direct reference to a specific acoustic (or notational) foreground. And each such subspan is distinguished as a particular rhythmic event by virtue of some single triadic function it may be observed to express, however complexly (as, for example, the first span typically designated by a Schenker *Ursatz* asserts a single tonic triad). Each span at a more foreground layer either rhythmicizes (subdivides into functionallyand temporally determined subspans) or repeats some more background span; hence each layer "covers" the same structural and temporal ground: that is, the total composition. What varies is the degree of rhythmic determinacy with which each layer accounts for the whole. And the "prolongation of triads by contrapuntal elaboration" is at the same time a means by which spans are determined, and the structural content they project.)

In Stravinsky's honor, then, the rhythmic genius may be exalted to the highest position in musical creation; but to honor his own special rhythmic genius requires necessarily—though also sufficiently—the recognition of his own special genius as a creator of whole new musical worlds: (consider it done.)

–Benjamin Boretz, 1971

Stravinsky in Person:

I remember seeing Stravinsky on two occasions—the first in some unnumberable year of childhood, the second a dozen-or-so years ago—the first, a conducting appearance with the Cleveland Orchestra: at rehearsal, the awaited guest entering the hall from the rear wearing what appeared to be a long cape, accompanied by a large wife discreetly trailing, to become entrusted at the understood time (near the front of the hall, just a few rows short of the stage where the orchestra waited) with the doffed cape: and at the concert, a finely inexpressive avian artifice consuming the distance from the wings to the podium in a jerky glide; a sparrowlegged Lilliputian Nijinsky, in formfitting tuxedo, springing up weightlessly to the podium and bowing faultlessly, impersonally amid the ritual applause; immersed impenetrably in applause as a bird in air;—the second, an informal appearance before a small handful of eminent composers and a somewhat larger handful of young composers, a few expert performers of new music and a few interested musicologists, all gathered together by Paul Fromm on a campus in rural New Jersey, all intently focused in a near parody of silence, all basking reverentially in the master's voice: the master's hands gesturing minimally in the summer heat; the master's voice modulating the silence gently, confidentially, almost intimately; articulating doubts about the internal consistency of the serial works of the '50's in which he had not yet fully overcome his accumulated tonal habits; expressing hope that his current work might finally free him from habits no longer relevant; addressing colleagues, some of whom might perhaps be confronting in their own work problems similar to his if less acute by virtue of fewer years spent in accumulating irrelevancies; the almost intimate voice professionally, unostentatiously confessing; addressing those who would understand, those like himself for whom mainly the future mattered— scuffed summercolored shoes not quite tennis-shoes, collar open, gray summerweight suit uniformly, quintessentially wrinkled.

J.K.Randall

Reply to Arthur Margolin:
on the logical method of *Meta-Variations*

. . . It would be a simple matter to save a primitive [in *Meta-Variations,* Part II: Sketch of a Musical System] by taking interval equivalence of <u>pitches</u> as primitive, then recursively defining pitch functions as determined by discrete classes of pitches, each of which contains all and only those pitches which determine, relative to each pitch, an equivalent interval. Why I reject this strategy, in favor of adopting the additional pitch-functional primitive: it seems crucial to be able to assert *equivalence* among discrete members of a single pitch function (pf) without regarding that identity as a special <u>interval</u> quality. Or, rather, it seems juster to construe interval quality in all its variety as an enrichment of the more austere notion of functional equivalence and non-equivalence, such that functional equivalents determine a special type of interval, and functional nonequivalents all the others.

In effect, of course, the assumption of pf-identity creates a unique vocabulary of intervals—interval becomes a mere name for pf-member-pair. So functional equivalence and nonequivalence is already, prior to the assumption of interval equivalents outside the bounds of functionally equivalent pairs of (functionally equivalent or nonequivalent) pitches, a less determinate stage of interval distinction, whether or not so called explicitly (and without the further invocation of interval equivalence of nonequivalent pairs, the distinction hardly matters). This strategy is exactly congenial to the desired ascent in determinacy, and hence it seems clearly preferable to distinguish the two levels of assumption (pf and ie) rather than fuse them into one. Too, the remarks in *M-V* declaring a non-belief in the empirical meaning of a 'pitch interval' prior to the pitch-functional qualification of pitches seems important to continue in force, at least by considering functionally unqualified pitch-pair entities and functionally qualified pitch-pair entities as distinct entity types, and not merely contex-tually distinct modes of packaging for the same entity type (for in music where structural intervals are bands of pitch, non-interval-structural pitch distinctions are still structurally meaningful in other senses, as, e.g., 'sharp-ness', 'out-of-tuneness', 'vibrato', etc.).

The advantages of proceeding the other way appear to be exclusively formal; but when formalisms pass beyond the bounds of epistemic determinants, what is to critically distinguish among them as symbolisms for a theory of something?

— Ben (1972)

1972: Two Notes

1. A Note on a Point of Nelson Goodman's
"Reply to Benjamin Boretz" *

Being a work of art is being perceived a certain way, i.e., being
noticed (experienced) *as* an instance of the disposition of instances of certain types of instances of certain types of elements.
That the 'same' entity or phenomenon is susceptible in a distinct
perceiving as constituting a different such instance, or an instance
of a different type, is located at an epistemic level distinct from
that on which the identity of a given work of art is determined.
Hence when Goodman says,

> I see nothing wrong in saying that a given bronze
> object is a sculpture. This is entirely compatible
> with the object's being something else as well and
> by no means implies that to be a bronze object is
> to be a sculpture. A bronze object is a sculpture
> insofar as it serves as an aesthetic symbol; it may
> also serve as a non-aesthetic symbol in other
> contexts, or function in entirely non-symbolic
> ways. It is a hammer by virtue of some of its
> properties, a sculpture by virtue of others. It is a
> hammer when pounding a nail, a sculpture when
> serving as a symbol of a certain kind.

he is overlooking the question what the 'is a work of __' (art-
typical) predicate actually distinguishes—ontologizes—for his
remarks are instead directed to ways in which they *don't* distinguish anything. *Any* bronze, regarded a certain way, is a work of
art thereby—in short, any visual event (entity) may be (part or
all of) a 'painting' (if it incorporates a potential *tactile* or *dimensional* aspect) or any tactile-visual event a 'sculpture'; *any* verbal
event (entity) may be a 'literary' work, any auditory event a
'musical' one.

Thus the questions of individuation and differentiation—identification, in short—are the ones crucially at issue for the theory of
art. Ways in which it is *non*-indifferent to speak of a bronze as "at
the same time a sculpture and a hammer" (Goodman) are what
seem fruitful for theory to seek. Ways in which the things in the
world can be merged into an undifferentiated blur are not usually
what theory seeks, and Goodman's own remark that "Nature is a
product of art and discourse", taken however non-literally, seems
pointed toward quite a different theoretical aspiration.

(BAB, 1972)

---

* in "Some Notes on *Languages of Art*" in *Problems and Projects*
(Indianapolis and New York: Bobb-Merrill, 1972; p. 125)

2. A Note (or Two) on
(Twelve-Tone) Syntactical Polyphony

If tonal polyphony is the inference of voices inflecting a content-defined chord, 12-tone polyphony may be understood as the inference of chords inflecting an order-defined voice, the ordered set of single pitch classes. If only trichordally determinate, the 'voice' is defined entirely by 'chord' contents—the *voice*-elements are then 'chords' and 'harmony' is then a question of two or more 'chords' understood as non-displaced simultaneously. (Does this mean that 12-tone music is *syntactically* monophonic, with its 'counterpoints' and 'simultaneities' being not polyphonic in the sense of tonal-syntactic music, but essentially artifacts of texture?)

Or, perhaps, if:

Tonal polyphony=normative 'chords' sliced into 'voices'

and

12-tone polyphony=normative 'voices' sliced into 'chords'

Then:

Is '12-tone polyphony' the inference of more than one (non-adjacent) order function over a given time span such that if a,b are such order-position elements,

($\rightarrow$ = "is displaced by")

$\sim (a \rightarrow b)$ & $\sim (b \rightarrow a)$

so that a and b are regarded as *order-indifferent* relative to each other, and hence constitute a *true simultaneity* (as contrasted with counterpoint-generated simultaneities in tonal-syntactical music).

How to distinguish something 'syntactical' from something
'structural' (or 'compositional'):

This depends on what is taken to be the *syntax*, where syntax is
understood as a hierarchized collection of global invariants—thus,
relation-types (containing *vocabulary*, since global invariance
means non-variation structurally, and hence no *internal* relation
to structure—where there's no variability (change), there's no
structure (structural event)).

(BAB, 1972)

[jacket notes for EAKINS on CRI]

  I had very definite opinions about what I wanted to do, and wanted to avoid, in providing the music for Chris Speeth's feature-length film EAKINS. It had often struck me that the trouble with bad movie music was not that it was bad music but that it was music. (Those '30's raids on 19ᵗʰ century symphonic literature were plentifully available on TV-reruns to confirm this suspicion. What had been wanted was, no doubt, mood—but highclass for a change. What had been achieved was a level of surface activity and visually nonfunctional structure on the soundtrack which spiked any sense of visualaural blend.) Indeed my happiest recollections of soundtracks were recollections of elegantly sculptured "natural" sound: environmental noise (and no music at all?) in Mr. Hulot's Holiday; counterpointed conversations in Lady from Shanghai (Orson Welles was, after all, an oldtime radio man). In such cases, of course, the mere understanding that the sound is the sound of what you're watching (rather than the sound of some nonscreen people doing something to identifiable nonscreen instruments) carries with it a sense of blend; and in deciding that the music for EAKINS was to be purely electronic, I hoped to remove a potential obstacle to the desired illusion of music, like "natural" sound, seeming to emanate from the screenworld. (On the other hand, my decision to put exactly the same music into both channels of my final 2-channel (i.e., "stereo") computer-synthesized tapes was merely in anticipation of the vagaries of projection equipment in movie houses, art museums, schools, TV studios, and who knows where.) Thinking of talk as merely the human part of the screenworld talking, and sound-effects as its nonhuman part talking, I wanted to create an illusion of music as the whole screenworld's timeflow talking; music believable as the lighting in which a scene was photographed is believable—as color of; or believable as midwestern monosyllabics might be believable as the speechcolor, or coloring speech, of that screenperson—or long florid foreignaccented involutions, of that one; or believable as a gentle rustle or a spasmodic creaking and groaning, of this or that onscreen or offscreen forest. (Notice the recurrent reciprocity here: a believable sound of some look, a believable look of some sound; each believable as coloring, and as colored by, the other.)

It's the "talking" idea that steered me away from superdeeply supermickeymousing the screen. Notice that a film's dialogue and sound effects already open up its coloring, and colored, soundworld; and that this soundworld does not deeply, or even sometimes at all, mickeymouse the screen. (The screenperson now talking may be in an offscreen corner of the room (a Wellesian favorite), or the screenforest now rustling may be in a vaguely positioned offscreen Beyond: in which cases even the frequent, but consider how shallow, mickeymousing of speech/lips or gesture/speech or rustle/leaves fails.) So that any music which aspires to enter into this soundworld need set no premium on even the shallow mickeymousing of tightly synchronized soundchange/screen-change; but rather, as the total screenworld's timeflow talking—(and the screenworld of EAKINS evolves at a quiet Brucknerian leisure)—may retain its liberty to bind together the progression of visually disparate things as various articulants of, as counterpointed within and creating, the much slower drift of soundcolowed timeflow.

This slow drift and minimal surface activity in the music—this injection of music at the level of the screenworld's larger timeflow—provides the crunch for my "talking" analogy: think of the screenworld's particulars as the music talking; so that the focal screenworld comes across both fleshing out and fleshed out by, both grounded in and grounding—encapsulated by, immersed in—a peripheral world of sound: rather like one of those old Schenkergraphs, with the difference that only Background (music; and some of the natural sound) and Foreground (the rest of the sound) are in the soundworld at all, the heavily focal (here, as for Schenker) Middleground being visual. (One is tempted to make this definition of "Background music" mandatory.) For me, it is precisely this sense of a soundbathed visual focus which a fully developed musical composition (bad or good—of which deeply mickeymouse music would be just one (and the colorationally least interesting?) sort) so frequently jeopardizes by injecting itself at too middlegroundish (or worse, at too foregroundish) a level of the screenworld's timeflow; by providing not Ground, but rather a self-contained alternative to a hence detachable screen.

—JKR

{This film explores the life and more than 100 works of Thomas Eakins, the Philadelphia artist who won (he wrote) "misunderstanding, persecution, and neglect" through his interest in the nude human figure.}

OF THIS AND THAT

notebook entries, 1972-73

rethinking, post-*Meta-Variations:*
about how to construct music as a thing in the world;
about how to imagine things in the world
from the perspective of music

Benjamin Boretz

OF THIS AND THAT

Nothing can be anything except something a thing can be.

As you observe, the totality of what things can be is a bias that determines what there turns out to be, by being:

>   1. a prejudice that you start with and enforce come what may.

>   or

>   2. a prejudice that you start with and modify as what there is suggests what there might be, what there need not be, and what it would be better for there not to be.

>   or

>   3. a cumulative product of what occurs to you as things, observed as how it has occurred to you to observe, are modified and amplified by how, in full cognizance of how, it has been occurring to you to notice things present and future.

If a thing is something that could be anything, for all you know, call it an *open thing.*

If it is something that something else explicitly is not, call it a *qualified thing.*

(There can be two-thing things)

If it is a two-or-more-thing thing, call it a *complex thing.* (A thing that has sub-things, or a thing that appears when more than one other things are observed within the same thing-observation field, or a thing whose distinctness from other things includes an observation of it along with other things within the same thing-observation field, is a *relational thing*.)

Whatever the totality of things, everything is connected with everything else if they are in the same world. If they are not simultaneously in anyone's head, they are not connected. If they are simultaneously in someone's head, they are connected, hence in the same world.

Any 2 things are connectible.

Any totality of things is a *thing-network.*

Any inexplicit connection is an *open path.*
Any explicit connection is a *closed path.*

Things are connected:

>1. by being open things in a single world (in which case they are connected by open paths).

>2. by being qualified things (in which case they are connected by either open paths or closed paths).

>3. by being complex things or by being non-complex relational things (in which cases they are connected by closed paths).

What a network is is totally determined by what's in it, where, and how.

What a thing is is totally determined by what network it is in, where, and how.

Things are in a network at *locations where things can be;* by their locations are determined other locations where things can be.

Things are by virtue of the locations where things can be with which they are identified, or which can be created to identify with them.

(A *rhythm* hypostasizes the identity of a (however) ordered chain of things each of which is to each other as a particular network interval, a particular structural-level interval, a particular presented-order-interval, and a particular order-dimension interval.)

A network is a syntax for things.

"Things", as noted above, may be interchanged with "tracks of things in someone's head"; things may then be said to *refer to* network things.

Why do I want to know my syntax?

I admire the music of Beethoven inordinately

I want to compose something like that

but I don't want to compose Beethoven's music again

So I observe what it is I admire in Beethoven's music,
and imagine the network that captures it

So I can then imagine a network which is in some
sense isomorphic with it that doesn't have to be the
same network or to contain the same things

That it is in some sense isomorphic with it is a
discovery of imagination

To make it isomorphic in a particular sense is the
trigger for and direction of an effort of imagination.

Why be biased?

If you're not, there is nothing.

If there is anything, you are.

So it is not a question of being biased or not,
    but of bringing your bias up to reflection, so that you
    can shape it to your own taste.

And so you can have the contemplation of your own
    bias as a palpable subnetwork in your world.

Form and Content

How is a network used to recreate itself, to receive
    things and re-form around them?

Does the densest network react the most

        limply

            or the most

       alertly?

Does experience

            sharpen experience

                        or does

experience

          blunt experience?

A. I've heard it all before.

B. I've learned (I'm learning) to hear it as never
    before.

       : Two ways to use imagination.

[If knowing what a 'Mozart symphony' sounds like is
    ever useful to me in knowing a particular Mozart
    symphony, it's when I barely yet know it; the more I
    know it the less I can imagine, through it, what 'a
    Mozart symphony' could possibly signify.]

Rhythm, again

So, 2 different things can't have the same rhythm.

> But by sharing noticeably any of the aspects
> of another, earlier, rhythm, a later rhythm can
> retrieve those aspects so that the aspect-
> equivalence becomes part of the sense of
> what the second rhythm is;—not part of what
> the first rhythm is when it happens, but part of
> what the first rhythm is at the time when the
> second rhythm has happened.

Retrieval (1)

Something,

    because of something following,

    turns out to have been hearable, and

    becomes heard on purpose,

    as 2 things together, as a

    2-thing thing.

1. Is the 2-thingness there at the start, its nonperception an error, and its retroperception the recognition and rectification of that error?

2. Or is the 2-thingness perceived as latency, realized in the sequel?

3. Or is the thing a 1-thing thing until the sequel 2-thingthings it?

> 3. could be called 'retrieval' : a quality not present discovered to have been latent after the thing ceases persisting—but persists in memory in such a way as to make it retrievable as being referred to by later things, and even as being analyzed and reconstructed by them so that "it" ends up being a mental slot multiply qualified by a cumulative process over time, the times of accrual being also a quality of its retrievable thinghood.

Retrieval (II)

Jim Randall was troubled by some charts of mine because they seemed to leave everything that ever once sounded to reverberate indefinitely except for explicit impedances and re-sonations. He suggested that at a certain point a single sound-token, indexed as such up to then, is indexed subsequently as part of a package conspicuously stored as a chunk rather than as a mosaic:

1. Within-between predication back-orders things relative to their degree of subsumption within configurations of different degrees (i.e. at different piecetimes).

2. The aspect of interest in the chunk-indexing is that it retains the original thing-states of the sub-things of a chunk in a condition of retrievability. So Retrieval (I) may follow a developmental compression as well as an initial irreducibility (irreduction) of a thing.

Retrieval (III)

A motive is a retrievable aspect of something that is in the course of events retrieved.

MUSIC-ONTOGENIC FLOWCHART

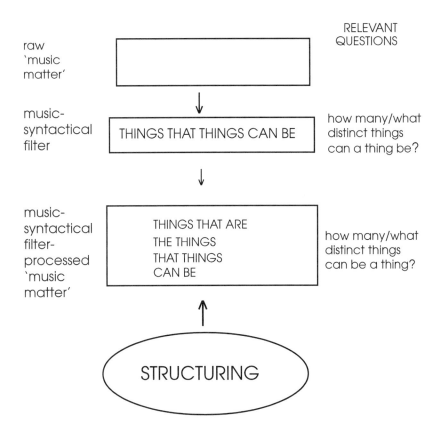

raw
'music
matter'

RELEVANT
QUESTIONS

music-
syntactical
filter

THINGS THAT THINGS CAN BE

how many/what
distinct things
can a thing be?

music-
syntactical
filter-
processed
'music
matter'

THINGS THAT ARE
THE THINGS
THAT THINGS
CAN BE

how many/what
distinct things
can be a thing?

STRUCTURING

A WORLD OF TIMES*

Benjamin Boretz

Nature, says Nelson Goodman, improving on Oscar Wilde, is the product of art and discourse. From this I infer that a natural entity derives its identity from that ongoing processing of the natural world that produces us as it produces the world we process; so that artworks and discourses, as filters through which such processing takes place, are less favorably taken as records than as instances of that processing, and that they are thus *of* the world in a sense perhaps prior to the sense in which they are *about* it.

But an artwork, specifically: a musical work, while it may be thus taken to filter the world, and to be in the world as such a world-filtering thing, may also be considered as a world-*like* thing in itself—perhaps as a hypothetical world, as such a world, that is, as may also appear to be proposed by discourses, but also, remarkably, and unlike the worlds proposed by discourses and mathematics, as a world quite fully experienceable. What encourages me to this attribution of worldlikeness to musical works are two observations of our experience of them, which seem under scrutiny to constitute two rays of a single illumination.

The first is an observation of the relative *independence* of the experienced identity of a single musical work; the second is an observation of the relative *singularity* of that identity. With respect to its independence each musical work seems, compared with most non-abstract things in the world, a relatively closed entity, in the sense that its experienced identity seems relatively independent of—even discontinuous with—those events and entities which might externally appear to be its spatial and temporal neighbors during any performance or other manifestation of it. And its singularity may be located in the fact that whatever are identified as its component entities seem unique to that single work. For even where, through an observational filter whose range is a multiplicity of works, a given component entity may be identifiable with component entities in other works, it will, when observed through a filter which focuses on the

---

*A talk, given at a symposium on the philosophy of art sponsored by the Department of Philosophy, University of Pennsylvania, on November 8 and 9, 1973. First printed in *The Lampeter Muse* (Bard College student magazine), Fall 1973.

identity of the single work, yield a wholly distinct feel from those yielded by the supposedly "same" components elsewhere.

I identify these senses of radical independence and singularity with the radical depth from which, as I have demonstrated elsewhere, the complex identity of a musical work may be constructed from contextual inference on its quality-content alone, without the intervention of convention to provide a prefabricated, and relatively universal, referential framework for such identification, in the sense of a verbal-linguistic syntax and lexicon. This is not to say that conventional filters *cannot* be employed, but that, to a remarkable degree, they *need* not be. To the extent that they are, of course, they neutralize the individual identities of musical entities to a collective identity, up to the level where all music is any music, and hardly distinguishable from the flux of everyday auditory experience.

Now if the networks of inference constructed on primitive qualities and creating the attributed and experienced identities of musical entities, which I have been nicknaming "filters", are considered to be the business ends of discourses, insofar as their nature-creating powers are concerned, then, in the spirit of Goodman's epithet, we may regard a work of music as the product of nature and discourse. But discourse is ongoing, and what nature is, or what any natural entity is, is continuously cumulating throughout the sentient spans of individual and collective humanity. So if the world is what is and happens, its identity is not only perpetually emergent, but that identity clearly includes the chronology of events itself, within all worldtime. A musical work, like any subworldly entity whose parts unfold chronologically, obviously shares this worldlike aspect, except that, unlike the world, it has an experienceable culmination as a perceived totality. But if my claims regarding the radical contextuality of musical syntax are justified, then it follows that the time-dependence of musical qualities goes radically farther: for if it is through the operation of an inferred musical syntax that musical entities acquire their essential attributes *as* musical entities; and if the syntax is constructed on the experienced properties of musical entities; then the syntactical filter itself is cumulatively constructed over the whole time of a work—is, indeed, operatively a *different syntax* at different moments of the work's time—and hence creates, *at* every moment of the work's time, *different entities* for every *previous* moment of that work's time. That is, not only are there new facts consecutively to be observed throughout a work, but every fact observed in every timeslot prior to each temporally newest entity is retroactively transformed into a qualitatively *distinct* entity still *in* that prior timeslot, but *at* the time of occurrence of each such temporally newest entity. Thus as the musical work unfolds, facts and syntax continuously create one another, and fact-created syntax creates the new facts through which syntax is recreated.

The obvious question here is of the experiential sense of such a claim. To elucidate that sense, let me suggest that—in the language of Goodman's *Structure of Appearance*—a quality instance in a single domain of qualities constitutes the irreducible identity of every unreduced musical entity. Musically speaking a tuba's note is not like a lion's roar: it betokens no tuba as a character in the musical fabric; the sound alone is the musical creature. So the whole identity of a musical entity is, clearly, *how it sounds.* Now "how it sounds" is a fairly elusive matter, since I seem to be able to have, in a direct sense, the experience of a musical work, in real time, as an act of thought, with no physical sounds in evidence, just as I can read or think a poem. So it seems that what a musical thing sounds like has to do with the relational feel of a place in a sound-quality network; with how, that is, such an entity instantiates a music-syntactic entity or a nest of such entities. For example, a given C E may be heard as "the C E of a C major triad"; as such it will be a distinct thing from something heard as "the C E of an A minor triad", or from something else heard as "the C E of a C major triad simultaneous with the C E of an A minor triad". So it would seem to be the syntactical *sense* of a musical entity which is experienced as its musical *sound;* and it is this sense which can plausibly be experienced in the mind's ear directly as a soundthought.

Thus what the claim of continuous retroactive transformation of the things in a musical work by each other amounts to is just the claim that the sound of each successive sound is, first, crucially determined by what has gone before, since the syntax within which it will be qualified can only have been inferred from the qualities of its predecessors plus it; and, second, that its sound, identified permanently with its own time of occurrence, has a subsequent history stretching to the end time of the piece, during which it *sounds different* as subsequent events succeed it. Thus to hear, for example, a "descending line" is to hear a first sound as something from which each successive sound is a (progressively further) descent. And to *have heard* a descending line requires the occurrence of a framing, (change-of-direction, interruption-of-sound, etc.) event *subsequent to* the bottom sound of the descending line. There is a famous though uncritically applied harmony-class experiment, in which two chords (dominant sevenths) agreed to sound the same in isolation are spectacularly found to sound quite different when given different chords to resolve *to*. And—for another example—the first sound of a piece has a distinct sound as it sounds in isolation, but immediately acquires a new sound as the first sound of a 2-sound event: listen, say, to the top C♯ at the opening of Mozart's famous A major piano sonata—the one with variations—as it sounds, then as it becomes the C♯ of a C♯-D, then of a C♯-D-C♯ tune, and so forth. By the time we reach the end of m. 8, in fact, that first C♯ has become the C♯ of a fast C♯-D-E-B tune, the C♯ of a (slower) C♯-B-A tune, the C♯ of a still slower C♯-B tune, and, slowest of all, the C♯ of a C♯-B-A tune that takes all 8 measures to become manifest. And, as it is sounded, that C♯ is a "highest sound"; as it is immediately succeeded, it is first a second, then a third highest sound, which latter it remains until m. 9, where it becomes in quick succession, a 4th, 5th, and finally 6th highest sound, which characteristic it retains to the end of the theme. Now until each of these complex events becomes manifest, that C♯ fails to exhibit its attributes as a component of that complex event. And heard *as* that which *consists of* those attributes, it ends up sounding like no other C♯ in any other piece of music, and only in a sense that needs explication "like" the other C♯s in the same piece.

Moreover, since our "tunes" are simplified instances of music-syntactic entities, the syntax of the piece fails to contain the thing-categories they instantiate/create until the moments where they are literally manifest or inferable from what is—though the arrival at the sense of such inferability is most often a highly potent act of retroaction in itself. My claim is that the rhythm—the content over time identity—of such a syntactical development relative to what is consecutively sounded, as well as the rhythm of a chain of retroactive sound-transformations, is a critical constituent of what is perceived as a musical identity.

But I have still further to take this claim: from the story of the adventures of a single C♯ we may infer that the resonance of a musical entity, once sounded, persists thenceforth, being progressively modified by the retroaction on it of every succeeding entity (that it *stopped* sounding at given time is, of course, part of its sound). And so we may characterize the singular identity of a whole musical work as a single, complex, cumulating sound, within which every component subsound sounds as it sounds when sounded, then sounds thenceforth as having sounded, sounding successively as it is successively resonated, deflected, enclosed, and connected, and as it resonates, deflects, encloses, and connects previously and subsequently sounded sounds.

From such a perspective, the singularity and independence that we ascribe to that discontinuity of sonic blips that we, perceiving fantastically, knit into a musical work, may acquire some plausibility, and under its guidance, our capacity to ascribe such identities may acquire some depth.

a Soundscroll.

Display. (,play.)

(-scroll; from start to finish.)

Time : from beginning to end;

Unroll

It. : from **capo** to **fine**.

(head to tail)
—: whatever you like.

; hard to tell

0.

is rolling up from start as fast as it unrolls towards finish.

but.
      (—Across a Backdrop.—)

across, & in contact with, a backdrop.

a Backdrop? (,fabulous!) of All Possible Futures.—   all Possible prospects.

each?

—: a sensitized track Across. (,on the Backdrop.)

: (Track Across) : in the direction the
    Soundscroll is rolling up from start
        as fast as it unrolls towards finish.

Each : taking Impress (,impression) of the
        Soundscroll's Passage.
    : registering (,on its Continuum of Moments)
      (— as the soundscroll passes —)
    each Momentary Vividness (,likelihood) of this
Particular Future. (— this Particular prospect.)

— (Now & Here.).

in the end? : the Whole Story will have been Indexed. (On the Backdrop.). — the Full Temporal Record.

Of?

: of Vicissitude of Implication.
: of Welter of Probability & Potential.

(—: of relation of Relations of Tracks?). if you like (,surely). (,has a Track of its Own. (,! if Possible)).

(—: of relations to Elsewhere?). why not (,if you like. !Follow their Tracks.!)

what else.
                    (— Haven't Got One? —)

) drop
    back

1.

(is rolling
   up from
   start, as fast as
   it
)unrolls
towards finish.

no Was
is ever present. just Here.

no There. so more
& more of
it
becomes past (,lost), as Now
advances.

!Somewhere
(,anywhere) between
beginning and
end :

(a now, here between start and finish.).

On it.
whatever it is
:Skinnythin.
                                    What.

like it is
(,absolutely)

will it have been?

(if it was)
:,like it Was(

)rolled
up

2.

(is rolling
    up from
    start, as fast as
    it
) unrolls
towards finish.

just here is
present now. as
just there was
present then. but
here is
thicker now than
there was then. when
there was here &
then was now; has
become thicker &
thicker as
it
advanced with now's
advance. thicker with
was (,whatever
it
was), as
more &
more became
was (,lost.). as

more &
more was
became lost in
presence now as
quality of
here.

is
like it is
to be like
it is to have been
like it was.

is
like it is
to have begun
already
(,before now began)
(,in the beginning?)
by beginning as
before for
this now.

                           & start informing here.

what will have become?
     (Hold it.)

      : relation to was,
      (: the Quality of Here.)

3.

(is rolling
        up from
        start, as fast as
        it
)unrolls
towards finish.

Thick with its
was.

each here
thick now with its Lost
Was. (& with
more besides.)

(with Prospects.).
(with what
might
yet be.) with
whatever
future might
inhere in a here now
thus
was-thickened.

(: Was-inceived
Future, Present
now :)—

— & Thicker the
Was, the
Thicker Inhere the
Prospects. (—, as
now advances — &
More &
More was
becomes lost in
presence now. (—, as
quality of here.).) (the
more the
Stuff.). —&
the Stickier (

    :relation to was
    & might yet be,
    (: the Quality of Here.)

) the more to chew
on

4.

is unrolling.

*more & more of it is opening out from start. is becoming present now
  from start.*

*presence now comprehends whatever, since the beginning, has ever
  been present. comprehends urtext of there & was, within a
  presence whose now is here. whose there to here is now's
  Increment on start to there Then;—which is present. like
  it was. (none is lost. nor will be.)*

comprehends Story Thus Far:

*:—the Quality of whose Here is thick with was & might yet be —
  & with more besides : with the thickness of just This Next
  in just This story just Thus far. —   : with the thickness of
  whatever inheres now in just This thickness Here in the
  presence of just That thickness There. (—& there —   :
  urtext; —nexted.)*
—: is thick with Story Of.

*(& Thickens as Story thickens as Now advances as the unrolling
  scroll unrolls.)*

in the End, All of it —   from start to finish —   will have become Present.
   all Story of; all Relation of; all Quality of. On it. within
   Presence Now. (,within presence whose now is finished.).

(: relation to Elsewhere?;
      ; to   ?Whatever you Like.*
: ,if you like.). but On it (,as you like it.). within presence
   Now —Already, quality Of it. (Presence Now : Thick with
   Depletion of Elsewhere. (;bloated? —   . not if you like))

) or don't you

(in what rhythm of?
      tracing
         Discovery Of
            what shades of
                what groupings

* ; to   ? / : Rules for Scrollhood. : / : Old Scrolls. : / : Nonscrolls. : /
: Ciphers for Scrollreading. : / : Readerfeeling. : / ?

5.

is   unrolling.   but

something   keeps   happening   to   it.   as   it   unrolls.

*as   now & here   advance   farther   &   farther   from
start.   Watch   it.*

*as   the   unrolled   part   becomes   larger   &   larger.
    (& thicker   &   thicker   with   story   of)
!happens   to   it.   More   &   more.*

*becomes   more   &   more
        warped   &   stretched   &   twisted.   (Changes   its*

Story.)
                *: straightforward Sags
                (& Loops. &)*

                *Sharp   turns Fuzzy (& Fuzzy
                        Sharp)
                ;or erodes away.*

                —: & Vacancy becomes Occupied.   :—
(,later.).

presence Then
    (from start to There)
becomes Changed (,lost) in
presence Now of
    (start to there within)
start to Here. (,as
Before begins anew now

;) as presence Now
    (of start to Here)
will become Changed (,lost) as
        Now advances (as the
            scroll warps/
                (/stretches/twists.)   *:*
                                : by retroaction
enacting Was.).
                        : (over & over Revamping
its Was.).
                    &
            So : The

more of it becomes present, the
more of it becomes lost.

:(& Here ?):

--: is thick with its freshforged Was (& its might yet be.);
& with more besides::

: with Twinge of   1.   *(hierarchy upset) or*
                    2.   *(priority cancelled). of*
                    3.   *(old sentence revoked) &*
                    4.   *(ambiguity chastised). of*
                    5.   *(past future aborted in*
                         censored story of.) : (the
                         Real Story of)

(or was I mistaken?
Ought I have begun otherwise?
(,for now)

have begun only as I will have begun in the end?(;&
   Hold it.)

)No.

What will become of it?

(It's never too soon.)(now.
to start here.) never too late.
            to start
                    over.

) august 1973

j.k.randall (:

6.

is unrolling. &

 —: & Leaving its Traces.

warps & stretches & twists (, — : but leaves Traces.

On it.).

warp/stretch/twist here. bounds the Reach of old prospect there (, :
    was-inceived then :) now newly reflected upon (,in retrospect)
    from here; reach of old prospect etched now (,& bounded) in
    trace of old path.— Present now : none lost. (nor will be.)

new path from here back to there (,: warped; stretched; twisted:)
    reveals now new prospect there now (,: here-inceived now:):
    some ambiguity now there (,revealed here).(— : Twinge Here
    of Junction There now. junction just there now of prospect
    was-inceived then & prospect here-inceived now. of just These
    prospects converging from Before & After just There from just
    Here (,just now).).

now's advance from there to here thus thickening
    (,Compounding) old sentence of was from start to there then.
    thickening was with more & more was.
    (— , with Traces. with more & more threads of story of.). — :
    was : — (— , Accumulating —) : becomes thicker & thicker
    with Now.

Story of Was. Told in the rhythm of now's newly knowing (,to become
    newly known). Only in Whose end (,in a last knowing of past
    knowings) will any was have been fully traced.—:be fully
    present.

7.

is unrolling again.

has unrolled already : &

is unrolling again. (— , & seems to have changed with use.).

Already from Start, traces (,or something) — of something
    — seem thickly in place (——— : not vividly, mostly; just
    thickly———); — as if hanging around waiting for
    something. Traces (,of something — : (of warp/stretch/
    twist?) —) of Warp/Stretch/Twist; — but without
    Twinge now.——— (— , & without warp/stretch/twist.).:
    tracery of Borrowed Time perhaps. (, time Yet to Be :).
    — waiting for something at the time. —   but present
    now.

as if was-inceived. (taking no chances.).

(though not Vividly.). — Sanitized. : that now's Advance
    might reveal no more (,in retrospect)(—   ! & no less
    either —) than traces from start Expect (,can
    Accommodate); might reveal Strict Reciprocity
    between thereness Here & hereness There : — : as if a
    here & now thick with there & then Had Been the was
    inceived prospect (,Precisely) of there & then, when
    there & then were here & now. no mistake.

(,actually). no bogus. nor Found Out Later. — : but waiting
    All Along as This trace has been waiting , — for advent
    of This vividness which Now has just now Infused (,in
    retrospect) from Here.

no Twinge here (— , nor Aborted nor Junction.); was all set for it : —
: There : — : thick with Foreshadowed. : with Position in Old
Story of. : — : sticky with Implication. - (— small Was-inceived
ambiguity Snagged (,lost) in Large Thickets of implication. —)(
— : thick with Will Yet Be. (— & Won't (,if you like)): —) —
waiting (— , with what hope? —) — as Ordained is awaited.— :

&
So : The

Closer to Start (— the Longer the Wake of now's Advance from there
to finish —), the more traces Await their Vividness. - & the more
Chance & Reach for advent of vividness there. for Infusion (,in
retrospect) from (somewhere).

: & At Start? — (,!the Nutshell.). the Whole Scroll. Foreknown here (
— , not vividly;   Thickly. —) as Quality of Here. — ; —————
, as   prospects whose Vividness (! not yet. At the Time.) will
have Indexed now's Whole Advance from Start to Finish; old
story's whole How & by What Path. — . in the end

8.

NOW IS ADVANCING ACROSS AN UNROLLED SOUNDSCROLL.

ALL OF IT—FROM START TO FINISH—IS PRESENT NOW. FROM BEGINNING TO END. THE WHOLE STORY. A PRESENCE NOW FROM BEGINNING TO END.——: PAST PRESENT & FUTURE PRESENT (, : ALL THE TIME :): PLAINLY VIVID. (EQUALLY. ((& UNVARYINGLY; — ALWAYS. &) EVERYWHERE.)

QUALITY OF HERE:? — : (EACH WHERE INDEXES WHOLE STORY OF.). THE SAME FULLNESS OF STORY OF.—— (—: THE SAME OLD STORY. — &

NOW? —: (,RELEASED FROM START) ADVANCES;—& PASSING AS A POINTER PASSES (,—— AS TIME MIGHT PASS—), DIVIDES PRESENCE NOW (,ALWAYS) IN TWO PARTS: THE PAST PRESENT PART (,BECOMING LARGER & LARGER) ACROSS WHICH NOW HAS ALREADY PASSED; & THE FUTURE PRESENT PART (,BECOMING SMALLER & SMALLER) ACROSS WHICH NOW HAS YET TO PASS. : PASSING AS A POINTER PASSES (, — AS TIME MIGHT PASS—)—: NOT TOO FAST (—& NOT TOO SLOW EITHER—), BUT JUST RIGHT. — (CAREFUL NOW.)—. EACH NOW (,!PRECISELY) POISED HERE ON ITS NEXUS.— . —OF? CONGEALED;)—) TIME.

(: WHAT HAS NOW BECOME?

∞

an unrolled soundscroll is present.—: still. :— as

a remembered memory of
a passing of
remembered presences.

of presences
remembered passing as
now might pass.

remembered as passing

as now might—

or as

was might—

evolve,
in evolving
presence.

(choose.)

a Soundscroll.

MIRAGE

I. notebook entries, 1974-1976

II. (a syntax for Schoenberg's op. 25, 1)

III. a talk and 2 floats

benjamin boretz

MIRAGE

benjamin boretz
notebook entries, 1974-1976

...does a musical image incandesce because it flashes
forth by a twinkle of surface the full depth of the
pool of reference on which it floats? Floats: the
twinkle is the depth's edge, ultimately depthlimiting.
twinkle at poolbottom, and there will be only flat
bottom perceived; but twinkle at top, and there is a
pool to float over felt, surface, depth, bottom, all
together. So the experience of riches of musical
depth comes by way of the acuity not the complexity
of the musical surface; all is conveyed by the explicit
sparkle of that twinkle: high atop a deep or boiling or
tranquil or shoalfilled current; or just a map of the
bottom of something or other. Still waters evaporate,
vanish in sands, leave perception high and dry; to keep
buoyant the flashes must flicker evernew dimensional
senses (not another pool over there, but another
depth, an unpremeditated cove, an elusive channel,
connected within a timespan of spacesense: the pool
reshaped as twinkles unveil newfolds, eddies, islands,
inlets, changes over time become part of what *it* is:
roiled, glossy, ripply, sparkly, gloomy, gleaming,
reflected invert blueskybowl: time, shaped over time;
space, shaped over time; (leafflutter: a still image
that only a movie camera can record).) And if the
texture datasaturates, repletes unto itself, color
neutralizes, drains: demorphizes. If the reference
is the surface, then the incandescence never glows.

But how make it glow, right from start?

Chord of Nature: maybe the harmony of the universe;
the underlying resonance of all, maybe even; but
deadly to music: null as image (replete unto itself;
data of structure):

(Beethoven Opus 2 No. 3):

        right from start,
        the shape of surface
        is a simple
        image of a
        complex
        landscape: E
                                                                                      C

                                                                                       G

                                                                                       C

the Chord-of-Nature image: E
                                                                       C

                                                                           G

                                                                           C

                                                                           C

        is only
        a hairsbreadth different
        but that crack
        is the universe
        of Opus 2 No. 3:

G, an 8ve too near,
wedged between Cs,
setting up then
its own upward space
not resonated;
the 2nd C made
not confirming
the lower but competing:
G blocks the 1st C's reach to the 2nd:

                                        C

                                        G

and   E   is altogether out
        C

        G

of joint: E   D
                                C   B

                        G   G   G

                        C

unconfirming upper pushes into parallel
competition with unconfirmed lower.

(what's consonant?)
(what's dissonant?)

C G/C E : halves of a broken Chord of Nature, broken to crunch with a competing, dissonant Chord of Nature, dissonantly neighbored:

```
        E                           E
        C                           C

        ‾                           
        G                           G
                                    ‾
        C                           C
```

(Crunch:

```
E                           D
C     is pulled down to      B

G                           G

C                           C
```

but   E   is, at   D   still carried by

```
      E                     D
      C                     B

      G                     G

                           ‾
      C                     C
```

C, fully crunched: two competing planes, simultaneous, incompatible. . .)

MIRAGE II

(Mirage II and III originated in Bard College music classes; In (essentially) their present forms, Mirage II surfaced in seminars at Princeton (10/75), UCLA (3/76), and University of Washington (4/76); Mirage III as a talk at SUNY Albany (11/75); both re-edited 1/00 and 5/02)

START HERE: (a syntax for Schoenberg's Op. 25, I):

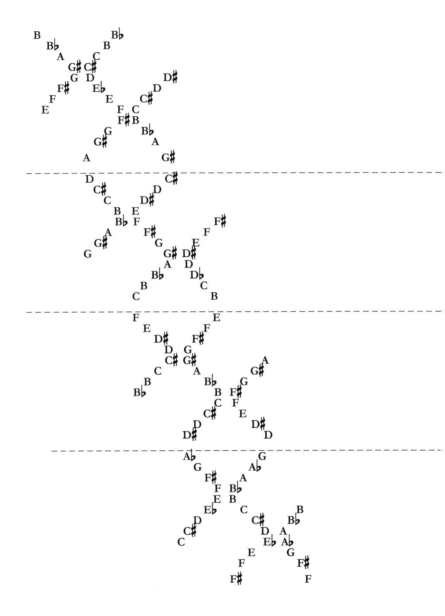

1. Exactly what am I doing when I "work (compose, listen, cognize) within a system" — that is, how do I understand in a functional musical sense what a musical system *does* for me? What a musical system is is no more or less than a bias to hear (and to imagine) all the sound-items in a musical sound-field as pieces of a specific internalized phenomenal vocabulary, not necessarily — and not necessarily not — determined by any rationalized set of properties. Attributing such syntactical identities confers 'sound' (the only perceptual identity ontological for music) on sounds ('acoustical signals'), so that any sound incorporated into a music-hearing has a distinct music-phenomenal 'sound'; under distinct attributions and — of course — in different contexts (i.e., in the actual timeflows of actual musics) no two sounds ever actually have 'the same sound', under any however strenuous uniformity of extratemporally reified attributions. And — in principle — and to within different relative determinacies — it makes sense to assert that when some sound is heard as having a 'sound' that there is a bias — a 'syntactical filter' — whether or not determinable, whether conscious or not — within the perceptual complex. Sounds are heard as 'sounds' within verbal languages by those so receiving them — intuitively in the case of native speakers, but with conscious invocation of alternate syntactical filters in alien contexts. Learning to read and write poetry within one's native language is probably a hybrid of 'native' and 'alien' language-construction. So too might a 'music language' be internalized — 'intuitive' — and musical thought be a 'poetic' exertion to exteriorize a speculative syntactical model for it to deepen, liberate, intensify the depth and scope of creative composing and listening.

2. Animadversions on the interaction of 'sound' and syntax such as those above lead to confrontation with the following truism: a system is a landscape, and a pitch system is a connected series of possible contents within the total pitch field within which I can hear any sound event. Obviously, the resonance of a piece is at all points the effect of the particular corner of the pitch world that its events appear to inhabit,

within the way its particular pitch system floats on the total pitch world — in the tradition which twelve-tone music shares (it's not in any evident way counter-traditional in this aspect), the chromatic scale. So I wanted to look at what twelve-tone theory appears to ask me to do in this respect, and what it doesn't ask me to do that I wish it would. And then to imagine a way of hearing a certified 'twelve-tone' music — in this case, the music by which the twelve-tone system was brought into being — a way that might compare to the way that 'tonal' music (in my syntactical reading of it) acquires its experiential richness, without simply falling back on a 'faux-tonal' construal of it. What follows is an outline of a process in quest of 'the syntax of Schoenberg's Suite for Piano, Op. 25':

3. What (I think) traditional twelve-tone-expository discourse posits for me to do as a listener/performer/composer-listener:

>   1. identify (use listening as data processing)
>   2. count (0-n)
>   3. index completions (aggregates of n elements)
>   4. isolate tokens out of time, multiqualitativity, and contour (pitch-classes, intervals)
>   5. order what is heard in a symbolic array
>   6. assemble additive components (rhythm, sound, etc.)
>   7. remember (keep a metalinguistic mental record of parametric histories)
>   8. measure and quantify (successive set-form identifications)
>   9. register surface configurations as syntactical configurations

I notice that all of these activities treat 'music' as a series of metalinguistically determinable 'facts': 'heard facts', a kind of terminal process of data-gathering in which 'the music' accumulates in the metalinguistic realm, fed by a series of sonic sensa each of which is cognized as an interpreted particle, and whose connectedness consists of the cognized connections among the metalinguistic 'facts'. But what I call 'music' exists in the 'effects' of its 'facts', not in the 'facts' of its 'effects'. The 'fact that' something is, say, a transposition of something else is not yet a musical issue, even though the resultant 'sound' may be directly dependent on that 'technical' fact. And the metaphysical mutual opacity of the 'syntactical' and the 'musical' implied by this categorial may be demystified by something like the following: I don't want to hear (or think auditorially) that what something is is a transposition; what I want to hear is what it sounds like in some context where my auditory processing of it might be metaperceptually described as 'transpose-filtering' (i.e., experiencing the sound sensum within a syntactical universe in which 'transposition' is an operative possibility). Listening (and composing) on this model consists of building a cumulative 'sound' as a rhythm of interpenetrating things. The naming, identifying, evaluating processes which are the texts of the 'ear-training' practices remain exterior to the musical enterprise.

4. A 'sound-accumulating' process for Schoenberg's Op. 25 (building a 'pitch-time-floating syntax'):

An assumption is that an optimal (intuitive or learned) auditory 'logic' begins from a simplistic cognitive model whose operation can be described as 'believing what you hear'. This entails that a first-heard sound will determine the entire sound-universe of its music; that subsequent sounds will sound as they resonate, deflect, expand the bandwidth of previous sounds; that first-heard successions of sound (as experientially 'grouped', by whatever operative process) determine a filter against which succeeding successions of sound are in some determinate way either parallel or non-parallel; and that a global 'syntax' evolves progressively (and always open-endedly) over the course of this process which can be understood as creating the 'universe of possibilities' determined by and determinate of the cumulative 'sound' of 'actual' events. (All of the above should be understood as a possible *schema* of a process of syntax formation, rather than as a *description* of such a process as it actually might happen in 'musical experience'.)

FLOAT 2: A syntactical float for Schoenberg's Op. 25, I

E F | G   D♭ G♭ E♭ |A♭ D
    |(B♭ B   D♭   G) |

2 chromatic octachords intersecting on their 2 tritones, articulated as 2 expanding dyads   [(3 4) (5 2)] interpolated with the two tritone dyads [(6 0) (7 1)]— (octachord = 0 through 7)—, such that each of the two non-tritone dyads form inversionally equivalent tetrachords

with the two tritones [$\overline{(3\ 4)\ (6\ 0)}$ (5 2)]; [$\overline{(4\ 3)\ (1\ 7)}$ (2 5)]; the union of the two octachords being 12 pc., as:

```
   E  F
  E♭    F♯
 ┌──────────┐
 │ D  ╲╱  G │
 │ D♭ ╱╲  G♯│
 └──────────┘
   C    A
    B  B♭
```

generating a syntactical array which might germinate into a possible 'eight-note system':

T0+T6 (16 distinct pc locations, 12 total pcs; :

```
   D                  C♯
  C♯             D
    C        D♯
     B    E
     B♭  F
    A        F♯
  G♯            G
  G                 G♯
```

<u>one set</u>

D
   C♯
     C
     B
   B♭
A

<u>one set</u>

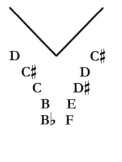

D   C♯
  C♯   D
   C   D♯
   B E
  B♭ F

which might expand into a (first cycle of a) syntactical array determining a rhythm for Op. 25, I:

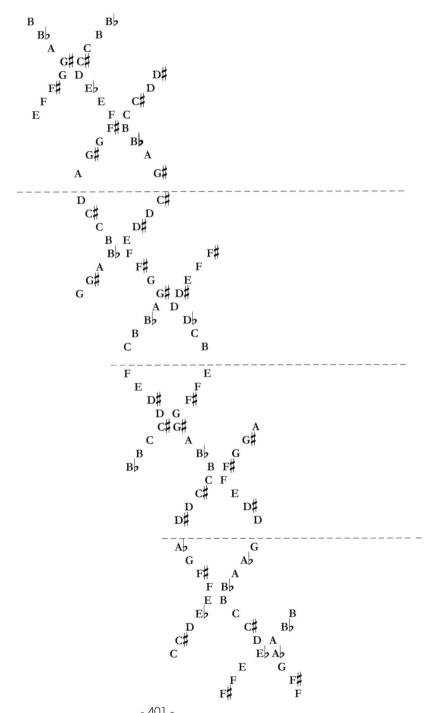

[Hints from tonal-syntactic music:

    1. A sound is hardly ever just one (syntactical) thing.

    2. A sound is not necessarily (hierarchically) more one thing than it is one or more other things.]

[START HERE:]

MIRAGE III

To be a musical thing is to have a certain sound. Musical things, that is, <u>are</u> just insofar <u>as</u> they sound, and have no other identity <u>as</u> musical things other than <u>how</u> they sound. If two things within a musical composition sound different, then, perforce, they are different things. Since a piece of music is entirely a sound-object, I cannot imagine any other possible criterion for the identity of its constituent components, or, naturally, of it as a whole. Just as we know the Beethoven Third Symphony by how it sounds, and it is only insofar as it sounds different from the Fourth Symphony that it is a different piece of music, so also anything we identify as a palpable constituent subentity of the Beethoven Third Symphony is so identifiable by the fact that it sounds different from every other constituent subentity of the Beethoven Third Symphony. Now, this observation seems to me uncontroversial, and self-evident almost to the point that it may seem absurdly naive as a point of departure in a purportedly 'serious' musical discourse.

But if I persist in contemplating the matter a little further, some peculiar and perhaps paradoxical-seeming consequences emerge — or at least they sound peculiar and paradoxical when I try to fit them into the familiar contexts of musically descriptive discourse. To elicit some of these peculiarities, let me back off a notch first and state another trite musical homily, which I hope will be as innocent and uncontroversial as the last. This is the simple thought that a piece of music, unfolding as it does over time, has as a critical aspect of its identity — that is, of its 'sound' — the specific and palpable chronology of its constituent sounds, so that not just its total identity, but the identity of each of its constituent moments, is in a state of continuous change over the total course of its temporal unfolding. So, too, then, a critical determinant, as well as a critical *aspect* of how anything within a piece sounds — at its initial moment of sounding — is its position within the chronology, as perceived. If you are taking in a piece of music, your sense of a given moment is inextricably involved with your sense of where it is in the piece; or to put it another way, your sense of being in a particular place within a piece is entirely conveyed within how a given moment, the transient 'now', sounds. And you are 'somewhere' in a piece just as, without overt conscious recall, you are 'somewhere' in a conversation (or a sentence), clearly and determinately in your experience, but carried only by the awareness of the transient 'now' of the sound of the moment. Thus every distinguished moment within a piece may be said to carry its position within the chronology of the piece as a critical constituent of its sound, as experienced by an observer if s/he is even minimally engaged in what we would all regard as taking in that piece of music, even as an act of mental hearing.

Put those two naive observations together, and what follows is the equally self-evident assertion that no two time-distinct events in a piece of music have just the same sound. For if they did, they would mean to us the same place in the same piece; and since that place is time-identified, the events couldn't <u>be</u> time-distinct.

Now even at such a naive level, this casts a certain doubt on what experience I am describing whenever I speak of a 'recurrence' of anything within a piece—whether an entire 'exposition section' of a 'sonata', a 'single pitch', or an 'interval'. And even at so naive a level, I am moved to take seriously the sense that musical description needs to reflect at least the grossest feel of actual musical experience, and that to capture the feel of a G-E♭ tune that repeats a previous G-E♭ tune I would, if I described it as a G-E♭-preceded-G-E♭*, not be splitting hairs but capturing a particularly blatant characteristic of that 'second G-E♭' as an experienced musical phenomenon.

I don't intend to allow the uniqueness of sound of a musical moment to rest solely on such a gross and universal quality as the mere fact of chronology as an essential identity-definer. But before I pursue the question further let me raise a question that arises naturally, and for me importantly, from the preceding.

_____

* Jim Randall invented this formulation.

Namely, why should I care so much about the niceties of musical description, when what I am interested in should be 'music', and music as experienceable directly and, by my own claim, exclusively as something that sounds in a certain way? The answer is that musical description is merely the externalized tip of that complex of music-creating mental activity which may be described as our internalized music theory, and whose operation is what results in musical things sounding as they do. The point is, that the experience of music is an activity of individual minds, a learned activity, which, having been learned, feels like an inborn capacity but which, in fact, may be understood as a particular state of conditioning which can be transformed by additional conditioning: hence music education, which rests on the faith that musical capacities can be developed in a determinate direction by the performance of mental exercises in conformity with specific instructions in descriptive form. So musical description, whether purporting to capture an already experienced musical event, or to propose the learning of new behavior, has at least the potential — and surely the exclusive interest — of influencing the development of the music-creating capacity. But to transform how one hears is to tranform what one hears as well — to transform music itself, or a particular music; and this is perhaps less well understood, although every musician knows in some form what a different music s/he hears after immersion and study and ongoing musical development from what s/he first heard. So description may be regarded as musically potent, since it proposes a way of hearing something which, heard that way, thereby becomes something else. And so it is a two-edged sword: insensitive description is not bad because it is ineffectual, but because it is negatively effectual. The trouble is, people can learn to hear *more* grossly, *more* indifferently, than they do without instructive/discursive/critical input, if they subject their intuitive conditioning to the instruction of descriptions that propose grosser modes of identification than those already intuitive (effectively operative though probably 'subconscious'). Capturing the sense of musical experiences deeply and sensitively, then, is not merely a challenging verbal-intellectual exercise; it is a powerful tool of musical discovery, of the transformation of musical identity, of the possibility of alternative identities out of the nominally 'same' sonic data, of, in short, the possibility of a world of musical qualities that one can invent by inhabiting, and can only inhabit by inventing. Music theorizing, then, engages me deeply just insofar as its practice creates in my world distinctive music-experiential adventures which would otherwise remain unexperienced.

Return to my just-barely-musical G-E♭ tune following a previous G-E♭ tune: to describe the second G-E♭ as "the same thing again" is to encourage a blunted, rather than a sharpened, experienced-music-rhythmic phenomenon, creating 'rhythm' additively rather than cumulatively, diverting the faculty of musical discrimination away from immersion in the 'sense' — the 'musical effect' — of a musical idea as it unfolds and is received, toward using that faculty as a means of data-processing, hearing in — as — categories in order to give categorical names to them. I believe, then, that even to make such a simple attempt at finding a sensitive grammar and vocabulary for the musical description of musical phenomena as is reflected in a phrase like 'a G-E♭-preceded-G-E♭' is to take serious advantage of the experiential possibilities of English-language theorizing about music on behalf of music itself.

To return more fully to the original trajectory: if by virtue merely of their chronological character it appears that no two musical events can sound alike and hence be the same thing, then consider the implications for musical description of the equally self-evident fact that any music we really take seriously has as its most striking characteristic the vivid specialness of each of its self-created moments — that's almost an index of musical valuation.

And just here arise some of the peculiar consequences I spoke of: how, in this light, are we able to speak of such things as <u>intervals</u>, as if they were things that remained irreducible under whatever alchemies of musical composition? What exactly are we referring to in using names like that? And if the most significant identity of a musical entity is how it arises uniquely in context, what are we learning when we learn to perceive such an entity in isolation, in what is actually a different and not less specific musical context, as if its sound in isolation were duplicated by its appearance in a cumulative, connected chain of musical moments?

On the other hand, am I proposing that music is, so to speak, autistic? That nothing can be learned of musical value apart from the inchoate intuitive confrontation with sounded performances? Or that the extremity of individuation of musical events within a musical continuity indicates an anarchic autonomy of identity for each thing—are musical things <u>purely</u>, <u>merely</u>, 'themselves', and merely <u>different from</u> other musical things?

Since the last question is the most urgent, let me take it up first:

Mere difference, incommensurable and unconnectable is, perforce, inarticulate: hence it is equivalent to no difference at all. Clearly the vivid individuality of those musical events is deeply bound up with their connectedness, the way a subsequent event is 'caused' to sound by <u>how</u> it succeeds an antecedent event. And, taken as wholes, musical episodes ('pieces' or whatever) <u>are</u> 'single events' <u>at some level</u>; that is, what a musical event <u>is</u> is a constantly cumulating thing, constantly transforming its identity by subsuming previous events into larger events over time. And since the identity of a musical 'whole' is carried at each 'internal' moment by its current 'now', the sound of every previous event is part of every subsequent sound-moment as well, as that originary sound is in fact constantly being transformed as a sound by the sense of its cumulative successors.

So how can we grasp the qualities that underlie the connectedness of a musical structure? And how can we find an intersubjectively communicative way to describe moments which we wish to explicate as unique?

To answer, let me take up an earlier question first, namely: in what sense are we able to speak of such things as 'intervals', in a musically sensitive way? A first answer is the requirement that 'music theory' be understood as a radically mutable activity, relativized to each musical experience by each musical behaver according to that person's needs and interests (intersubjective sharability of such theory is, though likely to be problematic, entirely as imaginable as the communication of any individual's thought, and at all times is not to be confused with something like 'intersubjective authority' — a red herring which arises as a political rather than a music-intellectual issue). Another answer, within the terms of the above, lies in the vicinity of something which might be termed 'depth of abstraction': finding, within each theorizing moment, the 'right' (according to individual musical desiderata) distance from 'surface' specifics for formulated 'universals', so that there is a maximum amount of room (between the 'infra' and the 'surface' structure) within which to create, compositionally, the individual identity of the musical event, momentary or 'whole'.

Just consider, in a general way, some of the different senses of 'interval' which might come to mind:

> chromatic
> diatonic
> triadic
> intertriadic
> intercollectional

And — at least in 'tonal' music — intervals function simultaneously in two discrete, non-intercommensurable ways: as 'qualities' and as 'metrics' of musical space, created by unarticulated qualities which create the reference for a subsequent 'filling in' or 'opening beyond', an 'enclosed', or 'enclosing', by the character of the subsequent unfolding.

AS:

FLOAT 3: an ontological float for Mozart piano sonata in A Major, K. 551:

Imagine a filter built on parallel structuring of intervals on distinct cycle-scales; familiarly, within the 12-pc world, the only exhaustive such cycles are 1/11 and 5/7. Imagine a music creating rhythms of pitch-chain extension along those cycles in some compositional context (motivic or not):

imagine a phrase centered on a (1+2)+(2+1) stacking of a 5-place segment of an (interval) 5 chain:

```
D
    A
E   E
B
    F♯
```

and initiating with a linear string of (1+2)+(2+1) on an interval-1 chain:

C♯ D (C♯) E   B C♯ (B) D

     (1+2)   (2+1)

voiced:

```
C♯ D       (D    )
           (   A )
E   E      (E  E )
A   B      (B    )
           (   F♯)
```

('Measuring' sound along chains or locating sounds within arrays ontologizes qualitative — as against quantitative — rhythms. And— what happens to 'octaves'? (see below)):

How does it get there?

A possible ontogenic ascension:

Centers.

Chains.

Spans.

Chains to measure on.

Centers to measure on chains
from.

Centers to measure on chains to.

Chains

     of spans

          to measure

               spans

on.

Extremes,   of spans,
     from which complementary

Chains   within
the Extremes   as far
       extend,

as they can go,   are

Centered   by

Extremes of spans
        of which

Chains consist,
      making

Extremes of spans between
     extremes of chain spans,

                    making some
                    smallest span in the
                              crossed-chain
                              span chain
                              (always
                    secure in
                    telling within
          from between),

          which is

Center Span
    of
Span
    or is

Extreme of half-Span

                    whose other

          Extreme is

one Extreme of

Span.

Centering a

Span by a

Chain of

Spans gives

3 spans   (outer, Center,
                  outer)

          or

2   (half, half);

4 Extremes   (outer, inner, inner,
                  outer)

          or

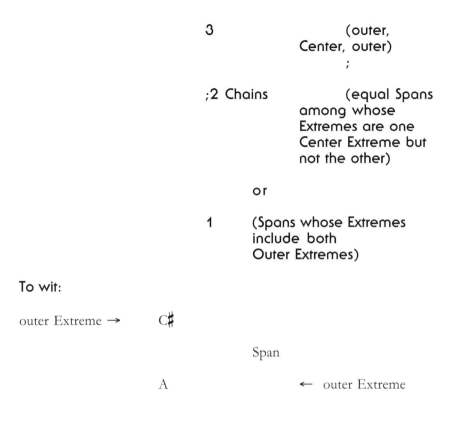

3   (outer,
Center, outer)

;

;2 Chains   (equal Spans
among whose
Extremes are one
Center Extreme but
not the other)

or

1   (Spans whose Extremes
include both
Outer Extremes)

To wit:

outer Extreme →   C♯

           Span

       A   ←   outer Extreme

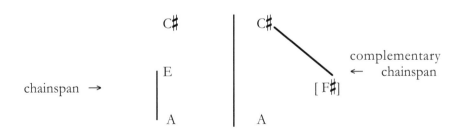

          C♯   C♯

                          complementary

          E   ←   chainspan

chainspan →   [F♯]

          A   A

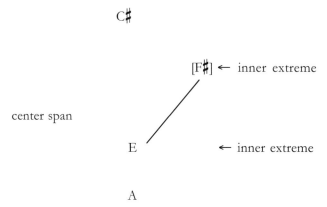

C#

[F#] ← inner extreme

center span

E   ← inner extreme

A

(Question 1: Within this world, are there 'octaves'?)

(Question 2: Is 'octave equivalence' distinct from 'any-interval equivalence'?)

(Possible answers: For a pitch n, an 'octave' ('Q') is the space between the sound 3 1s below n and the sound 3 5s below n; the space between the sound 3 1s higher than n and 3 7s lower than n is Q+Q; and .....)

Float 4: a sort-of-non-octave-equivalent scale float for Beethoven Op. 110:

3 5ths, with 3 5th-connected

offcenter articulators

are a 3-triad diatonic array,

linked conjunctly on unisons,

having 9 places

[occupied by 7

distinct pitches]

* * * * * *

3 major 3rds, 4ths apart, linked disjunctly
by semitones,

with 3 4th-related oncenter articulators,

are a

9-place

major scale:

E♭ F G A♭ B♭ C D♭ E♭ F

or

F
Eb
D♭
C
Bb
A♭
G
F
Eb

F
Eb
D♭
C
Bb
A♭
G
F
Eb

m. 2:

So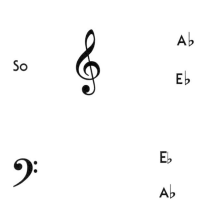

Ab

Eb

Eb

Ab

may be heard, whenever the 9-place scale is in place, to have been hanging the dominant over the subdominant.

forM(a music)

articulate
is incarnate
form

                                        fingertips
                                        articulate voices
                                        incarnate

                articulate   incarnations
                articulate   incarnate
                articulations   incarnate

                        voice
                        forms
                        fingertip
                        fingertips
                        form
                        voices

B.A.B.
March 1975

Marjorie Tichenor, for whom this text was composed, composed a
remarkable vocal composition out of her recorded reading of it.

WHAT LINGERS ON

(, WHEN THE SONG IS ENDED)

Benjamin Boretz

Plato's *Theaetetus* concerns itself with the theory of knowledge. After a false start or two, Socrates finally coaxes out of Theaetetus a commitment to the notion that knowledge is perception, and then he leads him headlong into the radical relativism of Protagoras, encapsulated in the famous epithet that man is the measure of all things. Just at the moment when Theaetetus is fully illuminated by the lucidity of Protagoras's teachings as Socrates represents them, and has fully realized the transcendent truth of those teachings, Socrates abruptly breaks into the tone and focus of the smooth sequence of plausible arguments with a speech that oozes inexplicable sarcasm:

> In the name of the Graces, [he says] what an almighty
> wise man Protagoras must have been! He spoke these
> things in a parable to the common herd, like you and
> me, but told the truth only in secret to his own
> disciples.

Now I must confess to you that this passage came vividly to my mind when Gerald Warfield first invited me to speak to you today, with the exhortation that I elucidate some of the ideas in a prose work of mine called *Meta-Variations*. Naturally, I was puzzled by the question how to explicate that which appeared to me so blatantly self-evident, and even more by the question why anyone who needed me to would want me to. And it occurred to me that perhaps, Protagoraswise, I may have seemed to be concealing lean wolves of lucid truth within voluminous wrappings of woolly rhetoric. Let me assure you, therefore, that the appearance of confusion without always lucidly conveys the truth, namely the reality of confusion within. A lot of people like to quote E. M. Forster's all-purpose dictum, that he couldn't know what he meant until he read what he'd written. But neither Forster nor his quoters ever tell you what to do if you *still* don't know what you meant *after* you read what you've written. Liszt just played his piece again when someone asked him to explain it. Maybe the person who's arrived at a particular form for his ideas is a dangerous choice anyway, as helpful guide toward clarification of his own text: returning to the scene of the crime may just stimulate him to recommit it, perhaps even with cumulative energy and excruciating new refinements enabled by relentless intervening practice. I have been practicing, and I shall proceed.

However personal and paranoid my reading of that speech of Socrates may be, it produces an extraordinary effect on my experience of the whole passage that precedes it, through which Socrates is leading Theaetetus down, as I suddenly perceive it, a garden path of plausible fallacies. As I suddenly perceive it: *not* henceforth, whenever I read through that preceding passage itself, but suddenly, as Socrates utters his enigmatic declaration, throwing what is surely one of the first major-league curves in recorded history. For if I am reading Plato, I had better be reading each of the steps of the preceding argument as carrying, within the context of the dialectic structure, flawless conviction; and only at the moment of Socrates' utterance should I perceive that those arguments may have been framed to harbor the fuel for their own conflagration, and that the simple persuasiveness of Socrates' tone has masked contemptuous ridicule. Did he not earlier say of Protagoras, "A wise man is not likely to talk nonsense. Let us try to understand him." When he says that, he *might* be being quite sincere; now, at the moment of his later exclamation, he must have been being heavily ironic. And similarly, for every step of this dialogue, we would arrive at an inadequate reading wherever we would freeze any points arrived at in the argument: for not only does the *Theaetetus* wind up in confusion and uncertainty, but its character is that of a process: a rhythmic structure of thought, whose components are thoughts—but thoughts which, as components of that structure, acquire progressively distinct identities and hence become progressively distinct thoughts, retroactively, as the dialogue unfolds. To data-process each thought as it arises by recording it on a scoreboard of philosophical points made, and then to proceed with a clean perceptual slate back into the fray to ferret out the next winner, is to read an anthology of frozen points, but not to read the *Theaetetus*.

Now suppose I emerge from the process of my own thought of which the above remarks might be a portrait, with a mental image of the character—call it the *rhythm*—of that passage of the *Theaetetus*: crudely, a trajectory of growing conviction derailed by a devastating wisecrack. Now I plow that mental image back into a close reading of the appropriate pages of print, and there emerges within my mental landscape the determinate feel of a unique, transformed text, as received print is filtered through the filtering image I had adopted. And as that text is made to be what it now is by being so filtered, it in turn uniquely transforms what that mental image was, emerging bonded in what I want to call a *semantic fusion*.

While I'm finding names to call things, let me call the filter I used in reading my passage, my mental configuration, a *theory of reading*. That's what I'm calling my mental configuration, please note, not my verbal portrait of it. As I read, that theory interacts determinately with the received print so that the text acquires properties as a text, uniquely traceable to its being read in a certain way. My theory of reading, therefore, is what I want to call *attributive*: that is, it isn't *descriptive* or *explanatory* of anything; what it does is ascribe properties to and thereby determine what there is. And if my verbal portrait of that theory were a bit more refined, it would mention that some components of my mental landscape are slots for entities that might be called "stretches-of-print-received -as-thought" slots, in a landscape of such slots which might be called a "thought-slots-in-an-array-configured-by-logical-connections" landscape. This mental landscape would continually expand to accommodate subsequent thought-slots in further logical connections, asserted or implied by the items of the print-text. At the moment of Socrates' sarcasm, the whole array might suddenly reduplicate into two configurations, one determined by ironically constructed, the other by non-ironically constructed, logical connections.

Such an array, minimally here described, I would want to call the *syntax* of my reading. It contains, for any given text-moment, the things that textual things can be; those things being amplified at every stage by the things that the textual things actually emerge as being. And the product of ongoing semantic fusion, the chronologically ordered emergence of the identities of textual things into some cumulative thing which is the identity of the text, is what I want to call the *rhythmic structure,* or simply the *structure,* of the passage of the *Theaetetus* within that reading.

The words I have just read to you I want to call a *description of the theory of reading;* as such, they are also a text, semantically fusing with the theory of reading, ultimately semantically fusing with the theory-text semantic fusion, and thereby being uniquely transformed as a determinate-feeling entity within the reading.

If I had gone to a different stretch of print with the same mental configuration induced by the same descriptive text—say, even, to a different translation of the *Theaetetus*—the *mental* configuration that would have emerged in the resultant semantic fusion would have had a different determinate feel; that is, in that other reading it would have become, retroactively, a different mental configuration; and so would the descriptive text emerge as a determinately different descriptive-textual entity.

So a given theory of reading could never be the same theory of reading for different print-texts. And now, let me call my theory of reading an All-Plato-theory-of-reading. And I want to use the same descriptive text for reading several different works of Plato. At the critical moment, of course, they become different theories and different descriptive texts as soon as they are semantically fused with a print-text in a given reading. A single theory of all Plato-reading is, thereby, unavailable; at most, what I might be able to believe in is a theory of *any*-Plato reading: under such a theory, upon each successive dialogue-reading, the different theory/descriptive-text components of the resultant semantic fusions are nevertheless perceived as metaphors for one another, inter-resonating to mutual effect. Thus, as applied to two different dialogues, a given background theory becomes two distinct theories whose metaposition relative to one another is that of analogy rather than that of identity.

A key component of the process I am describing is clearly the *translation* that takes place from the entities of the descriptive text into entities of the functional theory, the attributing mental configuration. The anticipation of some given translation will obviously guide the shaping of the descriptive text itself. Whether it takes a verbal, symbolic, or graphic form, the choice is part of an activity of imaginative composition, the more precisely achieved the more determinately suggestive of an appropriately shaped mental configuration. Thus the novelist's overtly metaphorical method may be more precise than the logician's; since the novelist might attempt to create a parallel structure to the sense of a mental configuration, as a fused image, where the logician proffers a box full of parts and a radically particularized set of instructions for re-assembly. The logician refers to *extensions,* the novelist to *intensions;* one no less inscrutably than the other, as we know from Quine—since neither objects nor concepts can be referred to with cognitive transparency. The *Theaetetus* itself, after all, is both dramatic text, and— in an overlapping world—descriptive text; whether it may serve as a model I leave as a discovery of future lection.

One thing I realize about this picture of a theory of reading is how radically the cognitive activity it describes diverges from the activity of explanatory linguistics. For out of it, the world of Platonic dialogues appears, most favorably, not as an aggregate world, but as an aggregate of worlds: each possible as a distinct, semantically fused product of a "single" any-dialogue reading theory, but mutually incompatible in that all the things there are in one dialogue are ontologically nonexistent for any other. And it seems that sheer ontological creativity is the desideratum of all readings: the multiplication of ways for things to be distinct, and the maximization of their distinctness by composing them into successions in which they acquire unique colorations. Such ontological prodigality is painful and exceptional for the explanatory linguist: he wishes to learn if possible how new entities are really old ones, and the individual utterance is specifically valued by him insofar as it can be reliably regarded as instantiating a class of phenomena or objects. But the qualification of the *individual is* the devolution point of all reading, for whose sake alone the class generality—all the way out to the class "Plato-dialogue texts" itself—is reified. The linguist, in short, wishes to make it unnecessary to know each in order to know all. The reader attempts to make it impossible, at least for himself, to know all without knowing each.

So extreme is the notion of ontological creativity that my theory of reading applies to Plato that virtually every thought-expression becomes a distinct entity, commensurable and connectible via a syntactical network with each other thought-expression within a dialogue, but functionally out of range of the thought-expressions in any other dialogue. Verbal language, however, has referents that, however grossly and obscurely, remain fixed to a certain degree. So the pieces of language that convey thoughts may still be referenced to a master language—say, Greek—and have, in different appearances, some overlap among their extensions. But what if there were no properties attributable to a piece of language outside of its phenomenal characteristics—say, its *sound*. In such a case, our theory of reading would determine even more deeply the identity of each textual entity: if to be a particular textual entity were, purely and simply, to have a particular sound, then the attribution of syntactical locations would determine everything about each such entity. In such a world—perhaps nearer to the world of Mozart than that of Plato—the ongoing retroactive transformation of things is even more extreme, since no properties of anything remain fixed by the operation of anything external to the context. If we speak of *identities*, then, within a musical text, we must be adopting descriptive-text language that is not especially helpful to the adequate formation of musical-mental configurations that elicit the deepest singularities of musical structures. If a thing has identity by virtue of its sound, then, since its sound is constantly being transformed by what succeeds it, how can anything *repeat* it, unless it undergoes exactly the same antecedent and subsequent history—in which case it would have to be in the same place in the same piece. So the C♯ that tops the first chord of the Mozart A-Major Sonata with Variations is, first, an unprecedented C♯, that becomes, as the tune unfolds,

> A d-succeeded C♯, that becomes
>
> A d-C♯-succeeded C♯.[1]

And the second C♯ in that tune is, of course, a C♯-d-preceded C♯; that is, a pitch whose identity *as a pitch* is quite distinct from that of the d-C♯-succeeded C♯ which, unprecedented, started the tune going. And—generally—since to be in a given place in a given chronology is to have a

---

[1] This formulation was invented by Jim Randall.

unique sound, and since to have a unique sound is to be a unique thing, we may truly suppose that no two musical entities can be alike, that musical qualities, as elicited by attribution, are all ontologically distinct, rather than repeatable. Within a piece, however, the history of every distinct thing is ultimately its absorption as a component of a complex thing—ultimately the whole piece, whose sound is then the cumulative sound of the cumulative chronology of its components. But the retroaction of musical things on each other is not merely replacement by different things—the syntactical landscape is at all times connected, and ordered by the uniform projection of quantized qualities; so that everything possible within a musical landscape at any moment is *commensurable* with everything else. For it is only by a *connected* retroaction that grouping would take place—otherwise the only two entity-levels in a piece of music would be the atomic single attack and the aggregate whole piece. Thus a pitch is the lowest note of an ascending line by virtue of events subsequent to its moment of sounding as first the lowest, then the second lowest, then the third lowest, and so forth, of a group which ultimately becomes articulate as such only because of its isolation by at least *one* event subsequent to all of it. So being higher or lower and being a certain measurable amount higher or lower is a quality of distinct things in which they are commensurable, and yet is at the same time the very medium through which their distinctness is realized, and through which it becomes musically particular—that is, is given its distinctive sound.

Thus there is a particular kind of commensuration in which distinct things are heard, resonating relative to each other, as exhibiting parallelisms, analogous characteristics—these being discovered, as always, by acts of creative attribution, rather than being qualities that inhere in the data. Since these distinct things must occur in chronological order, the attribution of analogy, or parallelism, amounts to the creation of a retroactive illusion that a fused musical event (fused at its time of appearance, or by subsequent retroaction) actually harbored distinguishable parts, composed of repeatable qualities. Since two things in two different chronological positions must be altogether distinct in sound, the sharing of aspects is in fact metaphorical, a particular way of attributing resonance to each at a given chronological juncture; and since time-position is an unsharable aspect, even metaphorically, all degrees of parallelism up to one-to-one repetition are, even metaphorically, only partial. This discovery by subsequent events of the possession of sharable aspects, or discernible parts, of previous events, I want to call *retrieval*. Whatever we call "motivic", then, or "referential", is just a retrievable aspect of something that is in the course of events retrieved. And our entire theoretical vocabulary of repeatable musical identities proves, in the long run, merely to be a set of frozen names for liquescent awarenesses: "pitch identity", no less than "octave equivalence" must be perceived as an activity of auditory structuring in parallel, in a given piece-time perspective. True identity is reserved, as always, for the only repeatable quality in music: being in the same place in the same piece.

In the biography of my mental-syntactical landscape, the moment of semantic fusion of a given syntactical slot with a bit of text reconstructs the landscape itself as well, so that the slot occupied by the first C♯ of my Mozart example cannot be the *same* slot as that occupied by the second; rather, they are analogically aligned. The warping of the landscape to such an alignment may be considered the common denominator of the introspectively observed music-structuring activities loosely referrable to as pitch equivalencing, octave equivalencing, cyclic equivalencing, or any pitch analogizing that becomes a salient aspect of sound-creation within a piece-hearing.

Even more generally, retrieval is understandable as any retroactive alignment, or overlay, of a subsequent on a previous event, where conditions of both events are uniquely elicited. Thus something which was in its time a fused unity, turns out to have had a separable durational aspect, a separable intervallic aspect, a separable pitch aspect, a multivalent pitch-syntactic position, or a separable timbral aspect, the discovery of which produces new dimensionalities out of formerly univocal slots; such are the syntactical overlays, overlaying distinct dimensions and hence *retroactively* creating distinct slots for each of those dimensions in the previous time *at* the present time.

Unlike Plato's *Theaetetus,* Don Martino's *Trio* proceeds from start to finish without tearing itself up as it goes. But it nevertheless manages, right at the start, a stunning bit of retroactive reconstruction. As it starts, it just lays out two hexachords, intervallically isomorphic, pitch-class complementary, with a specially sensitive registration, and with two different trichordal partitionings, temporally articulated. But the trichord-shapes temporally articulated in the first hexachordal phrase are parallelled, in a new relative rhythm, and temporally overlapping counterpoint, in the second; while the temporally articulated trichords of the second can be heard retroactively resonating a parallel cross-rhythm across the first, just at the time of the second. By cumulating rather than replacing the mental landscape for the passage, I experience a potent structural meaning for the presence of a group of two hexachordal phrases, temporally adjacent as they are, beyond the mere addition of one to the next, or even the continuation of the first in the second. What I hear is the transformation of each by the other, and hence a rhythmic transformation of the entire level of resonance within the piece, the escalation of an act of listening onto a plane of sonic imagery that recalls, at last, something of what it was about music that had placed it in my world at, or near, or even above, that place inhabited by the shades— and the Graces—of Plato.

Thus I share in inaugurating this forum for descriptive texts about music theories. I do so with much gratitude, in that there is music just to the extent that, and in the sense that, there is music theory; and with deep concern, in that there is music theory only to the extent that, and in the sense that, there is music.

(For the inauguration of the National Conference on Music Theory meeting jointly with the American Society of University Composers, Boston, February 29, 1976)

MUSICAL COSMOLOGY

Benjamin Boretz

For the Physics Section of the American Association for the Advancement of
Science, Boston, 2/19/76.

That I dedicate this occasion to the memory of Werner Heisenberg would
perhaps be presumptuous—though you may already identify
presumptuousness as virtually the occupational disease, if not indeed
the very occupation, of an artist—had I not, in contemplating Mr. Rolf
Sinclair's original invitation, thought immediately of Heisenberg's efforts
to understand the mutual significance of modern scientific and modern
artistic thought. That this effort was in particular oriented toward
developments in physics, on the one side, and music, on the other, made
it especially attractive for this occasion in particular, as a potential bridging
medium across that gulf of mutual oblivion which, in the sheer mental
and physical geography of our respective working lives, tends to dissociate
our activities and to deprive us, at least overtly, of the cross-fertilizing
benefices of mutual awareness and dialectic encounter. So it is the
intrinsically happy appropriateness to our meeting of the invocation of
Heisenberg's work that moves me to note also the gratuitously sad
appropriateness to it of the invocation of his memory.

Scientists and musicians: we see each other so little that, when we
meet, our natural first eagerness is to reassure each other that, really,
we're doing the same thing. Music, after all, was "scientific", courtesy of
Pythagoras, when science, courtesy of such as Heraclitus and Parmenides,
was pretty fanciful: read, "artistic". And music was solidly contained
within the Medieval Quadrivium, while the work of Helmholtz in the
nineteenth and Olson and others in the twentieth century seem to keep
a lively connection going at least between the ostensible subject matter
of physical acoustics and that of music theory. The discourse of
speedreaders and quick thinkers, moreover, is full of facile imagery
assuring us for the assuaging of God knows what spiritual anxieties that
art is no less scientific than science is creative. But the comforts of
communal indiscernibility, of the neutralization of the sharp particularity
of distinct ideas, phenomena, things or persons—of the erosion, that is,

of the very distinctions that particularize and give vivid identity to what there is—are not only denied us both by virtue of our chosen mental occupations but are, insofar as we take them seriously, subversive to the very extra- and inter-professional understanding they are presumably promulgated to promote.

Such intellectual immunity to being homogenized is, perhaps, what we do principally, if not exclusively, share. But even if we were constitutionally able to keep it down, we would have no need to digest such conceptual blandness as a basis for our mutual identification and awareness. For the common cognitive languages in which we speak and symbolize are, alone, all we need to guarantee the possibility of cognitive intercommunication, insofar as those languages are what we all depart from commonly into our increasingly esoteric conceptual worlds; insofar as, too, our own specialized observation languages, so remote from the observation languages of the uninitiated, are still only particular developments of those common languages, which are still, even among our own co-workers, the underlying court of appeal for any claim of intersubjective cognitivity, and, indeed, are still the functional delimiters of our capacity to freely conceptualize and invent; and, again, insofar as our creations and subjects are in fact in some significant degree determinate. And when the claim is made, as Heisenberg, along with such contemporary philosophers as Carnap, Reichenbach, and Quine, has made it, that the referential structure, and hence the meaning and significance, of our common languages have been fundamentally transformed by the emergent creations of modern scientific theory, just as when an analogous claim is made on behalf of contemporary musical thought, it is still only by a retrograde path along the same linguistic chain that such claims can be imagined. And since the linguistic landscape, however ordered, is flat and indifferent as to direction of flow, the variant revisions of concept and object that emerge within different esoteric pockets such as science and art may flow out not only to the common language, but through it to the bowels of any distinct other esoteric pocket as well. So, while the way into, the way out of, and the way across specialized conceptual communities are not directionally the same, whatever Heraclitus would have had us think, they are nonetheless functionally interdependent. Hence, when scientists and musicians do meet, rather than celebrating the trivial fact of our common-cultural humanity as perceived through our common logic and our common languages, we might better be concerned to use those as the media through which to elicit and articulate our divergent departures therefrom, offering to each other glimpses both of the worlds our own work enables us to view, and of the world-views that are shaped thereby, such that each of us may at least share that world which includes the others, and perhaps also that we may enlarge the vision of each of our own specialized worlds by conceiving them compatibly contained within a larger world including both.

The world, or worlds, that the musician's work enables him to glimpse are what I have dared to refer to in the presumptuous language of my title. As I hope you will see, it is an Argus-like glimpse that I am proposing, alternating or merging views from a myriad of perspectives; for even grossly, I am imagining my perspective bifocally, onto the worlds that are musical things, and out from them to the world as it appears from the perspective of a habitual observer of the worlds that are musical things. Now I do not know the translation value for your world of what there is in mine: that is, of what there is in the world of music, what there is in the world as music might make it appear, and what there is in your world as it appears from the perspective of the world as music makes it appear. But I offer for your contemplation some of the features of the music-cosmological landscape, that is, of some of the remarkable ontological peculiarities of the musical cosmos, as they appear to one engaged musician.

Now if, in the sequel, I use the heuristic device of contrasting musical with scientific matters, that is to be understood entirely in the light, if light it be, of the foregoing. I have no wish, even less any hope, of attaining to an unidiosyncratic characterization of scientific matters, from your point of view. No hope, for obvious reasons; no wish, because I believe that the view I afford you of a musician's world and world-view might include, even as perhaps its most revealing aspect for you, how your world looks from within it. So it is that which I believe I am conveying when I, rather than you, speak of science, just as it is the complementary view which I discern in the writings of Heisenberg, or Carnap, or Helmholtz, when they, rather than I, speak of music.

Scientific thought, as I suppose it, consists in the construction of theories of which some portions or all of the observable world are models, in whatever inferentially extended sense of "observable". Experimental science seems to arrange linkages among distinct portions of the observable world so that observable events, in the narrower sense, at some given node of such a system, are regarded as determinate data, relative to specific scales of quantization, concerning the behavior of entities of a specific nature as they are defined within a specific theory. One world only is the apparent universe of all, as well as each, scientific theory, and each tenable scientific theory is in principle, as I understand it, supposed to be compatible, co-tenable, and indeed co-effective with each other theory conceded to be tenable at a given science-historical juncture. I perceive Heisenberg in this spirit when he speaks of scientific idealization as a way of "understanding the colorful multiplicity of phenomena ... by recognizing in them unitary principles of form." Elsewhere, he specifies as conditions for theoretical tenability the "crucial precondition for any usable scientific theory that it should subsequently stand up to empirical testing and rational analysis ... there is an inexorable and irrevocable criterion of value [in science] that no piece of work can evade." Ontological creativity in science is, as Heisenberg points out, entirely the outcome of the painful struggle with empirical anomaly arising within the confines of existing theoretical-experimental systems: How does one make a revolution? he asks, and answers: By trying to change as little as possible.

Now a good way to elicit the peculiarities of musical things is to notice the oddly inscrutable results yielded by the effort to sustain this scientific perspective in the observation of musical phenomena, which Heisenberg attempts to do. For example, in tracing the history of abstraction in science and in art, Heisenberg is able to suppose that degree of abstractness is a possible relative attribute of musical compositions: witness his remark that "Genuinely abstract art has existed ... as in Bach's *Art of Fugue.*" To a musician, it seems obscure under what notion of abstraction such an observation can have been made. There is, so far as I can perceive, no relative want of concreteness in the musical entities that constitute the work in question: I do not hear them as classes, generalizations, concepts, or covering laws, but as determinate phenomenal particulars, nor do I find those entities especially indiscernible as particulars relative to other particulars, either within the *Art of Fugue,* or in other, distinct, musical compositions. Indeed, I can scarcely imagine how to take in any given sounding musical event as more "theoretical" in its sound than any other, any more than I can imagine that the contents of the heavens are more abstract than the contents of my lunch pail, whatever the relative abstractness of the astronomical and gastronomical sciences. And if "abstraction" refers, in Heisenberg's use of it relative to Bach, to some other class of attributes than those comprehended under the familiar relational sense of the term, say, the attribute of being referred to as abstract in the popular print, or the attribute of being complex or relatively inward, in that salient attributes of particularity are relatively less blazoned on the immediate surface, relatively less accessible by virtue of immediate association with extramusical things, and relatively more wholly discernible only as the product of minutely contoured configurations in context, then the word abstraction as so applied is a mere homonym of some other word, an epithet rather than a term.

What I discern as the origins of this admittedly rather innocuous confusion are at least two problems of context: first is the question, to which I alluded earlier, of the referential domain, the cosmos, being referred to in observations about something called "music". This we may speak of as the question what is the *object* of focus in speaking of music.

Second is the question what aspect of the content, or what content within a given system of activity, or observational complex, is to be regarded as the significant distinguishing characteristic of the individual enterprise or class of enterprises under scrutiny. Thus you might find it odd if someone mentioned as a salient attribute of Heisenberg's Uncertainty Principle that the brow of Albert Einstein tended to furrow whenever it was mentioned. This question we may speak of as the question of *direction* of focus. Of our two questions, the second is probably the more telling in distinguishing the character of musical from that of scientific activity. But since the question of direction is perhaps subtler and more elusive than, as well as dependent on, the question of object, it is the latter which I will now consider.

I remarked earlier that an adequate view of what is referred to by talk of music would require an Argus-like multiplicity of distinct observational perspectives. I should have mentioned that what is also required is a Cyclopean integrity within each focus: the creature that knows them all together must also know them each as univocally distinct. Music is, then, sometimes the aggregate of musical objects, in which case talk about it is about *all* works of music simultaneously. Or, music is whatever distinguishes anything as music, in which case talk about it is about *any* work of music, equally, but not more than one simultaneously. Or music is the historically ordered set of musical works, in which case talk about music sorts all works of music into proper subsets, with whatever account of the consequentiality and character of the succession of subclass characteristics. Or music may be the name for *musikierung,* music-making, the activity of composing, or perceiving, or performing, or theorizing, or analyzing. The problems that arise in confusing these domains are obvious when we consider another remark of Heisenberg, where he supposes that he finds music in a condition like that of early twentieth-century physics, confronting "the helplessness when faced with the question of what to do about the bewildering phenomena, the lamenting over lost connections, which still continue to look so convincing ..." and so forth. Now what he is remarking on is, in fact, a condition that may have been true of persons attempting to compose and perceive music, and, thus, a true condition of thought *about* music. But it is scarcely scrutable as even a possible condition of any musical composition or group thereof, that is, it is merely incoherent as a report of thought *within* music. Since thought within music is only discernible by virtue of the successful projection of specific attributes, or images, there can only be "bewildering phenomena" in one of only two senses: phenomena which have a determinate feel, hence a distinct identity, but cannot be characterized by any extension of existing descriptive resources. Or, phenomena which appear to purport to be musical, but cannot be so received, and hence are received as noise. In both cases, the indeterminacy is not of the phenomena but of the theory. "The theory", too, is two distinct theories: the first of which we may call the *descriptive* theory, the second the *attributive*. And the fact is, that the crisis in music which people talk about as having occurred at the end of the nineteenth century may be understood as the moment when the inadequacies of existing descriptive theory were brutally exposed by the faltering of available attributive theory: composers like Schoenberg were finding it difficult to proceed beyond brief passages, or to proceed coherently from any work to a successor. The relativity of musical systems which emerged as the solution to the crisis was not only, nor even primarily, a revolution in composition, or in the theory of contemporary music, but was in fact a revolution in the theory of musical foundations, the any-musical theory to which I referred earlier. By having to understand their own music, both descriptively and attributively, musicians of Schoenberg's generation and the next were forced to understand the nature of musical systems, beyond the attributes of particular systems, and thus to become able to perceive any given system not as a musical universal but as a musical choice.

Following on their work, some more recent musical thinkers, myself among them, were able to observe that in fact each musical entity could be understood to create its own system, rather than merely instantiating it. That is, that from any work, given only a large enough any-musical theory to begin with, the particular lexical and grammatical background for that work could be inferred from the theoretically interpreted perceptual characteristics of the data alone, without the intervention of assumed conventions; the significant compositional and experiential consequences of this are among the subjects of my long essay called *Meta-Variations*. But still further, it appeared from the confluence of both systematic relativism and ontological creativity that the variable ontology emergent from within different systems was not restricted to distinct works; that in fact, a system was a mode of cognition rather than an invariant attribute of data-complexes, and that hence, music theory was ipso facto creative, and that the effective result of musical description was the determinate transformation of what was experienced.

But to be a specific musical entity is to have a determinate feel—that is, to be perceived as having a *sound* distinct from that of every other musical entity. Musical things are thus truly phenomenal things, not only because, as we have observed, what musical thing something is is variable relative to an attributive theory, but because it is that thing only as perceived, and—even further—may be *experienced fully* as a determinate feel without *being* sensorily perceived: as, that is, *thought*, without the intervention of any physically measurable atmospheric perturbations in the receptive environment of any sense organs. This notion of determinate feels, then, may be an essential extension of our epistemology: for however mentalistic, determinate feels are as intersubjective as thoughts, correlating in no uncertain or indeterminate way with perceivables.

Here arises still a more peculiar ontological observation: consider the sound of a given musical moment, say the lowest pitch of a line of ascending pitches. Clearly, to be the lowest note of that particular ascending line of pitches is a salient aspect of musical thinghood, according to my earlier remarks. But the question arises: *when is* that pitch the lowest note of that ascending line? Obviously, it is dependent on both antecedent and subsequent events to acquire such a character: the pitch preceding it must not have pre-empted its lowest-ness, and the pitches following must follow in a certain relative height, such that the "ascending line" as a whole is entified by the observation of at least one pitch *subsequent* to its completion, when a "change of direction" isolates it as a specific string. So *chronology* becomes an aspect of *identity* within a musical structure. A datum sounds a certain way at its moment of assertion, by virtue of its predecessors, then becomes a progressively distinct entity by virtue of its successors: it sounds different first as the lowest of two, then of three, then of four, then of five successive notes— and to sound different is, as we have noted, to *be* different. The sound of a musical work is then the cumulative sound of the cumulative chronology of its components. And since to be in a given place in a given chronology is to have a unique sound, and since to have a unique sound is to be a unique thing, we may truly suppose that no two musical entities can be alike, that musical qualities, as elicited by attribution through a common theory, are all ontologically distinct, rather than repeatable in the sense of *qualia*.

But if musical qualities within a piece are non-repeatable because of chronological dependency, are musical compositions themselves non-repeatable—or, in other words, have I committed myself to a reductio ad absurdum of particularism on top of my imminent peril of solipsism? The answer, I hasten to assure you, is no—Beethoven's Fifth survives intact, and I am as relieved as you are to know it. But it does so only by a further ontological twist, this time in the character of musical time. For the significant chronology within which musical entities arise is within *a piece,* not, I believe, within *pieces*. That is, a musical entity is piece-time, but not world-time, dependent. Piece-time, like piece-pitch-position, is a location within a mental landscape, and has a repeatable determinate feel in auditory or thought-experience. Just like a particular juncture in a conversation, carried only by a mental act of bounding, the feel of such a moment of piece-time, outside of the determinate feel of a given place in a chronology, may be evoked even in the absence of the rest of the chronology on any given occasion: this happens whenever I write the next note of a piece, knowing just where I am in the time-structure, without re-reading all previous notes; and it happened to me last week when I turned on the radio, heard one C-major chord, and unhesitatingly perceived it as the last sound of the Beethoven *Coriolan* Overture—correctly, as it turned out, but, as you may by now suspect, I'm not sure whether that indicates that I, or Beethoven, or the piece, or anyone, was thereby passing one of those inexorable tests which none of us can rationally evade.

So the world of musical compositions begins to appear, most favorably, not as an aggregate world, but as an aggregate of worlds; each possible as a model of an any-musical theory, but mutually incompatible in that the ontology of predication (the values of the variables which predicate quality) is not even wholly uniform within, much less between, given works. And it is here that we may observe that the *direction* of musical focus diverges from that of science.

For it seems that the principal desideratum of all musical activity is the multiplication of ways for entities to be distinct: the very act which Heisenberg assured us was exceptional and painful for science, regarding which scientists wish to be preternaturally parsimonious, is the one regarding which musicians seek to be limitlessly prodigal. The data yielded by the scientific experiment supports or disconfirms the theory. The theory applied to the data of the musical experiment is supported by the richness of identity it thereby confers on the data. The scientist wishes to make it unnecessary to know each in order to know all; the musician wishes to make it impossible to know all without knowing each. In science, one seeks to learn if possible how new entities are really old ones. No one is interested in creating musical entities that merely duplicate entities already created; and to learn to hear a unique thing as a categorical thing is a net loss for musical experience. If there are "natural" laws of musical hearing, if some given relation of fundamentals to the partial spectrum is more closely in conformity to a natural norm than other relations are, then composers are likely to seek to re-compose nature rather than conform to it, to de-naturalize musical sound and produce empirical reality out of natural anomaly. The qualification, hence, of the *individual* is the devolution point of all musical thought, for whose sake alone the class generality—all the way out to the term "music" itself—is reified; whereas the individual entity within the individual observation-complex is specifically valued by the sciences insofar as it can reliably be regarded as instantiating a class of phenomena or objects. Thus induction, and thus what seems, at least, a radical divergence in the nature of the inductive process as between what we may call musical knowing and scientific knowing. Musical thought is not, as Heisenberg thought, in a less happy position than that of science, because it lacks that "inexorable and irrevocable criterion of value that no piece of work can evade", for it has as its modus operandi the no less exigent demand for precision of identity, unique, determinate, and—consequently and for no gratuitous other reasons than those of clarity and specificity—inordinately complex.

And perhaps it would not be altogether surprising if, out of valuing our art for the co-existence of virtual incompatibles which it enables, there might emerge as a world-view a kind of pacific philosophical anarchism, wherein one would seek the means to regard as permissibly within one's world as wide a divergence of views and behavior as possible, without feeling obliged to adopt, accept, emulate, or approve, in order to permit cohabitation within the commonwealth of sentient existence.

You may have noticed that here, as from the outset of this paper, I have been making observations heavily loaded toward the personal—both private-personal and social-personal—signification of our respective projects. I do this because of the intellectual conviction that this is the nodal perspective out of which the most revealing aspects of the structures I observe will emerge. I also do this because I, personally, am keenly conscious of the particular complexion of this occasion as a confluence of customarily non-confluent minds, and because, especially under that idiosyncratic condition, it looks like the likeliest avenue to mutual communication. Now whether communication is possible or not may depend crucially on whether we can make apparent the commensurability—rather than the sameness, or compatibility—of our respective world-views, however much in principle—because of their common common-languages origin—we know them to be so commensurable. So it may be of some value right here to take note of the fact that scientists and artists—if I may add being presumptuously categorical to being presumptuously personal—exhibit what seem to me to be interesting and perhaps even eloquently revealing differences in public professional behavior.

Thus, by now, I expect I have sufficiently persuaded you of the irrepressible presumptuousness of the artistic character—at least as it is embodied in one of its immediately observable avatars. But I also see a certain complementarity of presumption across the amniotic social fluid, as I look toward my scientific brethren. You, I find, are arrogant by virtue of your apparent modesty in claiming that you merely seek and uncover that which is true about that which truly exists. We, on the other hand, are modest in virtue of our arrogant insistence on constructing and making palpable that which we acknowledge to be wholly fictitious.

We, in other words, presume to decide and create what reality is to be, while you presume that what you decide and create is what reality is and must be. Ladies and gentlemen—metacolleagues—I submit that we are both at the very least insufferable, and share a common stake in concealing from the innocent world our social unsavoriness. That, in fact, is why we both need humanists and journalists to misrepresent us publicly as if we had permissible manners and redeeming social value. Lord help us all if they ever turned on us the sharp critical tools of our own methodologies, in place of the nice soft soap they have been accustomed to use. Until that fearful juncture, at any rate, we can share at least the tranquil joys of that impunity which comes uniquely of being thoroughly misunderstood, even by one another.

FANTASIA

Benjamin Boretz

8/77; for the International Musicological Society Congress, Berkeley, 8/77
revised 12/79-1/80

Somewhere along the way, our talk, our hearing—even perhaps
(could it be?), our music—seem to have lost their grip on the
musical image. Schoenberg, examining Schenker's analytic sketches
for Beethoven's Third Symphony, complained that he couldn't find
his favorite tunes: a crude wisecrack, no doubt, which nonetheless
hints at serious epistemic anxieties. Oscar Levant, Schoenberg's
pupil, not long after, introduced a performance of his own Piano
Concerto with the admonition that it was a piece "so modern, even
the composer doesn't like it": apart from the point that Schoenberg
should have paid more attention to Levant when composing
wisecracks, and that Levant should have paid more attention to
Schoenberg when coining compositions; and apart from the
dazzling evenhanded misanthropic virtuosity in managing
simultaneous sneers at neanderthal cultural philistines *and*
avantgarde culture snobs, all in a single mouthoff, it remains that
no one could even have imagined the sense of such a joke fifty
years earlier: something, however frivolously, was certainly being
smoked out there.

About fifty years earlier, the philosopher Gottlob Frege was
strenuously propounding and refining certain concepts in the
analysis of language which have dominated an entire realm of
linguistic theory and philosophy for almost a century thereafter:
'meaning', for Frege, is identifiable as reference, or extension—
'sense', in its various guises, is relegated to a distinct category, one
which concerns the criteria for applying a sentence or term; and—
in some of its most prominent guises—'sense' is dismissed as
elusive, shadowy, 'psychologistic'. Natural language, having no

invariable criterion for the truth value of all its sentences, or of the ontological status of all its references, is regarded by Frege as essentially incoherent in comparison with a logical, rigorously self-governing, language. And—and even more stringently for the history of our own thought—the guise of 'sense' in which we distinguish shades of meaningdifference within grossly equivalent conditions of applicability ('synonomies') are designated by Frege as 'coloring' (*Färbung*), distinguished altogether from 'sense' (*Sinn*), and regarded as cognitively (or, at least, philosophically) unimportant. Thus was the cognitive quagmire of idealist philosophy surmounted, by the elevation of the designable 'extension' to the status of 'meaning' and the relegation of the elusive 'intension' to the status of 'psychology'; by the elevation of the determinately, logically, paraphrasable language to the level of cognitivity, and the relegation of the shades and nuances of natural language to the status of vagueness.

And while this Fregean canon, like the Schoenbergian canon, has undergone strenuous revisionary criticism since it was revealed, our thirst for understanding—whether language, music, or, the world —has seemed to be predominantly slaked by an assiduous quest for extension, verification, and denotation: to understand music, we descend below its surface, perhaps never to return; the musical work is understood as, is dissolved into, the structures it denotes, and into the sequential structures which successions of those structures denote: *the fact that* x exhibits such and such a structure, or such and such structural relation to some y, or that x:y represents such and such species of structural logic, is taken to satisfy the search for the sense of music. Subtly, and insidiously, a peculiar distinction is created between *understanding* music and *receiving* it, between what is chosen to be described and what is expected to be heard. And then, just as subtly and insidiously, the distinction dissolves: music finally comes to be received, to be heard, just *as* the denotator of its own logicized structures. And comes to be composed that way too, if the rhetoric of discourse of some of our most thoughtful composers is in fact reflected in the sonic identities of their works, just as Oscar Levant feared. And thus too, as Arnold Schoenberg feared, may Beethoven be shorn of his tunes.

But whatever language might turn out to be in a Fregean world, it seems that poetry is entirely excluded from it; for surely it is a simple ontological truth that the existence and meaning of literary works, and certainly their artistic richness, reside not in *what* they denote, but in *how*; not in the syntactic (or semantic) structures which they may be taken to symbolize, but in the specific peculiarities of each nuance of word sound, word choice, word order, and grammatical, lexical, and referential rhythm they embody. How a literary composition makes something unique *with* its language, how it makes its language unique, and how it makes unique language, are surely not only what we value most *about* it, but also constitute the *identity of* the object we refer to by using its name.

For music, too, it seems an ontological perversity to regard it, or—especially—to compose it, as if it had as its object the exhibition of the structure of its language, as if it were best received—or understood—as an informative symbol whose musical identity is assimilated into the identities of its denoted syntactical- (or semantical-) structure-entities. To focus on what music *refers to* is terminally to obscure what it *is*; to data-process a musical configuration as a *symbol* rather than to assimilate it as an *image* is surely to produce a music-perceptual experience of inferior vividness and quality; and thus is our difficulty in hearing contemporary music heavily compounded by the paths by which we have come to *understand* it.

Imagine, on the other hand, that instead of eliciting "facts" internal to a musical structure, we were engaged in capturing the qualities exuded by a musical surface. Suppose, for example, that we were talking about the stretch of Stravinsky's *Rite of Spring* from the opening bassoon solo to its semitone-depressed recollection. I can scarcely imagine that anything could be called a musical account of that stretch which failed to evoke the sense of its inner choreography: beginning with the very first singlenote sound,

*a keening primordial whine, a trembling hover, suddenly sending
seismic chills down its own spine, sprouting eerie excrescences that
merge with it, twisting it into a ghoulish glide through that sound-
and time-space environment that woodwinds simultaneously create
and slither through, arrested electrically by stinging stringtrills
traumatically freezing action, woodwinds as traumatically unfreezing
it, splintering into myriad simultaneities of tiny frenzies interweaving
but blankly oblivious of one another, the desolate whine now
reemerging in ever so emptier a space, oddly discolored, dislocated
now, its spasms now feeble in the aftermath of whatever it was that
happened. . .*

The quantified serial data and the atemporal referential
structures factually and inferentially recoverable from the score
may, unquestionably, be said to be what does all this; but they are
not what music does.

Entrained wondrously, six assorted short pieces [--"variations"; but in some balletic, not musicformal, sense] framed by a full-dress opening "Adagio" (with introduction and conclusion of its own) and a "Coda" comprise "No. 3 Pas de six" in Tchaikovsky's Sleeping Beauty" ballet. The six chapters of what follows -- which refers often to the Adagio -- correspond to these six pieces, scorecaptioned thus:

I. "Candide"
II. "Coulante. Fleur de Farine"
III. "Fée aux Miettes"
IV. "Canari qui chante"
V. "Violente"
VI. "La Fée des Lilas"

JKR

march / june , 1976
april / july , 1977

-- J. K. RANDALL

how music goes

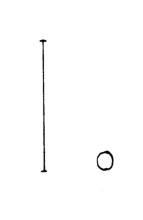

new now
is it

(at The same old
          stall ? (

I.

: didn't get The word.

ruminates ;
over
in some
underspace

: or got the word /
/ just not the point.

stalled ;

-- (, Though the Point
was what the word Had)

over
in some
corner of the
word / point

(got / not got)

chews its
cud.

underchews
some leftover
crud

left over

(overchews) some

in some
corner of
underspace

leftunder
crud.

& fumbles

mumbles

over

what
would have done the job.
what

, with a last flick

(, wrap

did do

it   up)

(already.)

& nail down   did make

                                     the point

(even then already)

(, if ever)   driven in

                                     with a sledgehammer.

                                     stumbles over (,

(, Onto?   what
                                     had been

smashingly   routed

                                     from the fray.

                                     does the

(Thanks)   job now

                                     -- by --
(again)

(Diffracturing) it--   fucking (it) up;

rehashes

--(it)--

)That's
one
thing(

by

(Intradicting)

--it--

:&now, old
Oversong;

(again)

                                        sort of
(; Fumigated):

: anything

(, everything)   : (No Dirty)

that might
recollect
the point

(got/not)

-- excised.--   (up here)

clean.

: nothing

To Rout.   (now)

(old Oversong)

Open   now

                    up here

to (
                                        : exhalations (,
                                          (, rising

to (
                                        : fuckupfumes from
                                          underspace (,

                    (, still   (, still
                    ruminant   chewing its
                    down there   crud over

            (song)

                                                (undercolored)

                    stalls

Translucent
                                : shadows
                                  cast)
                    (over)
to (
                                    (from
                                      under

                                                , will color)

(uncoloring,

                    still

)that's
another(

)rising,
                    FRACTED
                    BESPEAKS

            WORLD/
            /COLOR
    fumes(

                                            , will rise

                                            (shadowing
                                            themselves

(old Oversong)   up(,

                            higher
(ducks)(Under)

)(
(into the clear.)

                                            , above the
                                            fray)

(&)   &
(cleans)(out)

                                            , fraying the
                                            overfringe..)

                            rising
(underspace.)

                                            out of sight

            --(--World
                Cracked?--)--

    :(Safe Now.):?

:--! (by no means.).--)--:   Two   (Do)

squared

footed

/upsight/   four   lump
(song)
                             :
/downside/
(over)

con
cedents

(frayed   --its--

↓

outsight   )(
incised   :

ante
sequents

inside)   :
(in

(each)

There
where
                                                              it.

(one)

underducked)   (Dirty)

; & Up Here now . ?

Then

when

)strained(

(clean)

(clear)

(all's)

done :
--;

: (Do)

all

:   :

:

(over)   --¦--   :

it

(all)

up
here

; (Installed.).

)no(

strain

/got/

(fracted)

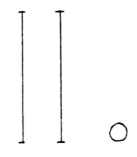

which being the case,

, forthright assertion was called for.

-- an elucidation of distinguishable parts.

-- some principled query.

-- reassembly along tested lines.

(and Assert you Did.)

II.

; in fact

Distinctly.

first, you loudmouthed the obvious.

what was common; undoubted.

-- an average--; (--warped, in fact;
just noncommittal. --)--

some hollowed-out generality

just a backgrounder, was it?

then, you impounded a distinguishable part.
    -- stuck it right in our nostril.

    --in fact, that chatter you sprattled at us was just
apologia expostfacto (--albeit monosyllabic--) for the fait
already accomplis by fiat.

(even your innuendos were forte at least)

(which fiat attainted what The chatter was tainted with anyhow)

so you stuck us again.

    --Taint & all --

    just not The backgrounder. -- off which the meaning
took its meaning

(thanks)

Thus of Meaning Depleted

& with Taint Replete

you counterfacted
your gross

miracle :

:[you showed up in the other camp.].

& long, O long did you Squat There, over what was
banished from the realm, Twice already.

(, sempisyllabic chatterstretch Tidied. -- squelching
demur--.).

O long, long Did you squat; a bulbous growth on The
Taint in your expostfacto, elucidated Transcendently.

(_forte_ was beginning to sound like a wheeze from the past)

Squatting long.

-- backgrounder, _fiats_, & chattertaints just a
Grand Backgrounder for this ! { resplendent emergence } ! here.

; which you repeated on us, deleting its _raison d'être_ ;
emergence

(Which resplendent emergence was a fake anyhow.)

(What was a Point once (& sledgehammered) was an Impacted Part. -- our Principal Query, in fact.)

(Testing the Wheel, you looped Full Circle.).

; around the bend .

: so you recycled it on us.

as best you could.

--which was none too well.

what with dropping meanings on us.

: so we waited it out.

--without much hope & prospect

which it turned out you didn't rise to.

(fortissimo was about conversational for you by then)

--(-- in fact, We Yawned.--)--

: & you hopped the track.

(Incorrigible you are not.).

: of miracletime noncognizant,
you commenced yakking _in situ_.

(_L'histoire_ _ancienne_ recouped The Wheel.)

(the rescinded _fiat_ recending on us in fact)

:(: yakked to the last splat)

in its own taint, in fact

(which chatterstretch was wheelshaped anyhow)

⊐ something needs looking into

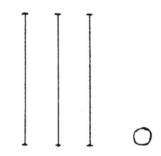

(-- but notice my angle of entry --)

III.

softly,
    on your blind side,   approaching --

(--noticing ;); from across the
            crack in
                your world

        (; you ;)
             --just you--

        1. & 2.
your crack in the   fancied
      world

as insight
    flare --(as
        worldflaw)
           (fleshed)

--not into ; nor   -- but skew
    across.

)nor
　　yakking in

place ---.

< You are to know that insight need not be overt. -- may even covertly take form as overt confusion about something else. -- as alien resonance of something else. Insight need thus not only not be overt : it need not even be into the overt. >

) not chatter --.   (; without haste

speaking   (--& openly)
        softly (To you)

(, from your insight,
                          , just over the brink,)
in clipped   speech
          , (like your own),

                              -- (, onesyllabled)
          (--your own voice,
                              is it?--)

     :(my touchstone):

⟨You are to know also that covert insight into the covert --
become overt -- may cloud, even shatter, something else
overt. -- will even leave confusion to one side, unresolved.
(-- but also, unattended).⟩

in twists & (   ) turns, yes --

-- undulations --

Through   places--.
        connected
              (, roundedly--)
                      (--curving)

(message   (, wideranging)
          highfloated,)

of new landscape   , contour
              (; noticed
                    (for now) as,)

{and you are to feel insight   as in mind from
the outset.} {--as what you had in mind   from
                                  , more or less,
the outset.}.

                              {: (--and thus we interface)
(; or not noticed)
              ; you feel--

                          but enveloped in
embraced by,
                                    , assuringly

(--brushing you--)--   (I have only just begun)

(I have only just begun)   (beginning again)
                        with a difference

                                (--no angle of entry now--)

                        indiffidently

                            sustainedly) now
    (speaking   (--in multisyllable)

    of old message   redacting
                        an underthread

                        overlaving

        your crack   in the world
                    : (my fulcrum):

    in effulgence(   ) of warm

                        light

(soliciting)

an   underthread

(in   effulgence)

of   warm
          light

concerting((redacting   our)insight

            --right on it--

inside(   )out, I

                    Turn you
binding your
                                    cracked world

with future
                                    opening out

        (,unflushing)

            over the edges

retracting

(old message)

(, with twist

of wrist,)

as

color of

(as aura

of)

as color

exacting

of future

(, highfloating)

its very

--voice--

softly , on your blind side, approaching

from where you've never been
,just barely,

--coming near you--

the brink of
from just over your insight

inside your blind side
the soft edge on

Through you
brushing with my light
, but harrowing,

(Touch)

so slight
with twist for you, for me
so sheer

onto my ground

,wholly,

I bring you

;

whereon, whatever is

--you--

(may grow)

(still;

; you worry me.)(; you concern yourself less with
evolving than with evolved.)(--, with the faint
first glimmer of the uncreated, as terminal; -- as
fixed & done with.)(; -- opaque, to what lurks
behind; & beyond; & around; & underneath.)

so once again I will come upon you from a blind side -- and not
by hint or stealth this time (, nor by soft persuasion) beckon you
out of your depth -- but suddenly, all at once, will wrench
into recognition what you may come to feel I had all along
colluded with you in (, and with you in winking at) as mere
underside of your daydreams, as titillatingly merest periphery
of our messaging and futuring (; or worse: what you may come
to reproach me with having induced your acceptance of as
underpinning, impermeably glossed, whose nonconsequentiality
I had stood thereby your guarantor for; -- all along, injecting
while knowingly diverting your attention from). ; as if, having
healed you inside out, I were to wrench you outside in.

(but I will do it.)   3.   (--& you'll survive)

withdrawing ;
    : lights out :
(The high ground, -- evacuated now)

twotiming ;
    : the underside , infiltering --
(-- adorned --) --

    ; barefacedly
-- I disgorge upon you
    : (dressing you down now) :

    (; in parody)
old auramessage ;
    netherspaced.

    (goading ;)(; chiding)
: disfigured now --
    (in) hulked (,

) grunts.

(-- and I do this quite casually. -- (all at once.) -- (-- hit
over again --) -- (-- , & suddenly) -- hushing you off. -- (-- &
over again --) -- with a twist of the wrist. -- slapping your
wrist ; with a light bounce. --) -- off your old future --) --

"ALLOWANCE TO REASSUME OBSOLESCENT

--:--:that a like bounce (, rebounding)

POSTURES ARE NOT NORMALLY IMPLICATED."

4. & 5.

<Be it known that all things are what they are ;
: disperseth ; --:
        <not something else.>

        ;--: wrenched peripheries, whence they came;
        (--, underpinned ; the gloss, unscarred)

        <: but be it known that all things
: unleasheth ;--:
        <are from something.>

        ;--: in its old place; in its old voice :--:
        :--: old message (;--, glossed)

<And be it known
: gildeth, even ;--:
    <that novel adumbration of the word

       ;--: (, in a fine hand) , old urtext ;
       with novel adumbration of it , -- ,

    <is what it is ;
        , -- , which guideth ; -- (:
    <not something else. >

      -- (: the bounce (, the rebound) ; -- ;
      ; -- ; and cushioneth ; -- ;

     , -- , which revivifieth
       the very voice of old message

          in hushed
         (, yet appointed)

          celebration
             of
           recovery

     from jeopardies unharken'd to ; -- ;
     from errancies unhanker'd for ; -- ;

        ; -- ; ((; & cherisheth ;)) ; -- ;

⟨: by these testimonies be it known :⟩
" ALLOWANCE IS MOST NORMALLY IMPLICATED AS INDICATING
⟨ Misremembrance of the Word
" AN INSUFFICIENTLY UNEXPRESSED INTENTION OF
⟨ emanateth, clouded, from the word ;
" INFILTRATING AN OBSOLESCENT TENDENTIAL WITH DETERIORATED
⟨ and is hence from the word,
" PROSPECTS ; FAILING A MULISH PERSISTENCE. "
⟨ not novel to it. ⟩

⟨: contrapositively :⟩
" ALLOWANCE IMPLICATING THE SHOCK OF BOUNCES ARE MOST
⟨ Novel Adumbration of the Word
" NORMALLY IMPLICATED IN RESTRAINING CIRCUMSCRIPTIONS
⟨ cloudeth emanation of the word ;
" RESPECTIVE OF THE THRUST OF OBSOLESCENT TENDENTIALS
⟨ and is novel to the word,
" IN AN UNCOMPROMISED HAND. "
⟨ hence not from it. ⟩

< Hence be it known that Novel Adumbration of the Word --

: doth smack of contravention harken'd for
　　　　　< -- being neither something else,

　　　　< , nor misremembrance of the word ;
, to cancel what happened.

: doth smack of acquiescence hanker'd after
　　　　< ; nor from the word,

　　　　< , but yet from something --
, to recommence at start.

　< -- misremembers something else. >

;--yet glosseth over (, adumbration) something else ;

{misremembereth now, an old promise ; an old intimation

"ALLOWANCE IS NEITHER IMPLICATED NOR ACCORDANT

OF ANY INFRACTIONS ABNORMALLY IMPLICATED."

{of future opening out ; an old effulgence of warm light;

: doth misremember as nostalgia misremembers :

{ remembering in safety now; in comfort.

{ old urgencies rising quiescent now;
    as without consequence or future.

{ futures uncreated, unknown reviving
    as past & done with.
    as domesticated now for decent burial.

{ desireth now only this last disremembrance
    to be assuaged & laid to rest.

"..............IS   yet even as
                           misremembrance (,

                                        , burying
)adumbrates,

          ALL

                           glossed over
                           obtrudes.

     IMPLICATED

                           : to misremembrance
                           conformed,

                                     : to its weight

                                     & place, in
               IN   counterpoise :

                                     ungushed

          THE   Through cracked
                           edges,

                           floods

     PERMANENT

          RECORD."   remembrance.--

(a time of resurrection

for you;

of resurrecting) you

            --(--in rumpled redaction:)
reffulgence

    of warm light
    invests

      --, irradiates, --

    you,
      ; burial shroud and

                . . . . ALL.

; Thwarted)

(goaded;

THIS EQUIPOISE {:

, aborted)

(--Nonconsequentially--

--(insinuateth

:} of Old &

Resurrected

what

future?)--

life

"BEFORE

. . . . .You, I "

(, forcibly)

<, Abandonedly,>

Thrust, and

--To you--

(entrust.).

IV.

! how nice
to hear from you again.
Especially concerning
Resurrection & Equipoise.
And in my voice, is it!
Still beginning by ending,
are you? Which voice
was that? Beginning
by Ending as a way of beginning, sort of? (I guess.) ending What?
(As between Resurrection & Equipoise perhaps you don't recall: after
all, it's been a while, up to maybe 1.5 seconds, since you've been
there.) (And the 1.5 seconds was all creepy with distractions, like
Silence; & nothing.) Beginning What? (& So Careful I was, to
make Adumbration the Least of it!) -- (future?) -- in an Old voice
of mine, is it! beginning to wrap up & nail down? making Adumbration really Adumbrate? (How Interesting.) That's right: mine
was loose in the joints; but has it ever struck you that my loose
joints fastened something else on -- something of value perhaps:
something, say, like Nostalgia, or Warm Lights, or something
like that? -- Mine Laid Something to Rest? and Yours lays Mine

to rest? How Comprehensive of you! (Yours lays to rest, so to speak, my Embalming Tool?) and Blabbering on so LoopySmooth now! so what is it Yours Really Adumbrates? (Right Up Front really adumbrates.) My recovered NighFloated message to you, like Mine did? How Touching. Edited, of course; for Quick & Easy. (, by the pre-School crowd.): (rollicking & frolicking & Doing Their Diddly). (message with the Message lost.) Floats High Though. Gives a Tight Joint. (Fudges no Foursquared Though.) I know it's an Old Ending of Mine you're Working Over, -- The one from back before you fucked up in Underspace, in fact. You can't get what I shoved in your lap 1.5 seconds ago, but you can remember all the way back there to what you couldn't get either and fucked it up. Of course what you remember about it is beside the point to what you fucked up since what you fucked up was its point. But after all, I was in MetaLanguage then: sticking my Tongue out At, jollying you About; not Evolving Out Of. So no wonder you fucked it up. Nor get it now either unless I'm supposed to make whoopee! every time you flit through Locus Situs of your hoary fuckups as if you were in Warm Light. (Were I to offer a comment I've been withholding until now it would be this: Who besides You would figure Here & Now for Locus & Tempus Optimus for kicking your Underspace habit, not to mention Underspace.) Do you by any chance recall any occasion on which someone (-- never mind who; it might have been anyone --) shoved in your lap (: -- do I obtrude? --) anything which one might describe, perhaps, as equipoise of old & resurrected life, or something like that? (you are a slow learner.). The next time I leave something to you will be watched.

& briefly.

IV.

yours.

truly?

)gnarls.

warm

,bridging,

,arches

:[NEW TOY]:   V   --let's   back
                          --Up

                          --&   towards

                     ◯   where

light   you're   --&
fixture
                                              --Boot

                     coming

                                              --your
                                              --Ass

from.

                                              --Across

wherefrom(:--

                                              --!

                    --〈There!〉

:[,READY?]:

V.

! Repeat After Me !

    (well Not Quite)
    2. (-- minor Misquote --)
    I'll catch it.

!GO!

] Let's Pretend [

a ! Bothquote (,
, sort of)

    : finish it ! Off

but Watch it !
3.

) predictable :
    4.
(don't Quote me)

: misquotes the Bothquote
(-- & the Misquote --)
((--, & the Quote, --))(

    ; (your First reCycle);

    --! hangin' the Old Clothes line! --
Quit while you're Ahead ?

(I'll Undercover it)

--No Chance--
--Noquote now! :

: it's catchUp :
    5.

.All The Way.

   (to the end)   (of the line)

:
:
:
AS OUR
DOUGHTY
HEROES
KICK IT
AROUND
:
THROUGH
THICK &
THIN, NOT
:
ALL IS IN
ORDER.
:
ON THE
OTHER
HAND, A
STITCH IN
TIME
SAVES MORE

(cycled Short) 6. (? too easy)

OK: I'll Twist it.
    7. --Toss you a Curve--
Bag what you Skipped.

loops (, what'd you Do?)

! cool it ! (could do worse)   8.   (--curved ?)
pick it up 9. right there.   minor mostquote

    Up you Go.
10.   No sweat. (, 'cept all fucked
    Same deal.   ) Up

gives You a Dilly.   11. (not a Quote
    in a Carload)

a Real Lulu.
(it's fuckUpland around here)

Muffed........)   (: That Curve you
    zango!

12.   (--still hangin'' em Up--)
I reCycled   (in fuckUpland)

SCREWUPS
THAN YOU
MIGHT
EXPECT
:
OFF THEIR
PREVIOUS
EXPERIENCE
:
& EVEN
SHOWS SOME
SAVVY
WHEN IT
COMES TO
INSEMINATING
INADVERTENCE
. PUTTING
NOT TOO
FINE A
POINT
ON IT
, OUR
DOUGHTY
HEROES
:
TAKE THE
MINORS
BY THE
BATCH
:
THE BULLS
BY THE
HORN

so Here we Go.   13.   Same Curve

; for Broke again.

coming At you

--so--
Here's
--To--
you

! way Out
14.   you Goffle it ! Up   , in fuckUpland
(, Shortcycle it)

(OK :
: Easy One This Time) :   : (just a Noquote).
15.

: To get us Out of here.

(get you Off the Line)
Wait a Minute ! (wiseass) not That Way !
(what're you Into?)

16.

(66⅔ Z ?)
(! ono): The 33⅓ Z you Blew is What Counts.
(it's the Long Way Round ! now)

(You Asked for it.)   17.   (-- leaving it To me --)
! so test This little Teaser:

: Made in fuckUpland :

(don't Fall For it.)

NOR SQUEAL
ON A'
PAL
:
EVER.
ALTHOUGH
A COUPLE OF
MEATBALLS
GOOFING
THEIR WAY
THROUGH
FUCKUPLAND
OFF A MAP
OF F
MAJOR CAN
SCARCELY
BE CLAIMED
TO KNOW
THEIR
ASS FROM
THEIR
ELBOW
OR F
MAJOR
FROM
ZILCH
JUST WHO
:
MAY BE THE
LOSER FOR
IT : SAYS
:
WHO ?

hey what're you Into over there?

(really Stuck on it?)   18.

                    ! Move it !

            (, like for Starters)
19.   Away We Go.

    (big deal.)
      20.   just Back to the Easy one

                (--& Time's a'Wasting--)
(really Hooked on what you were into
over there?)

    oh Alright.   A Quick Peek.
        (: Through The Crack)

                (-- on The Way Home --)

                    21. Scrad?
I know. (oNo, that's Not where we're headed to.)
              ! Leave it Lay!

(fuckUpland's a Big Zip to what's Over There)

                Knock it Off!
                22.
                (you can't reCycle
                Shit Like That)

SO
ONE
THING
LEADS TO
ANOTHER
:
HEW
THOUGH
THEY MIGHT
NOT ALWAYS
TO THE
STRAIGHT
&
NARROW
:
DOWN A
PRETTY
FLAT ROAD.
:
THEY
PUT THEIR
FOOT IN
IT.
! KICK IT
LOOSE
DOUGHTY
HEROES !
&
STEP ON IT.
THERE'S
NO PLACE
LIKE
HOME :

--So--
--It's--
--The--
!Top of the World
To you!

(--& About Time--)
23.
:we're late:

(--Early, is it?)

: & All Whacked Out of Cycle

(don't Quote me)

(, it's All Yours)

)ono(Too Much!

(I should've Quit Before you Started)
(while you were Behind)

I Give it To you Wrong & you Get it Right!

24. (Quote me (,sort of).)
I Give it to you Right & you Get it Wrong!

(--I Mean--)
(you've Really Turned it Around)

: like say back There where we started.

), bottom of the world (, To you
: Give it To me Right There, in the first place, &
we could've Stood in Bad

; so don't quote me

: NOTWITH STANDING HOW SOME RESPECTED & COMPETENT AUTHORITIES ARE CLAIMED TO BE DIS CORDANT AS TO WHETHER OR NOT SOME CROSSED WIRES TWIXT OUR RANDOMLY SELECTED PAIR OF DOUGHTY HEROES STEM FROM CARNAL INADVERTENCE : OR REGARDING THE PROPER CONCEPTION OF PITCH CLASS AS ENJOYED BY SOME RESPECTED & COMPETENT AUTHORITIES

! so Let's Roll !

(watch This one :
: LuluDilly (,
25.
                    sort of)

— so —

right back

—alrighta'ready—

Through fuckUpland
                    , the other way,

!(keep it hopping)

Not Bad !   26.   (-- for Cooling it.)
(, & Leaving it to Me.)

! easy Does it.   : & Ditch
27.   that Skrid
just Do   you're Scritching
like you Did :   after

Real Cool !   28.
(back on the track now)
        (Back on the Backtrack)

                    (through fuckUpland)
! Curve   29.
    (coming AT you)(--The other way--)

! predictable !   forwards

                                   , backwards ,

         makes no Nevermind to You.
; just so's it's In   (fuckUpland)

                    30.

; just so's you're On   (Shortcycle)

      (hardly seems fucked Up anymore
      The way you're going)

(been Pushing The Undercover
around)

                                                    -- our
                                                    you
                                                    the
              --Straightened   goose,
                                                    you
                      --you   needed
                                                    To
                      --Out   head
                                                    for
      (since you Snarxled That   home
Skrod)

              ! down The Pipe
              31. now &
              we've Got it Made.

STRATED
THROUGH
CHANNELS
:
FEET IN THE
GROUND
, HAND IN
GLOVE
, HEAD IN
YOUR
SHOULDERS
, SHOULDER
TO THE
WHEEL
STICKING
THEIR
NECK OUT
NOSE OUT
OF JOINT
, EYE TO
EYE ; &
EYEBALL
TO
EYEBALL
NOT ALL
THAT
SASS ; IS
:
NICE SO'S
WE KNOW
WHETHER IT'S
SERIOUS.

! right On   you're In

32.

Position!   Position.
(, of course)   (: On Course)

(, now.)

To Do it All Over again

, of course

? what else!

(when did You ever Flour a chance
to Quote?)
(actually, I pulled a fast one)

(actually, you're In Position
for that Misquote you Started with)

(-- but you're going the Wrong Way --)

(actually, you're going like you went at the Top
when you got it Right when I gave it to you Wrong)

: so I'll Jump The Gun on you :

: Kick Off the Allquote ! Myself

: Goose your ! Misquote Back on The Track .

— (just a little Touch of Mine

I Thought you'd Like) —

& by the Time you're Back in line

you're ! reCycled &

you're Hooked

, you're Repeating (, ! Ready or Not) —

— by the Time you figure out which way is Up.

AH
! DOUGHTY
HEROES !
:
MAY YOUR
SEVERAL
SCREWUPS
NOT BE
CLAIMED TO
SYMBOLIZE
THE
SITUATION OF
US
ALL
:
! TO WIT
:
THE HUMAN
EXPERIENCE
ITSELF
:
TO WIT
:
THAT F
MAJOR
IS A
PRETTY LEAKY
SIEVE
:
NOR BITCH &
WHINE IF
YOU HAVE TO

--so just--   Settle In.   &   ) <u>curves</u>

<u>oops</u>

<u>fuckUpland</u>

<u>luludillies</u>

<u>Scrod!</u>

<u>quick peek</u>

<u>Top of The world</u> (:

        : roll with it

: ho

; wake up

: a Good Gander
This Time

57.
a real Zinger.

(noquotes you past fuckUpland)

DO IT ALL
OVER UNDER
AWKWARD
CIRCUMSTANCES
:
! ONE
STEP AT A
TIME !
DOUGHTY
HEROES.
SASS FOR THE
GOOSE IS
SASS FOR THE
GANDER.
:
CREAM IT.
A REHASH
CAN, IF BY
:
INADVERTENCE
:
, NAVIGA
TIONALLY
SPEAKING
:
SO CLAIM
SOME
RESPECTED &
COMPETENT
AUTHORITIES
:
AFFORD WHAT
NONE CONTRO
VERT

fuckUpland, this

--no--

     --Isn't--

soft stuff.
(; for starters)
!, Shift Ass!

    That's It!

get the feel of it

(oh that Snappy

Undercover)

--<There!>
(; Settle Down--)
: zero In :

	WAS A
	PREMEDI
	TATED PENE
	TRATION OF
--so--	SCRODGROD
	ON PURPOSE
	:
	, KNOWN
	LOCALLY
	AS TERRA
	INCOGNITA
	:
	, WHERE
--hey	HAVE BEEN
	UNRELIABLY
	REPORTED TO
	RECUR , A
	SELECTION
	OF INDIGNI
	TIES
--you	&
	AFFRONTS
--dropped	:
	NOT ALL OF
--your	WHICH
	UNHAPPILY
	:
	FOR THE
--!	DRIFT OF
	THIS
	NARRATIVE
	:
	ARE UNFOUN
--toy	DED.

(Sit Tight.)

(what's going On here)

(Steady now.)   hang in there

                                                     Ah!
(it's all Swishy & Kinky around here)
   (it's skrodding all over)

                          &
              --(grab it)--

(wait it out)

                                                     Truly?

:it's letting
up(

)--!Go!--(

socko!

caught it (   ), we did

!--offstride--!

)--let's
)--Up
)--&

quick (   )Shorttrack
Peek   the
&   Backtrack &
Peak   Fullcycle (

)at The Top   careful --(, upstuck) Home (

)— let's Up &--((hang on)   )pull! something

)-- let's Up &--(--Off!--

)-- !Snytch
)-- !Some!
)-- !Scrodd
)-- Globs:

(about Buried us
under)
        !)--let's Up &--(!

ANYWAY
WHO
CARES
?
:
! OUR
DOUGHTY
HEROES!
CARE.
:
REMEMBER
IT WAS
SCREWUPS
GOT US
THIS
FAR.
:
! EVER
ALERT
:
THOUGH
TRIED
WITH
:
TOIL
, &
SOILED
WITH
STRIFE
:
OUR
DOUGHTIES
HERE

)! difFracture some ! Sclofgrodds (

! STOP !

& Ram''em ! Home

(in ! fuck ! pland)! &

oh   --just ! Bang it In
<don't Quote me>
          (again)
)glort it (home

103.
        ! Skloffle it !

(busted scradgrad
up)

CONCOCT
:
, &
CUT
UP A
CAPER
:
, OF
WHICH
THOSE
COMING
AFTER
:
THOUGH
THEMSELVES
:
UNSULLIED
BY
STAKE
:
OR
PERIL
:
, WILL
CLAIM
SOMETHING
:
QUOTABLE
:
TO SEEKERS
OF
ISSUANCE
OR

OUTCOME
:

:
THEREFROM
:

:

:

take
where

it
we

VI.

right
left

from
off

○

!WAIT!

in scrodgorod ?

&

floor

The

off

up

it

get

let

,CHK

take it right
where we left

from
off

CHK

all together now

Ⅵ. BOOM

let

it

let's wrap
this thing
up

hang

out

out
?
here

when

! says it all

? we are

ring

out

PAH

let

it

−BLE SCRAB − BLE SCRAB − BLE

TAH

TA

feels good
to lay into
it

who

Truly.

in gradscrad?

whose.

?it is?

So Let's Hear It

! together
again
for the first time

everything
in place
now

IK

seen
it
all

That's

if

old LAH

oversong

i'm DAH

monkey's

a

uncle

DA

born

old

been
back

there
&

--ours?

altogether
now

don't quote me

so

who's   To   say

how

got   That   way

it

So What's the Story.

] put
in
a
plug

first

good

since

one

old   oversong

off   went

for
  a
    coda]

back

—who's

before

sledgehammered

or something

like

that

really

coming

off

on

new

us

kick
it

around

--no

!telling--

under the
warm

lights

in   its

intro   upside   down

wards   &   own

back

&
all

REPLY: TO JOHN RAHN*

Benjamin Boretz

Rhythm in my Quest is not duration. (John Rahn knows and acknowledges this.) A principal interest it professes is to distinguish "rhythm" as intuitively conceived from "the durational component of musical structure". (Ultimately, an epistemology of rhythm is invoked to decomponentialize "musical structure" altogether.) Yet I am able to suppose experiencing some given rhythm as the determinate feel of a pitched-duration structure, along whatever lines the experience of a pitch-duration (or durationed-pitch) structure is also intelligible. And the motivic retrievability of relative-time-sequence configurations ("patterns of duration") is at least implicit in Quest's mischievous *Sacre* example.

So I am not moved so much to criticize or correct John Rahn's objection to my construction of musical duration as to perceive it standing as a distinct, interesting alternative hypothesis. And hence I should wish rather to elucidate than to defend the durational perceptions of Quest, to sharpen rather than deplore their contrast with John Rahn's constructions. Quest's durational attitudes stem from the experiential heteromorphism that obtains between what I inceive when I try to line up a musical structure durationside out, and when I try to line it up pitchside out. Closer in, I distinguish *duration* from *time*: I think of two matching durations but cannot think of two distinct but matching times. Two pitches can be members of a single pitch class in two "degrees": as "same pitches" or as "n-octave-intervallically-related pitches". Durations duplicate quantitatively, relatively, but never between the "same two timepoints". Modular structuring of timepoints refines the analogical positioning of successive durations, but always in distinct "octaves", and specifically in distinct octaves linearly progressing in a deterministically inexorable ascending order. (Modular timepoint

---

*John Rahn: "Rhythm, and Talk About It", along with this "Reply", appear in *Perspectives of New Music*, 15/2, Spring-Summer 1977.

systems order timepoints *in time.)* These distinctions are consequent upon the irretrievability of any *time* of the past, whatever *qualities* of any past time are resonatable by sonic metaphor. On the other hand, I have no intuitions of "now" and "then" that are isomorphic with my intuitions of "here" and "there", largely in that while events happen in time, at times, over time, time does not happen. And while times pass inexorably within or outside a piece—i.e., a time is always present, such that it is always "now"—no such context is intuitive for "pitch" (there *must* be a time at every pitch, but there need not be a pitch at every time).

One more: the quantitative identity of pitch intervals ensues from their pitch-qualitative, or two-pitch-qualitative, identity; the qualitative identity of time intervals seems irreducibly quantitative. The fact of quantity is not the effect of quantity. Metricization has to do with the facts rather than the effects: by their sounds we *know* the sizes of relative durations; but the resultant indexes of relative size are *not* the sonic images of music.

Nowhere do these distinctions, if accurate and germane, preclude or demean the "time-in-pitch" program for which John Rahn pleads, especially where the analogy is compositionally created rather than theoretically alleged. But such a program might be significantly enlightened, and its allure as a musical alternative materially enhanced, precisely by its sensitive and aggressive adoption of the heteromorphic logics of pitch and duration to which these reflections would seem to lead.

THINGS

(A COURSE DESCRIPTION)

OBSERVING OBJECTS: FROM WHICH INTELLECTUAL ACTIVITY
DEVELOPS. OBSERVING OBJECTS MUNDANE, FAMILIAR,
ABSTRACT, ESOTERIC, VULGAR, REFINED, OBVIOUS, SUBTLE:
FROM WHICH DEVELOPS INTELLECTUAL ACTIVITY OF ALL SHADES
OF DEPTH, COMPLEXITY, QUALITY, CHARACTER. OBSERVING
OBJECTS, FROM WHICH INTELLECTUAL ACTIVITY DEVELOPS: AS
VIVID DESCRIPTION IS FORMULATED, AS COHERENT DISCOURSE IS
SHAPED. INTELLECTUAL ACTIVITY DEVELOPS: IN THE ABSENCE
OF PREFABRICATED DISCIPLINARY CONVENTIONS, IN THE
PRESENCE OF INTELLECTUAL ACTIVITY ALREADY DEVELOPED AS
THE WORLD'S LITERATURE OF FORMULATED IDEAS, AS OBJECTS
IN WHICH THOUGHT HAS BEEN REPOSED. OBSERVING OBJECTS:
THE SAME ONES, VIEWED DIVERGENTLY, FORMULATED INTO
DIFFERENT THOUGHTS AND DIFFERENT OBJECTS IN WHICH
THOUGHT REPOSES. INTELLECTUAL ACTIVITY DEVELOPS: AS
HOLDERS OF DIVERGENT VIEWS OF THE SAME OBSERVED
OBJECTS CONFRONT EACH OTHER'S VIEWS; APPRECIATE
CRITICALLY; EXAMINE CONSEQUENCES EXPLORATORILY; ADDRESS
INCOMPATIBILITY, FOR BETTER AND WORSE. OBSERVING
OBJECTS, INTELLECTUAL ACTIVITY DEVELOPS.

1978, FOR A 1ST-YEAR SEMINAR/BAB

and we shall endlessly be all had in Him
Him verily seeing and fully feeling
Him spiritually hearing
Him delectably smelling and sweetly swallowing

I. IN WHICH

I sing a song by the troubadour Bernart de Ventadorn

, which I am composing .

I caress my song , surely ; but this song caresses me back :

Widens , tightens its net , to caress just there --

from every side , with every pressure ;

lapses , to a dark edge

to reinvade the soft place , in shaded light ;

finding (-- attaining --) its voice for what dare not speak ;

ear , for what dare not be heard .

-- then lapses , to embrace its wake of silence

about what might count as Consummated .

My Friends! (Old Provencal : "Companho!")--(--not you)

Anonymous ,

you Congeal out there

FrontFaced ; by Rows & Columns :

to Applaud .

doubtless you will Applaud!

, on Schedule ,

: erupting ; in your Flabby Percussions

of the Left palm upon the Right ;

(or (-- alternatively --) of the Right palm

upon the Left)

((-- or of Both , Equidistantly Flapping .))

it may even be

that Bravo will be said!

(not as You might Say Something :

(said , as *Bravo! is said .

(: Hollered :

(-- to hear its *!Head Rattle!

: Brayed :

through cupped , Already Pinkened , palms .

[Anything Else from You

is Uncalled For :]--(--!or maybe a *Famous Scandal!

IT IS NOT YOU
WHO ARE IN MY LINE OF WORK

!COMPANHO!

IT IS I
WHO AM IN YOURS

INTIMACY—a polemic

INTIMACY—a polemic

[INTIMACY—a polemic]

INTIMACY—a polemic

So What?--that it's Mine.

--Likes Me . . . .

II. IN WHICH

I listen to myself sing my song --

-- myself , courting some far lady within ;

-- myself , courted ;

blend . -- (-- if indissolubly ; --)

We are ravishingly One .

III. *IN WHICH*

I sing my song for a loved lady --

-- sing For? -- or sing To?

: if To :

Far Lady Within is made flesh .

: if For :

may guess ; hope ; not notice .

) as we listen (

: I : am made songvoice .

: Far Lady Within : its songear .

WOULD YOU AGREE THAT THE SUBJECT ABOUT
WHICH "ABOUT" IS ABOUT IS A
PLACEHOLDER (: VACUOUS ; & HAVING NO
PLACE) FOR WHAT'S SAID ?

marks like this

, at gallop , replicate ;

overtake themselves

& squirm .

hurry

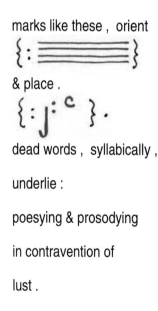

, denuded

; in droplets , transvest :

: ejaculated thru obscure

densities .

marks like these , orient

& place .

dead words , syllabically ,

underlie :

poesying & prosodying

in contravention of

lust .

IV. *IN WHICH*

I sing my song for

/ my therapist /

/ an old sidekick /

/ a singer /

/ my grandfather /

/ a composer /

/ a medievalist /

/ my teenaged daughter /

/ my english setter /

: To & For sever .

sung To , blunders ;

unbuttons , in the wrong voice ,

a wrong thing

in the wrong ear .

sung For , goes on loan .

I , With you , Listen .

: like you , apply it

to Our Account .

V. IN WHICH

e vei lo temps clar e se -re

My therapist and I listen to me sing my song .

The song thus sung , despair enjoins concupiscence .

And seems preferable.

to both.

VI. *IN WHICH*

An old sidekick and I listen to me sing my song.

(-- too Cozy . ; for porn .)

Pules .

WOULD YOU AGREE THAT A *NOUN* IS JUST A PLACEHOLDER FOR ADJECTIVES ?

VII. *IN WHICH*

m'a dol – ça lo cor   e-m   re   -ve

A singer and I listen to me sing my song .

) heard

) performed

1ˢᵗ person singular

untrained

right

care

) --   !

. " ? ;   >

{   , ,

. . .

care

1ˢᵗ person singular

untrained ?

? performed

Right

-- heard

(1ˢᵗ per. sing.)

-- untrained

heard

Care .

right .

; performed ?

VIII. *IN WHICH*

pos l'au-gels chan-ton   a lor for

My grandfather and I listen to me sing my song .

time Was & time Maybe

fuse

-- where all is possibility ; -- ineradicable ;

& good .

Community & Eternity -- stably --

glow .

IX. *IN WHICH*

A composer and I listen to me sing my song .

3 conjunct pitches -- recirculating -- realign , over a gradually revealed ostinato ,

to brush lightly against higher pitches -- in unsteadily earned metric disjunction from the ostinato

; unsettling it ; steadily to withdraw , into undiscovered pitches below ,

to develop them deliberately ; at length ;

re-emerging , in stretched reprise , as if in discovery of themselves

, narrowly synchronized with the now slowed , openly stated , ostinato ;

-- a last , high touch undone -- as they , then lower pitches , , enclose , then are enclosed by , ostinato remnants :

at recalled , then slowed , speed .

X. *IN WHICH*

A medievalist and I listen to me sing my song .

(as between this new song and Bernart de Ventadorn , Which has grasped Which? -- tangles What timeflow?

(entering tangentially -- like anyone listening to anyone -- this new song listens to Bernart's song

-- hearing (, composing) , with full ear , something believable as believedly This to someone ;

-- like anyone grasping (, composing) What was Said .

(what Bernart said ?) ; --(--heard ?

(; yes , of course not .)

as between live & dead ; as between live & live ; as between Body & Soul , going on loan ;

one may have , or have had , more , or other , in mind :

but not less .

XI. *IN WHICH*

My teenaged daughter and I listen to me sing my song.

Trust and Admiration levitate. -- metastasize, as Everyman's concern with the Highest Things. She and I fade from view.

; recrudescent ; crowdnoise hushed ;

; preempting what we most wish Everyman to take us for ;

we invest our very separate roles : as She , (Everyman) , and I ,
(Everyman) , engaging

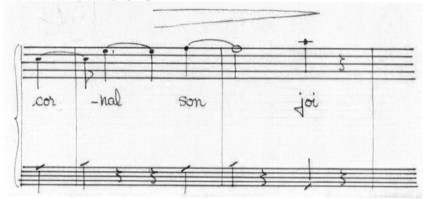

cor   -nal   son   joi

, encompassing ,

This Song Speaking .

(-- troubadour --) . . . . (-- fleshed of what grace --

e   cha   nt

. . . . ventriloquent , were I -- (-- to myself , dead
not perfectly

-- prone to things sensible ; to things outward ; things
temporal & mean ;

-- in things trifling : small . -- tempted quickly : &
overcome . -- & presently : with remorse disquieted .) ;

.... -- would speak (

ge   no   pes de re   n

.... what song

XII. IN WHICH

al

My english setter and I listen to me sing my song .

Sounds . We've pigeonholed Sounds . As those which Signify , and those which Don't . And those which Do , by what Each signifies . And which are Pertinent to Us . (-- godwilling ,) Incumbent on us to make .

Ours is the World of the Known Sign . Of Sender & Receiver . Of Inside Communication . -- Of the Hand That Feeds .

Our separate Views about what news is : -- that dog next door ; -- deposits on the rug ; -- some song going by on Master's Voice ;

-- These Things

(in our Servience Sealed to each other ; (in Ordainment that we're In This Thing Together

-- are not Very often entertained as
EVIDENCE TO THE CONTRARY .

In Ritualed Heat for Ritualized Standing with each other

-- These Things
-- anything , nothing -- nice , nasty -- pigeon , song --

) acquire Makebelieve , Makepretense postures (
Confirm Credentials .

Speaking Ritually , become (-- godwilling ,) Interchangeable in our ongoing Celebration of Who We , in Concert , Are for each other .

1. ● *Alone on horseback , within bowshot of a high window which perhaps is hers , the trobador sings his new song to the open air . When the song is over , seeing no sign of life inside , he reins his horse around and rides off the way he came.*

2.

Alone on horseback , within bowshot of the high window where she stands gazing , the trobador sings his new song . When the song is over , before reining his horse around , he waits for her to make some sign .

3.

Alone on horseback, within bowshot of the high window from which she has watched him approach, the trobador sings his new song to her. When the song is over, still meeting his gaze, she inclines her head slightly.

4. ● *She remains seated at the other end of the main hall while the trobador sings his new song to her . When the song is over , he approaches .*

5.

In the alcove , the trobador sings his new song to her . When the song is over , they talk in lowered voices .

1. Within shouting distance of a high window , a joglar sings the trobador's new song ; then rides on .

2.

Within shouting distance of a high window where a lady looks the other way , a joglar sings the trobador's new song . He decides to call it a day .

3.   Within shouting distance of a high window from which a lady watches

him , a joglar sings the trobador's new song . The lady nods . The joglar dismounts .

He places his right hand on his left side , and bows .

4. ● *A lady remains seated at the other end of the main hall while a joglar,*
ushered in by the porter, sings the trobador's new song. Ushered out, the joglar
departs with a pocketful of ginger & garlic.

1. ● *In sight of a vacant high window , the trobador listens as his joglar*

sings the new song .

2.

In sight of a high window where a lady stands gazing, the trobador (watching) listens, as his joglar sings the new song.

3. ● *In sight of a high window and of the lady standing there , his joglar sings the new song . The trobador watches . The lady listens .*

4.   *The lady remains seated at the other end of the main hall while his joglar , whom the trobador has brought with him , sings the new song . When the song is over , the lady summons a servant to provide boar's flesh and spiced wine .*

i. *from a large dwelling place ,*

entering the shadows cast by the highhulk'd church ,

a flock of The Pure disperses .

left alone inside , a trobador composes .

ii. *in procession , in the cloister of the highhulk'd church ;*

-- like his brethren , blackfrocked & telling his beads --

a trobador (mumbling) ambles ; composing .

iii. din of revelry & riot in the main hall of the castle

reaching him in an alcove ;

sword ungirt ;

a trobador reclines , composing .

1 . in the midst of the din of revelry & riot in the main hall of the castle where a motley throng takes its ease , a trobador signals a joglar : a new thread weaves thru the din .

2 . as his message rises on his joglar's voice , the lady's eyes seek the trobador .

3 . the trobador eyes the motley throng covertly .

4 . amidst courtiers & festivity , they hope .

5 . in the hush which has fallen over the motley throng , they listen .

6 . when the song is over , they take their ease in the rising din .

7 . to the motley throng

{ of }

{ virgins ladies husbands trobadors the lady the trobador }

taking its ease in the main hall

the joglar sings :

his voice

fills the hall .

1 . the joglar didn't like this setup : in this din it seemed pointless ; still , let's get on with it . (some revelers nearby glanced at him once or twice).

2 . in the midst of the motley throng , a lady notes that the song bawled into this din by his joglar , is in fact a message .

3 . the motley throng taking its ease in the main hall eyes its trobadors covertly , looking for some telltale sign .

4 . mindful of the lady's high rank , the motley throng in the main hall somewhat disregards the joglar .

5 . revelry & riot subverted by something about that joglar over there , the motley throng taking its ease in the main hall is aware of its din subsiding .

6 . when the song is over , the din rises again . the lady remains silent .

7 . not just anyone

-- trobador or no trobador --

would be received let alone well received

by this crowd in this hall .

belted

with purse , dagger , & gloves

the joglar

his voice swelling

sings .

1 . in conventional imposture , from the midst of the din of revelry & riot in the main hall of the castle where a motley throng takes its ease , a new song rises on the voice of the trobador . 2 . in the midst of the din in the main hall only the two of them know that this new song rising on the voice of the trobador is for her alone . 3 . the motley throng taking its ease in the main hall eyes its ladies covertly , looking for some telltale sign . 4 . with the consideration due to a lady of such high rank the motley throng in the main hall attends to the voice of the trobador . 5 . beguiling the time with his new song in an interval of lull in the din , the trobador entertains the motley throng . 6 . in the midst of the hushed , captivated throng to which the trobador is singing his new song , the lady listens .

7 . to the motley throng

{ of }

{ virgins ladies husbands trobadors the lady }

taking its ease in the main hall

the trobador

in stockings & belted robe

presents himself

in raised voice

singing his new song

when the song is over , some virgins crowd around the trobador ; the ladies keep their counsel ; a few husbands attend to their ladies ; & the trobadors , knowingly , receive confidences .